AUTOBIOGRAPHIES OF AMERICAN JEWS

THE PUBLICATION OF THIS BOOK WAS MADE POSSIBLE
BY A BEQUEST OF THE LATE LEE M. FRIEDMAN OF BOSTON, MASSACHUSETTS,
WHO HAD BEEN A TRUSTEE OF THE SOCIETY AND AN ACTIVE PARTICIPANT IN ITS WORK,
AS WELL AS THE AUTHOR OF
A NUMBER OF VOLUMES ON AMERICAN JEWISH HISTORY.

AUTOBIOGRAPHIES

OF

AMERICAN

JEWS

Compiled, with an Introduction,

by Harold U. Ribalow

078267

The Jewish Publication Society of America
5733   PHILADELPHIA   1973

For My Mother

My First and Most Faithful Reader

PREFACE

If we were to sum up the contents and aim of books such as this, we would do so in terms of the phrase from the Book of Job (33.30): *To be enlightened with the light of the living.*

For few things are as instructive as experience, and we are here permitted to watch sensitive men and women of almost our own generation adjust to or rebel against, but in every case make a valuable contribution to, the world that has shaped our destiny.

The Jewish Publication Society made use of the autobiographical approach when it published in 1955-6 the three volumes, *Memoirs of American Jews, 1795-1865,* by Jacob R. Marcus. In the present volume, Harold Ribalow covers the years 1880 to 1920. During these forty years, the entire tempo and temper of American life—and therefore of American Jewish life—underwent a radical change. We hope that the reception accorded this volume will encourage the undertaking of another, covering the decades between 1920 and 1960.

It remains for us to express our admiration for Mr. Ribalow's patience in examining the numerous volumes of this nature from which he selected the excerpts here published. We also express our gratitude to the publishers and copyright holders of the respective books who cooperated with us in permitting the free use of the material; their names are listed elsewhere in the volume.

The Jewish Publication Society

ACKNOWLEDGMENTS

Thanks are due to the following authors and publishers who were kind enough to give permission for the use of the material included in this volume:

Putnam's and Coward-McCann for the excerpts from *Challenging Years,* by Stephen S. Wise (1949), and *The Autobiography of Sol Bloom* (1948).

Mrs. Leon M. Solis-Cohen for the excerpt from *Memories of an American Jew,* by Philip Cowen (1932).

The Trustees of the Rockdale Temple, Cincinnati, the Union of American Hebrew Congregations, and John G. Kidd and Son, Inc., for the excerpt from *My Life as an American Jew,* by David Philipson (1941).

Houghton-Mifflin Company for the excerpt from *The Promised Land,* by Mary Antin (1912).

The Macmillan Company for the excerpt from *Loose Leaves from a Busy Life,* by Morris Hillquit (1934).

Eleazar Lipsky for the excerpt from *Thirty Years of American Zionism,* by Louis Lipsky (1927).

Joseph M. Proskauer, and Farrar, Straus and Giroux, Inc., for the excerpt from *A Segment of My Times,* by Joseph M. Proskauer (1950).

Label Katz, the American Association for Jewish Education, and the Bloch Publishing Company, for the excerpt from *In the Grip of Cross-Currents,* by Ephraim Lisitzky (1959).

Roger M. Straus for the excerpt from *Under Four Administrations,* by Oscar S. Straus (1922).

Julius Haber, and Twayne Publishers, Inc., for the excerpt from *The Odyssey of an American Zionist,* by Julius Haber (1956).

Mrs. Gustav Hartman, and the Citadel Press, for the excerpt from *I Gave My Heart,* by Mrs. Gustav Hartman (1960).

Samuel Chotzinoff, and Alfred A. Knopf, Inc., for the excerpt from *A Lost Paradise,* by Samuel Chotzinoff (1955).

Simon and Schuster, Inc., for the excerpt from *Ex-Prodigy,* by Norbert Wiener (1953).

Harry Golden, and Doubleday and Company, Inc., for the excerpt from *Five Boyhoods,* edited by Martin Levin (1962).

Marie Syrkin, and the Theodor Herzl Institute, for the excerpt from *Nachman Syrkin: Socialist Zionist, A Biographical Memoir,* by Marie Syrkin (1961).

Louis Waldman, and Dutton and Co., for the excerpt from *Labor Lawyer,* by Louis Waldman (1944).

Louise Lewisohn for the excerpt from *Up Stream,* by Ludwig Lewisohn (1922).

The Baron de Hirsch Fund for the excerpt from *Born a Jew,* by Boris Bogen (1930).

Irma L. Lindheim, and Thomas Yoseloff, for the excerpt from *Parallel Quest,* by Irma Lindheim (1962).

Anzia Yezierska, and Charles Scribner's Sons, for the excerpt from *Red Ribbon on a White Horse,* by Anzia Yezierska (1950).

Felix Frankfurter, Harlan B. Phillips, and Reynal and Company, for the excerpt from *Felix Frankfurter Reminisces* (1960).

Meyer Levin, and the Horizon Press Inc., for the excerpt from *In Search,* by Meyer Levin (1950).

CONTENTS

AUTOBIOGRAPHIES OF AMERICAN JEWS

INTRODUCTION
by Harold U. Ribalow

THE AMERICAN JEW is, in many respects, seeking to define his own special image as a Jew living within American society. The Jewish personality of earlier and other societies manages to stand out in sharp relief. When we say "German Jew," or "Polish Jew," or "Spanish Jew," fairly distinct images are evoked. Each of these Jewries was affected by its environment, so that different types emerged in different countries. Yet, the essentials of Jewish life and character were clearly delineated and recognizable.

But what of the American Jew of the present day? Is he clearly definable? Is he immediately recognizable? Does he have a distinctive and familiar image?

The Jewish experience in America has not yet been fully described. The very freedom—social, intellectual, political and economic—which the Jews found in the United States, and their eagerness to adjust to this new and challenging life, complicate the story beyond the possibility of easy generalization. Still, the challenge is there, and various attempts have been made to meet it.

The historian has tried his hand by means of research into the past. He has attempted to trace the broad outlines of the historical process by utilizing documentary material, personal letters and journals, newspaper references and statistics. No matter how heavily he leans on individual lives, they are not his chief concern. Here and there, of course, a particular individual emerges as a giant and symbolizes, in his own personal life, the hopes, the problems and the achievements of his group. Usually, however, the individual is lost in the group and his personality is blurred, if not distorted, by being fused into the mass.

In recent years, creative artists have attempted to portray the American Jew. The imaginative writer—novelist, dramatist, or short story writer—has drawn on Jewish character and issues and in this fashion has traced the experience of the American Jew in fighting his way out of his ghetto environment into the varied areas of American life. But the creative writer's picture of the Jew is not necessarily more accurate than that of the historian. An unhappily large number of Jewish novelists, writing out of a sense of dissatisfaction and rebelliousness, have elected to focus on neurotic and maladjusted individuals like themselves. These fictional creations of the American Jew, no matter how artistically persuasive they may be, are likely to be no more valid than the portrait of the Jew emerging from the work of the historian.

Biography would appear to be a useful third approach. A biographer, describing the interplay between the individual and society, between character and environment, could conceivably be more successful than either a historian or a novelist in creating an image of Jewish personality. Unfortunately, few biographies of American Jews have been written to date—not enough, certainly, to permit of any generalization regarding the effect upon the Jews of their American experience. It may be too early to expect such biographies because the raw material for them has not yet been made available. The time may be soon with us, however, when we shall see the emergence of Jewish biography even as we have experienced the breakthrough of Jewish fiction on the American scene. A number of documents and collections of letters have been published within recent years, and more are on the way.

Clearly, it is fairly simple to write the biography of a rabbi or a Jewish scholar; it is infinitely more difficult to do the same for a business man, an American political figure, or a member of the professions. It is no easy matter to trace the life of an important Jew who may have made his mark in the wider community but has not been especially active as a Jew. At the same time, there have been many Jews who simultaneously have been active and influential both as Jews and as men of substance in "non-Jewish" areas. It is these men whose Jewish personality would serve best to illustrate the nature of that comparatively new type, the American Jew. And it is here, in this field, that biographies are lacking.

It may surprise the reader to learn that a glimpse of this new Jew can nevertheless be obtained from still another literary source, one which is in a sense more direct, more informative and more interesting in human terms than any other. American Jews have written and published a considerable number of autobiographies. They represent a kind of self-revelation which has advantages and disadvantages. If autobiographical material suffers from being too subjective, it has the advantage of being dramatic. If its horizon is limited, the sensitivity it displays is apt to be more poignant, for autobiography recounts actual experiences, which are the bricks out of which a life story is built, and emotional reactions, which both exemplify and fashion character.

A collection of autobiographical excerpts was prepared by Professor Jacob R. Marcus for an earlier period of American Jewish history (*Memoirs of American Jews, 1775–1865*, 3 volumes, JPS, 1956). The twenty-five selections in this volume are drawn, in all but one instance, from formal autobiographies by American Jews, many of whom participated significantly in American or Jewish life in more recent times, from 1880 to approximately 1920. The one exception is Felix Frankfurter, the United States Supreme Court Justice, whose memoirs included here are excerpted from his talks with Dr. Harlan B. Phillips. Every other chapter is selected from autobiographies written without the aid of ghost writers.

Although this anthology does not pretend to be a history of American Jewry from 1880 to 1920, it does, I believe, illuminate many of the trends, facets and developments inherent in American Jewish society during that period.

The forty-year era covered by these memoirs was one of the most significant in American Jewish life, and it may be instructive to highlight some of the historical events and experiences of that time. In 1881, the first great wave of immigration from

Russia and Poland engulfed the United States, adding some two million Jews to the half million already here. Between 1881 and 1900, more than a million Jews left Russia, following the oppression and pogroms there after the death of Czar Alexander II. Of this million, some six hundred thousand found a haven and homes in the United States. From 1889 to 1910, Jews from Eastern Europe crowded the ships that crossed the Atlantic Ocean and came to this country, and most of them, on touching American soil, remained in New York City. From 1908 to 1912, some eighty-three thousand four hundred Jews came to this country annually. Of course, this flood receded, but the Jews who arrived here during this period were our fathers and grandfathers, and the way they lived, the cities in which they settled, the traditions they brought with them, and the jobs they found—all helped to color and influence Jewish life in our own time.

The Jews who came to the United States before and after the turn of the century were not pioneers in the same sense as the modern Israelis, or as the Americans who settled the West. They fled Europe because their lives were in danger; they didn't flee because they sought adventure. They were literate. All of them had profound respect for learning and they knew that they were Jews. They were, in the main, city folk, and so when they came to America they settled in the industrial centers and attempted to regain their middle-class status.

They moved into areas which rapidly came to resemble European ghettos. They worked at the needle trades; they became merchants; and they became skilled workers. They built their own synagogues, organized their own charities and fraternal orders. They established their own schools in order to transmit their Jewish traditions, even while they encouraged their children to attend the American public schools and to become thoroughly Americanized.

By 1914, when World War I began, the United States had the greatest community of Jews living in freedom. They had become dedicated patriots of their country and participated with great spirit in the war when the United States joined the fighting. The fact was, however, that millions of Jews were trapped in the war area and American Jewry was faced with the responsibility of coming to the aid of its fellow Jews. Their reaction was almost instinctive; Jewish philanthropy emerged on a large scale, and the American Jew, only recently removed from his European roots, found himself emotionally and philanthropically bound to the Jews he had left behind.

What the American Jew did for his fellows overseas had an indirect and highly favorable effect on his own Jewish life, in that it developed his communal awareness, cemented communal unity, and thereby strengthened local philanthropies. A variety of charitable organizations had existed in every Jewish community since Colonial times. They expanded and multiplied in the course of the nineteenth century. In the period covered by this book they achieved a degree of organization and effectiveness unparalleled in Jewish history.

The Jew in America decidedly did not find the streets paved with gold, but he did recognize that he had in this country an opportunity to live freely as a Jew. He worked hard; he laboriously learned English and tried to adjust to millions of Americans whose ways were strange to him; he wanted his children to feel at home in his new surroundings as he himself had felt in the old. At the same time, he managed to retain the eternal dreams of Jews everywhere. In 1896, Theodor Herzl wrote his classic *The Jewish State*, and a year later the First Zionist Congress was held in Basle, Switzerland. Soon thereafter, a group of American Zionists formed the Federation of American Zionists, headed by Rabbi Stephen S. Wise, Rabbi Gustav Gottheil and his son, Professor Richard Gottheil, among other descendants of an earlier immigration.

Now that Israel has been established, it may be difficult for readers to recall the difficult path of Zionism in this country. For many decades, most American Jews were too occupied with earning their daily bread to involve themselves fully in the promotion of the rebirth of Jewish nationalism. In the period under discussion here, there developed a hard core of Jews who believed passionately in the Zionist dream of resettlement in the Holy Land. The struggles and turbulence of Zionist history are described both by influential leaders and by little-known followers of the movement.

It was difficult for American Jews to maintain in this country the patterns of living customary in Europe. There were problems of cultural adjustment, and there came to be varieties of Judaism. At first, Yiddish journalism and Yiddish poetry, rather than American Jewish journalism and English literature, were more attractive to the newly arrived American Jew. But the pressures of Americanization were strong, and the old ways were not easy to maintain.

There was some hostility on the part of the non-Jews. It shocked the American Jew especially, because this fact clashed head-on with his faith in America as a land of freedom. To be sure, now and again, an American Jew rose to a position of prestige on the American national scene; he was admired and respected, yet he was the exception rather than the rule. It was a situation to which the Jews reacted vigorously, and several important defense organizations had their origin during this period. Leadership in this respect, as in several others, was provided by descendants of earlier migrations, American born and of German-Jewish stock. Their participation in and description of the new developments is further evidence of the growing unity within the Jewish group.

All in all, it was an era of excitement, tension and uncertainty. It was one of the most fruitful periods of American Jewish history.

The material included in this collection falls into recognizable patterns. We have here first-hand reports from statesmen, politicians, philanthropists, and communal workers in American national life and Jewish community endeavors. There are also accounts here of Jewish labor movements and unionism in the United States, written by men who were movers and shapers in the labor movement.

Many of these memoirs were produced while the experiences were still fresh in the minds of the authors, as in the case of Mary Antin. More frequently, however, the autobiographies were written decades later, at a time when the writers recalled the past with affection, as in the case of Harry Golden. All of the contributors to this volume have made their mark on American Jewish life. Some of them are well known to the contemporary reader; others to the historian; still others to an older generation of Jews.

Each writer has had something to contribute to his time and, I think, to our own. I do not intend to recapitulate or to summarize their stories here, for they are to be found within the pages of this volume and each selection stands on its own. Yet is is worth making a few observations about the material the reader will find in this book.

Joseph M. Proskauer and Sol Bloom, both of whom became distinguished Americans, have written with warmth of the years when they were young boys growing up in cities where few Jews lived. The late Congressman Bloom recalls life in San Francisco in 1880, when the city was not yet full-blown and where a poor boy had many opportunities to earn money. Joseph Proskauer, who later became quite affluent and a leader of the American Jewish Committee, thinks back upon life in the Southern city of Mobile, Alabama, in the 1890's, when life was slow-paced and gracious. While the age of which these men write seems very far away today, their chapters reveal the great progress American Jews have made since the days when they were young boys in a pioneering America.

Cyrus Adler, Rabbi David Philipson, Oscar S. Straus and Rabbi Stephen S. Wise have been among the outstanding Jews in American history. They achieved much and, because their lives were so rich in experience, it has been impossible, in the material included here, to indicate the extent and depth of their influence and significance. Dr. Adler's modest account of his relationships with famous men and the part he played in founding the American Jewish Historical Society and the Dropsie College help to make clear how difficult it was for American Jewry to establish institutions which we now take for granted. Rabbi Philipson's report of important rabbinical conferences and his account of the establishment of the Jewish Publication Society of America are valuable contributions to Jewish history in this country. The accomplishments of these two men indicate that the period between 1880 and 1920 saw the establishment of organizations whose value has increased during the decades that followed.

Oscar Straus' chapter on his intimate friendship with President Theodore Roosevelt and on the impact on American Jewry of the Kishinev pogrom in Russia again make vivid to us events in both American and Jewish history which deserve to be remembered. Stephen Wise's dynamic account of how he fought for a free pulpit is relevant to our own time and helps us understand that Rabbi Wise was a major figure in Jewish life, not only because of his leadership in the Zionist movement, but also because he recognized in the rabbinate one of the most influential platforms of American Jewish life.

There is a vast literature on the American labor movement, written by scores of historians, economists, sociologists, novelists and labor leaders. Yet few men have written more convincingly and passionately about strikes, trade unions and social justice than Morris Hillquit and Louis Waldman. In their memoirs we learn of the birth of Jewish labor unions, of the formation of the first Yiddish-language Socialist newspaper, of the horrifying Triangle fire, and of the stirring, seething masses of Jewish workers who helped make American Labor a powerful factor on the contemporary scene. It might be pointed out here that while Dr. Adler, Rabbi Philipson and Rabbi Wise, as well as other contributors to this volume, were totally committed Jews, the labor leaders who were Jewish were less concerned with Judaism, with religion, or with national Jewish movements than they were with the Jewish working people. Thus, the contributions of men like Hillquit and Waldman, while significant, were not "Jewish" in the sense that the efforts of Jewishly-oriented leaders were.

American fiction today is a fairly accurate gauge of the increased influence of the Jew in all walks of American life. Early Jewish fiction dealt largely with the immigrant Jew, the conflicts between fathers and sons, the struggle to adjust to America, and the painful attempt to break out of the Jewish ghettos in the large American metropolitan cities. This fiction, beginning with novels by Abraham Cahan and Anzia Yezierska to the more recent work of Charles Angoff, has done much to explain the immigrant generation to the more Americanized Jews of our time. Yet the cumulative effect of autobiographies written by immigrants also has served to make the Jewish image vivid. Ephraim Lisitzky, a Hebrew poet and teacher who wrote and died in comparative obscurity, offers us a moving and poetic chapter on his life when he was a boy in Boston in 1900. This selection predates the novels of Charles Angoff and makes equally clear the sense of bewilderment of a young boy who cannot cope with the tensions and pressures of the rapid American pace and the materialistic American society. Lisitzky was a highly gifted poet with a dark and pessimistic turn of mind, and so one need not wonder that he draws a bleak picture of his experiences. Still, the late Samuel Chotzinoff and Harry Golden, more optimistic men who gained both fame and fortune in this country, stress in their memoirs the grinding harshness of poverty, and the conflicts inherent in the Americanization of immigrants and in the indifference of non-Jewish Americans to the Jew struggling to find his own way in this country.

Since the establishment of the State of Israel, a library of books has been published on Zionism, on Israel's wars and economic problems, on the mass immigration into the country and on its leaders. Zionism in America, however, has not inspired as many books as has the rebirth of the Jewish State, a fact which is not surprising. There have been volumes on Zionism in the United States, some of them good, and others indifferent. I believe that the selections included here by Louis Lipsky, Irma Lindheim, Felix Frankfurter, Marie Syrkin and Julius Haber illuminate the role of American Jews in the creation of Israel. The late Louis Lipsky writes from the highest levels of the movement, as does Justice Frankfurter. Mrs. Lindheim, who served as a president of Hadassah, is a remarkable but modest woman, and her description of how Zionism became important to her is moving and memorable. Marie Syrkin, in writing of her father, Dr. Nachman Syrkin, a provocative and original Zionist thinker, evokes an era as well as a personality, while Julius Haber, a modest soldier in the ranks of Zionism, remembers the impact on New York Jews of the death of Theodor Herzl. It is fitting, at a time when the leaders of the past have become shadowy and fuzzy in our memories, that we be reminded of those men who made possible a strong Zionist movement in the United States.

Philip Cowen, Boris Bogen, Rebekah Kohut and Mrs. Gustave Hartman have intriguing stories to tell. Their experiences were wide and they knew, worked with, and lived among some of the most important Jews of our time. To read their autobiographies, or chapters from them, is to learn about Jewish history and American Jewry. Cowen was the editor of *The American Hebrew*, once a widely-read and important journal. Although he writes a great deal about his problems as an editor, he has also taken the trouble to record his impression of Emma Lazarus, a poet and essayist who has become part of the American legend because of her emotional sonnet, which we all remember as part of the story of the Statue of Liberty. Boris Bogen was a Jewish social worker in New York and Cincinnati and his autobiography, long forgotten, does not deserve obscurity. There are now massive Jewish philanthropies with tens of thousands of lay leaders and fund-raisers. When Bogen did his work, the machinery of Jewish philanthropy was less developed but no less significant, considering the size of the Jewish community of his time.

Mrs. Hartman, married to Judge Gustave Hartman, was a partner in his efforts to help orphaned Jewish children. She recreates the New York East Side of an earlier age, and recalls a period in Jewish life when poverty was so prevalent, and orphaned children so helpless, that orphan homes were absolutely necessary because there was no one overall philanthropy to care for these children. Of course, philanthropy has become "big business," and a single orphanage is no longer such a major matter. The Hartmans, however, raised their money through shows in which noted entertainers participated. This pattern has been continued to the present day by other, more ambitious, fund-raising organizations.

Mrs. Kohut, like Irma Lindheim, was an unusual woman. She had largeness of soul, raised a large family, respected learning and education, and with her own heavy personal responsibilities, managed to become a dynamic and influential communal leader.

She wrote more than one volume of her memoirs, but I believe that the selection printed here depicts those characteristics which made her a unique personality.

In recent years, various Jewish magazines have published symposia on the problems of Jewish intellectuals. There have been "dialogues" in Israel on the meaning of being a Jew, on the importance of Jewish religion to creative writers, on the relationship between Jews in Israel and Jews in the United States. The question of Jewish awareness, its meaning and its depth, has disturbed novelists, sociologists, commentators, rabbis, of course, and leaders of national Jewish organizations. A number of Jewish writers, although their creative fiction concerns Jews almost exclusively, reject affiliation with the Jewish community and frequently are caustic in their depiction of Jews, their customs, their culture and their religious habits. They think they are being original and bright. They do not know that other, and perhaps better, writers before them fought through their own neuroses and emerged whole men as a result of their internal struggle. In *Up Stream*, the late Ludwig Lewisohn produced a classic statement describing how he was first assimilated and then returned to Judaism. His awareness of being a Jew changed him, turned his writing and his life into totally new directions and made him a man radically different from the one who had been cut away from his people. Norbert Wiener, a great scientist, was one of those Jews who did not know he was Jewish for a surprisingly long period of his life. In the selection included here, we share with him his shock of discovery and recognition of his being a Jew. It is an instructive chapter and from it we can begin to understand the intensity of Jewish self-hatred and its effect on the most intelligent of men. Meyer Levin, a talented and sensitive novelist who has written important American Jewish works of fiction, informs us in his autobiography, *In Search*, what being a Jew means to him. The result is a significant contribution to American Jewish literature, for he has given us a lyric and vivid memoir.

This volume limits itself to excerpts that do not go beyond 1920, and since that time literally dozens of autobiographies have been published by American Jews. No doubt, these books have lessons for us all; but history, contrary to Carl Sandburg's phrase, is not "a bucket of ashes." To understand the present we must know the past. The twenty-five chapters in this anthology give us many valuable insights into the American Jewish past. It has been satisfying for me to read the books from which this material has been drawn as well as hundreds of others. I have been impressed with the Jewish "stubbornness," idealism, talent and industry which have marked the work of these men and women. We have every reason to be proud of the Jewish contribution to American civilization. I believe that the selections in this volume justify the hope that a distinct American Jewish personality will emerge and faith that the Jews of America will contribute in the future even more richly to American and to Jewish history than they have in the past.

SOL BLOOM

Sol Bloom, a member of the United States House of Representatives from 1923 to his death in 1949, was a powerful figure in Democratic Party politics and, for many years, was Chairman of the House Foreign Affairs Committee.

Representative Bloom was born in 1870. Before entering politics he had had a varied career as a music publisher, a realtor and a builder. He constructed the Midway at the Chicago World's Fair in 1893, and built a number of theaters in New York City.

While serving in the House of Representatives, he held several other important positions. He filled the post of United States delegate to the Anglo-American Conference on Refugee Problems in 1943, and was a member of the United States delegation to the conference which established the United Nations in 1945. While a Congressman, he was also National Director of the George Washington Bicentennial in 1932 and of the Constitution Sesquecentennial Commission in 1939.

The Autobiography of Sol Bloom *deals not only with the author's experience in government, but with his life in the business world as well. His account of life in San Francisco in the 1880's is of special interest as one of the few descriptions we have of Jewish life on the West Coast at that early time in American Jewish history.*

Boyhood in San Francisco*

SOL BLOOM

IN SPITE OF my preoccupation with the theater, my occupation within the theater actually took only a small portion of my time from one year's end to the next until I was fifteen years old. Six days a week, rarely taking time off (and then nearly always to improve an opportunity to make extra money), I worked at the California Brush Factory. After hours, when there was nothing for me in a theater, I would peddle violets to theatergoers; middle-aged gentlemen accompanied by young ladies were my best customers. On certain evenings I would sell newspapers,** and for a time I had a regular job in the folding room of the *Chronicle,* which then was housed at the corner of Bush and Kearny Streets. This was a morning paper, and the bulldog edition started running through the press around nine in the evening; after coming off the press the papers had to be folded by hand, and I was one of the kids who performed that tedious but necessary task. I got this job direct from the publisher, Michael H. de Young, who was a customer of Figer Brothers. From the day I first talked with him until his death in 1925, Mr. de Young was my friend, and to none of the men who helped shape my career do I owe quite so much as I owe to him. This is not an idle expression of gratitude, as I think later happenings will bear out.

On Sundays I usually worked too, at least during part of the day, peddling novelties and souvenirs to picnic and excursion

---

* Reprinted from *The Autobiography of Sol Bloom,* G. P. Putnam's Sons, New York, 1948, pp. 47–56.

** Among them was the *Examiner,* then a feeble publication with a circulation of perhaps 5,000, which was owned by George Hearst, later to be Senator Hearst. When in 1887 he gave his son, William Randolph Hearst, the choice of managing any of a number of the great family properties, William chose the *Examiner,* and from it he built the chain of newspapers which today reaches across the country.

crowds. San Francisco, with its large groups of first-generation Europeans, went in for the Continental Sunday to a degree that amazed and often shocked visitors from the "Puritan" East. Mild climate and ease of access to numerous places of great charm abetted old-world temperaments and habits, and thousands of people regularly passed their day of rest out of doors. For those with money there was the Cliff House, outside the Golden Gate, where sea lions played on the rocks just off shore and gulls floated overhead waiting for handouts. For others there were Golden Gate Park, where less than a dozen years earlier nothing but sand dunes and tufts of grass had been known, and the Presidio. Across the Bay, to the north, was Sausalito, which has been likened to Sorrento and other Italian coast towns, and, not far inland, the grove of magnificent redwood trees that has since been set aside as a national monument under the name of Muir Woods. And across to the east was Alameda, which was then hardly a town at all and was thought of by San Franciscans simply as a place of rural refuge.

These and other romantic spots I knew in early boyhood only by repute. When the excursion steamer pulled out I was still standing on the pier with my canes and such other wares as convention deemed desirable picnic paraphernalia. There would be another steamer leaving in a little while, or at another pier, and my job was to earn money. Had I gone off on one of those trips, I would not only have limited my market but been forced to spend money, for excursion tickets never cost less than fifty cents.

My brother Mose could go on Sunday excursions, and that was all right, because it never cost him anything. He was one of those lucky fellows who are always finding things. Week after week he would come home, always on a Friday or a Saturday, and announce that he had found an excursion ticket. He just had an uncanny eye, it was clear to me, for spotting a ticket that somebody had dropped. I was proud of him, rather than envious, and attributed his gift to the same sort of genius that enabled certain individuals to gather a dozen four-leafed clovers while a fellow like me was still searching for his first one. Even after I had taught myself to look for lost tickets as I hurried along Market Street or some other likely thoroughfare, I had no luck. It took me several years to figure out just what it was that Mose had. It was the gift of deceiving his brother. I caught him buying a ticket one day.

At this time I was also trying to make up for my lack of schooling by spending at least an hour daily reading and learning to write. My hours were so irregular that I seldom had any meal but breakfast with my family; I did most of my studying while eating lunch at the factory and again during my late supper at home. This unavoidable peculiarity of mine brought peculiar results. In the evening I learned Hebrew by reading, under my mother's tutelage, the Old Testament, and English through the perusal of *The Argonaut,* a local theatrical review. My literary style must have been extraordinary, and I regret exceedingly that none of my early works have survived for possible quotation here.

During the noon hour (actually a half hour) I studied arithmetic, only this activity was in no sense a task, for I pursued it incessantly throughout the day, noting lot numbers, prices, costs, and practical calculations of all sorts that had to do with the manufacture of brushes. Before many months had passed I knew the exact specifications of every article we manufactured. I knew the precise number of holes that had to be drilled in every brush block, the amount paid at piecework rates for every single operation, and the selling price for each item, whether it was sold over the counter at retail or in job lots to dealers. With no conscious effort I made up imaginary orders in my head, and I could have set down almost instantly the price, the gross profit, and the net after wages and operating costs had been deducted. It was fun to toss the figures around while my hands were occupied with some dull routine job.

As time went on I discovered that my store of detailed knowledge was useful. If a customer was asking for a quotation on a mixed order, it might take the clerk ten or fifteen minutes to figure the answer. Even then he might be uncertain, and he would perhaps have to check the stock room for specifications and consult with the foreman on piecework pay. This exchange of information was accomplished by shouting from one room to another and, needless to say, it was not very efficient. But we were a small establishment, and no one ever bothered to think up a better way of doing things simply because it wasn't absolutely necessary. One day, however, when one of the men called to the stock room I piped up with the answer.

"How do you know that's the right answer?" he shot back.

"Oh, I just know," I said. It would have been impossible for me to explain my processes. I never worked out the answers on paper.

"A smarty, huh?" he grunted. "Well, you better be right!" Then he went to work with a pencil and a scrap of paper. Several minutes later he walked over to me.

"Now let's see whether you were just lucky the first time," he said. "What's the price for making up two dozen Number Forty's with long handles?"

I gave him the answer without hesitation, and after he had tried two or three more he walked away visibly shaken. But he passed the word about my memory for figures, and after that a day seldom went by without a test of it. It made me feel important to be consulted by grown men, and for some reason it didn't occur to me that there might be money in my "trick." I just kept on having fun out of doing what for the men was real work. (In later years I continued to use the arithmetical methods of my childhood, and I know that my lack of proper instruction not infrequently was the very thing that dropped a contract in my lap. When I was in the construction business in New York I knew building costs as I once had known brush costs, and I could listen to the reading of a long list of specifications, estimate the quantities, multiply them by the prices, calculate the total— sometimes in millions of dollars—add my profit, announce the figure, and offer to sign up then and there. I never needed a pencil and paper. They would, in fact, have encumbered me.)

One day in the early part of 1880, about the time of my tenth birthday, Ben Figer called me into his office and began to ask me questions. He found that I knew not only specifications and costs but piecework rates—in other words, that I was able to figure payrolls. He realized, what was more, that I would be able to work them out without having to refer constantly to schedules. That was more than his chief bookkeeper was able to do. I was a freak, a veritable *lusus naturae,* and a valuable one to boot!

"On Monday, Solly, I want you to start working in the office," said Mr. Figer. "Somebody else will have to handle the things you've been doing. I don't want you to waste your time running around out there any more." He waved his hand in the direction of the workrooms. "Remember that."

At the end of the week I found that my pay had been raised to three dollars and a half. If that seems small, even for a ten-year-old, I can give my assurance that it loomed very large in the life of a family that paid six dollars a month for the rental of their house. It was not until some months later, after I had been raised another dollar, that we felt secure enough to move from Brannan Street to a larger and more comfortable house around the corner on Sixth Street, where we had to pay ten dollars.

If at this point it should occur to someone that I would have needed days that were seventeen or eighteen hours long for the regular accomplishment of all my tasks, both in and out of the factory, and that such an account of my life as I have given must therefore be regarded as preposterous (to use the most charitable adjective), let me answer in this way: it *is,* by virtue of the fact that my early career was, contrary to normal experience, quite preposterous; and I *did* need days that were seventeen or eighteen hours long.

Never within memory have I slept longer than six hours at a stretch. My boyhood days began around five in the morning and ended somewhere between ten o'clock and midnight, and from the moment I got up until I went to bed I was in action. The necessity of childhood became the fixed habit of later life. Even today, although I sometimes spend more hours in bed, I find that five or six hours of sleep are enough. When I go to bed early I read until a late hour; when I wake up in the morning, whatever the hour may be, I get up at once. I have never known the experience of being awake without being in action. It has been a great help to me to be able to start my day's work at full speed instead of warming up gradually.

When I am asked whether the fast tempo of my childhood didn't have adverse effects on my health, I can only answer that I don't know how it could have. Except for an occasional cold, I escaped all of the illnesses that a child, even in the present relatively advanced age of sanitation and medical science, is expected to suffer. In recent years I have continued to enjoy almost perfect health, and although I go regularly and frequently to see my doctor—partly as a matter of good sense, but largely because Ben Salzer, whose patient I have been for years, is one of the most stimulating men I know—I have never in my life, thank God, been really sick. I don't even believe that the long hours of work and the short hours of sleep stunted my growth. My parents were both of small stature, and I am satisfied that genes, not too much work, determined my height of five feet, six inches.

One thing that my eccentric routine did affect was my religious observances. As I have already made clear, we were Jews of the strict Orthodox faith. That meant a close adherence to ritual in all things. There could be no exceptions.

We began our Sabbath (as I still begin mine) in accordance with the ancient ordination that the seventh day of the week— "and God blessed the seventh day and sanctified it"—commences at sundown, an hour recognizable by all men, in every era, with or without the aid of mechanical means for computing time. Since the seventh day of the week (even in the civil calendar) is Saturday, the Jewish Sabbath is observed on that day; since the sundown that introduces our seventh day comes on the sixth day of the civil calendar, our Sabbath begins on Friday.

At that hour, in every Orthodox household, comes the ceremony of lighting the candles and the taking of wine and bread. A simple prayer follows. I learned it first in Hebrew, from my mother:

Blessed art Thou, O Lord our God.
King of the Universe,
Who gave us the light.

Blessed art Thou, O Lord our God.
King of the Universe,
Who gave us the fruit of the vine.

Blessed art Thou, O Lord our God.
King of the Universe,
Who gave us the bread of the earth.

I repeat this prayer in Hebrew every Sabbath.

On Saturday devout Jews, if they are able to, worship in a synagogue. Mother never failed to attend this Sabbath service, and Father was almost as faithful. We children regularly went to the synagogue too when we were small. Later on, for various reasons, we became less regular in our attendance. For me, working all day in the factory, it was difficult; but once in a while during my lunch hour I managed to take a little extra time and hurry to the synagogue that my family attended. It was on Turk Street, fully a mile from the place where I worked; but any inconvenience I experienced was more than repaid when I was able to tell my mother that I had gone to the synagogue where the venerable Dr. A. J. Messing was rabbi.

When I was growing up it used to trouble me to miss Sabbath worship in a synagogue. The sense of original sin was strong in me, as I am sure it has always been in most children, whether Christian or Jewish, brought up in homes where the Bible is constantly read. And although I didn't have a great deal of time for philosophical contemplation of my own wretchedness as a son of Eve, when Saturday came round my essential wickedness preyed upon me and I sought the soothing atmosphere of the synagogue.

Happily my attitude changed as I grew older; the notion that any temple of worship should be regarded as a place where one goes to discharge an obligation, as a man might go to his bank to pay interest on a loan, is one that I now find as ludicrous as it is pathetic. Whenever it is possible I go to a synagogue. But I go because I wish to go, in order to commune with my Maker, never with the idea that I am thus laying up treasure in Heaven. The absence of a synagogue does not interfere with my worship. I can have my own communion with God just as well in any other place. To me the differences are inconsequential. There are perhaps five thousand creeds in the world, five thousand ways that may be followed to reach God. They are all good ways, for there is only one God.

The one thing completely lacking in my boyhood was play, at least play in the ordinary sense of carefree, undirected activities with children of my own age. When I was very small I undoubtedly had toys, but I cannot remember any specific objects that might have beguiled my days in Illinois, and after I arrived in California I know that there were no playthings. Not only had we no money for such luxuries, but life was far too grim a reality to have allowed for even the slight detachment needed for the establishment of a mood of play. The older children did not play; they all had serious tasks to perform. Following their example, I did not play either, and it was not long before I had other completely occupying things to do.

This early elimination of certain conditions that characterize childhood for most of the population of our country has had, I feel, certain lasting effects upon the course of my life. Some of them seem very obvious to me. Others, no doubt, while their existence has eluded *me,* are apparent to those who know me.

It is clear to me, for example, that my emergence in infancy from a world of childish fancy into the world of men exerted a strong influence on my imagination. Never as a small child did I inhabit the land of elves and fairies, in which dumb animals converse and experience human emotions, in which castles and armies exist in one's own back yard or in the shadows of a bedroom after dark. There were no reveries of golden-haired princesses while idling on the bank of some bright stream, there was no transformation of myself into a hero rescuing a child from a burning building while flames held back all the firemen, and I never discovered a pot of gold under a storied oak.

My imagination belonged to the world in which I lived, the one I could see and touch. It has always been intensely practical.

I could imagine how my mother would look in a new bonnet, and then I would try to get the money to buy her one. I could imagine, when I passed a bank, how it would be to work there, and then I would decide that, after all, I preferred to keep on at the factory during the day and in the theater at night. I could hear a new song, imagine how Anna Held or Nora Bayes would sing it, and then I would arrange, if possible, to have one of them introduce it for me. I could pass an old structure on Broadway and imagine the kind of building I would put up in its place, and then I would bring together the persons needed to consummate its erection. I could imagine a population of 130,000,000 uniting to celebrate the two-hundredth anniversary of George Washington's birth, and it became my privilege to bring that dream to fruition. I could even imagine a world in which all nations had agreed to unite and compose their differences under law—and I believe, whether or not I live to see it, that our own world will one day be like that.

And so it came about that my only play was in my work. Conversely, by the time I reached a level of economic comfort, my work had become so absorbing that it was almost the only play I wanted. I have never found satisfaction in participating in a game like golf or tennis, and although I learned to play cards—strictly as a social duty—I never once enjoyed a game. But I like to organize games for other people. This, I suppose, a psychologist would call a form of egomania. Quite possibly he would be right.

I can name one exception to my experience that playing a game of any sort is little short of torture for me.

I like to play marbles.

This was the one game I might really have gone in for when I was a little boy, for it was played on every open lot and needed a minimum of equipment. But I was so effectively discouraged on my first attempt, by one of the few acts of open discrimination ever directed against me, that I didn't make a second try for a long while. As I tried to join the circle of players on Brannan

Street one day, a big boy hit me and snarled, "Go on home, you little Christ-killer!"

But I had a yearning for marbles that even such an act of childish cruelty could not destroy, and some fifty years later, while walking to my office on Capitol Hill one morning, I found my opportunity. Three or four boys were playing, and after watching for a few minutes I asked, somewhat diffidently, whether I might join their game.

"Sure!" they exclaimed, and one of them lent me a glassie to shoot with. To my delight I found that I had a great talent for marbles! Latent through all the years, it appeared on a fine spring day in Washington, and I played blissfully for half an hour.

I am still devoted to the game, and if on an April morning my secretary should ever say to a visitor, "The Congressman is out playing marbles," her statement ought not to be taken as a sign that one or the other of us in on the verge of being committed. No—I would be out playing marbles.

PHILIP COWEN

Philip Cowen was born in New York City in 1853, the son of immigrants from Germany, and he died in 1943. He began his career as a printer, and soon ventured into publishing. In 1879 he founded the American Hebrew, *a weekly journal of news and opinion, and served as its editor and publisher for twenty-seven years. This magazine exerted considerable influence on American Jewish life.*

Cowen left journalism in 1905, when he became connected with the Immigration Department and worked on Ellis Island, the gateway through which millions of immigrants were then pouring into the United States, among them hundreds of thousands of Jews. His official duties made it possible for him to present the problems of immigration to government officials who were disturbed by the flood of newcomers to American shores. It was understandable, therefore, that Cowen was chosen by President Theodore Roosevelt to travel to Europe to investigate the cause of the migration, especially as it concerned the Jews of Eastern Europe.

Cowen never relinquished his interest in publishing books of Jewish content. He sponsored and edited in the publication of such books as Oscar Straus' Religious People in the United States *and Alexander Kohut's* Ethics of the Fathers. *The excerpt from his autobiography,* Memories of an American Jew, *which is presented here exemplifies his concern with Judaism and Americanism, and shows his pride in the emergence of an American Jewish literature.*

Emma Lazarus*

PHILIP COWEN

IT WAS MY PLEASURE and privilege to come in contact with many men and women, Jews and Gentiles, during my connection with the *American Hebrew*. The mutual bond that brought together these diverse personalities, and put me in touch with all of them, was the Jewish question, or some facet of that cosmopolitan subject. Among these hosts one person stands pre-eminent: Emma Lazarus—the one poet of first rank American Jewry has yet produced. When the terrible Russian "May Laws" went into effect in 1881, great numbers of public-spirited Jews and Christians felt the urge to conccrn themselves with the fate of the unfortunate Russian Jews. In the forefront of those Americans who endeavored to help the Russian Jew stood Emma Lazarus.

It was the Russian persecution of her people that fanned her Jewish feeling to a flame; before that, as Ella A. Giles wrote of her in the *Christian Register*, "She had only a latent appreciation of Hebraism, and no enthusiasm for her own race." But it was not the first time, as is commonly believed, that she showed her interest in things Jewish. Miss Lazarus had previously written poems of a Jewish character that were published in the *Jewish Messenger*. Her *magnum opus*, "The Dance to Death," which gave the title to the volume of her work published later by the *American Hebrew*, had been written some years before, as is shown by her letter given below. Of course, it is altogether possible that her interest in this fourteenth-century tragedy was purely literary.

Miss Lazarus' first contribution to the *American Hebrew* was an essay on Henry Wadsworth Longfellow, written for the Literary Society of the Young Men's Hebrew Association. It was read

* Reprinted from *Memories of An American Jew*, The International Press, New York, 1932, pp. 332–344.

at a Longfellow Memorial Meeting on April 5th, 1882, by Mark Ash, and appeared in the issue of April 17th.

Miss Lazarus' growing Jewish spirit is shown therein by her criticism of this quatrain from Longfellow's poem "In the Jewish Cemetery at Newport":

> But ah! what once has been shall be no more.
> The groaning earth in travail and in pain
> Brings forth its races, *but does not restore,*
> *And the dead nations never rise again.*

The italics are Miss Lazarus'. And thus is she moved to speak in this Essay:

The rapidly increasing influence of the Jews in Europe, the present universal agitation of the Jewish question hotly discussed in almost every pamphlet, periodical and newspaper of the day, the frightful wave of persecution directed against the race, sweeping over the whole civilized world, and reaching its height in Russia; the furious zeal with which they are defended and attacked, the suffering, privation and martyrdom in the name of Judaism, prove them to be very warmly and thoroughly alive, and not at all in need of miraculous resuscitation to establish their nationality.

A few weeks later we received from Miss Lazarus the following letter:

To the Editors of
the *American Hebrew,*

A few years ago I wrote a play founded on an incident of medieval persecution of the Jews in Germany, which I think it would be highly desirable to publish now, in order to arouse sympathy and to emphasize the cruelty of the injustice done to our unhappy people. I write to ask if the American Hebrew Publishing Company will undertake to print it in pamphlet form. I send you also a poem which I should be glad to have you publish, if you can make room for it. Will you kindly return it if you do not care for it? It has a strong bearing on the question of the day, besides having a curious historic interest.

An early answer will greatly oblige me.
        Believe me, very truly yours,

                                            EMMA LAZARUS.
34 West 57th St.,
May 25, 1882.

This was the beginning of a heavy correspondence that continued for some time till Miss Lazarus went to Europe. At first she wrote from there only occasionally, then rarely, and ceased altogether, as ill health virtually incapacitated her.

The poem she enclosed was "An Epistle of Joshua Ibn Vives," based on an incident in Spanish-Jewish life of the fifteenth century. Thenceforward she became a regular contributor to the *American Hebrew*. Besides articles over her own signature, she sent communications, signed and unsigned, from herself and friends. On one occasion she even broke into our editorial columns to her infinite delight, for it was the first time any article had appeared editorially that had not been written by one of the Board of Editors. The incident certainly afforded her a thrill.

"The Dance to Death," which was the subject of her initial letter to us, ran through the columns of the *American Hebrew* and was then reprinted with nearly all of her poems of Jewish interest in a volume entitled *Songs of a Semite; The Dance to Death and Other Poems*. After her death her sisters Mary and Annie published her writings in two volumes, the second containing her Jewish poems. I have been advised that there is a desire on the part of some of her admirers to issue a definitive edition of her writings, as much that Miss Lazarus wrote is buried in the *American Hebrew*, in the *Century*, and other magazines and newspapers.

A sister, Annie Humphreys Johnston, living in Rome, has presented to Columbia University eighty-eight autograph letters sent to Emma Lazarus by various men of prominence. A quarter of them are from Emerson, at whose home she was a welcome guest. Others are from Browning, Whittier and Oliphant. Her unpublished annotations of Emerson's *Journals* are now in the custody of Columbia University and are being prepared for publication. Her sister Mrs. Johnston, in Rome, has refused, in response to a suggestion to reprint her "Collected Poems," to grant permission to include any items of a Jewish character, she being an ardent Catholic. Miss Lazarus' own personal copies of her printed volumes, bearing manuscript dedication, and other associational notations of interest, are in the possession of George Kohut.

The first two of her poems printed in the *American Hebrew* were "The Banner of the Jew" and "In Exile," published June 9, 1882. The former had been delivered at the closing exercises of Temple Emanu-El Religious School, and the latter was based on a letter received by Michael Heilprin from a Russian refugee who had been located in one of the colonies established in Texas.

After the final installment of "The Dance to Death," Miss Lazarus contributed a series entitled "An Epistle to the Hebrews." This may well be called her most fruitful work. She was indeed very proud of it, as well she might be. It was suggestively stimulating, and led to successful action, for the establishment of the Hebrew Technical Institute was the direct outcome of her "Epistle," and of communications by her, or inspired by her, that had appeared previously. These articles offered her the opportunity to go afield for broad topics on which to express her views. Thus Herzl's *Judenstaat,* then freshly before the public—almost a generation before it was made the Zionists' creed—was thoroughly discussed by her in the "Epistle." Here, too, came her opportunity to correspond directly with and get invaluable information from Laurence Oliphant, that valiant Christian knight-errant who dreamed of restoring the people of Israel to their ancient land. Here is a letter from her dated May 9, 1883, based on her correspondence with Oliphant:

To the *American Hebrew*:

I am in receipt of a letter from Mr. Laurence Oliphant dated Haifa, April 6th, in which he informs me, among other items of great interest to our people, that there are between three and four hundred Jewish families in Jerusalem and Jaffa, who are almost destitute and are now being mainly provided for by the Christian Missionary Society who are establishing them in a colony in the hope of making converts of them. The contract for building the houses for them has already been given out. "I think," says Mr. Oliphant with pointed brevity, "that these are people who should rather be looked after by their own coreligionists." The fact speaks for itself and seems hardly to require any other comment than the ardent champion of our race so mildly bestows upon it. I cannot resist the hopeful conviction that by merely bringing it to the notice of American Jews through the columns of your paper, it will arouse a deeper sense of the claims that these unfortunate outcasts have upon us, and the extreme necessities of their actual situation. If we have not yet succeeded in proving to Christian missionaries that "converted Jews" are probably not only the most expensive of all marketable commodities but also the most worthless after they are purchased, we might at least raise our own hands to rescue these wretched creatures, who from the pressure of material want, unrelieved by their own kindred, are thus almost inevitably forced into apostasy and moral degradation.

EMMA LAZARUS

This letter casts an interesting sidelight on the character of Laurence Oliphant. The series constituting "An Epistle to the Hebrews" was reprinted many years thereafter by the Zionist Organization for propaganda purposes.

From time to time—in between these longer articles—we printed some of Miss Lazarus' short poems. One of these, entitled "Consolation," was her special pride. It is reprinted here with the original Hebrew from which she translated it. Many of her shorter poems of the medieval Jewish poets were translated from the German of Michael Sachs and Abraham Geiger. She had become impressed with the beauty of these olden poets in the translations at her disposal. Though done into English by her from the German versions, which themselves, of course, were faithful renditions of the original Hebrew, so well had she caught their spirit that many believed the translations had been made by her from the Hebrew direct. But Emma Lazarus never did things by halves. She determined to master the ancient language for cultural purposes, that in her translations she might dip into the pristine purity of the sacred tongue. At the instance of Dr. Gustav Gottheil she studied Hebrew under Louis Schnabel, a pedagogue of rare ability. So assiduously did she work that she soon was able to read and understand the inner beauty of the

Hebrew language. In transmitting her first effort she wrote me with great pride:

"I enclose a stanza of poetry for next week's paper. It is from some Spanish-Hebrew poet, but I am sorry to say I do not know which one. I have translated this from the original Hebrew, and so am very proud of it as my *first* effort."

Consolation
Translated from the Hebrew by
Emma Lazarus

Oh were my streaming tears to flow,
According to my grievous woe,
Then foot of man in all his quest,
On no dry spot of earth could rest.
But not to Noah's flood alone,
The Covenant's bright pledge was shown,
Nor likewise to my tears & woe,
Behold once more revealed — the Bow!

[Following is the original Hebrew from which the above translation was made.]

אֵלוּ לְפִי אִדֵי דִמְעֵי יְזוּלוּן

לֹא דָרְכָה רֶגֶל אֱנוֹשׁ יַבֶּשֶׁת

אַךְ לֹא לְמֵי נֹחַ לְבַד כֹּרַת בְּרִית

כִּי גַם לְדִמְעֵי נִרְאָתָה הַקֶּשֶׁת׃

Miss Lazarus did not limit her part in Jewish work to the pen. At her suggestion a number of gatherings of small groups were held to exchange views on matters of Jewish interest. Several of these were held at the home of Augustus A. Levey on Lexington Avenue, attended by Minnie D. Louis, James H. Hoffman, who became first president of the Hebrew Technical Institute, Manuel A. Kursheedt, Miss Lazarus, myself and a few others. We talked over the possibilities of a technical school, and listened to the observations of those of us who had inspected such schools in Boston, Philadelphia and elsewhere.

I have a letter from Miss Lazarus asking me to attend a

Very informal meeting at Dr. Gottheil's house for the discussion of the Western Jewish Question. I write with Dr. Gottheil's permission to beg you to be present, as I am especially interested in the subject. We shall not be more than a dozen altogether.

Like many writers, Miss Lazarus liked the atmosphere of the printing office. As I conducted a printing business and during office hours was usually busy, she came to see me at odd times, especially on Sunday afternoons when I was likely to be in and have comparative leisure. I shall never forget one such visit. I had taken down a printing press to clean. I looked like a dozen printer's devils rolled into one. Old clothes, hands and face black with smudge, I felt rather uncomfortable. But Miss Lazarus refused to hear my apology, saying that if she broke in on me at such an inopportune time, she was the one who should apologize. She insisted on my going on with my job, while she set a typecase on end, and balancing herself on it told me of the cause of her visit, which was to raise some money to enable a young Russian named Finkelstein to complete his medical course at Yale.

As I have noted before, the religious side of Judaism had little interest for Miss Lazarus, or for any member of her family. I well remember the sting in the remark of a sister as she came into their home one day with one of the sons of Charles A. Dana of the New York *Sun*. As they went upstairs, possibly in reply to a curious look towards me, the sister said: "Yes; that's Emma's Jewish editor." But when a few months later Henry Ward

Beecher got off a joke at a dinner to Herbert Spencer about the Jews being a Chosen People, and "that God should have chosen such a people," her father was up in arms and wrote a communication which Emma sent us with the following note:

I enclose a communication of my father, the authorship of which I desire that you keep strictly confidential. Above all, if anyone ascribe it to me, please deny emphatically that I had had anything to do with it—which is the truth—for I did not even know he was going to write it, till he handed it to me in its present shape.

Miss Lazarus took a delightful personal interest in the paper and from time to time sent in communications and articles from friends here and abroad for publication. We welcomed her suggestions and were glad to have her criticism. Here is an instance:

I see a note in your editorial columns suggesting the name of "Washington" for the Vineland Colony. *Please don't publish this as coming from me,* but I hope, in the name of common sense, and in compassion for United States postmasters, that not one more addition to the American villages or settlements of any kind in the name of Washington will be made; every State has already an indefinite number of them, causing much confusion and unnecessary bewilderment. Why not, if a name must be found, select that of some friend to the Jewish cause, or of some distinguished Jew—such as Eliot, after George Eliot, who has such a noble and eloquent sympathy with us; or Montefiore, a beautiful name in itself, or Mendelssohn, or Beaconsfield, or Abarbanel? Anything rather than Washington, Lincoln, Jefferson or Garfield.

Our dear friend was deeply touched by a gift and letter that were sent to her by the American Hebrew Publishing Company in accordance with a resolution adopted at an annual meeting. Mr. Hart, to whom she refers, was Benjamin I. Hart, the President:

Dear Mr. Cowen:

I send herewith a letter of acknowledgment to Mr. Hart, which I shall be obliged to have you forward. I was completely taken by surprise on my return home late last evening to find myself the recipient of so much honor and such a splendid gift. I thank you most sincerely as a member of the society, as well as for the special trouble which I know has fallen to you in the selection of my book. I could not have desired anything more beautiful and appropriate. The work I have done for the Jewish cause seems to me painfully insignificant and slight, compared with the generous sympathy and encouragement I received from my people. I can only hope, by continuing my efforts, to be some day worthy of such kind words and deeds. . . .

Sincerely yours,
EMMA LAZARUS.

Half a century ago the American women who affected the pursuit of culture formed Browning Clubs at which they discussed the writings of Robert Browning, and sought religiously for the hidden meanings in his poems. One such club, of which a friend was a member, was unable to agree as to what the author meant by a certain line. In despair, they asked if it was possible for me to get in touch with the author, that the members might be relieved in their literary distress. As Miss Lazarus, who was going to England, was a protégé of the Brownings, and practically a member of their household, I transferred the inquiry to her. She told me that when she put the question to him, Browning queried with a smile, "how was he to recollect then what he had in mind fifty years before when he had written the lines?" I understand that a similar incident is touched on in the recent play, "The Barretts of Wimpole Street."

Much mystery surrounded the cause of the death of Miss Lazarus. But in a report by Rose Hawthorne Lathrop, who devoted her life to the relief of the cancerous poor, published a few years before she died, she tells the sad story. Here are a few extracts:

Among my valued friends at one time was Miss Emma Lazarus, the poetess, whose mind was lofty and pathetically unsatisfied.

I met her in the perfect atmosphere, that, never to be equalled, in the studio-home of Richard Watson Gilder and his wife Helena De Kay. Here the genius of the young Jewess was recognized to the brim, held up and rejoiced over in its rare vintage and purity. Miss Lazarus and I sometimes walked and talked together . . . I doubt if two more such fundamentally disconsolate minds, trying to carry a corner of the woes of the world upon their quivering shoulders, could have been found together in a search of years. But early discontent can sometimes produce a result. This young woman of finest promise and exalted perception died in her prime of cancer; but, though I grieve deeply for her, I would not pity her, for she never knew unaided suffering, but every amelioration. . . .

When I had settled down over a year later as a nurse in the lower East Side slums, Miss Josephine Lazarus, the sister of Emma, wrote me that what I was trying to do "could not be done." She had tried herself to establish a little hospital for this class in memory of Emma and had failed, in spite of wealth, paid trained nurses, and every advantage.

Emma Lazarus died November 19, 1887, after a long illness, during which she kept herself from the outer world. The reason for this may be found in the story told above by her friend. A few weeks after her death the *American Hebrew* published a Memorial Number devoted to her which brought together tributes from the foremost literati of the age, from men of affairs, and from those who were devoting their days and nights to the problems that affected world Jewry as a result of the Russian horrors. The last-named group felt especially the loss of a woman who for some years—though unfortunately not actively of late—had inspired them and spurred them on in the fine work they were doing. Hers was not a cry in the vast wilderness, for her voice struck a responsive chord and urged all on to still greater performance.

In the Memorial Number referred to, John Greenleaf Whittier paid this beautiful tribute to his sister-poet:

Her songs of the Divine Unity, repeated on the lips of her own people in all zones and continents, have been heard round the world. . . . Since Miriam sang of deliverance and triumph by the Red Sea, the Semitic race has had no braver singer. "The Crowing of the Red Cock," written when the Russian sky was red with blazing Hebrew horror, is an indignant and forceful lyric worthy of the Maccabean age. Her "Banner of the Jew" has the ring of Israel's war trumpet. Well may those of her own race and faith lament the loss of such a woman. They will not sorrow alone. Among the "mourning women" at her grave, the sympathizing voice of Christian daughters will mingle with the wail of the daughters of Jerusalem.

DAVID PHILIPSON

*David Philipson (1862–1949), a noted Reform rabbi, was a gradu-
ate of the first rabbinical class of the Hebrew Union College,
which he had entered on the urging of Rabbi Isaac Mayer Wise.
Upon his graduation in 1883, he accepted (1884) the pulpit of
Har Sinai Congregation of Baltimore. From 1884 to 1886, he did
post-graduate work in Assyriology and other Semitic languages
at Johns Hopkins University. In 1888 he became the rabbi of
Bene Israel Congregation in Cincinnati, where he remained
rabbi to the date of his retirement in 1938.*

*As a leading Reform rabbi he participated in the Reform Jew-
ish rabbinical conference at Pittsburgh in 1885. This was the
important conference at which the Reform rabbinate drew up
the "Pittsburgh Platform," which enunciated the principles of
Reform Judaism.*

*Rabbi Philipson was President of the Central Conference of
American Rabbis from 1907 to 1909, and was Honorary President from 1929 to 1934. He was a founder of the American Jewish Committee and a member of the Publication Committee of
the Jewish Publication Society. He was also a member of the
Board of Editors of the committee responsible for the Jewish
Publication Society's translation of the Bible, which appeared in
1917.*

In this selection from his autobiography, My Life as an American Jew, *he tells of his participation in the Pittsburgh Conference, in the establishment of the Jewish Publication Society, and
of his relationships with other outstanding Reform rabbis.*

Introduction to a Rabbinic Career*

DAVID PHILIPSON

MY FIRST DIRECT CONTACT with my rabbinical colleagues in the Eastern section of the country took place in January, 1885. I had received a note from Dr. Gustav Gottheil, the rabbi of Temple Emanu-El of New York, in which he informed me that plans were afoot to form an organization of the rabbis in the Eastern states and invited me cordially to attend. I had met Dr. Gottheil and Dr. Kohler on the occasion of my graduation from the Hebrew Union College, where they had both been present, but the other rabbis of New York City and other cities in the East were strangers to me. I therefore was glad of the opportunity to come into touch with them. I was by all odds the youngest officiating rabbi present at that meeting. An organization of the rabbis there present was effected with the Rev. Dr. Gustav Gottheil as president and myself as secretary. It adopted the name and title, Jewish Ministers' Association. A public meeting was held in Temple Emanu-El, at which I delivered an address on the Hebrew Union College. It was my first appearance before a gathering of rabbis and also my first public appearance in the metropolis of the nation. I presented the cause of my alma mater and of the Union of American Hebrew Congregations to the best of my ability. The address was well received. The New York rabbis were extremely cordial to their youngest colleague, especially Drs. Gottheil and Kohler. I was a guest at their homes. Dr. Gottheil's wife had died recently and his daughter was the head of the household. The hospitality of the home was charming. Gottheil was a suave diplomat of the pulpit. His was a hand of iron in a velvet glove. The congregation over which he presided was considered the Jewish "cathedral" congregation of the country.

* Reprinted from *My Life as an American Jew*, John G. Kidd and Son, Inc., Cincinnati, 1941, pp. 47–57.

Most of the prominent Jewish laymen of the city were members. Its beautiful temple of so-called Moorish architecture impressed me greatly. Gottheil was most kindly to me and in his home was a most gracious host. Probably as a result of this contact he stopped at Baltimore the following winter, on his way to the Southland, and offered me the post of assistant to him. I promised to consider the proposition and write to him shortly. After some thought, I came to the conclusion not to accept an assistantship anywhere, and so informed him by letter. This did not cause any coolness in his attitude toward me when I met him thereafter. The other great Reform congregation in New York was Temple Beth El, of which Dr. Kaufmann Kohler was the rabbi. Kohler was undoubtedly the most scholarly among the New York rabbis of that day. He, too, was most cordial to me during that meeting. I was quite overwhelmed when he took me into his library in the rear room of the top story of his residence. The library was replete with Judaica. Kohler at that time was a little over forty years of age. He was of a fiery temperament, quite a contrast to the suavity of his colleague Gottheil. He gloried in controversy and was a fighting champion of the Reform movement. He was a son-in-law of the famous Reformer, Dr. David Einhorn, and his successor in the pulpit of Temple Beth El. I can never forget his kindly reception. The hours that I spent with him in his library, where he showed me the classical works of the liberal Jewish movement, were indeed inspirational. I returned to Baltimore from that meeting with the feeling that I had gained much through the first contact with my senior colleagues. Their attitude was more than kind; it was indeed hearty.

My introduction into the communal activity of Baltimore was through my appointment as a member of the Charity Organization Society. Here I was associated with a number of the most prominent men and women of the general community. Two ladies on the board were members of aristocratic Baltimore families. One in particular I recall, Miss M. Of great beauty and charm, she seemed to me the embodiment of the finest in American womanhood. My service on this board was an education in the principles and methods of organized charity. Those were the early days of charity organization. The doubting Thomases were many. The traditional idea that charity was only giving, without professional supervision, was still largely held. At the annual meeting of the Baltimore Charity Organization Society that year, Henry C. Potter, the famous Episcopal bishop of New York, was the speaker. His theme was charity organization. I recall his *bon mot* that in the thought of most people the charity organization movement was no charity and all organization. Why employ professional workers and not use all the money contributed by generous givers for the relief of the needy? Sixty years after, that is still the feeling of many. But the cause of the intelligent administration of charitable funds has made great advance. The head as well as the heart is now active in the cause of aid to the worthy poor.

The head of the Charity Organization Society was the famous president of the Johns Hopkins University, Dr. Daniel C. Gilman. He invited me to be the speaker at the next annual meeting of the society. The meeting was held in Baltimore's most famous Protestant church on Mt. Vernon Place, the city's loveliest section. I was young and inexperienced. Instead of speaking on the subject of organized charity, as I should have done, I used the occasion to deplore religious prejudice and intolerance. The audience was largely Christian—possibly ninety-five per cent. What right had I, a young "Hotspur," to use that pulpit as a sounding board from which to rebuke my hearers? After the meeting Dr. Gilman, in conversation with me, hinted in the kindliest way that he felt that I had made a mistake in speaking as I had. He attributed the mistake to my youth and inexperience. And so it was. The mistake had no ill results for me, as it might have had. My Christian colleagues on the board (in fact, I was the only Jew) showed no resentment and our relations continued to be cordial as before.

I was also a speaker at the annual meeting of the Hebrew Benevolent Society, the premier Jewish philanthropic organization of the city. The speaker who preceded me on the program was the mayor of the city, a a typical politician of the old school. His address was along the line usually employed by that gentry.

He told that gathering what remarkable people the Jews were; that there were few Jews, if any, in penal institutions, and further balderdash of that kind. In my address I took him to task. I said that I resented remarks of that kind. Why should Jews be flattered because they are not criminals or wrongdoers? And so forth and so forth. A number of my hearers felt that I had done an unwise thing in calling down the chief executive of the city. But this time I felt that I was in the right and had no compunctions such as I had had after my address before the Charity Organization Society.

During the second year of my ministry in Baltimore I formed a Bible class for the young women of the congregation. About twenty daughters of members of the congregation attended regularly each week. I took as the theme of my discourses the opening chapters of the book of Genesis. All these girls were eligible for marriage, but I had special feelings for only one. The brightest girl in the class was Ella Hollander, and she quite carried me by storm. Sweet, unassuming, and modest, she spread about herself an aura of maidenly charm and refinement. It was not long before I felt that she would be my helpmate if I could gain her consent. I began to call at her home more than at any other house and it was soon common gossip that the young rabbi had lost his heart. The gossip proved true and when the dear girl accepted my proposal of marriage, my cup of happiness was full. There was general approval of my choice, for it was felt that of all the girls in the congregation she was the best fitted for the position of "rabbi's wife." The engagement was announced in December, 1885, shortly after I returned for the most important gathering of Reform rabbis since the conference at Philadelphia in 1869. These rabbis convened at the call of Dr. Kaufmann Kohler, of Temple Beth El, New York. In his call for a conference Dr. Kohler stated that he was issuing the invitation to the rabbis of the Reform wing to come together "for the purpose of discussing the present state of American Judaism, its issues and its requirements, and of conferring upon such plans and practical measures as are demanded by the hour." In addition to this general call, I received from Dr. Kohler a special invitation couched in these words: "Dear Doctor, I hope you will not disappoint us. We cannot spare you, particularly at the prayer-book meeting. Besides, let us concentrate our forces and accomplish something creditable and worthy of a conference of rabbis! We must have you, and I wish you would prepare or suggest something in the way of practical reform! Yours cordially, Dr. K. Kohler."

As may well be imagined, I, who was little more than a boy, was immeasurably flattered to receive such a pressing invitation from so eminent a man. I went to Pittsburgh with heart beating high at the prospect of meeting and conferring with my colleagues, many of whom I had never met. This conference became very famous through the remarkable platform setting forth in eight paragraphs the guiding principles of the Reform or liberal movement in Judaism. This "Pittsburgh Platform" aroused intense excitement among the Jews of the country. In a paper which I read at the meeting of the Central Conference of American Rabbis in Chicago in June, 1935, on the occasion of the fiftieth anniversary of the adoption of the "Pittsburgh Platform," I used this language:

Immediately upon the reading of the report of the Committee on Platform, the President, Isaac M. Wise, asked, "Gentlemen, what are you going to do with this Declaration of Independence?" The platform thus strikingly styled was without doubt the most challenging declaration ever sent forth by a rabbinical assembly in the United States. And the challenge was promptly taken up by critics and opponents, notably the Conservative press and rabbinate in the Eastern section of the country. . . . Conservative rabbis raged and fumed. When I returned from Pittsburgh to Baltimore I found the Jewish community in a ferment because of the agitation against the conference by the senior rabbi of the community, who denounced the criticism. The best-known public structure in Baltimore was the Washington Monument. He compared the rabbis assembled at Pittsburgh to pygmies attempting to pull down the Washington Monument. . . . I felt compelled to enter the lists in defense of the belabored conference. Taking each of the eight paragraphs of the platform as a text, I delivered to crowded houses a series of eight addresses on these paragraphs, and a ninth on the other resolutions adopted at the meeting.

The local press gave much space to these addresses. It was my first experience in rabbinical polemics. I had acted as secretary of the conference and naturally I felt a particular duty to rise to its defense in answer to attacks. Many years later (1907) in my book, *The Reform Movement in Judaism*, I wrote, "This platform aroused the usual storm of opposition in the Conservative and Orthodox camps, but it still stands as the utterance most expressive of the teaching of Reform Judaism." And even now I feel that this remains largely true.

This meeting at Pittsburgh was the most exhilarating professional experience I had yet had. My elder colleagues (I was the youngest man present) were exceedingly kindly and gracious. I formed friendships there that lasted for years. Notably was this the case with Dr. L. Mayer, the genial host of the conference, who throughout his life remained a devoted friend. When his son, Harry (Rabbi Harry H. Mayer, now rabbi-emeritus in Kansas City, Missouri), came to Cincinnati to enter the Hebrew Union College, the father brought the boy to our home and asked me to take a particular interest in him. This I did, and today the son continues the warm friendship which existed between the father and myself.

In March, 1886, America's greatest preacher, Henry Ward Beecher, passed from earth. On the Sabbath morning following his death, I voiced a tribute to him from my pulpit in Har Sinai Temple. This was considered so unusual that one of the daily papers of the city requested a copy of the sermon for publication and it appeared in full in the columns of the *Baltimore American*. It created quite a stir, for it was the first time that a tribute had been paid to a Christian minister from a Jewish pulpit. Beecher had in a number of instances shown a breadth of spirit unusual in the Christian ministry. When Joseph Seligman was refused accommodations in the Grand Union Hotel at Saratoga, Beecher denounced the management of that hostelry with all the eloquence—and it was very great—at his command; he was one of the speakers at the great meeting held in memory of the leading

Jewish philanthropist of the nineteenth century, Sir Moses Montefiore. Beecher was truly a man who transcended the narrow limitations of creed and preached a religion of humanity. Thus it appears that from that very early day in my public career I entered upon a course which I have consistently followed through all the years, namely, the practical following out of the ideas implied in the doctrine of the Fatherhood of God and the brotherhood of man. Even in these most distressing days in which we are now living (1940), when Hitlerism has filled the Western world with prejudice and hatred, I cannot and will not recede from the stand that I have taken all my life, the stand indicated in the great queries of the ancient prophet: "Have we not all one Father? Has not one God created us?"

One of the prominent rabbis who attended the Pittsburgh Conference was Dr. S. H. Sonneschein, of St. Louis. He became the center of a fierce religious storm in that city. He was rabbi of congregation Shaare Emeth, the leading Jewish congregation of the Missouri metropolis. His course of life alienated a large number of the members of his congregation. He failed of re-election as rabbi. But he had many devoted friends and followers who seceded from the congregation and formed for him a new congregation, Temple Israel. The reason for my mentioning this unfortunate incident is that I was brought into connection with it by the receipt of a letter from the secretary of congregation Shaare Emeth, offering me the pulpit. I was asked to come to St. Louis to look over the ground. This I did. I preached several times. When asked if I would accept the position, I bade for time to consider the proposition. I promised an answer shortly after my return to Baltimore. I had married recently—in September, 1886. I did not feel it right to pull up stakes and take my young wife so far from home. I wrote a letter full of appreciation for the honor the congregation had done me, but refusing the proffer. My refusal aroused some indignation, but unjustifiably so. I had given no assurance that I would accept the position. It was thoroughly understood by the officers of the congregation that I would give my answer after due consideration. Thus ended that chapter.

The Rev. Dr. Samuel Sale, who had been my predecessor in

the Har Sinai pulpit and had gone from Baltimore to Chicago to fill the pulpit of congregation Anshe Ma'arab, was elected rabbi of the St. Louis congregation. Not long thereafter Rabbi Liebman Adler, rabbi-emeritus of the Chicago congregation, came to Baltimore, commissioned by the Board of Trustees of the congregation to offer me the pulpit. What a beautiful spirit was Liebman Adler! A gentle scholar, a rabbi in the truest sense of the word. I recall him so well, this lovely character. He was an ornament to the profession. He had published a remarkable collection of sermons in German, entitled *Tzeenah u'renah*, a title taken from the medieval collection of homilies for the Jewish woman. A selection of these sermons was published some years later by the Jewish Publication Society of America, under the title, Sabbath Hours. These sermons make no pretense at grandiloquence. They are heart-to-heart talks by a man grown wise in the school of life. The aged rabbi, whom I revered deeply as my senior in knowledge and experience, had come that great distance to urge me to go to the great Western metropolis. But Chicago had no charms for me. I was thoroughly content in Baltimore. I was happy in my beautiful new home, which my young wife and I had recently established. It hurt me to have to refuse the request of the saintly sage to occupy the pulpit that he had graced, but he understood the situation and, while expressing his regret that I could not see my way clear to give a favorable answer to the offer, he saw my side of the case and departed, giving me his benediction.

The mention of the Pittsburgh Conference brings to mind another gathering held in that city, namely, the convention of the Union of American Hebrew Congregations in July, 1887. I had induced the Har Sinai congregation to join the Union and I attended the Pittsburgh convention as a delegate of the congregation. That convention remains memorable for me not because of any startling resolutions like the "Pittsburgh Platform," but because of an important personal experience. Like all young rabbis, I was greatly troubled in the search of subjects for my addresses. I had instituted Sunday evening lectures. I had given a course in Jewish history. What in the world should I speak about in the coming season? This worry I carried about with me. It accompanied me from Baltimore to Pittsburgh. One day, as my foot rested upon the lowest step of the stair leading to the second floor of the hotel where a meeting was in progress, there flashed upon my mind from the unknown the query, "Why not deliver a course of lectures on the Jew in English fiction?" This was one of those inexplicable happenings that occur now and then. It was really an inspiration. The problem that was troubling me was solved. Upon my return to Baltimore, I at once set to work to outline such a course of lectures and to gather material. I announced the course in a communication to the members of the congregation and in the daily press. The announcement aroused great interest. I delivered the opening address the first Sunday evening in November, 1887. The temple was crowded by both Jews and non-Jews. I was told that a large number of Johns Hopkins students were present. I had apparently struck a new vein. I was here a pathfinder. I have had many successors who have found subjects for addresses and books in the novels and plays that have Jews as characters. Each address was given generous space in the Monday papers. A friend suggested that these addresses should be preserved in book form. That suggestion was acted upon after I removed from Baltimore to Cincinnati. This book has gone through six editions. After the appearance of Zangwill's *Children of the Ghetto*, I added, in 1902, a lengthy chapter to the original book. I was made very happy by the enthusiastic reception given the book in literary journals throughout this country and in England. It appeared that I had struck it rich.

My addresses on the Jew in fiction did not exhaust my literary activity. One of the leading Jews in the country, the Hon. Benjamin F. Peixotto, who had been U. S. Consul to Rumania, was editing at this time a magazine entitled *The Menorah Monthly*. This is not to be confounded with another far more recent publication, *The Menorah Journal*. I contributed several articles to this monthly, namely, "Jews as Physicians," which was the leading article in the issue of December, 1887, and "Jews and Industries," which appeared in the issue of February, 1888. During that same year I contributed a number of articles to the *American Israelite* in Cincinnati which I called "Jewish Celebrities."

The celebrities treated were Jehudah Halevi, the poet; Abraham ibn Ezra, the traveler and commentator, and Isaac Abarbanel, the statesman. This literary activity, in addition to my congregational and communal duties, kept me fairly well employed.

When I arrived in Baltimore to take charge of the Har Sinai congregation, I came into a religious atmosphere quite different from that which I had breathed during my college life in Cincinnati. I refer particularly to the interpretation of Reform Judaism. Isaac M. Wise was the dominant personality in Cincinnati, David Einhorn in Baltimore. True, Einhorn had left Baltimore many years before, but his influence was still potent. During his lifetime he and Wise had clashed frequently. Einhorn had for his motto, *"principiis obsta"* ("fealty to principle"). Wise had the more statesmanlike outlook; Einhorn was never willing to compromise. Wise felt that life frequently demanded such compromise; Einhorn went forward in a straight line. Wise felt that deviations from that straight line were often necessary in order to achieve necessary and desirable results. I have always considered myself particularly fortunate in thus being subjected to these two contrasting influences in my early professional life. I had been reared in the Wise school; I had my first graduate training, if I may call it so, in the Einhorn environment. This double interest led me to that study of the Reform movement which eventuated later in the writing of my book, *The Reform Movement in Judaism*. If I had remained in Cincinnati or taken a position in some Midwestern, Southern, or Western congregation, it is not at all likely that I would have obtained so vivid a knowledge of the Reform movement as was reflected in the teaching of Einhorn and his sympathizers in the Eastern part of the country. I had not been in Baltimore long ere an elderly member of the congregation, who had become impoverished, offered to sell me his file of *Sinai*, the magazine edited by Einhorn. The pages of this magazine opened an entirely new field. I studied intently the writings of Einhorn and other Reformers who were represented in its pages. Thus the two tendencies in the Reform movement found lodgement in my thinking. This helped greatly in my advanced education. The five years I spent in Baltimore were precious years in the pursuance of this advanced education.

For four years I had been the only graduate of the Hebrew Union College in the East. In November, 1887, my classmate, Joseph Krauskopf, who had been rabbi in Kansas City from the time of his graduation, came to Philadelphia to take charge of the Keneseth Israel congregation. This prominent Reform congregation had had Dr. Samuel Hirsch, one of the leading Jewish Reformers, as its rabbi. Krauskopf, who was a veritable live wire, soon set things humming. The congregation was roused from its lethargy. The community, too, sat up and took notice. Philadelphia, through the leadership of Isaac Leeser and Sabato Morais, had become the center of Orthodox Judaism. Krauskopf's addresses on Sunday morning embittered the anti-Reformers. The Jewish community was split into opposing factions. The fiery young rabbi constantly added fuel to the flames. Reports of the exciting situation were constantly reaching the neighboring city of Baltimore, where I was stationed. Shortly after Krauskopf's coming to Philadelphia, I was invited by a Jewish organization of that city to deliver an address. My classmate came to hear me and after the address we went to his house. He unburdened himself to me. He was in the heart of a determined opposition but he was determined to fight. And fight he did, and he achieved brilliantly. In that very first year of his ministry in Philadelphia, he advocated in a Sunday morning address the formation of a Jewish Publication Society. He had organized a society called the "Knowledge Seekers." The society, through his urging, arranged for a meeting of Jews in Philadelphia and neighboring cities to consider the advisability of organizing a Publication Society. The meeting was held in the city of Philadelphia in May, 1888. Men and women of all shades of opinion were present also from New York, Baltimore, and other places. The fur flew, for the discussions were hectic. But the organization was effected and the Jewish Publication Society was born! Krauskopf was really the founder of that society. His implacable foes, however, secured the upper hand; he was gradually forced out. As it chanced, these foes of Krauskopf were very friendly to me. But I constantly regretted what I felt was a great injustice that they had done to him. Fifty years have rolled around since the Jewish Publication Society was organized. A celebration of the Fiftieth Anniversary took place in December, 1938. I was asked to preside at the anniversary meeting. In my address I took occasion to pay tribute to the memory of Joseph Krauskopf as the founder of the society. I felt that in paying this tribute I was correcting the wrong that had been done him. Through my continued service as a member of the Publication Committee I had been for a long time a member of the so-called official family, and as a member of that family I spoke as I did in officially giving the credit that was due to my old friend and classmate of the first class of rabbis to be graduated from the Hebrew Union College.

My stay in Baltimore was coming to an end. Since May I had been negotiating with the Bene Israel congregation in Cincinnati, generally known as the "Mound Street Temple." I had frequently attended services there while a student in Cincinnati. I had been a great favorite of its famous rabbi, Dr. Max Lilienthal. In fact, he is reported to have said that if he could choose his successor it would be David Philipson. Although I had declined half a dozen calls to the pulpits of congregations here and there, when the opportunity presented itself of going to Cincinnati, I entertained the proposition gladly. True, I had been very happy in Baltimore; I had established a home there with a charming, congenial life companion; I had made many dear friends; but although I had refused offers to go to New York, Philadelphia, Chicago, and St. Louis, Cincinnati exerted a spell that I could not withstand. My alma mater lured me on. I saw things in the rosy light of retrospect. I had no idea of the difficulties that lay in prospect, and the disillusionments that would dissipate the glamor. Ambition spurred me on, the ambition to be connected with the institutions of Reform Judaism that centered in Cincinnati. I impressed my young wife with the opportunities that lay before me in the Ohio city. With superb loyalty, she said as once Ruth had said, "Where thou goest I will go." And this, too, although she was leaving her childhood home and all her fond home and other associations. Never has man had a truer mate. Through all the vicissitudes of a career that was frequently stormy, she never wavered, although frequently heartsick for her former home and associates.

MARY ANTIN

One of the most vivid and impressive books written about the Americanization of the immigrant Jew is The Promised Land *by Mary Antin, a chapter of which is offered here. Miss Antin was born in Russia in 1881 and was brought to the United States in 1894. She was educated in public schools in the Chelsea section of Boston and at Teacher's College, Columbia University. She died in 1949. Her account of her schooling is now recognized as an American classic. She also wrote* From Plotzk to Boston *(1898), which is a record of her voyage to America and, of course,* The Promised Land *(1912). Sections of* The Promised Land *have been used as text books in Massachusetts.*

The material included here gives her first impressions of America when she settled in Boston at the turn of the century.

The Promised Land*

MARY ANTIN

HAVING MADE such good time across the ocean, I ought to be able to proceed no less rapidly on *terra firma*, where, after all, I am more at home. And yet here is where I falter. Not that I hesitated, even for the space of a breath, in my first steps in America. There was no time to hesitate. The most ignorant immigrant, on

* Reprinted from *The Promised Land,* Houghton Mifflin Co., Boston, 1912, pp. 180–205.

landing, proceeds to give and receive greetings, to eat, sleep, and rise, after the manner of his own country; wherein he is corrected, admonished, and laughed at, whether by interested friends or the most indifferent strangers; and his American experience is thus begun. The process is spontaneous on all sides, like the education of the child by the family circle. But while the most stupid nursery maid is able to contribute her part toward the result, we do not expect an analysis of the process to be furnished by any member of the family, least of all by the engaging infant. The philosophical maiden aunt alone, or some other witness equally psychological and aloof, is able to trace the myriad efforts by which the little Johnnie or Nellie acquires a secure hold on the disjointed parts of the huge plaything, life.

Now I was not exactly an infant when I was set down, on a May day some fifteen years ago, in this pleasant nursery of America. I had long since acquired the use of my faculties, and had collected some bits of experience, practical and emotional, and had even learned to give an account of them. Still, I had very little perspective, and my observations and comparisons were superficial. I was too much carried away to analyze the forces that were moving me. My Polotzk I knew well before I began to judge it and experiment with it. America was bewilderingly strange, unimaginably complex, delightfully unexplored. I rushed impetuously out of the cage of my provincialism and looked eagerly about the brilliant universe. My question was, What have we here?—not, What does this mean? That query came much later. When I now become retrospectively introspective, I fall into the predicament of the centipede in the rhyme, who got along very smoothly until he was asked which leg came after which, whereupon he became so rattled that he couldn't take a step. I know I have come on a thousand feet, on wings, winds, and American machines—I have leaped and run and climbed and crawled —but to tell which step came after which I find a puzzling matter. Plenty of maiden aunts were present during my second infancy, in the guise of immigrant officials, school-teachers, settlement workers, and sundry other unprejudiced and critical observers. Their statistics I might properly borrow to fill the gaps in my recollections, but I am prevented by my sense of harmony. The individual, we know, is a creature unknown to the statistician, whereas I undertook to give the personal view of everything. So I am bound to unravel, as well as I can, the tangle of events, outer and inner, which made up the first breathless years of my American life.

During his three years of probation, my father had made a number of false starts in business. His history for that period is the history of thousands who come to America, like him, with pockets empty, hands untrained to the use of tools, minds cramped by centuries of repression in their native land. Dozens of these men pass under your eyes every day, my American friend, too absorbed in their honest affairs to notice the looks of suspicion which you cast at them, the repugnance with which you shrink from their touch. You see them shuffle from door to door with a basket of spools and buttons, or bending over the sizzling irons in a basement tailor shop, or rummaging in your ash can, or moving a pushcart from curb to curb, at the command of the burly policeman. "The Jew peddler!" you say, and dismiss him from your premises and from your thoughts, never dreaming that the sordid drama of his days may have a moral that concerns you. What if the creature with the untidy beard carries in his bosom his citizenship papers? What if the cross-legged tailor is supporting a boy in college who is one day going to mend your state constitution for you? What if the ragpicker's daughters are hastening over the ocean to teach your children in the public schools? Think, every time you pass the greasy alien on the street, that he was born thousands of years before the oldest native American; and he may have something to communicate to you, when you two shall have learned a common language. Remember that his very physiognomy is a cipher, the key to which it behooves you to search for most diligently.

By the time we joined my father, he had surveyed many avenues of approach toward the coveted citadel of fortune. One of these, heretofore untried, he now proposed to essay, armed with new courage, and cheered on by the presence of his family. In partnership with an energetic little man who had an English chapter in his history, he prepared to set up a refreshment booth on Crescent Beach. But while he was completing arrangements at the beach we remained in town, where we enjoyed the educational advantages of a thickly populated neighborhood; namely, Wall Street, in the West End of Boston.

Anybody who knows Boston knows that the West and North Ends are the wrong ends of that city. They form the tenement district, or, in the newer phrase, the slums of Boston. Anybody who is acquainted with the slums of any American metropolis knows that that is the quarter where poor immigrants foregather, to live, for the most part, as unkempt, half-washed, toiling, unaspiring foreigners; pitiful in the eyes of social missionaries, the despair of boards of health, the hope of ward politicians, the touchstone of American democracy. The well-versed metropolitan knows the slums as a sort of house of detention for poor aliens, where they live on probation till they can show a certificate of good citizenship.

He may know all this and yet not guess how Wall Street, in the West End, appears in the eyes of a little immigrant from Polotzk. What would the sophisticated sight-seer say about Union Place off Wall Street, where my new home waited for me? He would say that it is no place at all, but a short box of an alley. Two rows of three-story tenements are its sides, a stingy strip of sky is its lid, a littered pavement is the floor, and a narrow mouth its exit.

But I saw a very different picture on my introduction to Union Place. I saw two imposing rows of brick buildings, loftier than any dwelling I had ever lived in. Brick was even on the ground for me to tread on, instead of common earth or boards. Many friendly windows stood open, filled with uncovered heads of women and children. I thought the people were interested in us, which was very neighborly. I looked up to the topmost row of windows, and my eyes were filled with the May blue of an American sky!

In our days of affluence in Russia we had been accustomed to upholstered parlors, embroidered linen, silver spoons and candlesticks, goblets of gold, kitchen shelves shining with copper and brass. We had featherbeds heaped halfway to the ceiling; we had clothes presses dusky with velvet and silk and fine woollen. The three small rooms into which my father now ushered us, up one flight of stairs, contained only the necessary beds, with lean mattresses; a few wooden chairs; a table or two; a mysterious iron structure, which later turned out to be a stove; a couple of unornamental kerosene lamps; and a scanty array of cooking-utensils and crockery. And yet we were all impressed with our new home and its furniture. It was not only because we had just passed through our seven lean years, cooking in earthen vessels, eating black bread on holidays and wearing cotton; it was chiefly because these wooden chairs and tin pans were American chairs and pans that they shone glorious in our eyes. And if there was anything lacking for comfort or decoration we expected it to be presently supplied—at least, we children did. Perhaps my mother alone, of us newcomers, appreciated the shabbiness of the little apartment, and realized that for her there was as yet no laying down of the burden of poverty.

Our initiation into American ways began with the first step on the new soil. My father found occasion to instruct or correct us even on the way from the pier to Wall Street, which journey we made crowded together in a rickety cab. He told us not to lean out of the windows, not to point, and explained the word "greenhorn." We did not want to be "greenhorns," and gave the strictest attention to my father's instructions. I do not know when my parents found opportunity to review together the history of Polotzk in the three years past, for we children had no patience with the subject; my mother's narrative was constantly interrupted by irrelevant questions, interjections, and explanations.

The first meal was an object lesson of much variety. My father produced several kinds of food, ready to eat, without any cooking, from little tin cans that had printing all over them. He attempted to introduce us to a queer, slippery kind of fruit, which he called "banana," but had to give it up for the time being. After the meal, he had better luck with a curious piece of furniture on runners, which he called "rocking-chair." There were five of us newcomers, and we found five different ways of getting into the American machine of perpetual motion, and as many ways of getting out of it. One born and bred to the use of a rocking-chair cannot imagine how ludicrous people can make themselves when attempting to use it for the first time. We laughed immoderately over our various experiments with the novelty, which was a wholesome way of letting off steam after the unusual excitement of the day.

In our flat we did not think of such a thing as storing the coal in the bathtub. There was no bathtub. So in the evening of the first day my father conducted us to the public baths. As we moved along in a little procession, I was delighted with the illumination of the streets. So many lamps, and they burned until morning, my father said, and so people did not need to carry lanterns. In America, then, everything was free, as we had heard in Russia. Light was free; the streets were as bright as a synagogue on a holy day. Music was free; we had been serenaded, to our gaping delight, by a brass band of many pieces, soon after our installation on Union Place.

Education was free. That subject my father had written about repeatedly, as comprising his chief hope for us children, the essence of American opportunity, the treasure that no thief could touch, not even misfortune or poverty. It was the one thing that he was able to promise us when he sent for us; surer, safer than bread or shelter. On our second day, I was thrilled with the realization of what this freedom of education meant. A little girl from across the alley came and offered to conduct us to school. My father was out, but we five between us had a few words of English by this time. We knew the word school. We understood. This child, who had never seen us till yesterday, who could not pronounce our names, who was not much better dressed than we, was able to offer us the freedom of the schools of Boston! No application made, no questions asked, no examinations, rulings, exclusions; no machinations, no fees. The doors stood open for every one of us. The smallest child could show us the way.

This incident impressed me more than anything I had heard

in advance of the freedom of education in America. It was concrete proof—almost the thing itself. One had to experience it to understand it.

It was a great disappointment to be told by my father that we were not to enter upon our school career at once. It was too near the end of the term, he said, and we were going to move to Crescent Beach in a week or so. We had to wait until the opening of the schools in September. What a loss of precious time—from May till September!

Not that the time was really lost. Even the interval on Union Place was crowded with lessons and experiences. We had to visit the stores and be dressed from head to foot in American clothing; we had to learn the mysteries of the iron stove, the washboard, and the speaking-tube; we had to learn to trade with the fruit peddler through the window, and not be afraid of the policeman; and, above all, we had to learn English.

The kind people who assisted us in these important matters form a group by themselves in the gallery of my friends. If I had never seen them from those early days till now, I should still have remembered them with gratitude. When I enumerate the long list of my American teachers, I must begin with those who came to us on Wall Street and taught us our first steps. To my mother, in her perplexity over the cookstove, the woman who showed her how to make the fire was an angel of deliverance. A fairy godmother to us children was she who led us to a wonderful country called "uptown," where, in a dazzlingly beautiful palace called a "department store," we exchanged our hateful homemade European costumes, which pointed us out as "greenhorns" to the children on the street, for real American machine-made garments, and issued forth glorified in each other's eyes.

With our despised immigrant clothing we shed also our impossible Hebrew names. A committee of our friends, several years ahead of us in American experience, put their heads together and concocted American names for us all. Those of our real names that had no pleasing American equivalents they ruthlessly discarded, content if they retained the initials. My mother, possessing a name that was not easily translatable, was punished with the undignified nickname of Annie. Fetchke, Joseph, and Deborah issued as Frieda, Joseph, and Dora, respectively. As for poor me, I was simply cheated. The name they gave me was hardly new. My Hebrew name being Maryashe in full, Mashke for short, Russianized into Marya (*Mar-ya*), my friends said that it would hold good in English as *Mary*; which was very disappointing, as I longed to possess a strange-sounding American name like the others.

I am forgetting the consolation I had, in this matter of names, from the use of my surname, which I have had no occasion to mention until now. I found on my arrival that my father was "Mr. Antin," on the slightest provocation, and not, as in Polotzk, on state occasions alone. And so I was "Mary Antin," and I felt very important to answer to such a dignified title. It was just like America that even plain people should wear their surnames on week days.

As a family we were so diligent under instruction, so adaptable, and so clever in hiding our deficiencies, that when we made the journey to Crescent Beach, in the wake of our small wagonload of household goods, my father had very little occasion to admonish us on the way, and I am sure he was not ashamed of us. So much we had achieved toward our Americanization during the two weeks since our landing.

Crescent Beach is a name that is printed in very small type on the maps of the environs of Boston, but a life-size strip of sand curves from Winthrop to Lynn; and that is historic ground in the annals of my family. The place is now a popular resort for holiday crowds, and is famous under the name of Revere Beach. When the reunited Antins made their stand there, however, there were no boulevards, no stately bath-houses, no hotels, no gaudy amusement places, no illuminations, no showmen, no tawdry rabble. There was only the bright clean sweep of sand, the summer sea, and the summer sky. At high tide the whole Atlantic rushed in, tossing the seaweeds in his mane; at low tide he rushed out, growling and gnashing his granite teeth. Between tides a baby might play on the beach, digging with pebbles and shells, till it lay asleep on the sand. The whole sun shone by day, troops of stars by night, and the great moon in its season.

Into this grand cycle of the seaside day I came to live and learn and play. A few people came with me as I have already intimated; but the main thing was that I came to live on the edge of the sea—I, who had spent my life inland, believing that the great waters of the world were spread out before me in the Dvina. My idea of the human world had grown enormously during the long journey; my idea of the earth had expanded with every day at sea; my idea of the world outside the earth now budded and swelled during my prolonged experience of the wide and unobstructed heavens.

Not that I got any inkling of the conception of a multiple world. I had had no lessons in cosmogony, and I had no spontaneous revelation of the true position of the earth in the universe. For me, as for my fathers, the sun set and rose, and I did not feel the earth rushing through space. But I lay stretched out in the sun, my eyes level with the sea, till I seemed to be absorbed bodily by the very materials of the world around me; till I could not feel my hand as separate from the warm sand in which it was buried. Or I crouched on the beach at full moon, wondering, wondering, between the two splendors of the sky and the sea. Or I ran out to meet the incoming storm, my face full in the wind, my being a-tingle with an awesome delight to the tips of my fogmatted locks flying behind; and stood clinging to some stake or upturned boat, shaken by the roar and rumble of the waves. So clinging, I pretended that I was in danger, and was deliciously frightened; I held on with both hands, and shook my head, exulting in the tumult around me, equally ready to laugh or sob. Or else I sat, on the stillest days, with my back to the sea, not looking at all, but just listening to the rustle of the waves on the sand; not thinking at all, but just breathing with the sea.

Thus courting the influence of sea and sky and variable weather, I was bound to have dreams, hints, imaginings. It was no more than this, perhaps: that the world as I knew it was not large enough to contain all that I saw and felt; that the thoughts that flashed through my mind, not half understood, unrelated to my utterable thoughts, concerned something for which I had as yet no name. Every imaginative growing child has these flashes of intuition, especially one that becomes intimate with some one aspect of nature. With me it was the growing time, that idle summer by the sea, and I grew all the faster because I had been so cramped before. My mind, too, had so recently been worked upon by the impressive experience of a change of country that I was more than commonly alive to impressions, which are the seeds of ideas.

Let no one suppose that I spent my time entirely, or even chiefly, in inspired solitude. By far the best part of my day was spent in play—frank, hearty, boisterous play, such as comes natural to American children. In Polotzk I had already begun to be considered too old for play, excepting set games or organized frolics. Here I found myself included with children who still played, and I willingly returned to childhood. There were plenty of playfellows. My father's energetic little partner had a little wife and a large family. He kept them in the little cottage next to ours; and that the shanty survived the tumultuous presence of that brood is a wonder to me today. The young Wilners included an assortment of boys, girls, and twins, of every possible variety of age, size, disposition, and sex. They swarmed in and out of the cottage all day long, wearing the door-sill hollow, and trampling the ground to powder. They swung out of windows like monkeys, slid up the roof like flies, and shot out of trees like fowls. Even a small person like me couldn't go anywhere without being run over by a Wilner; and I could never tell which Wilner it was because none of them ever stood still long enough to be identified; and also because I suspected that they were in the habit of interchanging conspicuous articles of clothing, which was very confusing.

You would suppose that the little mother must have been utterly lost, bewildered, trodden down in this horde of urchins; but you are mistaken. Mrs. Wilner was a positively majestic little person. She ruled her brood with the utmost coolness and strictness. She had even the biggest boy under her thumb, frequently under her palm. If they enjoyed the wildest freedom outdoors, indoors the young Wilners lived by the clock. And so at five o'clock in the evening, on seven days in the week, my father's partner's children could be seen in two long rows around the supper table. You could tell them apart on this occasion, because they all had their faces washed. And this is the time to count them: there are twelve little Wilners at table.

I managed to retain my identity in this multitude somehow, and while I was very much impressed with their numbers, I even dared to pick and choose my friends among the Wilners. One or two of the smaller boys I liked best of all, for a game of hide-and-seek or a frolic on the beach. We played in the water like ducks, never taking the trouble to get dry. One day I waded out with one of the boys, to see which of us dared go farthest. The tide was extremely low, and we had not wet our knees when we began to look back to see if familiar objects were still in sight. I thought we had been wading for hours, and still the water was so shallow and quiet. My companion was marching straight ahead, so I did the same. Suddenly a swell lifted us almost off our feet, and we clutched at each other simultaneously. There was a lesser swell, and little waves began to run, and a sigh went up from the sea. The tide was turning—perhaps a storm was on the way—and we were miles, dreadful miles from dry land.

Boy and girl turned without a word, four determined bare legs ploughing through the water, four scared eyes straining toward the land. Through an eternity of toil and fear they kept dumbly on, death at their heels, pride still in their hearts. At last they reach high-water mark—six hours before full tide.

Each has seen the other afraid, and each rejoices in the knowledge. But only the boy is sure of his tongue.

"You was scared, warn't you?" he taunts.

The girl understands so much, and is able to reply:—

"You can schwimmen, I not."

"Betcher life I can schwimmen," the other mocks.

And the girl walks off, angry and hurt.

"An' I can walk on my hands," the tormentor calls after her. "Say, you greenhorn, why don'tcher look?"

The girl keeps straight on, vowing that she would never walk with that rude boy again, neither by land nor sea, not even though the waters should part at his bidding.

I am forgetting the more serious business which had brought

us to Crescent Beach. While we children disported ourselves like mermaids and mermen in the surf, our respective fathers dispensed cold lemonade, hot peanuts, and pink popcorn, and piled up our respective fortunes, nickel by nickel, penny by penny. I was very proud of my connection with the public life of the beach. I admired greatly our shining soda fountain, the rows of sparkling glasses, the pyramids of oranges, the sausage chains, the neat white counter, and the bright array of tin spoons. It seemed to me that none of the other refreshment stands on the beach—there were a few—were half so attractive as ours. I thought my father looked very well in a long white apron and shirt sleeves. He dished out ice cream with enthusiasm, so I supposed he was getting rich. It never occurred to me to compare his present occupation with the position for which he had been originally destined; or if I thought about it, I was just as well content, for by this time I had learned by heart my father's saying, "America is not Polotzk." All occupations were respectable, all men were equal, in America.

If I admired the soda fountain and the sausage chains, I almost worshipped the partner, Mr. Wilner. I was content to stand for an hour at a time watching him make potato chips. In his cook's cap and apron, with a ladle in his hand and a smile on his face, he moved about with the greatest agility, whisking his raw materials out of nowhere, dipping into his bubbling kettle with a flourish, and bringing forth the finished product with a caper. Such potato chips were not to be had anywhere else on Crescent Beach. Thin as tissue paper, crisp as dry snow, and salty as the sea—such thirst-producing, lemonade-selling, nickel-bringing potato chips only Mr. Wilner could make. On holidays, when dozens of family parties came out by every train from town, he could hardly keep up with the demand for his potato chips. And with a waiting crowd around him our partner was at his best. He was as voluble as he was skillful, and as witty as he was voluble; at least so I guessed from the laughter that frequently drowned his voice. I could not understand his jokes, but if I could get near enough to watch his lips and his smile and his merry eyes, I was happy. That any one could talk so fast, and in English, was marvel enough, but that this prodigy should belong to *our* establishment was a fact to thrill me. I had never seen anything like Mr. Wilner, except a wedding jester; but then he spoke common Yiddish. So proud was I of the talent and good taste displayed at our stand that if my father beckoned to me in the crowd and sent me on an errand, I hoped the people noticed that I, too, was connected with the establishment.

And all this splendor and glory and distinction came to a sudden end. There was some trouble about a license—some fee or fine—there was a storm in the night that damaged the soda fountain and other fixtures—there was talk and consultation between the houses of Antin and Wilner—and the promising partnership was dissolved. No more would the merry partner gather the crowd on the beach; no more would the twelve young Wilners gambol like mermen and mermaids in the surf. And the less numerous tribe of Antin must also say farewell to the jolly seaside life; for men in such humble business as my father's carry their families, along with their other earthly goods, wherever they go, after the manner of the gypsies. We had driven a feeble stake into the sand. The jealous Atlantic, in conspiracy with the Sunday law, had torn it out. We must seek our luck elsewhere.

In Polotzk we had supposed that "America" was practically synonymous with "Boston." When we landed in Boston, the horizon was pushed back, and we annexed Crescent Beach. And now, espying other lands of promise, we took possession of the province of Chelsea, in the name of our necessity.

In Chelsea, as in Boston, we made our stand in the wrong end of the town. Arlington Street was inhabited by poor Jews, poor Negroes, and a sprinkling of poor Irish. The side streets leading from it were occupied by more poor Jews and Negroes. It was a proper locality for a man without capital to do business. My father rented a tenement with a store in the basement. He put in a few barrels of flour and of sugar, a few boxes of crackers, a few gallons of kerosene, an assortment of soap of the "save the coupon" brands; in the cellar, a few barrels of potatoes, and a pyramid of kindling-wood; in the showcase, an alluring display of penny candy. He put out his sign, with a gilt-lettered warning of

"Strictly Cash," and proceeded to give credit indiscriminately. That was the regular way to do business on Arlington Street. My father, in his three years' apprenticeship, had learned the tricks of many trades. He knew when and how to "bluff." The legend of "Strictly Cash" was a protection against notoriously irresponsible customers; while none of the "good" customers, who had a record for paying regularly on Saturday, hesitated to enter the store with empty purses.

If my father knew the tricks of the trade, my mother could be counted on to throw all her talent and tact into the business. Of course she had no English yet, but as she could perform the acts of weighing, measuring, and mental computation of fractions mechanically, she was able to give her whole attention to the dark mysteries of the language, as intercourse with her customers gave her opportunity. In this she made such rapid progress that she soon lost all sense of disadvantage, and conducted herself behind the counter very much as if she were back in her old store in Polotzk. It was far more cosey than Polotzk—at least, so it seemed to me; for behind the store was the kitchen, where, in the intervals of slack trade, she did her cooking and washing. Arlington Street customers were used to waiting while the storekeeper salted the soup or rescued a loaf from the oven.

Once more Fortune favored my family with a thin little smile, and my father, in reply to a friendly inquiry, would say, "One makes a living," with a shrug of the shoulders that added "but nothing to boast of." It was characteristic of my attitude toward bread-and-butter matters that this contented me, and I felt free to devote myself to the conquest of my new world. Looking back to those critical first years, I see myself always behaving like a child let loose in a garden to play and dig and chase the butterflies. Occasionally, indeed, I was stung by the wasp of family trouble; but I knew a healing ointment—my faith in America. My father had come to America to make a living. America, which was free and fair and kind, must presently yield him what he sought. I had come to America to see a new world, and I followed my own ends with the utmost assiduity; only, as I ran out to explore, I would look back to see if my house were in order behind me—if my family still kept its head above water.

In after years, when I passed as an American among Americans, if I was suddenly made aware of the past that lay forgotten —if a letter from Russia, or a paragraph in the newspaper, or a conversation overheard in the street-car, suddenly reminded me of what I might have been—I thought it miracle enough that I, Mashke, the granddaughter of Raphael the Russian, born to a humble destiny, should be at home in an American metropolis, be free to fashion my own life, and should dream my dreams in English phrases. But in the beginning my admiration was spent on more concrete embodiments of the splendors of America; such as fine houses, gay shops, electric engines and apparatus, public buildings, illuminations, and parades. My early letters to my Russian friends were filled with boastful descriptions of these glories of my new country. No native citizen of Chelsea took such pride and delight in its institutions as I did. It required no fife and drum corps, no Fourth of July procession, to set me tingling with patriotism. Even the common agents and instruments of municipal life, such as the letter carrier and the fire engine, I regarded with a measure of respect. I know what I thought of people who said that Chelsea was a very small, dull, unaspiring town, with no discernible excuse for a separate name or existence.

The apex of my civic pride and personal contentment was reached on the bright September morning when I entered the public school. That day I must always remember, even if I live to be so old that I cannot tell my name. To most people their first day at school is a memorable occasion. In my case the importance of the day was a hundred times magnified, on account of the years I had waited, the road I had come, and the conscious ambitions I entertained.

I am wearily aware that I am speaking in extreme figures, in superlatives. I wish I knew some other way to render the mental life of the immigrant child of reasoning age. I may have been ever so much an exception in acuteness of observation, powers of comparison, and abnormal self-consciousness; none the less were my thoughts and conduct typical of the attitude of the intelligent immigrant child toward American institutions. And what the child thinks and feels is a reflection of the hopes, desires, and purposes of the parents who brought him overseas, no matter how precocious and independent the child may be. Your immigrant inspectors will tell you what poverty the foreigner brings in his baggage, what want in his pockets. Let the overgrown boy of twelve, reverently drawing his letters in the baby class, testify to the noble dreams and high ideals that may be hidden beneath the greasy caftan of the immigrant. Speaking for the Jews, at least, I know I am safe in inviting such an investigation.

Who were my companions on my first day at school? Whose hand was in mine, as I stood, overcome with awe, by the teacher's desk, and whispered my name as my father prompted? Was it Frieda's steady, capable hand? Was it her loyal heart that throbbed, beat for beat with mine, as it had done through all our childish adventures? Frieda's heart did throb that day, but not with my emotions. My heart pulsed with joy and pride and ambition; in her heart longing fought with abnegation. For I was led to the schoolroom, with its sunshine and its singing and the teacher's cheery smile; while she was led to the workshop, with its foul air, care-lined faces, and the foreman's stern command. Our going to school was the fulfillment of my father's best promises to us, and Frieda's share in it was to fashion and fit the calico frocks in which the baby sister and I made our first appearance in a public schoolroom.

I remember to this day the gray pattern of the calico, so affectionately did I regard it as it hung upon the wall—my consecration robe awaiting the beatific day. And Frieda, I am sure, remembers it, too, so longingly did she regard it as the crisp, starchy breadths of it slid between her fingers. But whatever were her longings, she said nothing of them; she bent over the sewing-machine humming an Old-World melody. In every straight, smooth seam, perhaps, she tucked away some lingering impulse of childhood; but she matched the scrolls and flowers with the utmost care. If a sudden shock of rebellion made her straighten up for an instant, the next instant she was bending to adjust a ruffle to the best advantage. And when the momentous day arrived, and the little sister and I stood up to be arrayed, it was Frieda herself who patted and smoothed my stiff new calico; who made me turn round and round, to see that I was perfect; who stooped to pull out a disfiguring basting-thread. If there was anything in her heart besides sisterly love and pride and good-will, as we parted that morning, it was a sense of loss and a woman's acquiescence in her fate; for we had been close friends, and now our ways would lie apart. Longing she felt, but no envy. She did not grudge me what she was denied. Until that morning we had been children together, but now, at the fiat of her destiny, she became a woman, with all a woman's cares; whilst I, so little younger than she, was bidden to dance at the May festival of untroubled childhood.

I wish, for my comfort, that I could say that I had some notion of the difference in our lots, some sense of the injustice to her, of the indulgence to me. I wish I could even say that I gave serious thought to the matter. There had always been a distinction between us rather out of proportion to the difference in our years. Her good health and domestic instincts had made it natural for her to become my mother's right hand, in the years preceding the emigration, when there were no more servants or dependents. Then there was the family tradition that Mary was the quicker, the brighter of the two, and that hers could be no common lot. Frieda was relied upon for help, and her sister for glory. And when I failed as a milliner's apprentice, while Frieda made excellent progress at the dressmaker's, our fates, indeed, were sealed. It was understood, even before we reached Boston, that she would go to work and I to school. In view of the family prejudices, it was the inevitable course. No injustice was intended. My father sent us hand in hand to school, before he had ever thought of America. If, in America, he had been able to support his family unaided, it would have been the culmination of his best hopes to see all his children at school, with equal advantages at home. But when he had done his best, and was still unable to provide even bread and shelter for us all, he was compelled to make us children self-supporting as fast as it was practicable. There was no choosing possible; Frieda was the oldest, the strongest, the best prepared, and the only one who was of legal age to be put to work.

My father has nothing to answer for. He divided the world between his children in accordance with the laws of the country and the compulsion of his circumstances. I have no need of defending him. It is myself that I would like to defend, and I cannot. I remember that I accepted the arrangements made for my sister and me without much reflection, and everything that was planned for my advantage I took as a matter of course. I was no heartless monster, but a decidedly self-centered child. If my sister had seemed unhappy it would have troubled me; but I am ashamed to recall that I did not consider how little it was that contented her. I was so preoccupied with my own happiness that I did not half perceive the splendid devotion of her attitude towards me, the sweetness of her joy in my good luck. She not only stood by approvingly when I was helped to everything; she cheerfully waited on me herself. And I took everything from her hand as if it were my due.

The two of us stood a moment in the doorway of the tenement house on Arlington Street, that wonderful September morning when I first went to school. It was I that ran away, on winged feet of joy and expectation; it was she whose feet were bound in the treadmill of daily toil. And I was so blind that I did not see that the glory lay on her, and not on me.

Father himself conducted us to school. He would not have delegated that mission to the President of the United States. He had awaited the day with impatience equal to mine, and the visions he saw as he hurried us over the sun-flecked pavements transcended all my dreams. Almost his first act on landing on American soil, three years before, had been his application for naturalization. He had taken the remaining steps in the process with eager promptness, and at the earliest moment allowed by the law, he became a citizen of the United States. It is true that he had left home in search of bread for his hungry family, but he went blessing the necessity that drove him to America. The boasted freedom of the New World meant to him far more than the right to reside, travel, and work wherever he pleased; it meant the freedom to speak his thoughts, to throw off the shackles of superstition, to test his own fate, unhindered by political or religious tyranny. He was only a young man when he landed—thirty-two; and most of his life he had been held in leading-strings. He was hungry for his untasted manhood.

Three years passed in sordid struggle and disappointment. He was not prepared to make a living even in America, where the day laborer eats wheat instead of rye. Apparently the American flag could not protect him against the pursuing Nemesis of his limitations; he must expiate the sins of his fathers who slept across the seas. He had been endowed at birth with a poor constitution, a nervous, restless temperament, and an abundance of hindering prejudices. In his boyhood his body was starved, that his mind might be stuffed with useless learning. In his youth this dearly gotten learning was sold, and the price was the bread and salt which he had not been trained to earn for himself. Under the wedding canopy he was bound for life to a girl whose features were still strange to him; and he was bidden to multiply himself, that sacred learning might be perpetuated in his sons, to the glory of the God of his fathers. All this while he had been led about as a creature without a will, a chattel, an instrument. In his maturity he awoke, and found himself poor in health, poor in purse, poor in useful knowledge, and hampered on all sides. At the first nod of opportunity he broke away from his prison, and strove to atone for his wasted youth by a life of useful labor; while at the same time he sought to lighten the gloom of his narrow scholarship by freely partaking of modern ideas. But his utmost endeavor still left him far from his goal. In business, nothing prospered with him. Some fault of hand or mind or temperament led him to failure where other men found success. Wherever the blame for his disabilities be placed, he reaped their bitter fruit. "Give me bread!" he cried to America. "What will you do to earn it?" the challenge came back. And he found that he was master of no art, of no trade; that even his precious learning was of no avail, because he had only the most antiquated methods of communicating it.

So in his primary quest he had failed. There was left him the compensation of intellectual freedom. That he sought to realize in every possible way. He had very little opportunity to prosecute his education, which, in truth, had never been begun. His struggle for a bare living left him no time to take advantage of the public evening school; but he lost nothing of what was to be learned through reading, through attendance at public meetings, through exercising the rights of citizenship. Even here he was hindered by a natural inability to acquire the English language. In time, indeed, he learned to read, to follow a conversation or lecture; but he never learned to write correctly, and his pronunciation remains extremely foreign to this day. If education, culture, the higher life were shining things to be worshipped from afar, he had still a means left whereby he could draw one step nearer to them. He could send his children to school, to learn all those things that he knew by fame to be desirable. The common school, at least, perhaps high school; for one or two, perhaps, even college! His children should be students, should fill his house with books and intellectual company; and thus he would walk by proxy in the Elysian Fields of liberal learning. As for the children themselves, he knew no surer way to their advancement and happiness.

So it was with a heart full of longing and hope that my father led us to school on that first day. He took long strides in his eagerness, the rest of us running and hopping to keep up.

At last the four of us stood around the teacher's desk; and my father, in his impossible English, gave us over in her charge, with some broken word of his hopes for us that his swelling heart could no longer contain. I venture to say that Miss Nixon was struck by something uncommon in the group we made, something outside of Semitic features and the abashed manner of the alien. My little sister was as pretty as a doll, with her clear pink-and-white face, short golden curls, and eyes like blue violets when you caught them looking up. My brother might have been a girl, too, with his cherubic contours of face, rich red color, glossy black hair, and fine eyebrows. Whatever secret fears were in his heart, remembering his former teachers, who had taught with the rod, he stood up straight and uncringing before the American teacher, his cap respectfully doffed. Next to him stood a starved-looking girl with eyes ready to pop out, and short dark curls that would not have made much of a wig for a Jewish bride.

All three children carried themselves rather better than the common run of "green" pupils that were brought to Miss Nixon. But the figure that challenged attention to the group was the tall, straight father, with his earnest face and fine forehead, nervous hands eloquent in gesture, and a voice full of feeling. This foreigner, who brought his children to school as if it were an act of consecration, who regarded the teacher of the primer class with reverence, who spoke of visions, like a man inspired, in a common schoolroom, was not like other aliens, who brought their children in dull obedience to the law; was not like the native fathers, who brought their unmanageable boys, glad to be relieved of their care. I think Miss Nixon guessed what my father's best English could not convey. I think she divined that by the simple act of delivering our school certificates to her he took possession of America.

MORRIS HILLQUIT

Morris Hillquit, the noted Socialist leader, was born in Latvia in 1870 and died in New York City in 1933. He built a distinguished career as a lawyer and as a spokesman for the working man.

Hillquit came to the United States at the age of seventeen. He became greatly depressed by the abject poverty he saw and in which he himself lived on the East Side of New York. He worked in a shirt shop and then a waist shop in order to earn his livelihood. At the same time, he studied English—which he later taught—and managed to learn Yiddish, a language with which he had no familiarity, although it was the daily tongue of hundreds of thousands of Jewish immigrants.

It was nearly inevitable that Morris Hillquit, given the circumstances in which he worked, become a union organizer. He established the United Hebrew Trades and was a founder of the first Yiddish-language Socialist newspaper, the Arbeiter-Zeitung, *in 1890.*

As a founder of the Socialist Party, Hillquit was one of its major ornaments. He ran for Congress on the Socialist Party ticket five times, and was a mayoralty candidate twice. Although he did not win office, he did gain the respect of the public, especially as a lawyer. He represented many unions before arbitration boards, and framed a labor code for the garment industry which was a model for future codes in the trade union movement.

The Birth of the Jewish Unions*

MORRIS HILLQUIT

ASIDE from the roofs on Cherry Street our favorite gathering places were the East Side tea shops. There, particularly during the long winter nights, we would pass many hours talking and occasionally sipping weak tea served in tumblers, Russian style. A glass of tea and a "coffee twist" of ample proportions were, as a rule, the limit of a guest's consumption. The price of each was five cents.

I often wondered how the owners of the establishments could keep going on such meager income, and I suppose the owners were kept wondering harder than I. But they somehow managed. In some cases, they were of the same kind and type as their guests, and they took it for granted that the tea shop was there not so much for drinking or eating as for discussions.

Of discussion there was plenty, but the purely vocal exercise did not long satisfy the enthusiastic young Socialists' yearning for action. They cast about for a promising field of practical work and inevitably discovered it among their own countrymen. The anti-Jewish riots or "pogroms" of 1881 and 1882 had set in motion a powerful stream of Jewish emigration from Russia and Poland. Thousands of immigrants arrived on the shores of this country every week seeking shelter and bread. By 1890 their number was estimated at no less than half a million. In New York they formed the largest Jewish settlement of the world, the largest, most congested, and poorest.

In two thousand years of homeless wandering among the nations of Africa, Europe, and Asia, in centuries of outlawry and persecution, the Jewish people had been largely excluded from productive work and had become a race of traders and money

* Reprinted from *Loose Leaves From a Busy Life,* The Macmillan Company, New York, 1934, pp. 15–40.

lenders. In the new world they evolved for the first time a solid proletarian block.

In the early days of immigration, many of them turned to the lowest form of trade—peddling; but that occupation proved utterly inadequate when their numbers rose to hundreds of thousands. They were compelled to seek employment at manual labor. The great majority of the new arrivals found work in the different branches of the clothing industry. Others tried to eke out a precarious existence as bakers, cigar makers, house painters, and factory workers. Their conditions of life and labor were pitiful. Ignorant of the language and ways of the country of their adoption, mostly without technical training of any kind, penniless and helpless, they were left at the mercy of their employers, mostly men of their own race. Many of these "employers" were mere middlemen or contractors acting as intermediaries between manufacturers and workers.

There were hundreds of these middlemen in the clothing industry, and they operated in fierce competition with one another. A number of hired sewing machines set up in a tenement-house room, often connected with their own living quarters, constituted their whole capital and establishment. In these close, dark, illventilated and unsanitary shops a welter of working and perspiring humanity, men and women, from three to twenty or thirty in number, were crowded together. Their pay was almost nominal, their work hours were unlimited. As a rule they were employed "by the piece," and as their work was seasonal and irregular, they were spurred to inhuman exertions in the rare and short busy periods.

Mercilessly exploited by their employers and despised by their American fellow-workers as wage cutters, they completely lacked self-assertiveness and the power of resistance. They were weak from overwork and malnutrition, tired and listless, meek and submissive. Tuberculosis, the dread white plague of the tenements, was rife among them.

Here was a situation that fairly cried out for sympathy and help. Our group was quick to heed the summons. We resolved to undertake the task of bettering the lives of our laboring countrymen, of educating them to a realization of their human rights, of organizing them for resistance to their exploiters, and of securing for them tolerable conditions of labor and life.

It was a task beset with baffling difficulties. Several attempts to organize the Jewish workers of New York had been made before and had failed. A few spontaneous strikes had been quickly quelled. A few nuclei of labor unions had been stillborn. The Jewish workers seemed to be unorganizable. They had not been trained in any form of collective action in the countries of their birth. They were dull, apathetic, and unintelligent. And worst of all, we did not speak their language, both figuratively and literally. Our language was Russian. The workers spoke Yiddish, a corrupted German dialect with several provincial variations. Few of us knew Yiddish well enough to embark on a campaign of propaganda. The only one among us who could speak Yiddish and did it fluently, lovingly, and artistically was Abraham Cahan, who subsequently made equally enviable places for himself in the English and Yiddish worlds of letters. Cahan was somewhat older than the rest of us. He was nearly thirty at that time, and we looked up to him with envy and respect, not only on account of his venerable age but also because of his incomparable knowledge of the language of the people.

We all began perfecting our Yiddish. Those of us who happened to know German had a somewhat easier task than those who spoke only Russian and had to labor at it word by word and idiom by idiom.

The next problem was to make contacts with the workers. This also proved a highly elusive undertaking. There were so many of them, and they were hopelessly scattered.

It would have taken decades to build a Jewish labor movement from the bottom up, educating individual workers, forming them into organized trade groups and finally uniting them into one cooperating body. We were forced to reverse the logical process and to attempt to build from the top down.

Taking the bull by the horns, we founded the United Hebrew Trades in October, 1888. It was a central labor body without affiliated labor unions, a mere shell within which we hoped in time to develop a solid kernel. The idea originated among the Jewish members of the Socialist Labor Party, the political organization of American Socialism at that time.

The party had two Jewish branch organizations or "sections" in New York, one composed of Yiddish-speaking members, known as Section 8, and the other, Section 17, whose members spoke Russian. The task of setting the contemplated organization in motion was entrusted to a joint committee of the two sections, each electing two members. The Yiddish-speaking section was represented on the committee by I. Magidoff and Bernard Weinstein.

Magidoff, who may be termed the father of the idea, was very active in the initial stages of the Jewish labor movement, but later dropped out of it and devoted himself entirely to newspaper work. Bernard Weinstein was and remained one of the best types produced by the Jewish labor movement in the United States. A native of Odessa, in the southern part of Russia, he came here as a boy with the first wave of Russian emigration in 1882, and found employment in a cigar factory alongside Samuel Gompers, then also an obscure cigar maker.

He associated himself with the early Socialist and labor movements immediately upon his arrival, and has remained wholeheartedly devoted to their cause for fifty years. Handicapped by a slight facial deformity, devoid of the gift of popular oratory and modest to the point of shyness, Bernard Weinstein was never very prominent in the leadership of the movement. But he did not seek prominence or even recognition. He served the cause for the sake of the cause, served it with simple and unwavering faith, steadily, unostentatiously, and with utter self-abnegation.

The "Russian section" was represented on the committee by Leo Bandes and by myself. Bandes was a somewhat maturer man than most of us. He had won his revolutionary spurs as a member of the redoubtable "Will of the People," and had served time in Russian prisons for his Socialist activities. He was a person of kind disposition and rare idealism and occupied a leading and authoritative position in our councils. But we were not long permitted to enjoy his companionship. He had contracted a tubercular infection of the lungs during his prison life, and the tenement air of New York was not at all conducive to recovery. He languished before our eyes and died in less than two years.

The organization meeting of the United Hebrew Trades took place at 25 East Fourth Street, the headquarters of the Socialist Labor Party, and the meeting place of the United German Trades (Vereinigte Deutsche Gewerkschaften). It was the latter organization that inspired the name of the newcomer in the field of organized labor.

The United German Trades was a powerful body in those days. It was a federation of labor unions composed of German workers, who practically controlled several important industries in New York. Originally called into being for the sole purpose of supporting the German labor press, it soon broadened its functions to include those usually exercised by central labor bodies in cities. It was a progressive organization and worked in close cooperation with the Socialist movement.

The United German Trades assisted in the formation of its younger Jewish brother by practical advice and made a generous contribution of ten dollars to its war chest.

Before we called the organization meeting, Bernard Weinstein and I made a minute and painstaking search of all nuclei or remnants of Jewish labor unions in New York. There had been, we knew, unions of shirt makers, cloak operators, and bakery workers at one time or another. We thought them dormant. We found them dead.

The only Jewish unions that could lay any claim to existence were two in number, the Hebrew Typographical Union and the union of chorus singers. The typesetters' union was only a few months old. It was made up of employees of the struggling newspapers and job printing shops on the lower East Side.

The Chorus Singers' Union was somewhat of an anomaly in the labor movement. It was composed of members of the chorus of the two Yiddish theaters then operating in New York. In the daytime they were employed at other trades, the men mostly as cigar makers and the women as garment finishers. The work at rehearsals and in the nightly performances was strenuous, and the pay ranged from three to four dollars a week. But it was not so much the hard work and low wages that drove them to seek protection in organization, as the brutal treatment to which they were subjected by the theater managers.

In membership the two "unions" together represented a grand total of forty. This was the modest beginning of the organization that in later years boasted of an affiliated membership of a quarter of a million workers.

Undaunted by the slim foundation, we proceeded to the formal organization of the United Hebrew Trades, with Bernard Weinstein as recording secretary and myself in the somewhat vague post of "corresponding secretary." The triple aim of the new organization was declared to be: (1) mutual aid and cooperation among the Jewish trade unions of New York; (2) organization of new unions; (3) the propaganda of Socialism among the Jewish workers.

A somewhat humorous sample of the work ahead of us presented itself at the very first meeting of our newly formed body. Just before adjournment a delegation from an actors' union appeared and applied for affiliation.

The Jewish theaters of New York were in their infancy and had a hard struggle for existence. The members of the troupes were not paid fixed salaries but worked on shares. The lion's share of these "shares," however, went to the numerous stars, while the lesser lights of the stage were left with little more than the gratification of their artistic aspirations. The class struggle in this instance was between the minor parts and the headliners, and the former had just formed a union against the latter. The definite organization meeting of the new union was to be held in a few days, and we were asked to send a speaker to initiate the neophytes in the principles and practices of trade unionism.

Of course, we were eager to serve, but the spokesman for the theatrical proletariat was careful to attach proper conditions to his request. Actors are artists after all, he explained, and cannot be expected to receive instruction in coarse and common Yiddish. Our speaker would have to address them in German, the language of the poets and thinkers. All eyes turned on me. I nodded assent, and this part of the problem seemed to be solved. But not so with the next condition of our theatrical comrade. "To have the attention and respect of the audience," he calmly proceeded, "the speaker will have to appear in proper attire, i.e., dressed in frock coat and silk hat."

Again all eyes turned on me, but this time not with confidence but with consternation succeeded by irrepressible mirth. I was nineteen and looked younger. Frock coats and silk hats were not among the customary articles of my wardrobe and were generally not sported at our meetings.

This was our first taste of some of the difficulties of practical trade-union politics, and we just gave it up. The organization meeting of the actors' union was held without a representative of our group and seems to have gotten along quite well, for the Jewish Actors' Union was definitely and firmly organized and has remained in continued and effective existence ever since. For years one of the favorite and exciting subjects of our debates was, whether actors were wage workers and had a legitimate place in the labor movement. The final decision was in the affirmative.

Our work among the genuine and simon-pure proletariat began very soon. Our first effort was to reorganize the defunct shirt makers' union. This was accomplished within a few weeks after the foundation of the United Hebrew Trades. It was a comparatively easy task because this particular trade happened to employ large numbers of Socialist intellectuals.

The problem was infinitely more difficult in the other branches of the needle industry, but gradually a technique of organization was developed.

I remember most vividly the origin and early history of the Knee Pants Makers' Union, and shall rapidly sketch them because they were typical of all tailoring trades.

In 1890 there were about one thousand knee pants makers employed in New York, all "green" and most of them illiterate. It was a sweat-shop industry *par excellence*. The work was done entirely on the contracting system. A contractor employed about ten workers on the average and usually operated his shop in his living-rooms. His sole function consisted of procuring bundles of cut garments from the manufacturer and having them made up by the workers. He did not even furnish the sewing machines. The operator provided his own machine as well as the needles and thread. The work day was endless, and the average earnings of experienced operators ran from six to seven dollars per week. Often the contractor would abscond with a week's pay; often the worker would be discharged because he was not fast enough to suit the contractor, and often he would be compelled to quit his job because of maltreatment or intolerable working conditions. Every time a knee pants maker changed contractors, he was compelled to put his sewing machine on his back and carry it through the streets to his new place of employment. It was at this point that their patience finally gave out. In the early part of 1890, they struck. The movement was spontaneous, without program, leadership, or organization. It was a blind outbreak of revolt and was destined to collapse if left to itself, sharing the fate of many similar outbursts in the past.

In this case the United Hebrew Trades stepped in during the very first hours of the strike. Through a committee of five, of whom I was one, it took complete charge of the situation.

Our first step was to hire a meeting hall large enough to accommodate all the strikers. There were about nine hundred, and we gathered them in from all shops and street corners. In the hall we held them in practically continuous session, day and night, allowing them only the necessary time to go home to sleep. We feared to let them go, least they be tempted to return to work, and we entertained them all the time with speeches and such other forms of instruction and amusement as we could devise.

While the continuous performance was going on in the main hall, we tried to bring order and system into the strike and to organize the strikers into a solid and permanent union.

In consultation with the most intelligent men and women from the ranks of the strikers, we worked out a list of demands centering upon the employer's obligation to furnish sewing machines and other work tools at his own expense. Then we chose pickets, relief committees, and settlement committees, all operating under our direct supervision and guidance.

The men did not know how to conduct meetings or transact business of any kind. They had never acted in concert. Our discourses on the principles of trade unionism and the philosophy of Socialism were interspersed with elementary lessons in parliamentary procedure and practical methods of organization. We tried to pick out the most promising among them and train them for leadership of their fellows. The strike was a course of intensive training and education, but it was of short duration. After one week without a break in the ranks of the workers, the contractors weakened; one Saturday night they became panicky and stormed the meeting hall of the strikers in a body, demanding an immediate and collective settlement on the workers' terms.

The United Hebrew Trades had scored a great victory and was encouraged to new efforts in other fields.

One of the most difficult tasks the pioneering group was called upon to tackle was the organization of the Jewish bakery workers. In the early days of Jewish immigration a limited number of bakeshops had sprung up on the lower East Side. They specialized in "Jewish" rye bread and other bakery products to which the Jewish consumers had been accustomed in the countries of their origin. These bakeries were in deep and dark subcellars, without ventilation or any hygienic accommodations. The walls and ceilings were moist and moldy. The shops were infested with rats and reeked with dirt. The air was pestilential. The bake ovens were primitive. No machinery was used. The work was all done by hand.

The new industry employed a total of a few hundred workers, mostly immigrants from Galicia, Hungary, and Poland. They were different from the bulk of the Russian Jewish workers, more stolid, unemotional, and irresponsive. They worked seventeen to eighteen hours a day except on Thursday, when their "work day" began early in the morning and lasted until noon on Friday. As a rule they boarded and lodged with their employers. They worked at the ovens naked from the waist up and slept in the bakery cellars. When they did not receive board and lodging, their wages averaged six to seven dollars a week.

Their only leisure time was between making the dough and its rising, and these hours they spent in their favorite saloons, drinking beer and playing cards.

The beer saloons, particularly one on the corner of Ludlow and Hester streets, provided the only romance in their drab lives. Here were their social clubs and also their labor bureaus. Here they would exchange information about jobs and here also employers would come in quest of "hands."

Pale-faced, hollow-chested, listless, and brutified, they seemed to be hopeless material for organization and struggle. In 1887 the newly organized Bakery and Confectionery Workers International Union of America had succeeded in enlisting a number of them into a Jewish local union, but the organization collapsed within a year, for a reason very characteristic of the workers' mentality.

Anxious to remove them from the demoralizing atmosphere of the Ludlow Street saloon, the secretary of the national organization of bakery workers had secured new headquarters for them. It was a room back of a beer saloon on Orchard Street. Meeting halls connected with saloons were the customary thing for labor unions in New York in those days. The saloon keeper would make no charge for the use of the room, expecting to be compensated in trade. In the case of the German and Irish unions the scheme worked well, but with the Jewish unions it mostly proved unprofitable from the saloon keeper's point of view.

The attempted removal of the organized Jewish bakers from the Ludlow Street saloon met with considerable opposition. They were used to their old gathering place and its ways, and many of them were suspicious of the proposed change. A severe factional fight broke out between the conservative adherents of Ludlow Street and the radical supporters of Orchard Street. To the Jewish bakery workers of that period the class struggle assumed the form of a fight between two rival beer saloons. With the help of the proprietor and the support of the employers, the anti-union Ludlow Street saloon won out. The union disbanded.

Undeterred by this miscarried attempt, the United Hebrew Trades launched a new campaign to organize the bakers in 1889.

After some preparatory propaganda, a strike was called. The principal demand of the workers was for the six-day week with one day of rest, on Saturdays, a radical demand in those days.

The strike call met with general response. The Jewish bakeshops were tied up, and within a few days their proprietors surrendered to the union.

As in the case of the knee pants makers, the strike was organized and conducted by a group of young Socialists acting in behalf of the United Hebrew Trades; and as in that case we tried to take advantage of the situation to give the workers an intensive course of instruction in the principles and methods of trade unionism. Our efforts seemed to be successful beyond our most optimistic expectations. Within a few months the organization numbered about four hundred members, constituting practically the whole body of Jewish bakery workers. The Union became their religion, and they zealously adhered to its tenets as they understood them.

A tragic incident which occurred shortly after the organization of the Jewish bakers' union served to call general public attention to the revolting conditions in the bakeshops of New York's East Side and led to important consequences in the field of labor legislation.

One early morning the secretary of the newly organized union reported to Bernard Weinstein at the office of the United Hebrew Trades that a baker had collapsed while working at night and was still in the bakeshop, critically ill. The secretary, as well as the employer, were at a loss as to what to do. When Weinstein reached the bakery cellar, he found a most appalling condition of filth, with three emaciated and exhausted bakers continuing to work at the side of their agonizing comrade. He made arrangements to have the sick man taken to a hospital and reported the case to the Labor Department.

An investigation of the bakeshops on the East Side followed and resulted in a sensational report condemning the inhuman labor conditions in these shops and branding them as a standing menace to public health.

As a consequence of this investigation and report the New

York State Legislature shortly thereafter enacted a law, limiting work in bakeries to ten hours a day. The law had an interesting career in the courts and largely served to determine the limit of protective labor legislation.

Contesting the constitutionality of the law, the employers fought it in all courts of the state and in the Supreme Court of the United States. It was upheld by the trial judge, whose decision was affirmed in the Appellate Division by the narrow margin of three to two votes and in the Court of Appeals by a vote of four to three. In the United States Supreme Court it was reversed by a vote of five to four.

"There is no reasonable ground for interfering with the liberty of person or the right of free contract, by determining the hours of labor, in the occupation of a baker," declared Mr. Justice Peckham, who wrote the prevailing opinion in the case of Lochner against New York. "There is no contention that bakers as a class are not equal in intelligence and capacity to men in other trades and manual occupations, or that they are not able to assert their rights and care for themselves without the protesting arm of the state interfering with their independence of judgment and of action."

The learned court held that the law curtailed both "the right of the individual to labor for such time as he may choose" and the right of the employer "to purchase labor" in such quantities as he may choose.

I have often wondered whether Mr. Justice Peckham and his four concurring associates would have felt quite so certain about the capacity of the bakers to assert their rights and to exercise "their independence of judgment and of action," if they had met the Jewish bakers in their hang-out in the Ludlow Street corner saloon, or gone through the numerous strikes with them, or accompanied Bernard Weinstein in his mission of help to the sovereign and independent baker who fell in the midst of his free labor like an overburdened beast. And I am still wondering why a few theorists, ignorant of the daily struggles and sufferings of the toiling masses, should be allowed to determine industrial relations, social conflicts, and human rights, irrevocably and regardless of public sentiment and the enactments of popularly chosen legislative bodies.

The bakers' union subsequently became one of the strongest, most progressive, and best disciplined organizations among the Jewish workers of America. But that development took many years of patient and persistent struggle punctuated by recurring disappointments, failures, and defeats.

In spite of its promising beginning, the union founded by the United Hebrew Trades had a short life. With the immediate objects of their strike attained, the members lost interest in their organization and within a short time the union disbanded. The lack of organization led to a new deterioration of labor standards and to a new revolt, another strike, and a revival of the union, followed by an inevitable decline and eventual dissolution. The disheartening process was repeated at fairly regular intervals every two or three years, each new organization being a little stronger and lasting a little longer than its predecessor, until stability and permanence were at last achieved after a zigzagging course of fifteen to twenty years.

Such also was the history of the Knee Pants Makers' Union and of practically all other Jewish trade unions organized since the advent of the United Hebrew Trades.

I have dwelt at length on the organizations of the Jewish knee pants makers and bakers because they were typical instances of the accomplishments and problems of the United Hebrew Trades. But these organizations were by no means the only ones called into life by the United Hebrew Trades, nor the most important ones. In its early career the Jewish Hebrew Trades was incessantly busy organizing and reorganizing Jewish trade unions. During the first eighteen months of its existence it had increased the number of its affiliated bodies from two to thirty-two. These included practically all industries in which Jewish workers were engaged in substantial numbers. Heading the list were the different tailoring branches, such as the cloak makers, men's tailors, furriers, and cap makers, but included in it were also such occupations as musicians, retail store clerks, book-binders and soda-water workers. And in practically all cases the unions were short-lived. They came and went and had to be reorganized every few years. In the minds of the Jewish workers of that period unions were associated with strikes and were little more than instruments of strikes. They were mostly born in strikes and died with the end of the strikes. It took twenty years of patient and persistent work to educate the Jewish workers to a realization of the value of trade unions in peace as well as in war, and it was not until about 1910 that the Jewish labor movement was organized on a solid and stable basis.

One of the important factors that contributed to that result was the consolidation of the multifarious organizations of separate branches of the needle-trade crafts into large unions embracing all parts of a related industry, such as the International Ladies' Garment Workers Union, whose jurisdiction extends to all branches of the manufacture of women's apparel and the Amalgamated Clothing Workers Union, which is composed of all workers in the men's tailoring industry.

At this time several hundred thousand Jewish workers are normally organized in national and local trade unions. They have been fully accepted by their fellow workers as an organic part of the American labor movement, and have made a distinct contribution to the general progress of the movement.

During the half-century of their struggles, trials, errors, and experiences, the Jewish workers in America have been strikingly transformed, mentally, morally, and even physically. From a race of timid, submissive, cheerless, and hopeless drudges they have grown into a generation of self-reliant, self-respecting men and women, conscious of their social and industrial rights and ever ready to defend them.

I was seventeen when I came to America with my mother, a younger brother, and two sisters. My father and an older brother had preceded us by about two years and established a "home" for us in a two-room apartment in a tenement house on Clinton Street.

It was the unanimous decision of the family that I resume my interrupted studies and prepare myself for a professional career.

My first step in that direction was to enroll in a public high school on Fourteenth Street.

I had come to New York with a smattering of school English, which served me very well in Russia, but proved utterly inadequate and largely incomprehensible in New York. My prime object in attending public school was to learn some real American English.

I liked the school, its friendly atmosphere and free and easy ways. Most of my fellow students were younger than I, and I must have appeared to them queer with my foreign ways and quaint English; but the boys were kind and helpful, and the teachers took a sympathetic interest in my progress.

After a short time, however, I was again compelled to interrupt my studies.

My parents were frightfully poor. My elder brother and the older of my sisters were working. I felt uncomfortable in the role of the drone of the family, and determined to go to work.

To decide to work was one thing, but to find work was, as I soon discovered, quite another thing. Because of my fragmentary knowledge of English and total lack of business connections I could not look for anything but manual labor. I was frail and untrained for any trade and almost inevitably gravitated into a shirt shop. For some fortuitous reason, shirt making had become the favorite occupation of the circle of young Russian intellectuals in which I moved. It was a trade easy to learn principally because of the minute division of labor that prevailed in it. Nobody made a complete shirt. The task of each worker was confined to one small and uniform operation, such as making the front or the sleeve, the collar or cuff, hemming the bottom or sewing some parts together. The cuff was the simplest part and required least skill and training. The operation of the "cuff maker" consisted of stitching together two square pieces of cut material on three sides and attaching it to the sleeve. I started my career as a cuff maker and never advanced to a higher stage of the art.

The work was not exacting, and the surroundings were not uncongenial. The operators in the stuffy little workshop spent at least as much time in discussing social and literary topics as in turning out shirts, and the whir of the sewing machines was often accompanied by the loud and hearty sound of revolutionary songs.

But the monetary returns were distressingly slim. The "boss," i.e., the contractor who ran the shop, took no business chances. He practically paid no rent, since the work was done in one of the rooms of his living quarters. He had no outlay on machinery because every worker hired his own sewing machine, at a rental of two dollars per month. Wages were low and were paid "by the piece." Work was seasonal and irregular. The machine rent was the only constant element in the peculiar industrial scheme, so that a worker of my skill and productivity sometimes wound up the month with a deficit in earnings.

Disappointed with the financial aspect of the shirt industry, I turned my talents to waist making. For a short time I also held down a job in a picture frame factory. But in all of these occupations my earnings were highly precarious, to say the least.

Stability of employment and income came to me only with what I may term my first political job. That was nothing less than a clerkship in the national office of the Socialist Labor Party. The party at that time occupied a four-story building at 25 East Fourth Street. The ground floor was used as a beer saloon, while the upper stories were divided into meeting halls, editorial rooms of the two weekly publications of the party—*Der Sozialist* in German and *The Workmen's Advocate* in English—and the office of the National Secretary. In the same building the party also conducted a bookstore and publication department under the firm name of Labor News Company.

I was attached to the latter. My salary, as I recall it, was four dollars a week. I was very happy in my new occupation. There was no rigid dividing line between the different departments in the headquarters of the Socialist Labor Party, and my work offered me a fine opportunity to familiarize myself not only with the Socialist literature then extant but also with the practical problems and methods of the organized movement. The National Secretary of the party, William L. Rosenberg, was also the editor of its German paper and the titular head of the whole establishment at 25 East Fourth Street. He was a poet of some merit, a sentimental idealist, and the kindliest of companions and teachers. He had taken a liking to me the first time he noticed me at a party meeting, and it was he who picked me for the job.

But again my employment was destined to be of short duration. After a few months of peaceful and serene work at the party headquarters, I was called upon to assume more responsible duties in a different field.

From the very beginning of our efforts to organize and consolidate the Jewish trade unions we felt the crying need of a labor paper as an organ of the movement, as a medium of communication between the unions and their members, and, above all, as an instrument of propaganda and education.

There was at that time a well-edited German Socialist daily newspaper in New York, the *New Yorker Volkszeitung;* but the Jewish workers could not read German. Nor could they read English. They knew only Yiddish.

Plans for the publication of a Yiddish weekly labor paper were often discussed among the leaders of the movement and in the fall of 1889 several formal conferences were held on the subject.

The original idea was that the paper be "nonpartisan" in editorial policy, and the conferences were attended by representatives of anarchist groups as well as the Socialist Labor Party and the trade unions. But the fundamental differences of view between the two wings of the radical movement, which found heated, vociferous and continuous expression at the conferences, soon demonstrated the impossibility of the project. The social democratic and trade union organizations separated themselves from the anarchists and decided to go it alone.

Months of incessant and enthusiastic preparatory work ensued. Funds had to be raised, the paper planned, and its management organized. Among the most active promoters of the project were Abraham Cahan, one Louis E. Miller, and I.

Cahan's life always was an uninterrupted succession of enthusiasms. Whatever interest happened to take hold of him at the moment dominated his thoughts and actions to the exclusion of everything else. He now threw himself body and soul into the new enterprise and never tired of discussing the proposed paper and working for its realization. He had two advantages over the rest of us. He knew Yiddish well, and he had the instincts of a born journalist.

The other member of our trio, who went by the name of Louis E. Miller, was a brother of Leo Bandes mentioned in the preceding chapter. He was a few years older than I. He had left his native Russia at a very early age and spent several years in Switzerland working, studying, and associating with the numerous Russian Socialist émigrés in Geneva.

In New York he spent his first years working by fits and starts in shirt factories and editing and publishing a Russian Socialist weekly of very limited circulation. Later he was admitted to the bar and practiced law rather sparingly, preferring to give his time to the Socialist movement and newspaper work. He was a person of persuasive eloquence, indomitable energy, and fanatical devotion to the cause.

Together we set out soliciting contributions for the projected paper. Almost every night we visited one or more Jewish trade unions and friendly German labor organizations, making our plea and receiving donations.

Within a few months we raised the enormous capital of $800.

On the 6th of March, 1890, the first number of our *Arbeiter-Zeitung* (Workers' Paper) appeared. It was an event of first magnitude in the Jewish Socialist and labor movements and an occasion for boundless rejoicing. For hours a throng of eager sympathizers stood in front of the printer's shop waiting for the first copies to come off the press. As fast as they did, they were handed out to the waiting crowds and snatched up by them with reverence and wonder. Here it was "in the flesh," a four-page paper neatly printed in the familiar Hebrew characters, all written for them and about them. Their hopes and dreams of many months were finally realized.

The paper was an instantaneous success. For weeks and weeks we had carefully planned every detail of its contents. It was our aim to conduct the paper along broad educational lines rather than to confine it to dry economic theories and Socialist propaganda. The Jewish masses were totally uncultured. They stood in need of elementary information about the important things in life outside of the direct concerns of the Socialist and labor movement. Without a certain minimum of general culture they could not be expected to develop an intelligent understanding of their own problems and interest in their own struggles.

Alongside a weekly chronicle of the Socialist and labor movements, the *Arbeiter-Zeitung* printed simple expositions of the philosophy of the movements in their different phases, articles on popular science, descriptions of travel, good fiction, and even poetry. Abraham Cahan largely supplied the "human interest" features. I contributed editorials, historical sketches, and articles on Socialist theory and a variety of other subjects. Other contributions came from the editor-in-chief and a number of volunteer writers who gradually augmented our forces.

The paper soon reached a circulation of about eight thousand copies, an almost fantastic figure in view of all our handicaps and modest expectation. Its size was increased from four pages to eight.

The *Arbeiter-Zeitung* exerted a powerful influence on the course of the Jewish labor movement and contributed materially to the intellectual development of the Jewish laboring masses. It retained the field until it was succeeded by the Jewish *Daily Forward*, which, under the able editorship of Abraham Cahan, became one of the great Socialist newspapers of the world and probably the most prosperous.

As editor we chose one Jacob Rombro, who wrote under the nom de plume of Phillip Kranz. He was considerably older than most of us, had established some reputation as a contributor to Russian magazines and was at the time living in London, where he edited a small radical Jewish weekly paper known as the *Arbeiter Freund* (The Workers' Friend). We lured him to New York by the promise of a larger and more fruitful field of activity and the offer of a princely salary of seven dollars per week.

I was the rest of the staff, combining in my own person the

offices of associate editor, business manager, bookkeeper, and official poet, for all of which I was paid five dollars a week.

As I look back on it in the calm judgment of sobering time, I rather think I was overpaid. I had no business experience. My bookkeeping system was reduced to the simple processes of addition and subtraction in one running account. The income of the paper I kept in a desk drawer, and the "petty cash" in my pockets. If there was a discrepancy between my accounts and my pocket, one or the other suffered the consequences. My weekly poems were a liability rather than an asset to the paper. As to my prose contributions I thought and still think they were tolerably good in substance, but Cahan severely criticized my language. "It is not Yiddish," he would assert, "it is German written in Hebrew characters." I did not and could not deny the charge, but attempted to justify the practice. There were practically no recognized authorities on written Yiddish at the time. The literary style of the language was in the making. What was it to be? Cahan advocated a faithful reproduction of the spoken Yiddish with all its crudities. I, on the other hand, argued since Yiddish is nothing but a corrupted, illiterate, and ungrammatical German, the task of the Yiddish writer was to improve and purify the language with the ultimate aim of converting it into modern German.

I did not maintain my end of the interesting controversy very vigorously or very long and ultimately Cahan's views prevailed.

When the paper became more prosperous and could afford to pay more adequate salaries, I resigned my multiple business offices on it. Although I would not say that my resignation was forced, I have a distinct recollection that it was rather encouraged by my colleagues.

I continued writing for the *Arbeiter-Zeitung* from time to time as a voluntary contributor, but gradually drifted away from the Jewish labor movement.

In the first few years after the organization of the United Hebrew Trades, a number of capable leaders had developed in the Jewish trade unions. At the same time some organizations of English-speaking members began to spring up within the Socialist Labor Party. I was quick to perceive the superior importance of that branch of the movement to the ultimate success of Socialism in the United States, and transferred to it the greater part of my activities.

I had learned English in the meantime and was supplementing my meager income by teaching this language to some of my less advanced countrymen.

In those days of heavy immigration and slow assimilation the task of teaching English to foreigners was one of great public importance, particularly in New York. Evening classes for that purpose were organized in the public schools in ever growing numbers and pupils were eagerly sought.

One day I made the acquaintance of one Joseph Darling, a man of charming personality and liberal political views, a devout follower of Henry George. Mr. Darling was a school teacher and had just been appointed principal of a newly created evening school for foreigners in Public School No. 1, on Vandewater Street, towards the southern extremity of the city and within walking distance from the Jewish settlement. The course of instruction in these evening schools consisted of ninety nights in the year, and the teachers were paid three dollars a night. Half of a normal weekly wage for two hours' work, what a lucrative compensation! "Is your teaching staff complete?" I asked Mr. Darling. No, it was not. "Could I apply for the position of a teacher?" "Yes," Mr. Darling assured me, "but on two conditions: First, you will have to pass an examination and secure a teacher's license and, second, I shall have to have students for you. This fall will be our first experiment and I do not know how many, if any students, will enroll."

The problems did not seem difficult. I took the examination at the earliest possible date and induced my friends Louis Miller and Phillip Kranz to do likewise. We all passed the test satisfactorily and were given licenses to teach English to foreigners in the public schools.

As the opening of the school term approached we hired a hall in the vicinity of the Vandewater Street school and inserted a notice in the *Arbeiter-Zeitung* calling upon all workers desiring to learn English under Socialist tutelage to meet in the hall at seven o'clock. About one hundred and fifty prospective students responded to the call. I explained the situation to them in a brief speech and concluded with the request that all those who desired to enroll in the school raise their hands. All hands went up.

"Well, then, let us go," I commanded.

Fifteen minutes later I arrived at the school auditorium at the head of an army of one hundred and fifty men in regular march formation. Mr. Darling, who sat at a desk in front of an empty enrollment book, looked up, and his eyes widened with utter amazement.

"What is this?" he asked me.

"These are students coming to enroll for your evening classes," I quietly explained.

"How many are there?" the principal inquired with growing bewilderment. I mentioned their number.

"But what shall I do with them?" ejaculated Mr. Darling. "I cannot put more than forty or fifty into one class, and I have no teachers for three new classes."

"The teachers are here," I informed him, introducing Mr. Miller and Mr. Kranz to him.

Then the humor of the situation dawned on him, and he broke out into hearty laughter. I was appointed a sort of foreman of the new crew and assigned the task of classifying and enrolling the students. The task was soon accomplished. I reserved the most advanced class for myself and divided the rest between my two colleagues.

I taught evening school for three years, and the recollection of these years is among the most pleasant in my life.

My pupils were about my age or a little older. Most of them had had a good education in the countries of their birth. They were intelligent and earnest and, with very few exceptions, of radical leanings. Our relations were comradely and cordial and sometimes, particularly at the close of the school terms, their demonstrations of genuine affection for me were touching. For many years thereafter, I would often meet men who had made their mark in liberal professions or in business, and who would smilingly remind me that I had taught them English in the Vandewater Street school.

During my leisure hours in these years I took up the study of law. Having passed the requisite "Regents' examination," I enrolled in the New York University Law School and was admitted to the bar in the spring of 1893.

I immediately settled down to the practice of the law and have remained active in it ever since.

LOUIS LIPSKY

Louis Lipsky is one of the great names in American Zionism. Lipsky, who was born in Rochester, N.Y., in 1876, and died in New York City in 1963, was one of the few important American Zionists of his generation who were native Americans.

In addition to his Zionist work, Lipsky also devoted himself to editing and writing. From 1899 to 1914, he was managing editor of the American Hebrew. *During part of that period, from 1910 to 1913, he also was on the staff of the* New York Telegraph, *for which he wrote drama reviews and fiction.*

In 1899, he established The Maccabaean, *the official magazine of the Zionist Organization of America.* The Maccabaean *was followed by* The New Palestine, *and Mr. Lipsky was its first editor. Throughout his life, he contributed to Zionist periodicals.*

From 1925 to 1930, he was President of the Zionist Organization of America, and he served for many years as a member of the Executive Committee of the Z.O.A. He attended his first World Zionist Congress in 1913 and was a leader and familiar figure at World Zionist Congresses in the decades that followed. At the same time, he was a founder of the American Jewish Congress and of the World Jewish Congress.

The author of several books on Zionism, Lipsky also wrote a volume on Yiddish actors, entitled Tales of the Yiddish Rialto.

The memoir included here, taken from his Thirty Years of American Zionism, *covers the period from the 1880's to 1914 and represents authentic Zionist history by a man who helped to shape it.*

The Founders of American Zionism*

LOUIS LIPSKY

I

ALTHOUGH I was born and lived my youth in a provincial American city, far from the pressure of the *Galuth,* I was always curious about Jewish life in general. My father was a *schochet,* fairly pious and learned, and our home was a rendezvous for functionaries of the community—teachers, rabbis and cantors. *Maskilim* were my father's friends. The Russian immigration poured into the city in a continuous stream from 1880 to 1897. I read about things Jewish with a strange avidity, and absorbed such books about Jews—there were not many of them—as could be found in English. At an early age I had acquired a general impression of the American Jewish scene. It was a picture of strange contrasts.

The early settlers, hailing from Central Europe, had already adjusted themselves to American conditions. They were prosperous middle-class people. They had built their temples, organized their charities, and established their social clubs. They had formulated a version of a pragmatic religion which they called American Judaism. Their manners and speech still showed traces of Teutonic influence, but they were American to all intents and purposes; they had more than a perfunctory love for American institutions; they shared the patriotic feelings of the early Germans who came to America to find freedom from Prussian oppression. Their Judaism being protected, in a way, by a Monroe Doctrine, it did not carry with it the pangs of the *Weltschmerz,* which afflicted the Orthodox. In comparison, it was a comfortable, easy-going, self-satisfied mode of Jewish life.

On the other hand, the new settlers hailing from Eastern Europe were then in the throes of the struggle to adjust them-

* Reprinted from *Thirty Years of American Zionism,* vol. I, The Nesher Publishing Company, for the Louis Lipsky Jubilee Committee, New York, 1927, pp. 5–47.

selves to the new environment. The process had just about begun. They still suffered the embarrassments of foreigners. They still felt themselves to be strangers in a strange land. They lived, for self-protection, in ghettos of their own making. Although many of them were petty merchants, the large majority went into the workshops. They crowded the needle industries. The pay of Jewish workmen was low, the seasons of employment were irregular, and they were with difficulty organized into trade unions. They persisted in being as Orthodox as possible, regarding lapses from piety as due to the *Galuth* which could not be overcome. (*Galuth* was still a living word in their vocabulary.) They fashioned their synagogues after the pattern of the synagogues they had left behind them in the old country. Their social life was segregated in their own fraternal lodges, their own *Chevras,* their own congregations. They were kept conscious of their past by the Yiddish and Hebrew press; and by the Yiddish theatre. The press gave them adaptations, reminiscences, knowledge of American conditions. The theatre was a vagrant beginning, living on historical operettas, melodramas and adaptations. Their children were beginning to enter the high schools; some of them had already reached the universities.

These two communities seldom met on equal terms. A chasm of social and economic differences divided them. The early settlers were interested in their co-religionists as poor relations. I remember an occasional visit to our synagogue by high-hatted *Yahudim* who walked gingerly into the crowded house of worship (it was usually a Holyday), donned strips of *Talesim,* went through the motions of prayer and soon stalked out, eager for a breath of fresh air. This was typical of their relationship. For these uncouth brethren they generously maintained charity organizations and settlements, and they were intensely concerned about their tardy Americanization.

II

An inventory of Jewish assets of the period could easily be made. The Jewish Publication Society had about started; its outstanding achievement was a translation of Graetz's *History;*

Zangwill's *Children of the Ghetto* had just been written and published. The Hebrew Union College was sending out its first graduates; rabbis from Germany were no longer imported. The Jewish Theological Seminary was in its infancy; it was on the verge of reorganization, with Solomon Schechter, who was to make a lasting impression on its graduates, still at Cambridge. The Independent Order B'nai B'rith was a purely German Jewish fraternity which, together with the Union of American Hebrew Congregations, maintained at Washington a Jewish Ambassador, in the person of Simon Wolf, to represent Jewish interests, which were then confined to questions arising out of immigration. An agent of the United Hebrew Charities of New York acted for the Jewish community at Ellis Island to receive the immigrants. The Hebrew Immigrant Aid Society was merely a hostel. To a noticeable extent American Jewry was not only intellectually and spiritually dependent upon the Jewish communities of Europe, but it received financial aid as well for the support of a number of its institutions from the Baron de Hirsch Fund. This generous philanthropist was interested in Jewish emigration from Russia. It was quite in order for American philanthropy to receive financial support from that Fund for institutions in America designed to improve the conditions of the Russian immigrants.

There was a fairly active Anglo-Jewish press, but it was largely rabbinical and congregational; its editors were rabbis, and its news interests were local. The Yiddish press had recently become diurnal, and was in a precarious financial and moral condition. Jacob Gordin had just come to the Yiddish theatre, pushed into it by the rising power of organized Jewish labor.

There was a Farm School at Doylestown founded by Joseph Krauskopf. The Jewish Chautauqua Assembly had been established by Henry Berkowitz. The Jewish Historical Society was engaged in gathering fragments of American Jewish history and publishing them in pamphlet form. The *Menorah* Magazine, edited by Moritz Ellinger, a German who wrote atrocious English, was the only monthly Jewish publication. Jacob H. Schiff was the outstanding Jewish philanthropist. Mayer Sulzberger of

Philadelphia was the leading intellectual personality. Emil G. Hirsch of Chicago was the premier Oracle and Orator of the Reform pulpit.

III

This was the prepared scene. Just as in Jewish life elsewhere, however, the seed of Zionism was already in the ground awaiting the fructifying stimulus of favorable conditions. There was a recollection of Mordecai M. Noah, who had enunciated a purely American version of Zionism. The old Sephardi community, disintegrating, and now being diluted by German infiltration, had given expression to Zionist aspirations in the stirring national poetry of Emma Lazarus. Not all the German rabbis were exponents of the anti-national reform school of Isaac M. Wise and Kaufman Kohler. Sturdy Zionist doctrine was preached by Bernard Felsenthal of Chicago, Marcus Jastrow of Philadelphia, Gustav Gottheil of New York, Benjamin Szold of Baltimore. A learned Jew, Louis N. Dembitz, of Louisville, wrote and lectured on Jewish subjects from a Zionist point of view. Aaron Friedenwald of Baltimore, a prominent physician, was one of the early Chovevei Zionists. H. Pereira Mendes, of Shearith Israel (New York), from his early youth preached a blend of Messianic Zionism and dogmatic orthodoxy.

But Zionism derived its strength and organized support chiefly from what may be called the Third *Aliyah*—the Jews of Eastern Europe. They brought with them living Jewish traditions; remembrances of *Chibath Zion* and Chovevei Zionism; there were many *Maskilim* among them; and the young people, including a segment of the youth born on American soil, made possible, eventually, the organization of Zionism in America. These were only slightly influenced by the early American pioneers. They received their inspiration from their own intellectual and spiritual leaders.

IV

I have already mentioned Hirsch Masliansky. Just as he made a deep and lasting impression upon my youthful imagination, so too he carried the inspiration of Zionist idealism into many corners of American Jewry, and kindled a steady flame of devotion and sacrifice. There is no doubt that the awakening of Orthodoxy in America (at first indifferent to Zionism and then resentful of it—a secular disturbance of a treasured religious ideal) was due in largest measure to the great eloquence and idealism of this man. Beginning his labors as a popular orator and *maggid* in the days of Pinsker, he came to America still in his prime and preached of the memories of Zion and of the Jews' duty to redeem themselves and their land. He was a voice of surpassing power. He had a remarkable arsenal of oratorical effects. He became the itinerant *maggid* of Zionism. He attracted large audiences in the bigger communities and was known and welcomed in hundreds of towns and hamlets. The Educational Alliance in New York engaged his services, and every Friday evening he preached to a crowded auditorium the truth of a living Zion, of Jewish ideals, of national traditions and aspirations. Through him, whom they knew from the old country, Russian immigrants coming to America were enabled to establish once more a new relation to the old ideal.

In this task of winning back to Zionism the new settlers, he was aided by other forces. There were Hebrew writers who made futile attempts to establish Hebrew periodicals that had a brief and sordid existence. These lovers of Hebrew maintained shabby Hebrew reading clubs; *Chibath Zion* flourished for a time and disappeared in a smoke of confused financial troubles; Chovevei Zionist groups were organized, some for a day, and a few extended their lives to come face to face with the Herzlian movement.

v

I think it will interest the reader to include in this narrative a few observations on several unusual personalities—to say eccentric would be inadequate and unfair—who played a strange but useful part in the making of American Zionism. Quite a number of the early Zionists were distinguished by picturesque manners and bizarre thought. They were streaked with queerness. they were romanticists or iconoclasts; to a large extent *kibitzers*. Relics of that age still abide with us. I mention Marco Baruch as an example of the type I refer to. The men I place in this gallery were pale shadows of that half-insane devotee. They lacked his daring, but they had charm, and a modicum of sweet reasonableness, and their talents were displayed in an atmosphere of peace where tea was consumed (or stronger liquor), or at small Zionist gatherings, or in dramatic entrances and exits on important public occasions. Marco Baruch left no vocal descendants, unless we take our Activists seriously. The men I have in mind exercised personal influence quite out of all proportion to their merits. What was rational in them was absorbed by scores of listeners. These vagrant types were the spice of the movement.

VI

I knew Naphthali Herz Imber for many years before his untimely death in 1909. He was the author of the text of *Hatikvah,* our national anthem. He was a vagabond, a drunkard and a Hebrew poet. He looked like a bronzed Indian with a long acquiline nose and hair jet black that hung loose over his shoulders. *Hatikvah* was one of the poems he chanced to write and forgot about until he heard it sung at Zionist meetings. He did not regard it as much of a poem, but he thought he deserved a pension for having written it. The last years of his life were spent in collecting toll from the Zionist public. He had played many parts in his lifetime—Hindu fakir, dragoman, editor—and finally arrived in New York to hover about the fringe of the growing Zionist movement, and to bask in the sunshine of a growing public recognition.

I met him for the first time in 1899 in Philadelphia at a Convention. Not much honor was given to him there. He stood on the platform unobserved, with a bottle bulging out of his coat pocket and a bundle of manuscripts and newspapers under his arm. He seemed to be drowsy, but when the audience sang *Hatikvah* he shook himself out of his sleep, stood to attention, and with a pleased smile bowed many times in response to applause which was not intended for him. He was a mocker of the serious. He used to say that he was the only Hebrew poet who wrote poetry like a man, and not like a lachrymose woman. He had translated Omar Khayyam into Hebrew. He used to say his favorite gods were Bacchus and Hebe, while all the other Hebrew poets paid homage to Minerva and her degenerate offspring, Niobe. He was a sardonic and vulgar jester, but he spoke to those who used to pay for his drinks, of lands far off in which *Galuth* meant sacrifice or defiance, evasion or compromise. He knew Rumania, Austria, Germany; he had lived in Constantinople and in Palestine. He had known men and women of prominence. Laurence Oliphant was his friend. His tales were filled with an elfish wisdom that made them peculiarly attractive. He used to write strangely incoherent articles and bring them to me for the *American Hebrew*. He had a friend in Mayer Sulzberger of Philadelphia, who provided him with the pension which Imber thought was due him from the Jewish people. But that pension did not suffice to slake his growing appetite for strong drink. The editors of the Anglo-Jewish and Yiddish press were called upon regularly to provide the deficit. He seemed to represent the Vagabondage of Zionism, its restlessness, its boundless hopes, its good cheer. In spite of himself, he carried the message of Zion into strange corners of American Jewry.

VII

Joseph Seff—a speaker of great talents, an acrid controversialist, a bitter partisan—was a man of a much higher grade. He claimed that Herzl had sent him to America, but his letters of reference were lost on the way. He was too proud to explain this to the Zionists whose addresses he had been given. He believed his failure to establish himself in America was due to his having arrived here penniless; his wallet had been stolen on board the ship! This at once placed him in the category of ordinary *maggidim*. His first addresses were delivered for pay. How, therefore, could he raise his head and ask to be received as Herzl's emissary? He therefore devoted himself to the business of life in his own way, without references and without patronage. He made himself at home in East Side restaurants and coffee-shops, in Zionist clubs

and at Zionist meetings. He was a political Zionist with a venge-
ance—nothing less than a Jewish State, negotiations with the
Turks, the organization of an Army (probably from Cyprus),
international law, diplomacy in general, but seldom a word
about Zion itself—that was the range of his conversation. Palestine was the Territory, but the less said about it the better. He
was an inveterate hater of Orthodoxy and especially of rabbis,
and had many a battle with the moderate Zionists who resented
his reckless attacks on piety. He was a thoughtful speaker, but
lacked an easy touch. He believed in the masses, but could not
reach them. In his later years he persuaded himself that the first
law of nature was self-preservation. Therefore he joined the
Tammany Hall organization and was appointed a Court Inter-
preter under Civil Service Regulations, and thus was protected
for the rest of his life from serious financial embarrassments. His
vagrant last years were disappointing. Soon sickness and bad
habits reduced him to a shadow of that virile personality who
had come to America in the flush of youth with Herzl's mandate
to conquer it for Zionism.

VIII

Of a still higher grade—he does not belong in this galley at
all!—was Boris Kazman, who came to us from Montpellier University, from the First Zionist Congress, from Vienna and from
Palestine. He was—still is—a restless being. In the early days he
was insatiable in argument—would spend days in debate, propose the most fantastic schemes of propaganda, and worried sick
many of his friends with proposals for action that would have
sent them all into mad adventure had they accepted them. He
was a Knight without blemish. He had fought duels with students in Vienna—had been expelled for registering as a Jew—
refused to study in Russia as a protest against discriminations.
He disregarded all passports. He was already a citizen of the
Jewish State and comported himself accordingly. He declared
that nothing should be done in Palestine—or could be done—
without a complete soil map, to be used to prove conclusively

that Palestine could hold the Jewish people. He was an agricultural chemist. He wanted the return of the Jews to be organized from the first detail to the last; all estimates to be calculated in advance, and every movement foreseen and provided for. He was one of Herzl's devotees, having travelled through Russia at Herzl's command to induce delegates to come to the first Zionist Congress. But life was cruel to him for many years. It took him further and further away from the Promised Land. He went to Cuba as a chemist, then to Lyons (New York), then to Battle Creek (Michigan), all the while protesting that his aim was to get to Palestine as quickly as possible. In spite of his far-flung Zionist notions, he was absolutely disciplined and loyal, devoid of personal ambition and interests. Around him gathered groups of young Zionists who loved him and caught sparks from the fire of his enthusiasm that lasted for years. (He is now in Rehoboth, working the farm his father left him, experimenting with the refinement of olive oil. He has a plan for extracting oil from lime-shale, and is expecting American capital to enable him to complete his experiments).

IX

You will find Nissim Behar—a soft-footed, clear-skinned, clear-eyed old man (he is probably nearly a hundred years old)—at all Zionist affairs now. He does this without fear or restraint; he has earned his freedom. There was a time, however, when he did not want to be known as a Zionist. He came to America as a delegate or representative of the Alliance Israelite Universelle, but he had lived in Palestine for many years and was the Manager of a Trade School maintained by the Alliance. He was already an old man when he arrived. It was his intention to win the non-Jews for Jewish interests. He went about the business in a sly, Levantine manner, and succeeded in winning many friends among non-Jews for Jewish rights, liberal immigration, defense against anti-Semitism. He was involved in all sorts of complicated activities and was not responsible to any known organized body in America. What he was driving at was a mystery. Many of the leaders of American Jewish philanthropy endeavored to suppress him, sought to thwart his plans, but the old man, grave and bland, persisted in keeping to his own course until the great War came on. He then disappeared for a while, and when he returned, lo and behold, he merged his interests in the Zionist stream, and made it appear that all this time he had been playing a game. He had been introducing Zionism in sugar-coated pills to persons who otherwise would not have received it. It must be admitted that many a non-Zionist was brought nearer to Jewish national thought by this stealthy emissary. (Who actually sent him to America is still an unsolved mystery.)

x

Adolph Radin was a rabbi, a graduate of the Wolozhin Yeshiva and a *bon vivant.* He was not Orthodox, nor was he ever an advocate of Reform Judaism. He hovered between the two. He was not a Zionist in his earlier days, but his deep and sincere interest in everything Jewish, his love for Jewish customs and habits, for Jewish food, for Jewish song, soon brought him into the Zionist movement, and he became one of the most alert, one of the most aggressive, one of the most effective speakers the Zionist movement was privileged to have in those days. He was a man with a strong sense of humor; if there was no humor in a situation he made it his business to find it. If there were a serious question being discussed it was his business to puncture the seriousness of it by introducing wit and repartee. He was not only a speaker, but knew all the trivial details of Zionist activities—the selling of shares, the collection of money for this or that purpose, the using of influence to draw strangers into our activities; in all these matters he could be relied upon day and night. He was a typical communal worker. Quite without wishing it he was entangled in Zionism, for many of his friends were Zionists. His knowledge of Hebrew led him to the company of those who were readers of Hebrew literature. His homely Jewish interests led him to homes in which Zionism was a general feature. When he died, many Zionists wondered why he had never written for

Zionism—tried to remember some of the wise words he had uttered—the anecdotes he had told—but all they could remember of him was his devotion, his zeal, his absorption in the every day business of Zionist life.

XI

I am reluctant to bring into this section the figure of Mordecai Brodsky, one of the founders of Hatechiya, the first Russian Zionist group in New York. There was nothing of the unusual or the bizarre about him. He was quite normal in every respect. But he was obsessed by a sense of responsibility for Zionist affairs. He obstinately insisted on sacrificing himself for the menial tasks of the movement. He was a workman—probably a furrier—who had long slack seasons, but he managed to save enough to keep himself in modest circumstances during the twelve months of the year. He had one vice—he had to smoke cigarettes. He never sought office, but always duties. He could be relied upon for any Zionist task, no matter how menial, at any hour, anywhere within reach of a street car. He was the chief in National Fund collections. He was the caretaker of the club-rooms. He had National Fund stamps always in his pocket and tickets to be sold for any and all Zionist entertainments and affairs. When *Dos Yiddishe Folk* was established, he became its volunteer subscription agent, collector of advertising bills and what not (and also the severest critic of its editorials). After many years of such labors, living a frugal existence—he never married—he was taken with consumption, and then began a desperate struggle to get out of the stifling atmosphere of New York into the open spaces. He contrived to get to Denver, Col., but it was too late. The disease could not be checked. But he pushed himself there also into Zionist work, and busied himself until the last days, in committees, meetings, plans, etc. The last I heard from him was in a letter describing the weakened position of the local Zionist group and what should be done to remedy it. Of himself he wrote not a word. He passed away remembered by only a few of his former associates in New York. It was upon the sacrifices of such willful beings that the Zionist movement was founded. You will find them in dozens of cities; to sing their praises would be to destroy the beauty of their lives. But of Brodsky one may speak, for he has passed beyond the reading of these words.

XII

From Odessa came Avrom Eliahu Lubarsky, the friend of Achad Ha'Am and Lilienblum, of Mendele and Shalom Aleichem. He knew all the Hebrew writers by their first names, and had spent most of his life in Odessa. He loved them all. He was the American representative of the Wissotsky Tea Company, with which Achad Ha'Am was also associated. Of course Lubarsky was a lover of Hebrew and a Zionist. But he was the first broad-minded, open-pocketed man of affairs we had thus far encountered. He loved to play the part of a Maecenas, but in spite of his bragging about his wealth he had not enough money to go around; there were too many of the *literati* who knew of his existence. All Russian émigrés of the Zionist school passed through his home and—more or less—his checking account. He was a hearty full-blooded man with a rare sense of humor, oozing stories and anecdotes—some of them rather salty—and generous to a fault. When stolid business men expressed a protest against the aggressions of the journalists and speakers in the Zionist movement—a protest in later years lodged against paid Zionist officials—it was Lubarsky who fumed and spluttered against the argument. If it was necessary to collect a purse for an impecunious Zionist, Lubarsky held the bag. He was friendly to all groups—with Dr. Schechter as well as with Dr. Syrkin, the Poale Zionist; with Jewish labor leaders as well as with Mr. Marshall. He was a disciple of Dr. Magnes; he thought that Dr. Magnes was an exponent of the doctrine of Achad Ha'Am. He went so far as to join Temple Emanu-El when Dr. Magnes became its associate rabbi. In the Self-Defense movement he was a busy man. He liked to be in on political secrets. Revolutionists from Russia always found him an eager listener and contributor, especially if the work to be done had the earmarks of a conspiracy. He was not much of a scholar himself and had great respect for Jewish learning. He sought the company of learned men, of men of wit, and could easily be found at different hours of the day in the coffee-houses frequented by one class or the other. He suffered business reverses during the War; and, what was worse, was over-taken by ill-health which pursued him with malicious thorough-ness and killed him within a few years, after much suffering.

XIII

The Dreyfus case brought Theodor Herzl back to his people. The sensational incidents of the trial, cabled to the four corners of the earth—the frank expression of anti-Semitism revealed for the first time in a forum which assumed the aspect of an interna-tional sounding-board—the isolation of Jewish life which it revealed, produced a universal racial resistance. I remember dis-tinctly how many Jews who were utterly indifferent, read day by day the detailed story of the Dreyfus case. In America it was an event of the highest importance. It made American Jewry for the first time conscious of a direct relation to world Jewish problems. But the advent of Herzl was passed unnoticed. That was some-thing that had happened over there. American Jewish news-papers regarded him as a fantastic figure, a strange intrusion, lacking all the attributes and qualities of the Redeemer or Emancipator. Vienna suggested lightmindedness and lighthead-edness. The *American Hebrew* regarded Herzl as a curious portent, liable to degenerate either into a false Messiah or an out and out imposter. So far as Herzl was concerned, America was an unknown continent. He included it in one corner of his vision as a possible source of support, but for the moment it was a pawn in reserve. The call to attend the First Zionist Congress did not reach America; it was disregarded or unnoticed by American Jewry. International Jewish action or international discussion of Jewish questions was something the leaders of American Jewry could not countenance. American patriotism implied observance of the Monroe Doctrine; not only that Europe should not inter-fere with this continent's affairs, but the reverse process also was taboo. Further, the First Congress was a beginning; provision was not made for formal elections, a constitution was to be adopted, and those who came would assume responsibility for the organized effort. Several American visitors—rather curious—came to Basle. Some left unrecognized and unconvinced; others remained, tremendously impressed by the personalities of Herzl and Nordau, stirred by the eloquent addresses delivered, and determined to assume whatever responsibilities arose out of the adoption of the Basle program. According to the official register there were present from America the following delegates: Adam Rosenberg of New York, who had been sent to Palestine for land purchase on behalf of the American Chovevei Zionist movement; Dr. S. Schaffer, a Conservative rabbi of Baltimore; Rosa Sonnenschein of St. Louis, a journalist. Professor Richard Gottheil and Mrs. Gottheil were present, although not registered, while a number of the European delegates later settled in America. They were, to give a few of the names, Reuben Brainin, Ephraim Ish Kishor, Avrom Eliahu Lubarsky, Jacob de Haas, Boris Kazman, Joseph Seff, Nahum Syrkin, Yecheskel Wortzman.

XIV

The modern Zionist movement in America was organized in 1897. Leon Zolotkoff, a journalist writing in Yiddish and Hebrew, a Zionist from his early youth, brought together a number of Zionist groups in the Middle West and called the organization the Knights of Zion. Then Richard Gottheil, returning from Europe where he had attended the Basle Congress by chance, assembled a few friends and organized the Federation of American Zionists. The inspiration for this act came from his father, Gustav Gottheil, who evinced a strong interest in the movement, although he was then in failing health and soon passed away. Professor Gottheil had the cooperation of a young theological student, Stephen S. Wise, who was then studying at Columbia University in the Semitics Department. The organization formed was not a real Federation at that time, but soon various Hebrew societies, Chovevei Zionist groups and Jewish nationalist clubs rallied about the Gottheil group and were transformed into Zionist societies. The Federation, as a loose union of groups all endorsing the Basle program, was legally established at a conference held in Baltimore. A constitution was adopted; Professor Gottheil was elected President and Dr. Wise, Honorary Secretary. Soon thereafter the Knights of Zion were amalgamated with the Federation, retaining their jurisdiction over the Zionist groups in the Middle Western States.

Briefly to dispose of details, it may be well to describe in sequence, leading up to 1914, the structural progress of the movement in America. I was a personal witness of this progress and gradually became more and more interested in it. I attended all the American Zionist Conventions with the exception of the first and second. I acted at these Conventions as the guardian of correct procedure. At first it was a bit of audacity on my part to make these Parliamentary intrusions at Conventions, but later it was recognized that somebody should be responsible for Parliamentary order, and my efforts were then received with a better grace.

As stated, Professor Gottheil was the first President of the Federation, and continued in office until the Cleveland Convention of June, 1904, when he was succeeded by Dr. Harry Friedenwald of Baltimore. Dr. Friedenwald remained actually President until large powers were given to an Administrative Committee consisting of Israel Friedlaender, Henrietta Szold, Joseph Jasin and myself. Dr. Friedenwald continued nominally as President, however, until 1912, when I became Chairman of the Executive Committee.

Dr. Stephen S. Wise was the first Honorary Secretary, and was succeeded after a year by Isidore D. Morrison. At the Boston Convention in June, 1902, Jacob de Haas, then of London, was elected Secretary *in absentio,* and came over to New York to assume office. He remained the administrative head of the organization for a year or so and was followed as Honorary Secretary by Dr. Judah L. Magnes. Dr. Magnes resigned because of his interest in the New York *Kehillah* and his place was taken by Joseph Jasin, who was brought to New York from Texas. Jasin was Secretary for two years. Miss Szold stepped into the breach caused by the confusion arising out of Jasin's administration, and after a year of unusual devotion retired in favor of a coalition administration made up of the writer as Chairman, Bernard A. Rosenblatt as Honorary Secretary, and Senior Abel.

In 1889, *The Maccabaean* was born. I was asked to become its managing editor by Professor Gottheil and Dr. Wise. What induced them to appoint me to take charge of this important venture I do not know. I understand it was done firstly because I was getting out the *American Hebrew,* secondly because I was a Zionist, and thirdly, because I had written a sympathetic report of the Philadelphia Convention in the *American Hebrew,* which was practically a non-Zionist publication. The *American Hebrew* was then edited by a Board among whom were Frederick de Sola Mendes, H. Pereira Mendes, Cyrus L. Sulzberger, Dr. Solomon Solis-Cohen, and Philip Cowen, also its publisher. (A majority of these men were Zionists in spirit, but had adopted a critical attitude towards the activities of Herzl.) I was the managing editor of *The Maccabaean* for about a year, when de Haas became Secretary and also took over the editorship of the Zionist organ, but I continued my cooperation throughout, and subsequently, after the retirement of de Haas, I again became its editor.

It was a tedious business. The publication was always in financial difficulties. It could not pay for articles or editorial services. It regularly skipped issues to save expense. It owed its continued existence to the devotion and patience of David H. Lieberman who, although engaged in an engrossing manufacturing business, spent all his spare time and much of his own money to maintain *The Maccabaean.* Lieberman was a remarkable personality; he applied to the business of *The Maccabaean* all his skill as an experienced manufacturer. He scraped and saved to keep *The Maccabaean* going. He himself kept its books; he supervised its mailings; he was its accredited beggar. He went about with a little notebook in which, in very small handwriting, he kept all the accounts, from year to year, tabulated, classified, and could at a moment's notice tell you how much money had been lost, how much less money was being lost, how many subscribers there were—in fact, the little notebook was a complete bookkeeping set. He was a young man when he died; his death was a great loss to the movement.

There had been several sporadic attempts to publish a Zionist Yiddish weekly, but they failed, both for dearth of financial support, and because it was impossible then to secure professional Yiddish journalists who were also Zionists and willing to take the work. In 1909, the Zionist Organization created *Dos Yiddishe Folk*. Its first editor was, I think, a young man named Lazarson, who soon left for Palestine, but the editorial influence in *Dos Yiddishe Folk* for many years was Senior Abel. A number of editors passed through *Dos Yiddishe Folk,* but Abel remained in editorial control. He was a very precise man, with a deep sense of responsibility towards the printed word. He suffered physical and mental pain because of typographical mistakes, inaccurate information, or loose discussion carried on by some of the contributors. Of the succeeding editors I remember Yecheskel Wortzman and Abraham Goldberg. Goldberg was the founder of the Poale Zion party—had had a hand in the territorialist movement—and subsequently entered the general Zionist Organization, in which he exercised considerable influence both as a writer and a speaker.

xv

The protocols of our annual Conventions reveal our provincial status—they must appear shockingly inadequate to our more experienced European parliamentarians. We exercised the free manners of the West. Our written constitution troubled us greatly; we spent much time in amending and revising it. We dealt with Zionist groups and not with individual Zionists. Our system of taxation was curiously ineffective. If a Zionist group wanted to send a delegate to the Convention, it paid the tax of its members. If it had no delegate to send, our treasurer had to forego the taxes for the year; and the arrearage could not be collected. I was constantly on the alert to prevent the amendment of the constitution several times during one session. This eagerness to amend indicated a fickleness I could not appreciate.

I would insist that there must be at least a motion to reconsider. But these objections were regarded as technical, and I was usually crushed by the gavel.

When Professor Gottheil was President, he did not attend the annual conventions, for he usually left for Europe early in June. There was no challenge of his perennial candidacy until it became apparent that no self-respecting body could for ever countenance the re-election of an absentee President. The last annual Convention Professor Gottheil attended was held in Boston in 1900. He did not reappear in our councils for many years, although he wrote an occasional article on a Zionist subject, and his *History of Zionism* appeared after his retirement. Dr. Friedenwald was also elected in his absence. Gabriel H. Mayer of Philadelphia, who was Vice-President under Professor Gottheil, thought that he was entitled to become President, and specially resented the naming of an absentee candidate, and rightly so. But we regarded Mr. Mayer as an undisciplined Zionist, for were we not inviting Dr. Friedenwald to become President for the good of the movement? And so we defeated Mr. Mayer's ambition. Mr. Mayer surprised us by retiring to the depths of seclusion, and from that eventful day in Pittsburgh he was seen no more by Zionist eyes. In a similar way, the resignation of de Haas, after a disagreement with the President, led to his general retirement. He left for Boston, became the editor of the *Jewish Advocate,* and for one reason or another washed his hands of Zionist reponsibility. Many of his personal friends urged his return in spite of what appeared to be adverse conditions; but it seemed that he could not travel with a movement unless all its policies met with his personal approval.

With the advent of Dr. Friedenwald, the influence of Dr. Schechter predominated. Within the circle of the Schechter influence were Dr. Magnes, Henrietta Szold, Professor Israel Friedlaender, E. W. Lewin-Epstein and many others. It was a beneficial, fructifying influence, although it slurred the political aspect of the movement and benevolently laughed at political negotiations. Dr. Schechter was a personality of temperamental force. He was a scholar with many secular interests. He had intense dislikes, but his support of a cause meant unqualified, vehement cooperation. His influence upon the students of the Jewish Theological Seminary was remarkable. He provoked allegiance to Zionism in all his discussions, and treated with withering contempt the unfortunate wight who venture to disagree. It was Dr. Schechter—and later, to an extent, Professor Israel Friedlaender —who made the Jewish Theological Seminary an institution for the graduation not only of rabbis, but also of Zionists. Without exeception its rabbis—leaders and workers—have carried the message of Zionism into all parts of America. To their splendid cooperation we owe a great deal.

Our education in Zionism came from our conventions and conferences. At that time, an open forum for the discussion of Jewish problems was unknown. Our discussions may not have been conducted upon a high intellectual plane, but they were imbued with fervor, with passion, with a sense of devotion, which enabled us to achieve a publicity accorded to no other annual Jewish gathering. Regularly, early in the summer, after months of preparation, we called together the leaders of our army. We were able to take them with us—in those days of comparative poverty—as far as Cleveland or Cincinnati. The convention was the annual reunion. We got to know the old faces—to distinguish between the workers and the shirkers. We knew the delegate who came to make personal capital out of the public event; and those who were present to merge their interests in the common weal. The resolutions adopted were not important, probably, but the discussions in Committee, the talks in the lobbies, the long sessions at midnight in the coffee-restaurants, made it possible for us to weld out of diverse elements a generation knowing its Zionist obligations, bound together by ties of spiritual and intellectual idealism.

XVI

Slowly the movement in America was being prepared for the historic task opportunity was later to assign to it. The field in which we labored was vast and hard. The Jewish population was growing in numbers; it was becoming affluent, and thoroughly American. Thriving communities were springing up all the way from New York to San Francisco. The Russian Jews were emerging out of their obscurity and inferior status. Yiddish was slowly giving way to English, although the influence of the Yiddish press was not diminished. Thus far we had scratched only the surface of our resources. We had not been tested yet in the crucible of the *Galuth*, for the Gates of the Republic were still open to all comers, and we could speak truthfully of our future as Americans. We saw *Galuth* elsewhere, far away. Echoes of its tribulations and complexities reached us. It was freedom with memory; and Zionism was a free expression of that memory without personal bias.

The Uganda issue was flung into the forum of Zionist affairs by Herzl probably—if the truth were known—as a maneuver and a bit of political opportunism. It was discussed with fierce partisanship in the European Zionist press. It almost tore the Congress asunder, threatening to disrupt the Organization, and gave birth to the Territorialist diversion, which Zangwill led to a smothered death. But it scarcely caused a ripple in our American Zionist life. A few American delegates were present at the Congress at which the issue was fought out. How they voted did not matter, for they had no instructions from those who had sent them. It was, in fact, an academic question. Herzl passed away soon after the Uganda incident, and David Wolffsohn took the reins of Government into his hands, transferring its seat from Vienna, the gay, to Cologne, the stolid. But we on this side of the water noted the events with proper regrets or appreciation and went on with out labors unconcerned. We were in the adolescent age.

What troubled us then was the charge of "double" patriotism, which at irregular intervals rose up to plague and disturb us. It was a heavy boulder in our path. Jacob H. Schiff, always speaking with a delightful German accent, used to emphasize it and elaborate upon its dangers. His words carried in the press, and we had to spend weeks to catch up with them. Sometimes we got our case into even the *New York Times*, which was indeed an achievement (then as now). We took up the cudgels against anti-

nationalist Reform rabbis, who in sermons or editorials in their
weekly publications treated us to pious argument or expletives.
We had many a tilt with Emil G. Hirsch, who once promised
Leon Zolotkoff to address a Zionist meeting in Pittsburgh and
then denied that he had made the promise. The advent of a
Reform rabbi in our ranks was the occasion for general rejoicing:
it meant that a breach had been made in the enemy's citadel. We
plunged into the organization of the New York *Kehillah,* led by
Dr. Magnes, but no sooner was it set up when it began to slide
back into the old groove, and made an alliance with the American Jewish Committee. That Committee, of which Judge Mayer
Sulzberger was the first President, was the object of our hearty
attacks. We just could not abide its undemocratic constitution. It
was a self-appointed body. It was contemptuous of public opinion, and invariably took the unpopular side. We, organizers of a
free Jewish opinion, upon which Zionist success depended, felt
that we had to fight the American Jewish Committee or be faith-
less as Zionists and Americans.

The Turks were given a constitution and Abdul Hamid ceased
to reign, and all that was evil in his regime passed away to
assume other forms. This was an event of the greatest importance. It was greeted by many as if it were the end of all our
endeavors. I remember that many of us took the position that it
would not fundamentally alter the situation so far as we Zionists
were concerned. Without a charter we would not budge. So slug-
gish was the Zionist mind, however, that when Dr. Magnes, then
the Secretary and our outstanding orator—Dr. Wise was still
away in Portland, Oregon—delivered an informal address at the
annual Convention (which was not scrutinized or censored by
either Dr. Friedenwald or the Executive Committee) and accepted the Turkish constitution as the fulfillment of the Basle
program, there were only six delegates to register their protest
and vote against his statement. But although the address got into
the newspapers (and also our six votes) the situation was not
seriously affected. We were concerned with matters closer to
home; the internal struggle interested us more than external happenings.

XVII

Even Palestine was far away. It is true that we had created a large public interest in the Jewish National Fund, and that required the use of Palestine as subject matter for propaganda. We had a brisk campaign for the sale of Jewish Colonial Trust shares; and we had to speak of banking operations in Palestine. But Palestine itself was not a vivid reality, except when Palestinians came to us and told us their colorful tales. It did not play an appreciable part in our calculations. We were probably too young to appreciate a glowing picture of the Orient; it was hard to visualize the descriptions; they were altogether too stunning.

E. W. Lewin-Epstein came to us as a representative of the Carmel Wine Company and opened a branch office for the sale of Palestine wines and cognacs. (His original home was Warsaw.) He appealed to us to aid him in disposing of his wares, which we did. In the course of time Lewin-Epstein became our expert on Palestine. Any knotty question that presented itself was referred to him, and his judgment was accepted without question. He was a cool man of affairs, and avoided exaggeration, but his presentation of Palestine facts did not inspire; we felt confident that he could be relied upon, but he was lacking in sentiment and emotion. Although bound by unbreakable ties to Palestine, he spent the larger part of the years 1900 to 1927 in the United States. He went with the Hadassah Medical Unit to Palestine in 1917, but soon returned.

I remember Zwi Cohen, who came to us direct from Palestine, representing, it was said, independent wine-growers, who were carrying on an agitation against the Carmel Wine Company. Zwi Cohen denied that he had beeen sent to us by interested wine-growers. He declared that he was a simple, public-spirited Zionist. It was charged that the Carmel Wine Company was deliberately restricting the production of wine in order to enable them to fix higher prices. Zwi Cohen thought that large sales would be better for the colonists, even though prices would be lower. In order to further this policy of the Carmel Wine Company, the agents of Baron de Rothschild at one time ordered the uprooting of acres of vineyards. This was made the occasion of a loud outcry by Zwi Cohen and his partisans. He was abetted by Solomon Frankel, one of our ablest propagandists, who made turbulent scenes at one of our Conventions. It was boomed into an issue of the first magnitude. Some vineyards may have been uprooted: I do not know. But there were Palestinians then whose principal asset was sentiment and against their onslaught it was impossible to contend. The Carmel Wine Company had a hard time of it.

Later came Simon Goldman of St. Louis who wanted our endorsement of his plan to establish a colony which he subsequently called Poriah. Years before settling in America, Goldman had lived in Palestine. He nursed a dream of returning to the land, went to St. Louis, and established a thriving optical business, accumulated a moderate fortune, and then prepared to go to Palestine. He persuaded a number of St. Louis friends to join with him in establishing a colony based upon individual ownership. He was the originator of the Achooza plan. He did not need official endorsement, but felt that if his plan received our approval others would imitate it. He was primarily a Palestinian. He did not have faith in political Zionism. But Mr. Lewin-Epstein had serious objections to his plans. These objections were passed on to us and we accepted them as ours. Furthermore, we were partisans of the Herzlian policy of not doing anything officially in Palestine until assured of political guarantees; we could not be asked to accept responsibility, even remotely, for a colonization scheme of a private nature. Goldman made a desperate fight at our Convention. He raved against us and declared we were going the way of ruination. He soon left for Palestine on his own responsibility. The colony Poriah was established. Thousands of olive trees were planted and houses were built. But Goldman had overlooked the fact that water would be required. He had been impressed by the beautiful scenery, the high altitude, etc., of Poriah, but these advantages were responsible for the fatal disadvantage, for water could not be obtained by drilling wells, and to bring it up from Lake Tiberias would be tremendously expensive. Then arose dissension among the stockholders. Poriah was soon involved in debts and litigation. Goldman fell sick and died, and today Poriah is a dead monument to his energy and will-power, unoccupied, with rotting olive trees, empty houses, and only Simon Goldman's son and a few strangers hold it to prevent its falling into the hands of aliens.

We knew of Dr. Arthur Ruppin, who had been sent to Palestine in a semi-official way to see what could be done to promote agricultural or industrial enterprise. He had been given all of Palestine as his field—and a small budget. He spent his time drafting plans, and sending them on to friends in different parts of the Jewish world. We had never seen him, but his communications were interesting and informative. He wrote of the Palestine Land Development Company, of the *Agudath Netaim,* and in recollection I seem to have heard of many, if not all, of our latest credit devices for the first time in the letters of Dr. Ruppin. A large part of his discussions was Greek to us, but we had an impression that great things were being done. I recall, in 1913, at Vienna, the able defense of Dr. Ruppin against the sour attack of Jacobus Kann, and it seemed to us then that the Zionist movement had produced a man of the first rank as an economist in the person of Dr. Ruppin.

Aaron Aaronsohn, of Zichron Jacob, was one of our early Palestinian visitors. He did not come as a propagandist, but as the founder of an institution. He had discovered the original prototype of modern wheat, and this was expected to revolutionize agriculture in Palestine. He did not work with the Zionist Organization, found friends in non-Zionist circles, but was guided in large measure by Henrietta Szold and Dr. Magnes. He won the support of a number of American Jews for the establishment of the Jewish Agricultural Experiment Station. Among his financial supporters were Jacob H. Schiff, Julius Rosenwald, Louis Marshall and Nathan Straus.

XVIII

It was the Kishinev pogrom that aroused, for the first time in *our* lives, the direct interest of American Jewry in an important "foreign" Jewish event. It was the first direct intrusion of a tragic

Jewish need emanating from the European Diaspora. The story of Kishinev awakened memories of all the Jewish tragedies of the past. Every Russian immigrant, his son and his grandson, felt a tremor of personal concern. It was the Jewish people who were attacked, and all Jews the world over felt the force of the impact. Kishinev gave American Zionists the first tangible opportunity to utilize their organized strength in action.

That was a thrilling, a moving time. Those who had voices used them to speak at meetings. Those who were good collectors went about soliciting funds. A tremendous parade was organized by Joseph Barondess, which made a stirring impression. The scenes at the mass-meetings transcended description. The sacrifices of the poor, the giving of jewels, the weeping that attended the simplest accounts of the riots, the passion in the giving—all this once lived through made impossible the easy-going, comfortable Jewish life of the past.

The Zionists pushed their way into the relief work—they were parties to the establishment of the relief committee—they were the speakers and the collectors. Out of the passion that was put into the demonstration arose the idea of Self-Defense. This was a radical new thought. It may not have had any practical bearing on the situation in Russia, but it served to give expression to Jewish self-respect. Fortunately for us, we found in Dr. Magnes an appealing protagonist of the movement for Self-Defense. Dr. Magnes was then rabbi of a Brooklyn Reform congregation. He had been forced to resign as an instructor in the Hebrew Union College because of his pronounced Zionist views. He was young and enthusiastic. He had not barked his shins on the rough edge of practical endeavor. He had audacity and a way of speaking that touched the heart. His youth made a deep impression even on those who did not share his views. The leaders of philanthropy were friendly to him. His ardor may have reminded them of youthful feelings they had suppressed in themselves.

We brought Dr. Magnes to our Cleveland Convention. He delivered an address on Self-Defense which was telegraphed through the Associated Press to all parts of the country. A new word was spoken which aroused great interest. Hitherto Jews speaking of their interests had uttered words of humility, had spoken of suffering unwarranted, had appealed for sympathy. The courageous words of Dr. Magnes (expressive of the ideals of Zionism) held a new content—it was the Jew courageous, the Jew self-reliant, the Jew protestant that appeared on the American scene.

' Through Self-Defense we made alliances with the unorganized Jewish democracy; the Poale Zion were greatly strengthened; we penetrated into the Jewish street and became known as an important party in American Israel; and Dr. Magnes became an influential personality. The leaders of philanthropy sought him out. He was brought into their councils. He was drawn into the pulpit of Temple Emanu-El. And through Zionist influence he was enabled to begin the organization of the Jewish community of Greater New York. The ideals of Self-Defense led inevitably to Self-Emancipation and Self-Government. Democracy was an inevitable corollary. The New York *Kehillah* was established.

· But there was not strength in us sufficient for a sustained effort. Democracy was a good word but a hard task. The New York *Kehillah* began under the most auspicious circumstances, but soon the insidious influence of philanthropy found a way to control its actions. There was always a lack of financial support from the democratic masses. The philanthropists had to be called upon. Soon the annual meetings of the *Kehillah* became farcically inadequate. The delegates did not provide the income; so how could they adopt an effective budget? They could not decide upon policy, for policy depended upon income. As a result, the *Kehillah* conventions met only to adopt ineffectual resolutions and to make hot speeches, and the Committee on Ways and Means—which found the means—decided what the *Kehillah* should do. Arising out of the organization of the *Kehillah* came the American Jewish Committee. The balance of funds collected for Kishinev—which was in excess of what Kishinev required—was transferred to the American Jewish Committee, which was set up to represent the Jews of America. It was intended that the communities of America should be organized on lines similar to the New York *Kehillah*, and the American Jewish Committee should eventually become the democratically elected representative of American Jewish life. This was never realized. Inertia set in. The original impulse of Dr. Magnes, which led him to the Jewish democratic "masses," died away; he made terms with the American Jewish Committee; and when the War broke out he was already far from all Zionist responsibility.

XIX

The man who then (and during the whole period of the War) made a profound and lasting impression upon the course of American Zionism was Schmarya Levin. It was he, with his passionate idealism and intense love of Zion, who made Palestine a vivid reality to us, and at the same time brought us to an appreciation of our intimate relationship to the European Diaspora. He made us understand the meaning of *Galuth* and the significance of Zion.

Dr. Levin brought with him the palpitating thought of a renascent Jewish life; he linked our national future with the modern nationalist development; he made us conscious of the spuriousness of much that was called Jewish life; he drew upon the treasures of the past to indicate the quality of the Jewish life that was to be; and he loved every nook and corner of Palestine and forced us to share that love. He spoke without a trace of the trained orator; he used none of the flourishes, the rhetoric of the professional speaker; but he could stir the emotions, clear the mind and make vivid both thought and scene. His addresses were filled with an astonishing combination of homely allusions and apt biblical and talmudic quotations.

He was then a dark-skinned, dark-haired man, eager for controversy, with an aggressiveness in argument that was overwhelming. In 1906, he came to us for the Haifa Technicum, for the founding of which he was responsible. (His breach with the Hilfsverein later led to a severance of relations with the Technicum.) He had been a Deputy in the first Duma and had left Russia for Berlin after the dissolution of the Duma. That was an unpleasant experience. Since then he eschewed all Diaspora political entanglements and although he lived in Berlin, he belonged to the Jewish world. Through Dr. Magnes he had been induced to come to America. He established a personal contact with Jacob H. Schiff and made his first public appearance, not as a Zionist, but under the auspices of a non-Zionist committee as an ex-Deputy of the Duma. He appeared again in the company of Dr. Paul Nathan, of the Hilfsverein der Deutschen Juden, also in the interests of the Haifa Technicum, for the management of which an international committee had been formed; the funds were to come from Germany and the United States. Thereafter he shunned the disguise of an ex-Deputy and entered into our propaganda with a zest and a lack of reserve that endeared him to all classes. He came to us with the regularity of winter and carried Zionism to all parts of America. He spoke to the Orthodox, to the half-assimilated, to the *Maskil* and the Jewish masses. He was the first nationalist Zionist we had met. All the others were either political Zionists or Palestinians. He made a unity of both. Under his magic influence Palestine seemed to reflect the personality of the Jewish people. As he often said, to every people is given a land; and to the Jewish people Palestine was given. Just what Palestine is, suits the Jewish personality; no other match is possible or desirable.

Having started the invasion of "foreign" Zionists with Levin, the next winter we brought over to America Benzion Mossensohn, who traversed the country with fresh accounts of the work of Jews in Palestine with special emphasis on Tel Aviv and the Herzlia Gymnasium. He was a trained orator, and his striking appearance made it possible for us to obtain audiences in B'nai B'rith Lodges, Reform pulpits, and in circles susceptible to the influence of Hebrew, its literature and art. Nahum Sokolow also visited us—with his amazing linguistic talent—speaking at the opening meeting for about two hours in Hebrew, Yiddish and English. For some unaccountable reason we invited Franz Oppenheimer to deliver a series of lectures in America. He knew German and just a little English. His economic attainments were known in American university circles; but he spoke to us of Merchavia.

XX

I now pass over to the period after 1914. The long-gathering clouds of war burst and sprawled over Europe, broke down the fragile defenses of civilization and drenched the world in blood. After a ferocious conflict that lingered on for over four years, the world, wounded almost to the heart, slowly and painfully, desperately, endeavored to erect new dykes to prevent the recurrence of a similar catastrophe and to assess the damages. Out of the War came the disintegration of European Jewries, the revelation of the unstable ground upon which the *Galuth* rested, and the need for remaking also the Jewish world.

All that had gone before—so far as we in America were concerned—was preparatory to the assumption of larger Zionist responsibilities. The elements of future action were being mixed in anticipation of Destiny. In the anxious days following the insane ultimatum to Serbia, we sat in coffee-houses, bewildered, wondering how the Jews would emerge out of the struggle. Was all this good for Jews? There were pro-Germans who believed that the struggle would last no more than three months: Germany would win. (What would we gain, or lose, out of that victory?) There were pacifists who, shocked and horrified by the sudden rush into Belgium, shouted for the delimitation of the area of bloodshed; they knew they were beating their heads against stone walls. (But what would we gain if we were to stand out as the world's fools, clamoring for a general "laying down of arms"? What would we gain by this martyrdom?) There were others who, remembering El Arish and Uganda, the ever responsive sympathy of the British people with Zionist interests—the land of George Eliot—felt that precedents and traditions accumulated might lead to far-reaching results. (They cast their votes and gave their voices to the Allies.) Without the slightest doubt the first period had come to an end. The old methods were now obsolete—nothing further to do with indirect approaches to a corrupt Turkish Government, no humiliating maneuvers to encounter by design or accident a German Kaiser at Jerusalem, no ostentatious receptions at the hands of Turkish Consuls, no more friends at

Court—the day had come for us (in our own name, through direct channels), to wrest something tangible and lasting out of the catastrophe. A new world would have to be set up, and in this world we must have a recognized place.

We made an inventory of what we possessed. The Congress had established a corporate responsibility for the future of the Jewish people. We had the Jewish National Fund and the Jewish Colonial Trust. We had a chain of colonies in Palestine, Tel Aviv in embryo, the Jaffa Gymnasium, the schools we had taken over from the Hilfsverein; a number of unofficial Palestine enterprises—all undergraduate experiences, maturing.

There were indications everywhere, even in our American Zionist youth, of a hoarse-throated adolescence, changing to virile manhood. Our isolation was a thing of the past. We knew what *Galuth* meant, here and abroad, and we knew more what Palestine was and could become. We had gone through the enthusiasms of the Self-Defense movement. We had given battle to the American Jewish Committee. We had had communion with Schmarya Levin, with Nahum Sokolow, with Mossensohn, with Franz Oppenheimer. About twenty American delegates had attended the Vienna Congress in 1913.

Our Organization, arising out of the impecunious era, could now boast of stability, variety and discipline. The Hadassah Women's Organization was formed in 1912 and it was already considering its special task for Palestine. The Intercollegiate Zionist Association was gathering in the college youth. The circles of Young Judea were teaching Zionism to the children. We had formed a Zionist fraternal organization, the Order Sons of Zion. The Poale Zion were a vigorous, able group of Zionists working in Jewish labor circles, with its Arbeiter-Verband reaching out to admit workmen into a fraternal association. (They were then in the best of condition, morally and intellectually.) The Mizrachi had been placed on their feet with the arrival of Meier Berlin. We had branches in every Jewish Community of any size. And we had created a Zionist Press—*The Maccabaean, Dos Yiddishe Folk, Der Yiddisher Kaempfer;* with the voluntary support of seven Yiddish daily newspapers, and many Anglo-Jewish weekly publications.

In general, the great War gave Zionists their first real opportunity to test their strength and ability. Herzl had labored under adverse conditions. He drew political opportunity out of the air. He wanted to meet the world in combat, but it would not accept his challenge. All his maneuvers were one-sided undertakings; the others had no interest in our proposed adventure. He spoke to unlistening ears. The Great War shook the world to its foundations. It created new interests; set in flux new fears, established new relations. Through this new world in travail Zionism pushed its way and forced the consideration of the Jewish problem as a matter of reality, national need and mutual concern. The Jewries of Europe fell under the burden of a double weight. They suffered as they had never suffered before. (Now, almost nine years after the Versailles Conference, their wounds are not yet healed.) But Israel was not left uncomforted. A remnant had been preserved to realize the hope of centuries.

XXI

In 1914 Schmarya Levin was lingering in New York through the summer months. He had attended our annual convention which was held at Rochester, N. Y., in June. Preceding the Convention he had spent several months in an attempt (partially successful) to obtain funds for the Palestine Hebrew school system, which had been taken over by the Zionist Organization as a result of the Hilfsverein controversy. He had interested quite a number of non-Zionists in the Palestine schools, notably Samuel Strauss, then publisher of the New York *Globe*. We had set up an organization budget at Rochester which was quite impressive and disturbing. I had been persuaded to agree to give all my time thereafter to Zionist affairs. I had resigned from the *American Hebrew,* and awaited the return of Joseph Jacobs, my associate, who was then in Europe, before shifting to my new office. We were making plans for a winter campaign for the school fund, and Levin was to return in December. It was a hot summer. Dr. Levin left New York in August on the *Kronprinzessin Cecilie.* While in mid-ocean, war was declared, and the ship was forced to return to its New York port.

Dr. Levin was then a member of the Zionist Executive. The headquarters of the Executive were in Berlin. With the Executive unable to maintain contact with Zionists in Allied or neutral countries, Dr. Levin was the only member free to act. The continuity of Zionist efforts was imperative. We could not allow the work in Palestine to suffer, our institutions to collapse. It was decided to call an extraordinary conference of all American Zionists—including Mizrachi and Poale Zion—under the signatures of Dr. Levin for the Zionist Executive Committee and myself for the American Zionist Federation. A manifesto was drawn up and issued to all our leading workers, and the Conference took place August 30, 1914, at the Hotel Marseilles, New York. It is necessary to point out that steps had not been taken by any organized body at that time to concentrate American Jewish attention upon any of the problems that might arise out of the fact that the bulk of the Jewish population lay within the war zone. Our Hotel Marseilles Conference was the first Jewish response at least to one phase of the situation.

At the meetings held in advance of the Conference, it was decided without a dissenting voice to call upon Louis D. Brandeis to take the Chairmanship of the organization we proposed should be formed. The Conference was a solemn affair. The addresses delivered were tinged with anxiety, not only for the future of Zionism, but for the welfare of the Jewish people in the countries in which they lived. It was not a time to speak of the practical aspects of Zionism. We were interested primarily in maintaining our Zionist possessions in Palestine, and at the same time in saving Jewish life in the Diaspora. Mr. Brandeis was elected Chairman of the Provisional Executive Committee for General Zionist Affairs, and at once threw himself with characteristic energy into the work that confronted him.

Through the generosity of Nathan Straus, offices were established in the Aeolian Building (our regular offices remained for a time on Henry Street, but they were soon removed to East 23rd Street) and a call was issued for an Emergency Fund to maintain Zionist institutions in Palestine and further Zionist propaganda in America and elsewhere. Authority for the action was derived from the Zionist Executive Committee acting through Dr. Levin.

XXII

The period from 1914 to 1920 was indelibly impressed by the personality and leadership of Louis D. Brandeis. He was one of the leaders of the American Bar. He had acquired an international reputation as a fearless advocate of human rights. He had given disinterested service to noble causes. He stood out as a man of sterling character and great ability. He had a keen analytical mind, the power to see through facts and figures, a talent for legal strategy and tenacity of purpose. But he was not known as a Jew. He had kept aloof from Jewish interests and was not a member of the Jewish community.

He came into the Zionist movement some years before he was called to assume office. His attention had been called to *The Maccabaean* by Bernard G. Richards on the tenth anniversary of the foundation of that publication. Mr. Richards lived in Boston; he had been engaged in journalistic work on the *Transcript*. From newspaper friends he learned that Mr. Brandeis was a Jew. And when the anniversary of *The Maccabaean* was being celebrated, he wrote to Mr. Brandeis on the chance that he would receive a reply. The reply came in the form of a modest check and a paragraph of acknowledgment and interest. Thereafter, as a matter of course, we sent Zionist pamphlets and *The Maccabaean* to Devonshire Street. When Mr. Sokolow visited us in 1912, Mr. Brandeis consented to act as Chairman at a Boston meeting which was to be held in his honor. At the suggestion of Mr. Sokolow, Mr. Brandeis agreed to come to New York to discuss a Palestinian economic project. In the meantime, Jacob de Haas, then editor of the Boston *Jewish Advocate*, had various opportunities of meeting Mr. Brandeis and subsequently prepared him to accept the invitation for the Hotel Marseilles Conference, and also the Chairmanship of the Provisional Zionist Committee.

Mr. Brandeis came to us as a Zionist novice, but soon was leader, not only in name, but also in fact. For he seemed to have been waiting for the opportunity of service. He plunged into the intricate responsibilities of Zionist action with such zeal and insistence that his associates were overwhelmed. He used to spend days in consultation with the New York Committee. He would brook no delays; the Provisional Committee was organized within a week; the Emergency Fund was set up in less than a month. He was eager for information, would meet all visitors, asking questions, saying little, making notes for things to be done just as soon as his visitor departed. He set up a special Zionist Office for New England in Boston and asked that Mr. de Haas be placed in charge, in order, more especially, to have somebody at his elbow to keep him properly informed. He travelled with Dr. Levin to a number of the larger Jewish communities. He brought back into the movement both Dr. Stephen S. Wise and Dr. Magnes. He induced a number of able young professional men to tackle some of the problems in preparation for peace. Among these men were Felix Frankfurter, Samuel J. Rosensohn, Walter Meyer, Howard Gans, and others.

He was not a brilliant speaker, but what he said had style, poise, accuracy and sagacity. The early days of his participation in our affairs were a source of joy and comfort to all who were involved in the Zionist responsibility. He was devoid of fear and never wavered in his faith. He believed that Zion would be redeemed, and that the dream of Herzl would come through, and that he was helping in the realization of that dream. When he was elevated to the Supreme Court of the United States, we rejoiced, for we felt that he could render even more important service from that exalted position. But he seemed to feel that he could no longer be as free in his movements, in his utterances. Perhaps that fear was accentuated by the incident which arose out of his participation in the American Jewish Congress, and for which Dr. Magnes was responsible. At any rate, whatever it was, he no longer mingled in our affairs thereafter, and retired to the smaller committees, the smaller meetings, spoke through intermediaries, was not accessible, and became a Voice, instead of that charming and persuasive personality he had been in the early days of his Zionist birth.

JOSEPH M. PROSKAUER

Joseph M. Proskauer was a notable leader in Jewish communal life and active in New York politics for many decades. He was born in Mobile, Alabama, in 1877 and was admitted to the New York Bar in 1899. For twenty years he was a member of an important law firm and in 1923 was elected to the New York State Supreme Court. Four years later Governor Alfred E. Smith named him Associate Justice for the Appellate Division. Later Mr. Proskauer returned to private practice.

He held many communal posts during a long career. He was a member of the executive committee of the American Jewish Committee and from 1943 to 1949 was President of the A.J.C. He was Vice President of the Jewish Board of Guardians and President of the Young Men's Hebrew Association at 92nd Street in New York City. He also served as President of the Federation for the Support of Jewish Philanthropic Societies of New York City. He died in 1971.

The author of an autobiography entitled A Segment of My Times, *Mr. Proskauer offers in the selection that follows a description of a young Jewish boy's life in Mobile in the 1890's.*

Southern Boyhood*

JOSEPH M. PROSKAUER

MY EARLIEST RECOLLECTION, keenly vivid, is of the overpowering sweetness of the magnolia tree, as I played by the open window of the cottage on Government Street at the foot of the Charles, where I was born. It was the day we were to move "downtown" to St. Francis Street, between Joachim and Jackson. Again, the very names had meaning in the subconscious of the child. Old Dr. Ketchum, who had brought me into the world, was driving by in his gig drawn by two diminutive "calico" horses which were in the nature of a local trademark. He gave me a ride to my new home.

Here was a new setting for boyhood. There was the central hall with the front and back parlors on one side, the dining room on the other; the front porch faced the street with its diminutive orange trees, and the steps led down to the "front garden," where Cary, the Negro gardener, used to astound us with the correct Latin nomenclature for every blossom. The "swing yard" lay behind it, while to the other side an alleyway ended in the back yard with its two big chinaberry trees. To the rear was the stable with the servants' quarters above; a wing connected it to the main house, consisting of the kitchen beneath and more servants' rooms overhead.

It was on the back porch of the main house that I used to sit and read until old Aunt Myra, ex-slave of my grandfather's, and second mother to me, would solemnly adjure me not to wear holes in the seat of my pants. And if I whittled or wrote on a Saturday she would, with an equal solemnity drawn from years of service in a Jewish household, warn me of the awful punishment that awaited a boy who would so desecrate the Sabbath.

* Reprinted from *A Segment of My Times*, Farrar, Straus and Company, New York, 1950, pp. 10–17.

My browsings in books were often broken by an afternoon journey in the mule cars to Frascati, with its beach bordering on the Bay, where sandpiles and fiddler crabs were the chief objectives once we had passed the old Confederate earthworks that had been thrown up in the last attempt to save the city from the Yankees.

And later, after Grandpa had purchased a horse and barouche, there was the afternoon drive down the shell road along the Bay, through groves of giant magnolias and live oaks festooned with Spanish moss. Fanned by a breeze redolent of salt-tanged bay and magnolias, regaled on special occasions with food and drink when we came to Fredericks at the end of the drive, I would come home fully convinced that I lived in a wonderful world where I could love and be loved and all was "right as right could be."

And it *was* a good world. I could sit on my own front porch and hear the minister in the Methodist Church across the street thunder the special horrors of hell that yawned for the evil doer. And, further up St. Francis Street, I could sit on my grandfather's back porch and hearken to the minister in the Baptist Church next door proclaim his version of salvation and damnation. On my way to school I would pass the Catholic Cathedral with *Janua Coeli* inscribed over the portal; and I soon learned that the Latin phrase meant the same as the Hebrew *Shaaria Shomayem*, the Gates of Heaven, which was the name of our Jewish Congregation.

It was a little later that I made one of the warmest friendships of my life with Gardiner L. Tucker, who lived and died an Episcopalian rector, even as his father, Gardiner C. Tucker, had done before him. There followed many hours in the rectory of St. John's, with my friend's father speaking of the law and the gospels. And, though my own Sabbath school training made me deeply conscious of my Jewishness and my home life emphasized it by ritual observance of Reform Judaism, the variety of my religious contacts in these very early years implanted the conviction that all religions were good if, as I naturally believed, mine was somewhat the best.

Then came the day when I graduated from Cousin Katie's tuition to enter on the sterner curriculum of the public school. Fronting on the wide expanse of Government Street stood the white-columned structure of Barton Academy. Its eastern half housed the girls' school under the tutelage of Electra Semmes Colson, daughter of the great Confederate admiral. The tradition of the ante-Appomattox days remained unchanged under the guidance of this patrician and learned woman.

The northern half contained the senior classes for boys. In the rear on Conti Street was one building for the junior grade and one for the high school. I entered the junior grade and there for the first time encountered the mystery of anti-Semitism. I was, so I believed, a good boy. I was a patriotic American, and my uncle had surely earned for my family a deserved reputation for loyalty to Alabama. My father had close Christian friends. I treasure still the silver cup which had been given to me as the first-born of a member of the Order of Myths, one of the societies responsible for those Mardi Gras pageants which gave Mobile the proud title of "Mother of Mystics." Membership in that order gave a sense of "belonging" in a common fellowship. I had indeed heard that neither my father nor any other Jew could join the Athlestane Club, but that was something remote from everyday life. So that day when the "Goubil Gang" bloodied my nose on the astounding theory that I was a "Christ Killer" is burnt into my memory as an unintelligible *dies irae*.

It was the earliest in a long series of bloodied noses, both physical and metaphorical, that have marked the life of myself and every other American Jew. And, as I still puzzle today over the why and the wherefore of this amazing phenomenon in free America, I experience the same sense of bewilderment that came over me when I backed up against the fence on Conti Street and tried to trade blow for blow with Rene Goubil and his followers. I sensed then, as I have since come to know, that at least one of my missions in life would be to do all in my power to destroy this ugly excrescence on the American way of life.

There have been compensations in the comradeship of many Christian friends. But none of them can ever know, I believe, the

poignant grief, the self-consciousness, the hindrance to free intercourse that stems from this cancer and from their failure, inexplicable to me, to excise it ruthlessly by action instead of
condoning it, at least in part, by inaction.

The years passed. The afternoons on the bayshore gave way to
afternoons on the wharves. There I watched the paddle-wheel
river boats echoing to the song of Negro deck hands as they
unloaded the cotton; the trim steamers discharging cargoes of
bananas into waiting freight cars on the dock; the fishing
schooners and the oyster boats; the great many-masted sailing
ships that still came in from faraway lands, emitting odors of
rosin and tar. On those wharves the boy saw visions of distant
shores and a great, unknown world and the romance of life that
lay beyond the confines of the home town.

From the junior grade I entered the senior class of Barton
Academy on Government Street, and went from there on into the
high school division. After the lapse of fifty years, I can still recall
vividly the personality of every one of my teachers. In the lower
grade there was Sarah Zelnicker, a gentle, sweet and efficient
woman, with a sympathetic understanding of small-boy psychology; but she imperiled my standing mightily one day by the
bestowal of a maternal kiss as school was dismissed. It took me a
long time to live that down among my schoolmates.

In the senior class, I came to know the sterner stuff of human
nature in the personality of John D. Yerby. We had discipline
under him. The ominous sentence of "2 in deportment and reported to the room" still represents to me the climax of terror. I
do not know whether that language is still intelligible to the
Mobile of today. To us of the 1880's it meant that our record was
sullied with two bad marks in deportment, accompanied by a
session in the room after school hours, at which time the strap
fell none too gently on the outstretched hand. We were taught
there to do our work. That senior department had the virtues of
the horse-and-buggy days, even if it had some of their defects,
and I shall never cease to believe that the virtues outweighed the
defects. It was the fashion of the time to read and study two
English classics. We studied them in such a way that through all

these years the lovely words of Goldsmith's "Deserted Village" course spontaneously through my mind and the rounded balance and eloquence of Macaulay's "Essay on Warren Hastings" affect to this day, though unconsciously, whatever I write or speak. The essay brought the breath of life to such characters as Georgiana Duchess of Devonshire, Fox, Sheridan, Burke and the Indian Princes. Its reading gave me my first inkling of an historical sense. Our instruction under Mr. Yerby was a thorough drill. We had to know what was knowable and to learn our lessons. Yet I still envision Mr. Yerby's face breaking into a smile which showed beyond peradventure that beneath his austerity there lurked a kindliness and understanding that made us boys like him even though we stood in awe of him.

In the high school the old principal was Benjamin S. Woodcock. Under him we boys savored the zest of a unique personality. His habit was to make us relate the things we studied to the life he lived and knew. We read Xenophon's *Anabasis* in Greek. Xenophon's army never marched "two stations" or "four parasangs" without a discourse from Mr. Woodcock describing how his brigade in the Civil War executed a similar maneuver, but much more skillfully. Those who follow the counsel of perfection may object that we learned more about that Alabama brigade than we did about the Greek army. But this I know—that Xenophon under him became human and the soldiers of the Greek army real men, and the battles real battles, and when the sea at last was reached, it had as much the same aspect of actuality as the Gulf of Mexico from the shore of nearby Dauphin Island.

Head of them all was Mr. Dickson, superintendent of schools. I wonder now if the old engine room which he set up to the northeast of the main building still exists. I hope it does; for to us boys it was the supreme privilege to be detailed in groups of two or three to go to that room in the afternoon and there learn the wonders of physics. And we had our chemistry, too, developed to an astounding extent for a secondary school. There was a good and serviceable laboratory in which we advanced through qualitative to quantitative analysis, and the work was so well done that when I entered Columbia I could pass the course required of freshmen or sophomores and was allowed to substitute an advanced course in chemistry. He had a real passion for fostering the instruction of the young in the natural sciences.

With the strands of this secular training were intertwined those of religious education. Our family was not piously orthodox, but it was observant. It was my proud duty as grandchild on the first night of Passover to read in the Seder Service the age-old questions: "Wherefore is this night distinguished from all other nights?" "Wherefore on this night do we eat only unleavened bread, whereas on other nights we eat bread either leavened or unleavened?"

On Friday nights we broke the Sabbath bread while my father invoked the traditional blessing. And, though we did not fast on the Day of Atonement, we did spend the day in the synagogue.

As I reached my teens, I passed under the influence of a sanctified personality that deeply influenced my future course of life. That influence illustrates what an inspired rabbi can do to form the career and the ideals of an American Jewish boy.

This rabbi of my adolescent years died an untimely death as a very young man. His name, Oscar J. Cohen, is unknown today. But after I have passed my three score and ten, I still thrill as I remember the glee with which I celebrated, under his tutelage, the Maccabean victories, the delight I had when Haman was caught in his own toils, the sense of glory I felt in Miriam's Song of Triumph. But much more than to the glory of these merely historical phases of our Jewish life and tradition, I warm to the recollection of my response as I sat there, in our little synagogue, with the windows open and the sunlight streaming in. When I heard the choir intone *Lift up your heads, oh ye gates,* I felt that the gates of the Ark were really lifting themselves up, as Rabbi Cohen took out the scrolls of the Law from which to read the morning lesson. He gave me a sense of immanence of a divine spirit, firing me with a glow that made me Jew through and through, loving my religion and its traditions. He greatly influenced my secular education, but his priceless gift was to my soul.

This is the great function and opportunity of a rabbi. It is obscured sometimes today by the growing tendency of many rabbis to emphasize the secular phases of Jewish life. A similar tendency shows itself among the clergy of other faiths. Being a true priest is a full-time job—too much of that time is often expended by our ministers in political controversy, in secular movements where the office of the minister gives no special sanction to speak, and sometimes in acrimonious debate over the things "that are Caesar's." Oscar Cohen was exemplar of the faith that the rabbi's true duty was to further "the things that are God's."

Yet Rabbi Cohen also shaped my future beyond the limits of religious influence. I was graduated from high school in 1892. A Columbia man himself, he persuaded my father that a metropolitan college was the best place for a southern boy. I had relatives in New York with whom I might live. In the summer of that year, I came to the city that was to become my future home. A few hours of tutoring had added somewhat to my scant preparation.

In October, 1892, I was admitted to Columbia—with heavy "conditions"!

CYRUS ADLER

Cyrus Adler was one of the great leaders of Conservative Judaism in the United States. He was President of the American Jewish Committee from 1929 to 1940, and, in behalf of the A.J.C., accompanied Louis Marshall to the Versailles Peace Conference in 1919.

Cyrus Adler was born in Van Buren, Ark., in 1863 and died in Philadelphia in 1940. He was an educator and Orientalist. He received his Ph.D. in 1887 at Johns Hopkins University, where he was an Associate Professor of Semitic languages from 1884 to 1893. He was an Honorary Assistant Curator in 1898 and Curator of Historic Archaeology and Historic Religions of the United States National Museum in Washington from 1889 to 1908. He also was Librarian and Assistant Secretary of the Smithsonian Institution.

Dr. Adler was President of the Board of Directors of the Jewish Theological Seminary when it was reorganized in 1902. When Solomon Schechter, the head of the Seminary, died in 1916, Dr. Adler was named Acting President and assumed the post of President in 1924.

He was a founder of the Jewish Publication Society in 1888 and served from the outset on the Board of Trustees of its Publication Committee. He was Chairman of the Committee in 1923. Dr. Adler edited the American Jewish Year Book *from 1889 (the first year of its publication) through 1905, and again in 1916. He was Chairman of the Board of seven editors of the J.P.S. committee in charge of the translation of the Bible into English. He was founder and President of the American Jewish Historical Society and served as President of Dropsie College for Hebrew and Cognate Learning in Philadelphia.*

His autobiography is I Have Considered the Days. *In the chapter that follows, Dr. Adler describes the founding of the*

American Jewish Historical Society, his leadership in the estab-
lishment of Dropsie College, and his friendship with scores of
prominent Jews. This period covers from 1895 to the early 1900's.

From Washington to Philadelphia*

CYRUS ADLER

WE LIVED in an apartment called The Mendota, then on the
outskirts of Washington and overlooking Rock Creek Park. It
was very comfortable and provided us with sufficient wall space
for books. We had very happy years there, and in this little
apartment our daughter was born.

While there was plenty of work, there was also enough social
life, not too intrusive. This was during the presidency of Theodore Roosevelt; and Oscar Straus, a close friend of ours, was a
great part of this time a member of the Cabinet. Mr. Straus lived
on 16th Street, not very far from us, and it was our custom, even
in bad weather, to walk downtown together. This gave us the
opportunity for healthful exercise and many pleasant chats.

On several occasions we were at the White House, notably, I
remember, one evening when Mr. and Mrs. Roosevelt gave a
musicale. An American, Arthur F. Nevin, had written an opera,
the themes being from American Indian music, and the scenery,
Indian life. The Metropolitan Opera Company had declined to
perform it, and President Roosevelt decided to give it a chance.
So there was a rather unique performance of an opera at the
White House, the scenic background being supplied by colored
lantern slides, and the composer himself playing the various
themes on the piano, interpreting them as he went along. After

* Reprinted from *I Have Considered the Days*, The Jewish Publication
Society of America, Philadelphia, 1941, pp. 264–298.

that part of the evening was over, the President moved around among the guests. My wife and I were standing, chatting with Mr. and Mrs. Thomas Nelson Page, and President Roosevelt came up and spoke about the music of the evening. He said: "It is my desire, in addition to having Washington the political capital of the United States, also to have it the scientific and artistic capital," and then he turned to my wife and said: "Your husband knows what difficulty I have had with Congress in preventing them from building atrocities." Just at that moment Mr. Taft approached. The President beckoned to him and said: "Will, come over here." Mr. Taft came over: Mr. Roosevelt put his hand on his shoulder and said: "My friends, here is the next President of the United States. I hope Congress will be better to him than it has been to me." It seeemed to me that that was the first nominating speech for Taft.

I should like to record here an example of the remarkable memory exhibited by Mrs. Roosevelt. She had been down at the Smithsonian to inspect a large collection of beautiful fans which had been placed there as a loan exhibition by Mrs. Pinchot, the mother of the former Governor of Pennsylvania. In the absence of the Secretary, I accompanied her through the building and she greatly admired the fans. On a subsequent occasion, quite some time afterwards, we were at a reception at the White House. As I passed Mrs. Roosevelt, she stopped me and said: "Dr. Adler, I wish you would go into the room on the left, look in the drawer of one of the tables there, where you will find a fan; and if you think it is good enough for the National Museum collection, I should like to present it to them." This was said in the flash of a moment.

My wife and I had spent our honeymoon at Newport, Rhode Island. We were married in September, just before the Jewish holidays, and we chose Newport because the idea of attending services in the oldest synagogue still standing in North America attracted us. We spent three weeks in Newport and acquired an affection for the place, so that the summer our child was a year old we decided, in order to get away from the heat, to go to Newport again. Many people, outside of New England, consider

Newport a place only for the very rich and very fashionable, but we found that there were scientific people and artists and others that we knew, and that living in a good house there was less expensive than a cottage at the Jersey seaside resorts. One other reason for our going to Newport was the fact that the American Jewish Historical Society, of which I was President at the time, was holding its annual meeting there, on the 4th of July.

I was one of the three incorporators of this Society, whose aim was to collect and preserve all the materials concerning the history of the Jews and Judaism in America. The first meeting was held in 1892. I served as Corresponding Secretary and afterwards as President. I also edited the *Publications* from I to VIII, and remained a member of the Publication Committee. The method of work of this Society does not differ very much from that of other similar societies. It consists in associating persons of like taste for a given branch of knowledge; the making of collections of material on a given subject of common interest; the holding of meetings for the reading and discussion of papers, and the publication of such papers as are found worthy and within the means of the Society. Anyone who will examine the classified index to the *Publications* will see that every phase in early Jewish life in America has been touched upon. My chief contribution to the history of the Jews on this Continent was their treatment by the Inquisition, and these researches were rendered possible through the interest shown in the Historical Society by the distinguished historian of the Inquisition, Henry C. Lea, of Philadelphia, from whose manuscripts much of the information was derived. I have had two very distinguished friends as my predecessor and successor; Oscar S. Straus was the first President, and Dr. A. S. W. Rosenbach, upon my retirement, succeeded me as President.

In Newport, I became very fond of the synagogue and the Athenaeum. I read all I could about the local history of Newport, became more familiar with the facts concerning Rabbi Haim Isaac Carigal, whose portrait hangs in the Athenaeum and who was the first rabbi to preach a sermon in a pulpit in the United States, and certainly his was the first published sermon. He was a friend and the Hebrew teacher of Ezra Stiles, then

President of Yale University, who was also a frequenter of the synagogue at Newport and left accurate descriptions of it in his diary.

There were some curiosities in Newport, and a special curiosity was a Jewish butcher. He was a regular attendant of the synagogue. I remember one remark of his, which has remained a saying in our family. My wife asked him one day whether he could get some sweetbreads for her dinner, and his reply was: "Sweetbreads! You don't meet a calf once a month in Newport."

I also remember another curious incident in connection with our going to Newport. We had intended to go through from Washington; and I started alone, my wife being detained in Baltimore. It was deemed desirable that I should go ahead and see that the house was made ready, and take the cook along with me to Newport. This cook was rather stout and declined to get into the Pullman berth which had been purchased for her. She said she had never seen "one of them things" and would not get into it. The train was composed entirely of sleepers and a few coaches. These coaches did not go through; so I had the problem of seeing to it that the cook was not lost on the way and watched the process of her getting into another car, and finally, in order to soothe her feelings, invited her to breakfast at a way-station at 5.45 in the morning.

That summer, I remember, we had some very pleasant visits with the Arnold Hagues. Arnold Hague was a Washington man connected with the Geological Survey, and I particularly enjoyed their beautiful rock gardens. Albert Sterner, the well-known artist, lived on the same street with us. I also remember making the acquaintance of Mr. Theodore Davis, a lawyer, who lived in Newport. He himself conducted extremely successful excavations in Egypt for a number of years. He had taken up Egyptological work quite late in life, and was one of the first to get some very splendid things from Egypt into America. He had some of these objects in Newport, and they were most wonderful; but he was very modest about the tremendous finds that he made. On his death, in 1915, he bequeathed to the Metropolitan Museum in New York his entire collection, including all the Egyptian antiq-

uities, which is the pride of the present Egyptian Department at
the Museum. I recall Mr. Davis' giving a little address at the
National Geographic Society in Washington and showing slides
of all these very remarkable finds, which was an especially great
thrill to my wife as she was always fascinated by the results of
excavations.

In the year 1904–5, a committee took up the proposal to
celebrate the two hundred and fiftieth anniversary of the landing
of the first Jews in New York, and I occasionally went there to
attend the meetings. The celebration was a very great one, but at
the last moment I was prevented from attending it, because, a
few days before, Mr. Langley suffered his serious illness, of which
I have already spoken. Mr. Langley's death was a very great blow
to me. In fact, all three of my early closest friends of the Smithsonian, Goode, Winlock and Langley, were now gone.

I had, however, a very great affection for the place and still
have, and it was my intention to carry on there. When Langley
died, some of my friends thought that I ought to succeed to the
post, and I remember that Jacob Schiff, who was in California,
telegraphed me and offered to be of any service he could in my
behalf. I promptly declined this and had a very frank talk with
Rathbun, telling him that he was the senior Assistant Secretary
and that if there was to be, as it were, a promotion in the ranks,
it should go to him and not to me. The Board of Regents, however, offered the post to Professor Henry Fairfield Osborn, of
Columbia University, a very wise selection, I thought. But Osborn felt himself so tied to Columbia and the American Museum
of Natural History, and indeed to his pleasant work in New
York, that he declined the post, which was then, at least in my
opinion, the greatest scientific post in the United States. After
that, the Regents tendered the office to Charles D. Walcott, eminent geologist, a man very experienced in Washington affairs,
and he held it until his death.

Walcott and I were good friends, and I was very glad to continue to be of service to him and to the Institution, as I had been
under Langley, but I did feel that Walcott had not the same
need of me as Langley had. He himself was an experienced

administrator and devoted his time to the administration of the Institution, except during the summer, when he went to the Rocky Mountains, whereas Mr. Langley's scientific work occupied him virtually every day of the week and quite a number of hours a day.

One of the last incidents of importance concerning the Smithsonian Institution occurred in the summer of 1908, when I was Acting Secretary, and had to do with the expedition of President Theodore Roosevelt to Africa. Some time in June, Mr. Roosevelt, who had already gone from Washington to his home at Oyster Bay, telegraphed the Smithsonian that he intended immediately after the 4th of March, when his term of office would expire, to do a year's big game hunting in Africa, that he would get up an expedition, take his son with him and pay his own and his son's expenses, but that he could not afford to pay the expenses of the taxidermist and the shipment of the specimens, and that if the Smithsonian Institution could supply these two things, he would give all these specimens to the Smithsonian; if not, he would offer them to another museum. I was in a quandary. Owing to the system of government appropriations, item by item, there was not a single cent free in our budget for expeditions. I assembled the few curators connected with the Zoological Department, who told me that it would be very important if the collection could be obtained for the Institution, because Roosevelt was a good naturalist and there would be éclat connected with the collection made by a former President of the United States.

It was a very hot day in June and it was not my custom to go home for luncheon, because our apartment was several miles from the Institution. However, I thought I would take the best counsel a man could obtain, go home and ask my wife's advice as to whether she thought there was at that time any possibility in Washington of my raising the money toward such an expedition. She told me I ought to try, whereupon I did try; and the first man I went to was Oscar Straus. I told him the story, and he at once said to me: "I will give you $5,000 towards that." This start so encouraged me that I telegraphed Mr. Roosevelt that the Institution would accept his proposal. Four days after that, we got into telegraphic communication with Secretary Walcott, who approved my action, and when he came back in the autumn, he successfully collected the rest of the fund.

I remember an incident connected with this expedition of Mr. Roosevelt's for which he was very much blamed in Congress, though I was responsible for the proposal. When he came back to Washington in the early autumn, I saw him and we talked of the personnel of the proposed expedition. I said to him: "Are you not going to take a physician with you?" He snapped back "Why?" "Well," I said, "you are all right, but your son is rather young, Africa has a treacherous climate, and you might be in need of medical advice." He looked at me, thoughtfully, a moment and said: "Well, do you know anybody who would be suitable?" I said: "Yes, Major Edgar A. Mearns. He is a Major in the Army, a fine naturalist, he was the naturalist of the Mexican Boundary Commission, he is acquainted with tropical diseases, and is now in the Philippines." The idea struck him favorably, and through General Leonard Wood the release of Mearns was temporarily arranged. Roosevelt was later criticized for taking a man in government service on a private expedition.

One of the things that struck me about Major Mearns was the fact that he was a very careful man; I mean careful about the possibility of contagion or infection. He was fond of beer, and he always ordered bottled beer. He made it a point never to pour the beer into a glass, but drank it straight out of the bottle. I once asked him why, and he said: "It lessens the danger of infection."

In July 1905, there died in Philadelphia Moses Aaron Dropsie, well-known lawyer and an interesting personality. He was born in Philadelphia in 1821, of Dutch parentage, was an apprentice to a jeweler, and continued in this business until he took up the study of Law at the age of thirty, and became quite a figure at the Bar. He was one of the pioneers of the street railways of Philadelphia, President of two of them—the Lombard and South Street Railroad, and Green and Coates—and Chairman of the Commission that built one of the early bridges across the Schuylkill River. He left his entire estate, with the exception of some annuities to relatives, to found a college in the City of Philadelphia for the study of Hebrew and Cognate Learning, to be open to students without any restriction as to creed, color, or sex, and where the tuition was to be free, but the Governors and Faculty were to be of the Jewish faith. He named in his will as Life Governors of this College, Mayer Sulzberger, William B. Hackenburg of Philadelphia; Oscar S. Straus of New York, then Secretary of Commerce and Labor; Dr. Aaron Friedenwald of Baltimore, and myself. Dr. Friedenwald predeceased Mr. Dropsie.

As Oscar Straus could not leave Washington, we held our first meeting in his office at the Department of Commerce and Labor. It was due to Oscar Straus that the College was named after Mr. Dropsie. I had been rather inclined to give it some general name, using as a sub-title, "Founded by Moses Aaron Dropsie," holding that there are certain disadvantages in naming a College after an individual. Straus, I remember, said: "Did this man leave any children?" I said: "No." "Did he leave his entire estate to us?" I said: "Yes." "Well," he said, "by God, the College ought to be named after him even if there is a disadvantage," and so it became the Dropsie College.

It was really also somewhat at the insistence of Mr. Straus that I left Washington and became President of the College, because, as he pointed out, I was the one person among the Governors who was trained in the subjects it would have to teach. In addition to him, my dear friend, Dr. Francis S. Nash, a surgeon in the United States Navy and a devout Episcopalian, who was also my physician, when he heard about the offer to me to become head of a Jewish college, advised me strongly to accept. For, he said: "You can do so much more for your people, and someone else can do your work at the Smithsonian." He was always a great admirer of the work done by the Jews in Palestine, and during his life contributed most generously, usually anonymously. After his death, his daughter, Carolyn Nash, who had done fine work among the German refugees in Paris, sent $1,000 to the Joint Distribution Committee in memory of her father. The matter of my acceptance of the post was one of long discussion, because I had felt myself settled in Washington, but finally the move was decided upon.

The last thing I took part in before I left Washington was the building of the new National Museum, which came to a great extent under my direction. It was completed, but not occupied, before we went to Philadelphia. I returned to Washington in 1909, as there seemed to be a number of questions which my old friends at the Smithsonian wanted me to come down and talk over. I then had a chance to go over the new Museum, with its collections installed, and found it very impressive.

About a week or ten days before we were leaving, Mr. Straus said to me: "Are you going to see the President and say good-bye to him?" I said: "I had not intended to. I thought he was too busy to spend his time on mere courtesy calls." Mr. Straus said: "But he expects you to come to see him." So I dutifully made the appointment to call on Mr. Roosevelt. As I was ushered in, he arose and waved his hands and said: "Go away, go away. I do not like to see people who desert the government," and then, the next instant, said: "Come in, come in, sit down and tell me all about it." I explained the situation to him and told him that there were plenty of people at the Smithsonian amply able to take care of it, and this College seemed to be something for which I was specially fitted.

When I left the Smithsonian, they created for me the title of Honorary Associate in Historic Archaeology, and my name is carried on the rolls to this day.

We settled in Philadelphia on September 15, 1908 and rented a house at 2041 N. Broad Street, where we still reside, first and foremost because it was near our synagogue, and then because it was on a street on which there were no carlines. I had been living for a good many years in Washington off the carline and disliked the clanging of the bell of the trolley car. It turned out, however, in the days to come, when the automobile and the bus appeared, that Broad Street became the Lincoln Highway, and added to that, the subway was put underneath it, so that the looked-for quiet has not been attained. As we are not people who move very much, we have managed to go through with it. Still, I am becoming steadily more and more of the opinion that if our cities are not to be entirely deserted, some way will have to be found to abolish noise.

It was agreed among the other Governors of Dropsie College and myself that the first year should be spent in organizing the College, increasing the Board of Governors, conferring with heads of institutions of learning, and more particularly with professors in the departments in which we were concerned, in order to make a reasonably definite plan for the College before it was started.

The original Governors had elected, among others, Dr. Solomon Schechter and Mr. Louis Marshall as Governors of the Dropsie College, this with the idea of having a sort of interlocking directorate and a good understanding with the Jewish Theological Seminary. Dr. Schechter, Mr. Marshall and Mr. Schiff were very much concerned about the establishment of this College. They feared that, with its then relatively large endowment, much more than that possessed by any other Jewish college in the country at that time, it would draw students away from these other Jewish colleges and perhaps injure them in other ways. Mr. Schiff actually made a proposal that the Seminary and the Dropsie College should merge. The New York gentlemen were quite willing to move the Seminary to Philadelphia, but Judge Sulzberger and I, although we were Philadelphians, felt that it would be a great mistake to leave New York, the largest Jewish community in the world, without an institution of higher learning.

My first care was to organize the College. I had decided on a financial course of great prudence. Our lectures began in the building of the neighboring Gratz College; and Professor George Foot Moore, head of the Department of Semitics at Harvard University, gave the opening course of lectures at the Dropsie College. He afterward incorporated these lectures in his book called *Judaism,* which appeared some years later.

We erected a charming building, designed by William Tachau, formerly of Louisville, later of New York, with a considerable sunken garden in front. This, together with the Mikveh Israel Synagogue next door, and Gratz College back of it, made an ornamental corner at Broad and York Streets, quite refreshing after the regular rows of brownstone houses.

I commenced to take an active interest in the affairs of the synagogue, to which I was naturally glad to return after having been absent from its particular ritual for a matter of twenty-five years, except on holidays. I was President for several years, and one of my main concerns was to promote the cause of education in the congregation. I have always been gratified to think that we had the best congregational school in the country. I was chairman of the arrangements for the dedication of the new building of the Mikveh Israel Synagogue, which had been made possible through the bequest of Henry M. Elkan. The whole ceremony was one of great dignity, and the rabbis and heads of many congregations took part. However, there were one or two amusing incidents. The sexton of the congregation was found kneeling before the safe, which contained the silver ornaments for the Scrolls of the Law, and weeping because in his excitement he had forgotten the combination.

I was standing in the vestibule of the synagogue when one of the congregants came up to me and complained bitterly of the seat that had been assigned to her. I said: "Madam, this cannot now be changed. If it were myself, I should be willing to sit in the gutter, if it were for the good of the Synagogue." Afterwards I was told by the President that she had come to him and said that I had told her to sit in the gutter.

The College progressed far beyond my expectations. Indeed, I had been doubtful as to its success at all, thinking that the students who pursued our rather recondite subjects would prefer the Semitic departments of our great universities. But this turned out otherwise, and Dropsie College came to have more students than any of them. The cause of this was perhaps the excellence of the Faculty which was gathered and maintained, and the fact that the tuition was free.

It was about the time of the opening of the College that Israel Abrahams and Claude G. Montefiore of England announced their intention to cease the publication of the *Jewish Quarterly Review* at the completion of its twentieth year. I surmised that Mr. Montefiore had tired of footing the bills, and at my recommendation the Board of Governors of the Dropsie College offered a substantial subvention toward the upkeep of the journal, the only scientific magazine devoted to Jewish subjects in the English language; but to my surprise it was refused. Israel Abrahams wrote me that he was the deciding factor in giving up the journal, because of difficulties with authors. All of them wanted their articles printed in the "next number" and persisted in rewriting these articles in proof, so that, as he put it, he "had not a friend left in Europe."

Rather blithely, and with the warm support of Dr. Schechter, I took over the journal, made its character strictly academic, and now have seen through the press thirty volumes. For the first four years I had Dr. Schechter's invaluable assistance in selecting articles, although I did all the proof reading and saw each number through the press. The next years, Professor Max L. Margolis, who spent all his time at the Dropsie College, was of invaluable aid to me, not only as Professor of Bible, but also in connection with the *Quarterly*. He was later taken seriously ill, and I reduced his work to the minimum and took on as much as I could. My daughter then became a sort of assistant to me in preparing manuscripts and reading proof for the *Quarterly*.

I had a great many difficulties with the press. First I wanted to employ home talent and gave the work to a small printing office in Philadelphia, which, while it had Hebrew and also English type, had very little experience, and the compositors were in no way trained for scientific work. I then decided to transfer the printing to the Oxford University Press; and this went on very satisfactorily, until the war broke out, when transmission of proof was very slow and on one occasion the entire edition was lost, the vessel which carried it having been sunk by a submarine, and the number had to be set up over again. Quite a number of years ago, because I thought it necessary for the independence of Jewish scholarship and for the sake of the community here, I began to propose the idea of the establishment of a Hebrew Press. I should have been willing, at the time, to have it connected with the Dropsie College, but a gentleman whom I had interested in the project suggested the Jewish Publication Society, a more neutral organization. Hence the Hebrew Press was established there. We used the fund to build two monotypes, which in my opinion set a very beautiful Hebrew, but set it so that the points were cast with the letters, thus preventing the danger of breaking off. The type faces were very well drawn by Joseph B. Abrahams, Secretary of the Seminary. He used as his model the seventeenth-century type from the presses of Menasseh ben Israel, which I felt came nearest to my idea of what the new type should be. I took great delight in going over many of the old prints in the Seminary Library before coming to this decision. The original drawings are now in possession of the American Jewish Historical Society. The Press of the Jewish Publication Society, after a number of years, has turned out to be very efficient.

I think that the *Quarterly* takes as much, if not more, of my time than does the administration of the Dropsie College. I have persisted in it, however, and hope that there will be someone willing to do the rather thankless work of taking it up when I feel obliged to relinquish it. My authors have not always been easy to deal with, sometimes rewriting their articles in proof, and I have had to have quite a number of manuscripts copied in my office, because they were not legible to the printers. *The Jewish Quarterly Review* has, however, world-wide recognition and affords me great satisfaction, as being the medium of introducing a goodly number of young scholars to the learned world.

One of the great advantages of my coming back to Philadelphia was the fact that my mother was still living there. She was then seventy, and my uncle, David Sulzberger, a little older, was living with her. I had been away from Philadelphia for twenty-five years, and it was a real homecoming. Our return was a source of great happiness to my mother. She had seven grandchildren, all living in New York; but our child, the eighth, named for her, Sarah, was a great joy and the two became fast friends.

We had only been here a few months, when our small daughter, a little over two years of age at the time, got scarlet fever, and under the strict quarantine rules then in force in Philadelphia, I had to either leave the house or stay at home, which last I chose to do, so that, in the very beginning, my planning for the College was done through talks over the telephone. The child happily recovered, and the day on which the quarantine was lifted I felt like a boy loosed from school. My first visit was to a barber shop. I remember going to an Italian barber in the St. James Hotel, and he, seeing my long hair, asked me in his inquisitive way what was my business, and did I always wear my hair so long? I, feeling very jolly, said I was a pianist, but this time I wanted my hair cut short. He then picked up my hand and said: "You have not the hand of a pianist, your fingers are too short." I said: "No, I am not a pianist, I am an undertaker." He then said: "Have you been in Philadelphia long?" I said: "No, only a few months." "Well," he said, "there is a man here whom you resemble." I said: "Who is he?" He said: "A well known judge, Judge Sulzberger." "Well," I said, "that is possible because he is a cousin of mine." Thereupon the barber, looking most skeptical, ended by saying: "Now I know you are lying."

One of the great honors and privileges of my life was membership in the American Philosophical Society, the oldest scientific society in the United States, founded by Benjamin Franklin. I was elected in 1900 and was a devoted attendant at the annual meetings, coming regularly from Washington, so that when we made Philadelphia our home one of my real pleasures was my closer connection with this Society. I presided over a number of the sessions of its annual meetings. I was first a member of the Council, afterwards Vice-President, and also Chairman of the Committee on Publications. This became a pleasant duty when the Society was enabled to make so many more grants to scholars for scientific work, following the large bequest of Dr. Richard Penrose, in 1932.

In 1914, I presented the Society a portrait of Mr. Langley, by Lazar Raditz, with the following statement:

On behalf of a number of members of the American Philosophical Society I have the honor to present to the Society a portrait of Samuel Pierpont Langley, a member and Vice-President of the American Philosophical Society.

Mr. Langley, who was the third Secretary of the Smithsonian Institution, was a man of national and international fame, which rested primarily upon his epoch-making researches in solar physics. He was the first distinguished man of science to devote himself to the subject of aerial navigation at a time when this was hardly considered within the realm of scientific study, and from the mere fact of his taking it up gave standing and impetus to this important study. But he did more than give an impetus; for he not only discovered principles of prime importance in connection with aerial navigation, but was actually the first to produce a machine heavier-than-air which was supported and propelled by its own engine, and possessed no extraneous or lifting power, which actually made an independent flight.

I was one of a group of members of the Society to go to Washington to present a congratulatory address to President-Elect Hoover, the ninth member of the Society to be elected President of the United States. When I greeted Mr. Hoover, he looked at me quizzically and said, "Now all the intellect of the Philosophical Society is here." I also had the honor of being one of the four speakers at the dinner of the two hundredth anniversary of the Society. I was a member of the Building Committee at the time when it was proposed to erect a new building on the Parkway. This project has since been abandoned, although a great deal of time and money was expended on it. Alba Johnson was chairman of this committee, Eli Kirk Price was very much interested and was always present at meetings, and Paul Cret, who had been chosen as the architect, had actually made plans which have never been used. It was a relief to me when the decision was reached to remain in our historic surroundings, adjoining Independence Hall. Additional funds from the bequest of Dr. Penrose were used to improve the old building and place the library in a fire-proof structure across the street.

Philadelphia also brought me in contact with men with whom I had been in school and college, men who called me by my first name, which, with the exception of Oscar Straus, had never happened to me in the formal of life of Washington. My old friend, Charlie Audenried, did a whimsical thing about which we frequently had a good laugh. He was one of the most honored judges in Philadelphia. He was tall, impressive and usually of stern aspect. Two weeks after our arrival I received word from

his secretary that I had been appointed on a commission to inquire into the sanity of a prisoner in the Eastern Penitentiary. I
repaired to that elegant place, known to Philadelphia as Cherry
Hill, and found two college classmates, Charles W. Burr, the
distinguished nerve specialist and alienist, and Howard Wurtz
Page, a well known member of the Bar; for the law required such
Commissions to consist of a physician, a lawyer and a layman.
Later, when I asked Audenried why he had appointed me, he
said that he wanted, early in my stay in Philadelphia, to arrange
for a reunion of the Class of '83.

Not very long after my return to Philadelphia, in 1908, I was
appointed a member of the Board of Trustees of the Free Library
of Philadelphia. One of the trustees at that time was Thomas L.
Montgomery, who was a classmate of mine at college. John
Thomson, an Englishman, was then Librarian and did a great
deal toward building up that institution. John Ashhurst succeeded him as Librarian, a post which he held until his death, in
1932. I continued as a trustee for some time and then was elected
Vice-President, and upon the death of Simon Gratz, in 1925,
President of the Board of Trustees, a position from which I have
just retired, December 1939.

The Library was housed in an old building, situated at 13th
and Locust Streets, and it was John Ashhurst who undertook the
new building, now on the Parkway. This was completed in June
1927, and I was proud of the unusual experience of having a
goodly sum left over from the building fund. John Ashhurst was
a charming man, a great bibliophile, of an old Philadelphia
family, and always devoted to his native city. Dr. A. S. W. Rosenbach, a fellow bibliophile, said of him once: "John Ashhurst is
the wisest man I have ever known." We had one characteristic in
common. Neither of us ever hurried, but went about our work
deliberately. My association with the trustees and with the entire
personnel of the Free Library has always been most agreeable.

At the request of the Board of Trustees, Adolphe Borie was
commissioned to paint a portrait of me for the Free Library, it
being the custom thus to record each President. He chose to
paint me standing, and in my robes; and I have always thought

that the pained expression on my face was due to the fact that I stood so much. One day Mr. Borie asked my wife to come out to criticize the portrait, and he told her, rather whimsically, that a Paris artist friend of his had called him on the telephone that morning asking to come out to see him. When he said: "I have a sitter this morning and his wife is here to criticize the portrait," his friend said: "Oh, my God," and hung up the receiver.

In 1908–09 the long discussed project of a new translation of the Hebrew Scriptures under the auspices of the Jewish Publication Society of America took form.

Dr. David Philipson, of the Hebrew Union College in Cincinnati, and I, old friends and fellow students at Johns Hopkins University in our younger years, always maintained happy relations, but there seemed to be some difficulty about making this project one that would represent all the Jews, since the Central Conference of American Rabbis had felt that the translation should emanate from a rabbinical body and had already made plans to this end. I wrote to Dr. Philipson and asked him whether, if he were planning to come East, he would call on me in Washington, which he did. I think that he and his colleagues had pretty well made up their minds to have a separate project. We sat down in my little study in our apartment in Washington and talked it over without reaching a definite conclusion. I suddenly conceived the idea of a mechanical device. I said to him: "Philipson, suppose that I get a long sheet of paper and divide it in two. Let us put down all the points on which we agree and all the points on which we do not." He assented, and it finally turned out that we agreed on nine points and disagreed on two, and he was generous enough to say: "Well, if we only disagree on two points, we certainly must reach an agreement." While there were many more formal discussions in regard to the production of the Bible, it was on that afternoon in Washington that the matter was really settled.

My own part was the rather difficult one of Chairman of the Board of Editors. The company was made up of three men chosen by the Publication Society: Solomon Schechter, Joseph

Jacobs and myself; and three chosen by the Central Conference of American Rabbis: Kaufmann Kohler, David Philipson and Samuel Schulman. These six chose as the seventh member of the Board, Max L. Margolis, a distinguished biblical scholar, afterwards Professor of Bible in the Dropsie College, who was named Secretary and Editor-in-Chief. The Board met at first in a rather strained atmosphere. Margolis had, a couple of years before, left the Hebrew Union College after a serious difference of opinion between himself, Kohler, and most of the Governors of the College, amongst whom Philipson was prominent. This attitude of strain soon relaxed and, in the course of the seven years the Board sat together, clashes became less frequent, and it was in a spirit of thankfulness to God that we completed these labors. Although here and there a rendering crept in, by vote, which I thought was unhappy, on the whole I felt that a distinct contribution had been made to the interpretation of the Scriptures. The meetings of this Board usually lasted for three weeks and were held in Philadelphia at the Dropsie College, in New York at the Jewish Theological Seminary, several in Atlantic City in the summertime, and one in Cincinnati at the Hebrew Union College.

My wife and I devised various forms of entertainment for our colleagues—a reception, dinners, and the opera—and once we ventured upon a frivolity in the shape of a revue. The grave and reverend gentlemen were much absorbed by the current edition of the Ziegfeld Follies. Opera glasses were in constant use, and after the show was over, one gentleman astonished us by saying: "I never knew that so many girls were vaccinated on their legs."

One story that stands out in my mind was a quip of Dr. Schechter's. Dr. Kohler was a native of Fürth in Bavaria. Kohler told us at luncheon one day that during the many years the Prince Regent was insane and in an asylum, prayers for his recovery were regularly said in every church and synagogue, only not in Fürth. "Well," said Dr. Schechter, "perhaps in Fürth insanity is not considered a disease."

The last meeting of the Board was held on November 3, 1915. The whole question of the final manuscript, typography, proofreading, occupied quite a period of years. I think that every member of the Board read the proof four times, and Miss Henri-etta Szold, who was the Secretary of the Publication Committee, told me that she had read it twelve times. Strangely enough, we had the work printed in Chicago, which also made difficulties, but we found that at that time the best printing establishment for thin paper was located in Chicago, and so the work was awarded to the Lakeside Press. All these steps had been taken, the plates had been made, in fact two sets of plates, and a small advance edition was actually printed.

On Monday evening, January 22, 1917, the Publication Society celebrated the completion of the new Jewish translation of the Bible by giving a dinner at the Hotel Astor in New York. It was a very interesting and noteworthy occasion, but a strange thing happened. While we were seated at the table, Rabbi Charles I. Hoffman, of Newark, discovered two misplaced lines in the first chapter of the Book of Isaiah. Of course there was consternation among us, and since each person present had been given a copy of the Bible, as a souvenir at the dinner, we asked them all to return them and finally had the plates corrected. It seems that a printer's boy had dropped a page of type and covered up the fact. He had the whole page reset, and the errors occurred in that way. But it was very strange that Rabbi Hoffman, with his eagle eye, and possibly because his middle name is Isaiah, should have discovered this error in a few minutes. On April 12, 1917, I made a few remarks at the annual meeting of the American Philosoph-ical Society about the new translation, and gave a résumé of other editions of the Bible printed in the United States.

I allowed myself one personal touch in this Bible. The Intro-duction was written in sections by five of the original company that survived. I was to put it into final form and completed this, the last part of the task, on September 27, 1917. My wife and I had been married on September 27, and it happened that year to coincide with my birthday according to the Jewish calendar, the day before the Jewish New Year. So the Introduction bears the date, September 27. Someone said that the only way in which a modern literary student could be certain of immortality was to have his name connected with the Bible or Shakespeare.

In the meantime two of our company had died; Joseph Jacobs and Solomon Schechter. I had known both ever since my first visit to England in 1890 and felt their loss most keenly. Schechter's death, in November 1915, brought me more duties and responsibilities. It was war time; my colleagues of the Board of Directors did not feel it advisable that the headship of the Seminary should go to anyone but a native American. So I was asked to assume this duty temporarily, say for six months. Twenty-five years have passed, and I am still doing double duty in Philadelphia and New York.

In 1909, a number of us, including Jacob H. Schiff, Felix Warburg and Judah L. Magnes, projected a conference on Jewish education which we proposed to make very comprehensive and to include all types of Jewish education, even agricultural schools. I remember spending a good deal of time, over a period of years, in drawing up these plans. Mr. Schiff was so much interested that one summer he cabled me from Europe to find out how the plan was getting along. Mr. Warburg went to Cincinnati with the plan and stayed there for three days discussing it. Our friends in Cincinnati at that time did not seem willing to enter into such a proposal. Of course, the fear was that their autonomy would in some way be limited. There was no such thought, and the project was really planned along the lines of the National Education Association, but it fell by the wayside and has resulted in other Jewish national organizations, though none on so comprehensive a scale as this one.

While I was never a resident of New York and had no direct part in the creation of the *Kehillah* (Jewish community), I nevertheless was interested in it because I thought it was a step in the right direction. Dr. Magnes was the organizing spirit. I attended one of its very early meeetings, but had to leave because of a meeting of the Trustees of the Jewish Teachers College Fund. This was a foundation created by Jacob H. Schiff for the purpose of helping in the establishment of two Jewish Teachers Training Schools, one at the Seminary in New York and the other, as Mr. Schiff put it, in the Deed of Trust, west of the Alleghenies. It was actually established in Cincinnati. The first trustees were Judge Samuel Greenebaum, Mr. Louis Heinsheimer and myself. I am the only one of these trustees still carrying on.

I established a *Kehillah* in Philadelphia in 1911, because I thought it was a proper kind of organization in the community. I was its first President, but retired at the time of the war because of the introduction of questions which I did not consider germane to the local *Kehillah*. This too has finally passed away. I think upon the whole that it was rather an error for the Jewish community in America to reject this form of organization, because at present, through the Council of Federations, the only real organization that they have nationally rests upon the basis of philanthropy.

In December 1911, the House Committee on Foreign Affairs agreed to hold a meeting with the members of the Executive Committee of the American Jewish Committee with regard to the Russian Passport question as it affected the religious convictions of visiting Americans. For a period of forty years the Russian government has refused to honor the passports of American citizens of the Jewish faith, and had taken similar action with regard to American Protestant missionaries and Roman Catholic priests. Judge Sulzberger, who was then President of the American Jewish Committee, made the initial statement, and I think it was one of the most impressive and masterly presentations of the Jewish case that I have ever heard. He entered the room just as he was called and without hesitation, and with no notes of any kind, he spoke for thirty-five minutes, in a beautiful voice and most eloqent and perfect language. After Judge Sulzberger had finished, one could hear the members of the Committee saying to each other: "Who is this man and why haven't we heard of him before?" Mr. Straus, Mr. Schiff, Colonel Cutler and I also made brief statements before the Committee; and Mr. Marshall, acting as attorney, summed up the whole situation as only he could. One of the dramatic moments was when Colonel Cutler made the statement that his father had been killed in the Kishinev massacre. A day or two afterwards, the same subject was considered by the Senate Committee on Foreign Relations, after the House Resolution had passed. Again Judge Sulzberger, Mr. Marshall and I appeared, and Senator Lodge was the Chairman of the Committee. Senator Isador Rayner, of Maryland, made quite an impassioned address and was insistent that the Senate Committee take the same action as the House Committee did. It was Senator Lodge who stated that if the House did not take action with regard to the treaty, the Senate would probably pass it unanimously.

In the early pages of these memoirs I mentioned the fact that my father had owned a tract of ten thousand acres of land in Sevier County, on which he raised cotton. As time went on, after my father's death, there were many reports to us about the great value of this land. It was supposed to have oil on it, and through the Geological Survey and through one of the representatives of the Guggenheims, I had a careful examination made; but no oil ever resulted. There were also reports that there were diamonds on the plantation. The fact was that only very fine timber grew on the land. As long as my uncle, David Sulzberger, was alive, he looked after this for my mother, and on several occasions timber was sold off the land and a very good sum secured, and other trees planted.

My uncle died in 1910; my brother had died in the same year, and it seemed incumbent upon me, as the sole male member of the immediate family, the following year, in 1911, to investigate what the real conditions were and what could be done to make this land more remunerative to the family. I decided to revisit my native state and spend some time there in looking into the business which concerned the whole family.

I went to St. Louis. As usual, I utilized this trip for the purposes of Jewish affairs. I had a very good friend in St. Louis, Elias Michael, a very charming man, who was an active member of the Executive Committee of the American Jewish Committee. He introduced me in turn to a number of the Jewish citizens. At that time the American Jewish Committee and other organizations were very much engaged in making a fight for the rights of Jews to enter Russia under the American Passport, and Mr. Michael and his friends were prepared to help.

I proceeded to Van Buren and put up at what was said to be

the best hotel in the place, but it was a very primitive affair; in each room a single electric light dangled from the ceiling. Van Buren, already then, and even before the days of Bob Burns, showed signs of life and drew upon a large agricultural area. It had four banks, a little opera house, and a moving picture theatre. Many years afterwards I was on a train on my way to New York. I went to the smoking room and found two men discussing the relative merits of comedians on the radio. One of them said: "I think Bob Burns ranks among the first because it is so remarkable that he invented the City of Van Buren, in Arkansas, always discussing his relatives, which makes it all seem so real." I listened for a few minutes and then apologized for breaking into the conversation and said: "Gentlemen, I must contradict the statement that Bob Burns invented the town of Van Buren, as I happen also to have been born there."

The supper in this elegant hotel was at 5.30, and after that there was nothing to do. I went into the large room to write and a number of natives gathered in the room and commenced a discussion, and to my surprise it was directed against the shortcomings of the Jews. Arkansas had never had any but a very small Jewish population, and the question could not have been a living one. However, after listening as long as I could, I interrupted the gentlemen, told them that I was a native of Arkansas, and proceeded to defend the Jews. After that there was an ominous silence. Later on one of the men came up and tried to make amends. It is rather remarkable that this was the first time in my life that an anti-Jewish comment was ever made by Christians in my presence, and it seemed strange that I had to go back to my native town to hear it.

This of course was symptomatic of the whole situation in Arkansas. It is true that the Galveston Committee and other Committees were trying to persuade the Jews, who had settled in very great numbers in New York, to go to the South and the West, and a few had done so. The Arkansas attitude was that they did not want any Jews, they did not want any Italians, they did not want anybody except themselves. As one man put it to me, referring to the Negroes: "We have one race question in Arkansas and that is all we can stand."

I visited a man called Tot England, whose name I had heard
from boyhood. He was known to me because he was the man to
whom we paid the taxes. I was actually welcomed as a native,
and Mr. England introduced me to a good many of the old men
there, men who remembered my mother and my father very well.
My mother had told me particularly to go to see a man by the
name of Jesse Turner. His father had been the leading lawyer in
that section while my family lived there, and she told me that he
had a son who had succeeded him. I called on him and found a
highly cultivated man. He was a Harvard graduate, well traveled, he had good books and good pictures. All this seemed very
remarkable in a small village; which shows the different strata of
which America is made.

In the afternoon I went, at Mr. Turner's suggestion, to Mt.
Vista, a rise I think of about six hundred feet, where the people
of Van Buren go in summer. When I reached there I was rather
surprised to find something like a summer resort. There were a
number of bungalows; there was a small golf course, and some
amusements for the children. I went to see Mr. Turner again,
who at that time was crippled with rheumatism and could not
leave his house. I said to him: "This little summer development
looks like a very enterprising thing for the town to have done."
He said to me: "The town did not do it. This was done by a
foreigner from Iowa, about twenty years ago." I mention this
curious little incident to show that a graduate of Harvard and a
traveled man could still speak of a person from another state of
the Union as a foreigner.

The people all spoke very highly of my father, asked about my
uncle, David Sulzberger, and whether my mother was still as
handsome as she used to be. I then went across the river to the
larger town of Fort Smith, where some of my father's cousins still
lived. Besides prospering in business, the elder, Bernard Baer,
had built the Fort Smith and Little Rock Railway. I am not
going to give here the history of my family in Arkansas, but they
did stick somewhat to that quarter.

It was on the way down from Fort Smith that I had my chance
actually to see the property of which we had always talked so
much. There was no way of getting around it except by walking,

and the agent walked with me. I was enormously impressed at being a land owner. A thousand acres of tall pine is a beautiful thing to behold, and somehow or other the ownership of land does give one the feeling of property, which chattels do not give.

I came home by way of St. Louis, where I stopped again over the Sabbath, and then straight through to Philadelphia. It was the longest time that I had been separated from my wife and child.

The result of my visit to Arkansas was that the family authorized me to sell this great estate to a man who wished to use it for agricultural purposes. Quite an anti-climax to all the wishful thinking of the family, that great mineral wealth would result some day from their one joint possession.

EPHRAIM E. LISITZKY

Ephraim Lisitzky was ranked as one of the most eloquent and talented Hebrew poets in America. He was born in Russia in 1885 and lived in Canada, Boston and New Orleans after he left Europe. He not only wrote original Hebrew poetry but evoked, in the ancient cadences of Hebrew verse, the Negro rhythms of the South. He died in New Orleans in 1962.

During most of his life in the United States, Mr. Lisitzky was a Hebrew teacher, but he never ceased to write poetry. He translated Shakespeare's The Tempest *and* Julius Caesar *into Hebrew, and wrote his remarkable autobiography encompassing his earliest years, both in Europe and in America.*

Although this autobiography, called in its English translation In the Grip of Cross-Currents *(in the original Hebrew:* Eileh Toldot Adam)*, is full of personal anguish and contains "a superabundance of sorrow," it is also an ennobling narrative, for Lisitzky concludes that life, however bitter and wracking, can be redeemed by dedication, by striving to fulfill a purpose.*

Boston in 1900 has been described by many writers, from many vantage points. No one, however, has written of it in the style and with the approach of this Hebrew poet and teacher.

Youth of a Poet*

EPHRAIM E. LISITZKY

DURING ALL OF MY TRIP to America my imagination kept conjuring up a picture of my encounter with my father. The image of my father's face, which had dimmed in my memory, shone through a haze of eight and a half years as it had registered in it the night before his departure, as I lay at his side holding him in tight desperation. Only now, his melancholy look of compassion had brightened. Anticipation of reunion softened the trials of the journey—stealing across the border, wandering through thick forests in the dark of night, the ship tossed about by storm for three consecutive days.

The picture of our reunion became sharper when, in New York, I boarded the train for Boston. The entire trip I visualized my father at the station, waiting for the train to pull in. When the train arrived and I got off, he would rush over and embrace me. I could see him standing there and hear the clatter of the train wheels bringing his greetings to me: "Welcome, my son!" And my heart responded in joyful tones: "Papa! Papa!"

The train slowed down to enter the station and my heart beat faster, as though to prod the train to hurry. Through the coach window I could see faces and eyes happy, trembling with anticipation. I searched for my father but he wasn't there! I descended from the coach, still looking and my heart scrutinizing every face in the crowd. But my father was nowhere in the crowd! I trudged to my father's home, stopping passers-by on the street to show them the crumpled address transcribed in my strange tongue. When I finally got there he was not in—he had gone to work early, as he did every day, for the telegram from New York an-

---

* Reprinted from *In the Grip of Cross-Currents*, translated from the Hebrew by Moshe Kohn and Jacob Sloan and revised by the author, Bloch Publishing Co., New York, 1959, pp. 63–81.

nouncing the time of our arrival in Boston had been misaddressed and had not reached him.

At the entrance to the hall of a house populated with poor tenants, with one of whom my father roomed, I stood tense with anticipation. My eyes scrutinized every passer-by; perhaps father would be there, for his landlord had gone to look for him in the street to tell him of our arrival. The din of the city filled the street. Foot and wagon peddlers shrilly announced their wares. An Italian ground his organ as girls danced on the sidewalk and in the street. Boys skated madly along, holding on to one another's back in a long line that twisted and straightened, broke apart and joined again. In passing they glanced mockingly at me, eyeing my Slutzk garb which branded me as a "greenhorn," and my strange hat—a stiff Homburg acquired in Belgium after I had lost my Slutzk cap en route. They laughed and hurled at me names, which, though uttered in a foreign tongue, were clearly not complimentary.

Many tedious hours I stood and waited, rejecting the pleas of my stepmother and my father's landlady to eat and rest from the journey. I was not going to put off for one moment the anticipated meeting with my father. The hours passed. Standing there, all tensed up, my nerves on edge, the effects of the two weeks at sea overcame me and I swayed and sank to a step near the entrance to the hall. I fell into a kind of exhausted faint which lasted many minutes.

Suddenly, a figure came towards me through a rosy mist. As it approached, the mist lifted and I saw it, radiant and compassionate. I leaped up—it was my father.

In the dusk my father's face loomed up from the street. He walked heavily bent under a sack full of rags and bottles. His face was dark and hard, with an expression of mingled humiliation and forgiveness. I shrank back, offended and silenced.

At midnight, lying on the bedding they had laid out for me in a corner of the kitchen floor in the apartment where my father roomed, I cried in silence over the alienation that screened me from my father.

At the time I immigrated to America the Jewish community there was in a state of upheaval caused by the clash of diverse elements, each striving for supremacy. The equilibrium which was bound to be established was postponed by the constant arrival of new groups. The most important group were the Orthodox, stable Jews who came to America and brought their tradition with them. They founded synagogues, schools, associations and fraternal organizations for the fostering of religion. These they maintained by donations, after the Old Country manner. The Orthodox had a great deal of vital energy. But their influence was limited both by their numbers and by their economic instability. Strict observance of the Sabbath and the Jewish festivals lessened their income! This, in turn, lessened their influence.

The Orthodox were submerged in the mass which constituted the majority of the American Jewish community. This mass, which appeared united from the outside, was actually divided into several distinct groups. A significant part consisted of Jews who had sentiment for religious tradition and supported its institutions, even becoming their officers. But they were forced by economic circumstances to give up some observances of traditional Judaism. Another group of American Jews denounced all religious discipline gladly as a kind of emancipation from slavery. And then there were the spite-workers—those who belonged to the Jewish socialist movement, whose cardinal tenets then were: atheism, denial of all religious and national values, and disparagement of the Jewish cultural legacy. In this general mass, alienated from religious observances, the Orthodox element constituted a tiny, lonely and isolated minority.

To all outward appearances, my first days in Boston, when I was able to live as I had in Slutzk, were only a matter of change of locale: the synagogue where I prayed daily was always packed; the congregants gathered after the morning prayers to study the Mishna and between the afternoon and evening prayers to study *The Well of Jacob;* one group stayed on after the evening prayers to study the daily page of Talmud—everything in Boston was just as it had been in Slutzk. But in Slutzk, the learned and

the pious had been in the vast majority; here in Boston, they
were a small minority; so I felt like an alien in Boston.

I particularly sensed the spiritual decline of American Jews on
the Sabbath. I have never forgotten the impression of my first
Saturday in Boston. I compared it to the Sabbath in Slutzk, and
my heart bled. Actually there was no comparison, for Slutzk,
though poverty-stricken, dressed up in glorious raiment in honor
of the Sabbath. Even the horse grazing in the pasture, swishing
his tail and leaping on his forelegs, bound so that he might not
frisk beyond the Sabbath limits, was permitted to enjoy Sabbatical rest and partake of the goodness of the luxuriant meadow.
But in Boston very few Jews observed the Sabbath. In the Jewish
quarter through which she had just passed they trampled with
weekday shoes the train of her bridal gown and interrupted with
shrill weekday outcries the music of her angelic escorts on her
way to her betrothed. Leaving the synagogue after the Sabbath
eve service, the observants were confronted by a tumultuous
Jewish quarter: shopkeepers stood in their shop doorways, peddlers on their wagons shouted their wares. Mournfully I passed
through this Jewish quarter that first Sabbath eve. As I entered
our house it seemed to me that the Sabbath candles were bowed
in mourning, too. Sadly my father sang *Shalom Aleikhem,* usher-
ing in the Sabbath. The room was too cramped for him to walk
around it as he chanted, in the traditional manner. Sadly I sang
with him.

I was seized with a longing for Slutzk. In my mind's eye I saw
it day and night, its streets, its houses, its people, its meadows,
gardens and orchards—and it appeared to me like a heavenly
city in an ethereal world.

My father sensed my homesickness though I never put it in
words lest he construe my unhappiness as ingratitude or take it
as an insult directed against Boston and thus against himself. He
tried to get me to appreciate Boston, and to win back my affection for himself, who had brought me there. Every night on his
way home he would buy some local products—fruit, for example,
the likes of which I had never or rarely seen in Slutzk. While I

was enjoying these delicacies he would study my expression. If he detected the least sign of pleasure in my face his own would light up and he would exclaim: "That's Boston for you! Did you ever taste such delicious fruit in Slutzk?"

Saturday afternoons father would take me walking through town in the better neighborhoods. On such occasions father was like a king on an inspection tour of his capital with his crown prince. Having shown me the wonders of Boston, father would straighten up and lift his head and declaim: "Have you ever seen such a magnificent city? What's Slutzk compared to Boston— nothing!" I did not dare tell him that in this magnificent city of Boston I pined for the nothing of Slutzk. I would nod agreement, though at heart I was back in Slutzk.

All my life I had been gregarious. Now that I had left my Slutzk friends behind, I tried to find replacements in Boston. My soul needed a friend desperately. I looked around all the immigrant boys like myself but found none. They had adjusted all too readily to the new country and had accommodated themselves to their new situation—one had become a peddler, another a laborer, the third a shop clerk. They were satisfied with what they regarded as an opportunity to improve themselves, and there was no basis for friendship between us. This was even truer with respect to the American-born or American-bred boys: we lacked even a common language. I had only one friend in my loneliness, one whom I met every day in the synagogue and to whom I poured out my heart—the Talmud. . . .

The synagogue was bare. Its walls seemed to withdraw into the gloomy shadow and emptiness to which they had been condemned in an alien land. The lions' heads over the Holy Ark were bowed, the royal wrath in their faces gloomy; in their roar a cry of calamity. The Eternal Light flickered feebly.

I was alone in the synagogue, sitting at the table and swaying over the open Talmud, chanting in the old country tone. Loud sounds burst in from the street—the sounds of the new life into which I have been cast and out of whose turmoil I have fled into this desolate haven. The cries reproached me mockingly! What are you doing among us, you unworldly idler?

I grew silent, my head sank down on my arms. . . .

The question of my future began to vex me. My attention was
diverted from my talmudic problems to a much more serious one
whose solution could not be postponed: What was to become of
me? My father sought the advice of our fellow Slutzk immigrants
who used to drop in. They thought it over, discussed it among
themselves and concluded that my salvation lay in becoming a
custom-peddler. They preached the advantages of peddling:

In the first place it gives you a livelihood, meager to begin
with, but eventually plenteous. It does not require you to desecrate the Sabbath or holidays; if you want to, you can observe
them. At the same time, you get an opportunity to learn the
language and ways of America. To be sure, it's a small beginning
—but many people began carrying a peddler's notions basket
and ended up owning a business or a factory—and it wasn't a
matter of luck either. However, if you want to become a peddler,
you must decide to be aggressive and daring. The main thing is a
peddler has to be a talker—the more he talks the better. Suppose
you enter a house and the customer does not need or want what
you have to sell; you can't simply leave looking for another customer who may need and want it. You would go on looking till
the Messiah comes and never find him! You have to stick with
that customer until you get him to say, "I'll take it!" How? You
talk yourself into his good graces and once having won his heart,
you have won yourself a customer, and a good one! Do it this way
and you'll get customers and make money. First you'll just make
a living, but you'll end up making piles of money—and you'll be
all set.

I nodded involuntary affirmation mingled with self-pity: so
this is the end of the great achievements you aspired to—to be a
door-to-door peddler!

Still, repugnant as the prospect was, I decided to try peddling
and see whether I was fit for it. I talked to one of my acquaintances, a boy my own age, who was a peddler himself, and he
consented to lend me for a day his notions basket with the understanding that we would share the profits. I chose Tuesday, a

lucky day in Jewish tradition, to embark on my peddling experiment.

It was a rainy autumn day. The wind shook my basket and
whipped the shoelaces dangling from my hand into my face. I
trudged down the street like a doomed man on his way to the
gallows. Whenever anybody looked at me I lowered my eyes in
shame. I approached a house whose number was the numerical
equivalent of a verse of Scripture I had in mind, timidly
mounted the stairs—and couldn't bring my hand to knock at the
door. At last I knocked diffidently. The door opened. I stood in
the doorway with downcast face, and inquired clumsily in a low
voice:

"Maybe the lady wants matches?"

"Matches?" The woman at the door responded sardonically.
"Come in and I'll show you the piles of matches the peddler
already supplied me with—enough to burn up all the houses in
Boston!"

I tried to ask her if she wanted any of the other notions in my
basket, but I couldn't find my voice. I went down the stairs,
bowed and beaten, and trudged along. Before I had found another house whose number tallied with the numerical equivalent
of the verse of Scripture I had in mind, I reminded myself of the
passage of "the merchants of Lod," which I had studied in the
Talmud and knew by heart. In my fantasy I saw Lod and its
merchants. I pretended that Boston was Lod and I one of the
merchants. This parallel made peddling important enough to be
discussed by the talmudic Sages and to serve as a basis for the
formulation of certain rules of commerce. When I came to the
second house, I climbed the stairs with firm step, and knocked
boldly at the door. When the door opened I went in and raised
my voice—I was no common peddler now, but a merchant, one
of the merchants of Lod! Unluckily my voice collapsed into a
cough-like sound made by blowing the trachea of a slaughtered
goose.

"Maybe the lady wants candles?"

"Candles?" my customer responded in a tone of amazement.
"If all the days of the week were Sabbath Eve I would have
enough candles for a whole year running."

"Maybe you want shoelaces?" I asked again, in a pitiful voice.

"I have plenty of shoelaces, enough to make nooses to hang Haman and all his ten sons!"

I went down the street again, mortified at my second failure, attributing it first to bad luck and then to a lack of practical skill. "You schlemihl!" I scolded myself. "First principle of peddling, you must be aggressive, bold and talkative, and you mustn't let a customer go just because he doesn't need or want your merchandise—you have to make him want it, keep after him until he says, 'I'll take it!' Ask a woman if she needs what you're selling, you can be sure, she won't touch it. 'Lady! I see that you need such and such, and I can give it to you for next to nothing—' That's the way to talk to a customer!"

I stopped seeking Scriptural verses, assumed an air of aggressive boldness, went up to another house, and knocked at the door energetically, loud enough to waken the dead. The door opened and before me stood a woman with a sooty face and dirty hands who had left her stove to find out what all the pounding was about. I made myself aggressive, bold and talkative:

"I see, madam, that your face is sooty and your hands are dirty and they need a good washing with soap—not just ordinary soap, but a good soap. I have just that, here in my basket, and you can have it for next to nothing. As the prophet Isaiah said: 'And I will cleanse as with soap thy—'" The door slammed in my face! I never finished the verse.

That evening I went back to my acquaintance's house, and returned the basket with all the merchandise intact—not a thread or shoelace was missing. He checked his merchandise and gave me a scoffing and pitying look. I scoffed at myself: "Oh, you Slutzk unworldly idler, you good-for-nothing yeshiva student—there's no hope for you!"

I plodded wearily to the synagogue and stayed after the evening prayers to study my daily portion of Talmud. Mutely I looked at the Talmud, afraid to open my mouth lest the suppressed cry within me, about to burst forth, erupt.

The synagogue emptied. The distinguished scholars who had finished the portion of their nightly study left. Only an old Slutzker, Artche, the Hebrew teacher, remained to finish his study. He sits at his Mishna, intoning sadly, reading every chapter once in the book through a magnifying glass, and repeating it twice by heart. He is losing his eyesight, and before losing it entirely he is laboriously fortifying his memory with portions of Mishna, food for his soul in the days of blindness that were closing in on him. Upon completing his daily portion he shuts his feeble eyes, and ends his study with a portion of Psalms chanted in a melancholy undertone. Suddenly his voice rises and he begins to groan and cry out into the stillness of the synagogue: "My heart flutters, my strength fails me, and the light of my eyes is also gone from me—O God, my Light and my Salvation, the light of my eyes is gone from me!"

An autumn drizzle falls outside and covers the panes of the synagogue with tear-like drops. The synagogue sheds tears out of compassion for Artche, the Hebrew teacher, whose light of his eyes is dimming and for me, whose light of my life likewise is dimming, and for both of us, our world turns dark. . . .

My one day's unsuccessful experiment in peddling was enough to convince me that I had been born with no practical talents whatsoever, a fate for which there was no remedy. Clearly, heaven had ordained that scholarship was to be my trade. I decided to devote myself to study with all my Slutzk diligence, and become a rabbi. The rabbinate appeared to me the only practical way to make good in America. I set up a regular schedule of learning. But I had lost my Slutzk diligence, and I made no headway. The saying of our sages was fulfilled in me. "Torah can be acquired only in company." As I sat studying in the empty synagogue, I was seized by boredom, and sank into a sort of apathetic stupor, for long hours. When I pulled myself together, it was to stand at the window and watch the hustle and bustle in the street. Watching the shopkeepers and peddlers at their business and passers-by hurrying to their tasks, I became disgusted with my own indolence.

It finally became clear to me that I could never realize my ambition to become a rabbi in Boston. My only hope was to return to the Slutzk Yeshiva. True, the thought of leaving my father saddened me, for the wall of estrangement between us had begun to crumble and we were becoming close. But even if I could become a rabbi in Boston, I didn't want to burden my father with my upkeep.

My father was a peddler who sold two loads of commodities. During the day he peddled rags and bottles, in the evening he peddled Hebrew lessons to Jewish boys, whom he trained for Bar Mitzvah. Every morning, after the services and breakfast, he would stick on his hat a brass badge marked with black letters and numbers against a glossy background—the badge which the Boston authorities had ordered every rag peddler to wear—shoulder his sack, and leave for work. He walked his route through the city, crying: "R-r-rags and bot-tles!" He looked up to the tenement houses, looking at the windows for a sign that one of the tenants wanted to bargain over their discards and rags. Sometimes young rowdies threw stones at him, and in the winter snowballs with pieces of coal inside, sometimes hoodlums pulled his beard, sometimes he'd be attacked in dark hallways and his pockets emptied. "Rags and bottles!" he would call again after such a mishap, his voice ringing with pain and grief, but not with bitterness or protest. He was inured to suffering and submitted to it.

My father's sacred peddling of Bar Mitzvah lessons was essentially the same as the profane, except that here he functioned as a seller rather than a buyer. American Jewish boys in those days much preferred to play ball than to read the unfamiliar letters in the prayer book. They thought of my father as a kind of hangman, a cruel executioner come to snatch them from the street and rob them of the pleasure of their games and fun. When they failed to anticipate the exact time of his arrival and had no chance to hide, they went up to their apartments like condemned men for the half hour of tortuous study. Out of fear of their parents they submitted to my father, but in the end they repaid my father double for the tortures he inflicted on them.

My father made the rounds of the houses, selling pieces of his learning for pennies. His customers lived far apart, but the pennies he earned through so much toil were too precious to be spent on streetcar travel, so he half-ran, half-walked from lesson to lesson. Late at night he dragged his weary feet home. After prayers, he sat down to an appetiteless supper—work had killed his hunger. Father had a side line which he hoped would get him on his feet: the little money he managed to save by limiting his expenditures to the barest necessities, he invested in ship tickets to be sold on installment to poor immigrants who wanted to bring over their families from Europe. He took out his little notebook and checked his accounts. He reckons and groans: this one wanted to pay but couldn't; this one could but didn't want to. The upshot was that neither was paying, and his losses were eating up his profits!

For one month a year, between Purim and Passover, Father also sold Passover necessities on the installment plan. From morning to midnight he walked the streets, in search of customers. That month he was a beast of burden, carrying bundles of matzoh, jugs of wine, bottles of whiskey, and similar Passover necessities for delivery to his customers. The night of the festival, when he sat down at the head of the table to reign over the Passover seder, he was a sore and miserable king indeed, with swollen feet, bent back, all his joints aching, muscles cramped. Loudly he recited the Haggadah, singing cheerfully of the Israelites' deliverance from bondage to freedom, from servitude to liberty which he himself was experiencing that night, just as those who did march out of Egypt. But when he reached the passage describing the hard labor of the children of Israel in Egypt, his eyes would tear; he was in Egypt every day, body and soul. The holiday over, he drew out his little notebook to audit the meager accounts of his Passover business. The summation of these accounts was deplorable! Hard labor and a scanty profit.

My heart went out to my father at the sight of the miseries he endured to eke out a livelihood. I took myself to task for hanging around his neck like a millstone. Every time I sat down to eat his hard-earned bread, I felt like a criminal.

I felt it was my duty to relieve my father of the burden of my upkeep while I studied to become a rabbi. Returning to the Slutzk Yeshiva would help from the material point of view too—

the yeshiva would give me a stipend as it did other poor out-of-town students.

While I was still considering whether or not to return to the Slutzk Yeshiva, the Ridbaz visited America and my decision was made for me. News had reached him in Slutzk that his co-religionists in America responded generously to appeals for support of sacred institutions and enterprises. He came to secure funds for his commentaries to the Jerusalem Talmud whose printing he had been forced to interrupt for lack of funds. Shortly after his arrival he visited Boston, which was then considered a great Jewish center. The arrival of this renowned scholar was a great event. Rabbis, community leaders, and notables from Boston and the surrounding cities and towns came to the station to welcome him. He had an escort of honor to the house where he was to be the guest during his stay in Boston. This house became a center for all Orthodox Jews. Day and night it hummed with visitors who came to warm themselves at the flame of the "Light of the Exile." All the Jews of Boston were proud to extend their hospitality to this Slutzk sage! But the rabbi's presence shed particular luster on the natives of Slutzk, who led the reception at the railroad station and were the first to sit at the rabbi's table. I was from Slutzk, too, and I felt especially close to him as a former student at his yeshiva and as one he had known from earliest childhood. But I stayed away both from the railroad station and the house where he was staying, out of a natural shyness compounded with shame at having left his yeshiva without asking his advice and without taking leave of him. His first Sabbath in Boston he preached in one of the large synagogues, which was packed for the occasion. My father and I were among the audience. As he stood on the almemar preaching, his eyes fell on me, and from the expression of surprise in his eyes I realized that he had recognized me. After the sermon he hurried over, gave me a hard pinch on my cheek that surpassed all others he ever gave me before, and while pinching hurled at me a reproof: "What are you doing here, you heathen! Why have you left my yeshiva, exiling yourself from a place of Torah to a land that consumes its scholars? Return—return to the haven of Torah—I order you to return with me to Slutzk!"

Whenever a native of Slutzk returned from a trip to America, his townsfolk begged him to recount the wonders he had seen and heard in America. He was proud to have his townsfolk, including notable personages, sit at his feet like pupils hanging on to his every word. His account would be extravagant, loaded with odd Americanisms like the French words in the commentary of Rashi. He would flaunt his short and tight-fitting clothes, a very stiff derby, his wide-toed and laced shoes, and the pure gold chain dangling across his vest. "Ah, America, America!" his audience would exclaim.

After deciding to return to the Slutzk Yeshiva I toured Boston to see its sights in order to be able to tell my relatives and friends all about the wonders of this third America, as the people from Slutzk had dubbed Boston. Actually, I had really not seen Boston before—the image of Slutzk had always stood in the way. But now I was able to look directly at Boston and was pleasantly surprised. I strolled through the elegant neighborhoods, the rich quarters of the Boston aristocracy of the old families that had preserved the Bostonian traditions and I was delighted. There was a modest beauty in the old-style buildings, standing side by side in rows, screening themselves from the public gaze that might infringe upon their privacy. The streets where they stood were serenely silent, the tumult of the city that was filtered through beat like a remote pulse of the city's life.

The suburbs, too, had their native beauty. It was springtime in New England. Neatly painted houses of wood and shingles, well-constructed houses of stone and brick, decorated with vines climbing up to the cornices of roofs, stood in the shadow of the broad-crested trees green with first bloom rustling melodiously, caressed by the breeze. The houses were an ample distance apart. The spaces between were covered with fresh grass, newly clipped; here and there lilac bushes opened fragrant blue-white buds. Coveys of birds returning from the south flew over the rooftops. A row of brick houses, standing on the diagonal bank across the

Charles River, peered into its depth. Sunset crimson flickered softly on the red of their bricks. Their windows glowed majestically! A gate of heaven opened in the west and a hidden mysterious world peered through it, and its sublime image was reflected in the window panes, and radiated from them in awesome majesty and beauty, a spectral kaleidoscope, gleams of the wondrous light which God had brought into being on the first day of Creation and forthwith hidden. The houses gazed into the mirror of the river's deep and observed with awe the reflection of this mysterious world. The river's waves also observed this wondrous reflection in the window panes mirrored in their deep, and they donned a silky purple, a garb of glory, and floated together with the beryl-tinted clouds above westward to see the real image of this mysterious world before it sets and vanishes. A sailboat glided gracefully over the river emitting the sweet strains of a mandolin—a melody of farewell to the apparition of beauty which had appeared in this mysterious world and the boat flapped its sails to its tune and waved to it goodbye!

Sitting on the bench enjoying this view at dusk, another view, far across the sea, flashed before my eyes: Slutzk, as it really was, with its quarters so poor, that I, a native pauper's son, knew so well. Muddy, smelly courts and alleys. Dilapidated houses sunk into the earth, up to the windows leaning on wooden props like cripples on crutches. Inside, soot-covered walls, damp with mildew, a sooty oven in the far corner of the house, belching smoke and sparks, like a monster bent on burning down the house and its inhabitants. The sooty, sagging ceiling would collapse at any moment were it not for the supporting beams! A long-legged spider spinning in the corner a web of gray threads in which ensnared flies writhe, buzzing furiously.

Startled, I rubbed my eyes as if trying to erase the traces of a bad dream. But with cruel clarity I could still see Slutzk in my mind's eye. One image followed another. Here was the market place: Jews with distorted faces, furrowed brows, and dishevelled beards, frantically push to and fro, trampling mud and dung, squeezing in among the peasants' wagons to trade with them, for cash or barter, wrangling and bargaining, quarreling, placating and imploring—their hollow eyes glinting like the eyes of hungry animals. In the center of the market place Jewish women wearing tattered and frayed shawls, faces yellow as old parchment, lips bluish-gray, sat near mounds of dust covered potatoes and rotten apples crying their wares. And at their side young girls with bushy hair, pale cheeks, and ashen eyes, stood before boxes full of costume jewelry, ivory combs, small mirrors, colored ribbons, and other notions, dinning the praise of their wares into the ears of the passing peasant women. On the edge of the market place were crowded rows of shops, whose salesmen and clerks stood in the doorways grabbing peasants by the sleeve, pulling them back and forth urging and cajoling them to buy.

I shivered; to such a horrid place am I going to return?

REBEKAH KOHUT

Rebekah Kohut was one of the most unusual women in American Jewish communal work. Born in 1864, the daughter of a rabbi in Hungary, she came to the United States in 1867 and was educated in San Francisco and the University of California. In 1886 she settled with her family in Baltimore and, when she came to New York, met and married Alexander Kohut, a noted rabbi and scholar, who was twenty-two years her senior and a widower with eight children. They were married in 1887 and in the remaining seven years of his life, Mrs. Kohut worked with him on his sermons and books.

When Rabbi Kohut died, his widow became a lecturer and teacher. She taught English at the Educational Alliance and, in 1899, founded the Kohut School for Girls. She held many important posts, serving as President of the World Congress of Jewish Women, and as a member of employment commissions, under New York Mayor John P. Mitchel and Governor Franklin D. Roosevelt.

Mrs. Kohut, who died in 1951, wrote many interesting books and in one section of her autobiography, My Portion, *told of her Jewish activities. The chapter included here constitutes a significant contribution to American Jewish history.*

Emergence of the Jewess*

REBEKAH KOHUT

IT WAS A SUMMER of doubt and agony and loneliness. The men I had loved most, whose guidance had been a shining light in life, had been taken from the world. Brother, father, husband; all in four swift years. Though many friends came with sympathy and tried to lighten my sorrow, not only with words, but also with deeds, I felt alone, acutely alone.

"You have neither the means nor the right to indulge in grief." So said Dr. Isaac Adler, warning me not to let myself go under. "You were brave all through the trouble, and I admired you for it. Don't let me be disappointed in you now. You must find the lost threads, and pick them up as best you can, and remember: I shall be your friend."

Though Dr. Adler had attended my husband every day for seven months, he refused to accept a fee. A man of few words, he gave most people the impression of being austere. I knew better. During those trying days in the sick room I discovered the real him. A soft glance, or the terse expression, "brave girl" or "good nurse," spoke volumes. In after years, when he, too, was battling against the chronic disease that took him off, I visited him frequently. He dropped the mask of austerity completely, and enjoyed recalling the Beekman Place days. It amused him to tell me how seriously I had taken myself and my work and he teased me for my unconsciousness of my shortcomings.

Whenever I was discouraged, or faced by a baffling problem, I would find an excuse to go to Dr. Adler. Great in medical knowledge, he was greater in his understanding of human psychology. He could size up a situation in a flash, and his advice was always

* Reprinted from *My Portion*, Thomas Seltzer, New York, 1925, pp. 192–221.

worth following. When I assumed more worries than a person should, he laughed me out of my state of mind.

"Don't take yourself so tragically," he said once. "Do you want to go down in history as the best stepmother that ever lived? If you possessed three times your energy, and three times your ambition to devote yourself to your family, you'd still not secure the title. No one can."

That made me smile, of course, and I questioned whether there wasn't some truth in what he said—perhaps the smack of an overweening desire not to fail in anything I undertook. I had undertaken to be a stepmother; I *must* make the best of stepmothers.

But that wasn't all, was it? I asked myself. My father and husband had left me another heritage. In my loneliness I wrestled and groped. Something must come, besides the sheer struggle with the economic situation, to fill the void. What could I do to carry on their work to keep their spirit alive, to have them beside me always even if they were gone?

The answer to my queries did not come at that time. I saw no special fields in which I could do definite, concrete things in line with their humanitarianism and love of Jews and Judaism. I could not remotely dream that it was through the awakening of women that the spiritual solution should come, and that by the assertion of my Jewish womanhood as well as the Jewish womanhood the world over I should be carrying on the noble tradition handed down to me.

The immediate problem, however, was economic. The oldest son, George, was a mere lad whose health was such that he could only struggle to keep alive. The girls were helpless. We had some resources, but so limited that the day must be provided for when they would be exhausted. The six young children must not know want; the home, at all costs, must be kept intact.

Several months earlier, before leaving for Europe, Jacob H. Schiff had inquired about Dr. Kohut's condition and assured me he wished to be of service. After my husband's death I received a cable from him, then cruising off the coast of Norway, asking me to wait until his return before making definite plans for the future. This was encouraging, but my pride, amounting almost to vanity, made me try to do what I could, meanwhile, on my own account. I applied for various positions in city institutions, and even considered a journalistic career. After writing several articles for newspapers, however, I realized that the precarious existence of a freelance writer was not for me.

Then it struck me that the lectures I had written in my husband's sick room might be turned to good account. A fresh reading showed me that much recasting was necessary. So I spent days in the Columbia University Library at Forty-ninth Street and Madison Avenue reading up more comprehensively on my subjects and revising the manuscript in accordance with more mature judgment.

The writing finished, the next thing was to secure the patronage of a well-known woman who would permit me to deliver the lectures in her home before an invited audience. Parlor lectures were the vogue, and in the home of the rich there were frequent gatherings of friends to listen to the addresses of various authorities and pseudo-authorities on diverse subjects. There was no doubt that under the right auspices I could derive an income which would go part of the way toward providing our livelihood. Deep in my heart, I felt the amateurishness of my efforts, but it was no time to question one's abilities too closely. And in my trunk at home, to give me self-assurance, was a diploma from the Normal School of San Francisco which mentioned my qualifications for teaching English literature.

The summer moved along slowly. Most of the people I knew were away, and I spent long days in planning for the coming months. The natural state of society is indifference; it is only through a concerted attack that we less favored ones can command its attention. The fate of the children and myself depended upon me, and I felt my responsibility and marshalled my forces accordingly.

I speak as though I were alone in a hostile world, friendless and ignored. Such was far from the case. I had friends, well-wishers, sympathizers, yet, in the last analysis, I was alone. My future depended upon myself. Great is humanity's capacity for self-absorption; not so great its capacity for genuine concern about others. Most human beings are kind; they will go half way to meet a person; but if that person is a shrinking individual who expects to be sought out in his retreat, he will learn a very tragic lesson in superfluity.

My dear friend Dr. Gottheil returned to New York and soon visited me. Here was an eager listener to my plans. He approved whole-heartedly and left promising to help. But over and above everything, I awaited with impatience the return of Mr. Schiff. I expected that he would visit us on the Jewish New Year, as he had always done. He did not disappoint me. He called on New Year's afternoon. I did not know Mr. Schiff really well. It was my husband's friend that he had been, drawn to him by respect for his scholarship and personality. I wondered whether he would possibly transfer his friendship to me.

That New Year's afternoon I lost no time in telling him how necessary it was for me to earn money, how I had hunted for work, and that my efforts to write for newspapers had been unsuccessful. He listened without comment. Then I decided it was time to be bold, for the sake of my children. I mentioned the lectures I had prepared and asked whether I could not deliver them in his home under his wife's patronage.

To my dismay, he discouraged me. Another hope gone. The field of opportunities was gradually narrowing. I wondered which of my plans would materialize. Clearly, it was to be a hard struggle for existence. And just as clearly, so it seemed at the time, Mr. Schiff had no interest in the Kohut family, but had merely called to pay a formal visit of condolence to Alexander Kohut's widow.

How delightfully surprising, therefore, when two or three days later a note came from Mrs. Schiff saying she was deeply interested in my plan and would be pleased to have my lectures held in her drawing-room. The skies brightened.

The lectures were not to commence for several months. My oldest sister in San Francisco had been writing me letter after letter importuning me to pay her a visit. I had been unwilling to leave New York while there was uncertainty as to my future, but now that the lectures under favorable auspices had been arranged for, I was glad to go back to my old home. The strain of the previous year had told upon my health, and I felt that from my sister, who had always been like a second mother to me, I would gather new courage for the ordeal of life.

Eight years had passed since I had left San Francisco, fresh from the academic world. A girl of dreams, I had been put to no ordinary test in those years. The woman who returned had lived on an abnormal scale. She had risked all upon a great love and had known joys and heavy responsibilities and heavier sorrows.

I renewed my San Francisco friendships and found that here, too, life had marched on. Some it had seared, some crowned with glory. Others were as I had left them, merely older.

With Esther, sister of understanding spirit, I found peace. Whatever my experience of the last years, I was still the little sister to her, and she knew how to comfort and gladden little sisters.

And while I rested in the West, forces were at work in the East which were to bring the answer to my spiritual problems and put into my hands the means whereby I should always walk in the paths blazed by my father and husband and feel that they were constantly there with me, my deeply loved companions and leaders.

As I have already said, a new factor had come into the life of Jewish women in America, the National Council of Jewish Women. Each of the women who had taken part in the original World's Fair Congress had been charged with the organization of a Council section in her locality. While my husband was still alive, Minnie D. Louis had called an organization meeting in New York and had invited me to attend it. But at that time, I had no interest outside of my husband's sick room. I was later told of the clash that had occurred at the meeting, of the dissension between women of Orthodox and Reform beliefs, and the gloom over the differences, which seemed to preclude the successful organization of a New York section.

A few days after I arrived in San Francisco a telegram came from Minnie D. Louis asking me to accept the presidency of the

New York section. I was not at the house when it arrived and my sister told me nothing of it as she wanted me to have a complete rest during my stay and not be concerned about the future. But she was proud and elated over the honor done me, and believed that the responsibility would give me the desired interest outside the home. So she wired back acceptance. A few days later there was another telegram from Mrs. Louis instructing me to stop at Chicago on the way East and confer with Hannah Solomon, the national president, and Sadie American, the national secretary. This telegram, too, was withheld from me.

It was not until the end of my stay, when I was filled with new courage and the desire to live not in retrospect but in the problems of the present, that my sister broke the news. Conceive of my surprise. The thing was farthest from my thoughts. However, I approved of what my sister had done, and looked forward eagerly to my duties in this new movement which so completely had my sympathy. In Chicago I was apprised of everything that had developed since the National Council had been formed. The day after my arrival in New York the first meeting of the executive committee of the New York section was held. Mrs. Louis introduced me to the committee, most of whom were unknown to me, as I to them. Before the session was over, it was evident that we were all ardent Jewesses, anxious to make our contribution to the welfare of our people and the preservation of our religion.

It was a gathering of real Jewish women notables, women who, though they made a name for themselves in the world, were all lovable persons whom I think of with affection and tenderness.

There was Julia Richman, the brilliant educator whose name has been immortalized through the naming of a girls' high school in New York after her.

There was Minnie D. Louis, sweet singer in Israel and Southern aristocrat, who, as I have already mentioned, founded the Hebrew Technical School for Girls.

There was Esther S. Ruskay, the fine poetess and fearless champion of Orthodoxy. Her home was always the stimulating center of a young intellectual group.

There was Mrs. Frederick Nathan, later president of the Consumers' League, and Sarah Lyons and Minnie Isaacs, all three representatives of the Sephardi (Spanish-Portuguese) Jews, some of whom settled in America in pre-Colonial days and took part in the Revolutionary War. The father of Sarah Lyons was the minister of the Sephardi synagogue and was the childhood friend and neighbor of Emma and Josephine Lazarus. Minnie Isaacs, who became secretary of the council, and did her work with modest, quiet charm, was the daughter of Judge Myer S. Isaacs, whose father founded the *Jewish Messenger*.

Then there were two women who were among the first confirmants at Temple Emanu-El, Dinah Gitterman and the wife of Judge David L. Leventritt.

And finally there was one whom life brought closest to me of all and made my lifelong friend, though we had had a sharp clash of opinions the first time we met, and have had again several times since. That's the sort of person Hannah B. Einstein is. She has a marked individuality. There are no half-ways with her. Beautiful, radiant, maintaining a lavish house and table, you'd have taken her at first sight for a spoiled darling. The fact is that though she was born and raised in luxury, the sufferings of the poor, sufferings of any sort, obsessed her. I truly believe that the reason she was first drawn to me was that I wore a widow's veil.

She and I had come together at the Emanu-El Sisterhood, where she was for giving without too many questions asked. But the world had outgrown indiscriminate alms-giving; the era of "scientific charity" had begun, in which the head must rule—but not stifle—the heart. If a poor girl wanted a silk dress with a train, Mrs. Einstein was for giving her the silk dress and the train. My idea was to help the girl to secure the silk dress and the train herself by her own efforts. (Though, as a rule, when people work for a thing, they outgrow, metaphorically speaking, silk-dress ambitions.) The Emanu-El Sisterhood, I think, is a model of a relief-giving agency, in which the head and heart operate in perfect balance.

The Council brought every sort of personality into its fold, people of the aggressive organizing type, of the modest retiring sort, women who were lukewarm about their religion, women who were intensely religious, members of the old families, and some of the latest comers to America.

Mrs. Isabella Freedman, for instance, has an intensity of religious feeling such as I have seldom encountered, and it is natural that when the Council was organized her strong devotion to her people and her faith should have made her one of the first to join.

Mrs. Julius Beer, the mother of a large family, is a fine representative of one of the old German-Jewish families, the Walters, who could have boasted a coach-and-pair, having come to America and grown well-to-do decades before the immigrations of the 'eighties. Her parents were members of Temple Emanu-El when it worshipped on the second floor of a house on Second Avenue.

The situation in the New York section required delicate handling, owing to the dissension among the factions. As president I was acceptable to both sides. While my personal leanings were toward progressive Judaism, the fact that I was Alexander Kohut's widow gave me the approval of the Conservatives.

As soon as I could get my bearings, and after many conferences with Gustav Gottheil and H. Pereira Mendes, representing the two factions, I called the first meeting of the board of trustees and invited the Jewish Board of Ministers to be present. There were many questions to be settled, and many heated discussions might be expected before we could commence work of a constructive nature. I endeavored to be fair to both sides. After all, we were and wished to be known as children of Israel, and I felt that the principles of each of us was a matter of individual concern. Whether Orthodox or Conservative or Reform, we could meet upon the common ground of social service. As we expected tolerance from the Christian world, we could, by the same principle, be tolerant toward each other.

The Board of Ministers were patient and kind. I fear, though, that they may have been a bit skeptical. Perhaps they thought the future of Judaism was sufficiently safeguarded by the rabbis of the country. But they realized, I know, that a new movement had been inaugurated, and that the Jewish women of the United

States were not only prepared to take their place with the women of the world, but also would be in the forefront in congregational activities.

We planned that the first open meeting of the council should be conducted in peace. Nevertheless, it developed into a stormy debate. From the meetings of the Women's Health Protective Association I had learned the essentials of parliamentary procedure. I was by no means gentle and demure when healthy rapping of the gavel was required. Bang! Bang! Bang! "You're out of order. You, too. You, too." For the chairman to waver, would have been to jeopardize the meeting. Soon all was serene and dignified. The meeting was a success. When it was over, Esther Ruskay, whom I hardly knew, rushed forward and kissed me heartily. Dr. Kohler, ardent champion of Reform, congratulated me upon managing a difficult situation. Most of the rabbis credited me with having rabbinical training.

My first appearance among the Jewish women had not been a failure. I went home and wept—wept because Alexander Kohut was not there to share in my experiences, wept because after all I was a lonely widow.

So the first year of widowhood found me busy indeed. I had not much time for reflection. Between the managing of the home, the delivering of lectures in Mrs. Schiff's drawing-room, the presidency of the New York Council, and participation in the affairs of several other organizations, my daily life seemed apportioned not by the hour but by the minute. As a tribute to Dr. Kohut's congregation, I volunteered as teacher in the Sabbath School. The pressure of work in all directions made me feel that my life had not ended, but that only a chapter of it had been closed and I was beginning a new era. My circle of acquaintances widened rapidly. I was invited to speak before many of the new Council sections, which sprang up in cities all over the country in answer to a real need.

Many friends questioned the advisability of my attempting so much public work. There were moments when I, too, wondered whether my outside interests were not overshadowing my home life. It was a period in American history when women's careers were looked upon askance. There was much unreasoning objection to women's public activities. But I continued as I had begun. My sisters and I had always felt that while a woman's interests ought to begin at home and ought to end there, they need not necessarily confine themselves to it alone.

A number of positions were offered to me, one or two rather remunerative. But my lectures at Mrs. Schiff's home were proving financially successful and my outside work was so interesting that I wanted things to continue as they were. Though I had a lurking fear that of the two or three hundred women who attended the lectures, many came in a spirit of curiosity or perhaps pity, certainly not for literary information, and though I was quite sure the work was of no educational value, yet it was more pleasant than other methods of earning a livelihood and had more to recommend it than the editing of a social column in a Jewish weekly or the writing of a necessarily amateurish homiletic for Jewish mothers. Cheered by the encouragement of Mr. and Mrs. Schiff, and the devotion of some of my new-found friends, I determined to continue the lectures for at least another year.

In time one of my daughters became a kindergarten teacher and was able to support herself, but soon our regular source of income to the family budget, the money George earned by tutoring, was cut off.

He had been continuing his studies for the rabbinate, begun during his father's lifetime, at Columbia University and the Jewish Theological Seminary. The question of how they were to be concluded remained to be settled, and his health had also to be taken into account.

Delicate from birth, suffering from pulmonary weakness since early childhood, he had always been a subject of concern to his parents; and we had adopted the practice of having him follow the sun, going south in the winter and north in summer. Isaac M. Wise, who was in New York at the time, visited us. He urged George to attend the Hebrew Union College of Cincinnati, but we were loath to have him identified with an institution whose teachings were so opposed to Alexander Kohut's views. So Dr.

Wise, Dr. Gottheil, George, and myself conferred. The two fine, broad-minded ministers helped us to decide that perhaps a European training would be more sympathetic to his father's ideals. Besides, our family physician believed that Europe for a year or two would be better than America.

Dr. Gottheil, realizing better than myself the financial difficulties, insisted upon our accepting a small stipend from the funds of the Emanu-El Theological School—once quite active—to go toward George's European education. He overcame my scruples by citing the cases of one or two of the most prominent younger rabbis who had been sent to Europe in this way. Yet it was a great relief when several months later I was able to return the money.

I have never enjoyed being under obligations of this sort and have tried to avoid them as much as possible. Perhaps my efforts to provide everything for myself and my children have at times been too foolishly independent. I felt I could fight fate, carve out my own career and that of the youngsters, and carry the day against the cross currents of life, against those deep-lying, inscrutable forces which mold people willy-nilly. And so I laid out a stern path for myself to travel. I insisted upon carrying the financial burden alone. I even declined an offer from my oldest brother-in-law in San Francisco, who was in comfortable circumstances, to help me with the education and maintenance of the children.

About this time an unusual event was scheduled to take place in Washington, D. C. A movement had been under way to call a Mother's Congress to discuss the status of family life in the United States from the mother's point of view. The financial sponsor of the congress was Phoebe Hearst, famous California philanthropist, who had been a school chum of my teacher, Mary Kincaid. The honorary president of the congress was Mrs. Grover Cleveland, that charming woman whose radiant personality won the love of all American women. The active president of the congress was Rachel Foster Avery.

To my surprise I learned that my leadership in the Council in New York had reached the ears of some of the women who were organizing the congress. I received a formal invitation to represent Jewish women at the congress and to deliver an address upon the subject of "Parental Reverence in the Jewish Home."

The invitation came at a time when I was feeling the strain of my many activities. To prepare such an address required time and concentration, which I felt I could not give it. The problem for me was how to conserve energy rather than to add new responsibilities. The subject appealed to me, and yet. . . . In an impulsive moment I wrote to the secretary of the congress that I was unable to accept the invitation and asked to be allowed to suggest some other name.

The same day I met Dr. Gottheil. He was angry at me, and insisted that I telegraph immediately requesting indulgence of a woman's privilege of changing her mind. A reply soon came, expressing pleasure at the reconsideration. Dr. Gottheil and myself discussed the subject and I set to work to study it. Its importance grew on me, and I worked on it enthusiastically. Dr. Gottheil assured me I was performing a genuine mission. I rewrote the paper several times and submitted each draft for his approval.

In my father's home parental reverence had been the natural and accepted course. I remember his telling us of a great rabbi's statement that the fifth commandment, "Honor thy Father and thy Mother," had been placed between the other commandments as a bridge between man's love of God and man's duty to man. Both in my father's home and in my husband's home the children grew up imbued with love and reverence for their parents. I have stated often from platform and pulpit that if we were to go back to the old biblical standards, the future fathers and mothers of the race would be better equipped for their responsibilities, and the integrity of the home be safeguarded.

The Congress of Mothers was attracting nationwide attention. Mrs. Cleveland presided at the first session, and Mrs. Hearst crossed the continent to attend. There was such a large gathering that the great hall over the Central Market was inadequate. The speakers were asked to repeat their addresses to the overflow meetings.

When I entered the hall I saw, seated upon the platform, Mary Kincaid. Instantly the awe I had felt in her presence when a girl came upon me again. Gone were all my worldly experience, all the maturity of the crowded years. I was not the Council president, the widow, the stepmother of eight children, the lecturer and teacher, but a San Francisco school girl, afraid to approach her principal.

Stage fright was a new experience for me. Judge Mayer Sulzberger, a splendid orator, once told me he never spoke well unless he felt very nervous before his appearance. I recalled the judge's words as my knees trembled and my teeth chattered, and I tried to convince myself that I was going to speak very well. But I di-di-di-di-di-didn't thi-thi-thi-thi-thi-think so. My stage fright came as the result of the sudden sight of Mary Kincaid, and of my having exaggerated the importance of the occasion and the weight of my responsibility. I was the only Jewess on the three-day program. Suppose the audience, which seemed entirely Christian (later I learned this was not so), found the address not worthy of the meeting. Suppose I did not prove a fitting representative for my sister Jewesses. It was not until after I had commenced and heard the sound of my voice that I gained courage. I believe that my extemporaneous speeches have always been better than my set ones. I had only read a few words when, inspired by the scene, I laid the paper down and departed from the written address, though not from the subject.

After tracing biblical reasons for parental reverence, I told my audience that when the Jew was driven from the Temple and walked out into the world, he soon found that Christians locked him up behind ghetto walls, visible and invisible. They robbed him of the right to nearly every pursuit. All they left him was his home and the right to study the law. So he learned to value the only possessions he had and the love of the home and the respect of children for their parents were not only fostered but accentuated. Therefore, I concluded, I, as a Jewess, thanked those who had deprived us of so much that we might have contributed, because in doing so they preserved and strengthened the love of parents for children and the respect of children for their parents, which is a peculiarly Jewish virtue.

I resumed my seat amid applause, and was thanked by Mrs. Cleveland for my address. But neither Mrs. Hearst nor Mary Kincaid approached me, though they had congratulatd the previous speakers.

What was the applause to me, then? I feared I had not done well, and Mary Kincaid did not approve of me, and Mrs. Hearst was angry. As soon as the morning session was over, I hurried to my hotel, even neglecting to attend the White House luncheon to which the speakers were invited. Once more lonesomeness came upon me, and I bemoaned the difficulty of doing everything alone. I had the wonderful help of kind friends, but I needed that great moral inspiring influence which Alexander Kohut had been.

A few minutes later there was a knock at the door—Mrs. Hearst's coachman bringing a large bunch of violets from his mistress and a note from Mary Kincaid: "God bless you, Rebekah, I'm proud of you. Mrs. Hearst and I will be over soon." When they came in, I fell upon Mary Kincaid's shoulder and wept. She hadn't suspected that Mrs. Alexander Kohut was her one-time pupil, and had been so startled and dumb-founded that she failed to greet me.

My address was translated into many languages and distributed throughout the world. I received a letter from the secretary of the Congress informing me that at the request of the Empress of Japan it had been translated into Japanese. Thus, in a measure, recognition had come to me through my first appearance before a non-Jewish audience.

At the Congress I had the pleasure of meeting the Rev. Anna Howard Shaw and Susan B. Anthony, two of the greatest of American women. Dr. Shaw expressed considerable interest in my address, and asked me why the Jewess had not emerged from the home and taken up her position with the others of her sex in fighting for women's rights. I was glad I could inform her of the recent organization of the Council and the remarkable progress already made. Her face shone.

Of course, I placed no great value upon the literary qualities of this or any other address, but I did decide that if the Christian world could hear what we had to say, it would serve to bring a

AUTOBIOGRAPHIES OF AMERICAN JEWS

better understanding between Jew and Gentile. So I determined that no longer would I regard my personal interest but would also accept opportunities to appear before Christian audiences.

Later I was asked to address the pupils of the fashionable and exclusive Ely School. I could see that these lovely girl pupils giggled when I was presented as a Jewess. I was determined to have my revenge, and in my talk made them so homesick for their parents that they wept. Then I told them part of the story of Heine's *Princess Sabbath* and the *Rabbi of Bacharach,* in which the ghetto Jew carries the burden typical of his race through the ages. On Sabbath eve, returning from the synagogue and entering his little home, he finds the table set with snowy cloth and lighted candles and the Sabbath bread, and becomes transformed not only in figure but in face. The bowed shoulders straighten, light enters his eyes. Is he not then a Prince of Israel, and is not his home a palace? The girls giggled no more at the mention of "Jew."

One of the meetings I was asked to address was the Women's Christian Temperance Union. Obviously their idea of a Jew or Jewess had been built upon the sort of misinformation common to people who live remote from the world, as most of them did. They were one more confirmation of my father's statement that people with only a smattering of knowledge readily believe the fantastic. To these women, wholly unacquainted with Jews, it was a revelation to come face to face with a Jewess who had neither distorted features nor spoke a distorted language. Their imagination, fed on bizarre pictures and grotesque literature, had led them to expect a caricature.

Miss Ely and the Women's Christian Temperance Union both wanted to remunerate me. I refused a fee. I always felt that it would be exploitation of my religion and my Jewishness to be compensated for expounding my favorite subjects to Christian audiences. The once or twice in my life that I tried speaking for pay, I was an utter failure. Being at my best as an extemporaneous speaker, the thought that I was speaking for hire put a damper on my eloquence. To be paid for teaching seemed right, but not to plead the cause of Judaism, especially before Christians. Love of one's faith, and devotion to the cause of one's people, should be worth a sacrifice. During all the years when the family budget was so puny, I never accepted emolument for public addresses.

While pursuing his studies in Berlin, George became critically ill. Taking the two younger daughters I went abroad to be with him. In Berlin we were met by three of his fellow-students, Dr. Paul Rieger, Dr. Hermann Vogelstein and Dr. Samuel Posnanski, all of whom won renown later for scholarship.

The next three months were spent in nursing George and bringing back his strength. We left him reluctantly, but more or less consoled that he was to have the loving care and devotion of Moritz Steinschneider and his wife, who did all they could for him, and drew him into the family group not only because they had known his father, but also because of their deep personal affection for the son.

Professor Steinschneider was world-renowned as a bibliographer, and was known locally as one of the characters of Berlin's academic circles. There were many anecdotes in circulation about him, for one thing that he had worn the same overcoat for forty years. During my stay in Berlin he received an honorary professorship at the age of eighty. The university named a distinguished committee to make the presentation. At the head of it was Mommsen, Germany's greatest historian. But Professor Steinschneider was nowhere to be found. Finally they discovered him in a corner of the Königliche Bibliothek, engrossed in an ancient tome. With great formality they presented him with the parchment. "Ah, yes, thank you," the venerable scholar said, wondering what all the fuss was about, and returned to his reading. He stuffed the paper in his overcoat pocket, and then completely forgot about it. His wife, whom I had nicknamed George Eliot because she looked like her, found the honor certificate late in the afternoon as it fell out of his pocket, and cried: "Moritz, why did you not tell me you had become a professor?"

"I forgot," was his reply.

We were often invited to tea at the Steinschneiders' and spent many happy evenings laughing over quaint stories told by or about him.

From Berlin we went for the remainder of the summer to

Reichenau, a beautiful health resort near Vienna. Here my son recuperated wonderfully. The little hotel at which we stayed for many weeks was built almost into the mountain, and surrounded by a fragrant pine forest.

An experience I had there made our vacation a never-to-be-forgotten one.

It was the first Friday evening of our stay. As we sat on the veranda chatting with the inn-keeper, we saw a man approaching from the road who looked uncommonly like my husband. He was tall; perhaps not as tall as Alexander Kohut, but of imposing stature; his face spoke eloquently of the man's soul and self-command. He had very white skin, large blue eyes, and a blue-black beard, neatly trimmed. I started as if I had suddenly seen an apparition of my husband, though a changed one.

He ascended the steps of the veranda and greeted the landlord, who turned to me and presented, "Dr. Theodor Herzl," the great prophet of Israel who had founded the Zionist movement and fired the imagination of his people with his conception of a Jewish state, who sought to make his dream reality, and traveled throughout the world in an endeavor to enlist the sympathy and support of monarchs and governments.

He had come to pay his weekly visit to his parents, who were spending the summer at Reichenau. His fame had already spread over the whole globe, and the Zionist movement was growing with amazing rapidity. I had heard and read so much about his personality and his book *The Jewish State,* which so revolutionized the thought of Jews everywhere, that I considered it an almost sacred privilege to be able to discuss these things with the man himself. He presented me with a copy of his book and spoke quietly of the progress of his work.

At the time of my meeting with Herzl I was not in sympathy with the founding of a Jewish State. I was an ardent American, almost chauvinistic in my patriotism for the land of my father's adoption. In conversation with the Zionist leader, I told him that my husband's grandfather had gone to Jerusalem to spend the last of his life and had been buried by the wall there, and I also spoke of the yearnings of Alexander Kohut to live and die in the Holy Land.

"Speaking for myself," I continued, "I should like to visit Palestine, but I should want to be assured of a round-trip ticket."

Instantly I realized the bad taste of what I had said. To disagree was honest and fair enough, but my remark was tantamount to a sneer, and was in keeping with the legendary anti-Zionist statement: "I am in favor of a Jewish State if I can be appointed Jewish Ambassador to Paris." The remark caused me misery. Herzl, however, took it quietly and tolerantly.

He came to Reichenau every week-end for thirteen weeks. By the end of that time I was a Zionist, converted by the great Herzl himself. In several walks together and many conversations, he gave me a real understanding of the solution of the problems of thousands of our persecuted brethren, and the fulfillment of the prophecy that we should be returned to the land of our fathers.

His ideas came at a time in the world's history when Jews were ripe for the espousal of them; they have become a part of world affairs and world movements. Yet it is undeniable that his personal charm aided greatly in their acceptance. Without his personality—magnetic, inspiring, but not demagogic—the cause of Zionism would not have taken root so quickly in the hearts of Jews the world over. Strangely enough, this man who developed into the leader of his people, pleading their cause before Kaiser, Sultan, Prime Minister, President, had at first been apathetic to Judaism, and his sudden emergence is one of the most fascinating and inspiring chapters in the history of his race.

A few years later, again in Europe, I was aboard a train bound for Vienna. At daybreak the train stopped at various stations outside the city and took on great crowds. It was unusually heavy traffic for that hour. I noted also that most of the passengers were Jewish men and women. I asked if anything special was going on. The man I addressed looked at me in astonishment. Did I not know, he asked, that the great Herzl was dead, and that his funeral was to take place that morning. The sad and dreadful news stunned me.

As soon as we arrived in Vienna, after seeing to my luggage, I hurried to the Herzl home to attend the service.

It was not difficult to learn where his home was. All the streets seemed to be filled with processions going there. I was fortunate enough, through presenting my card as an American and a news-paper correspondent, to enter the home and finally to join in the immediate procession of mourners. The only other American at the house was Seraphine Pisko, Secretary of the National Jewish Hospital for Consumptives.

Thousands walked to the cemetery through a human aisle two miles long, through a chain of young Zionists who stood clasping one another's hands.

One of the mourners explained the significance of the chain. "The Jews will never forget the teachings of Herzl and the service he rendered, and the chain of those who loved him must never be broken."

I dispatched an account of the funeral to an American weekly.

OSCAR S. STRAUS

Oscar Straus was the first Jew ever named to a Cabinet post by an American President. In 1905, Theodore Roosevelt selected him to serve as Secretary of the Department of Commerce and Labor. This was the highlight of his public career, but it was only one of many significant posts held by this outstanding American Jew.

Straus was born in Germany in 1850 and died in New York City in 1926. In 1887, President Grover Cleveland named him Envoy Extraordinary and Minister Plenipotentiary to Turkey. He was reappointed to this position by President Benjamin Harrison.

Theodore Roosevelt chose him to succeed ex-President Harrison as the American member of the Permanent Court of Arbitration at The Hague. He was reappointed to this influential job by Roosevelt in 1908 and by Woodrow Wilson in 1912 and 1920. President William Howard Taft selected him as his Ambassador to Turkey. In 1912, Mr. Straus ran as a candidate for Governor of New York on the Progressive Party ticket. Although he was defeated, he made a better showing at the polls than Theodore Roosevelt, who was the Progressive Party's presidential candidate.

Straus, in his brilliant diplomatic career, frequently represented the Jews at conferences abroad, and was chairman of a fund-raising campaign following the Kishinev pogrom.

He served under six Presidents of the United States; met with Theodor Herzl; visited Palestine and was, altogether, one of the notable Jews of his time. He was active in the Jewish Publication Society, American Jewish Committee, and was President of the American Jewish Historical Society from its inception in 1892 to 1898.

In his autobiography, Under Four Administrations, *Mr. Straus detailed the activities of his life. In the chapter included here he recounts his relationship with President Theodore Roosevelt, beginning in 1901, and discusses some of the significant events in which he played a major role.*

Theodore Roosevelt*

OSCAR S. STRAUS

I BEGAN THE YEAR 1901 as a private citizen once more. I devoted much of my time, however, to public activities, giving close attention particularly to the international questions that arose.

The doctrine of citizenship and the rights of naturalized American citizens in foreign countries had for many years formed the major subject in our foreign relations, and it had been one of constant controversy between our own and foreign countries, especially Germany, Austria, and Turkey. In the spring I read a paper at a meeting of the American Social Science Association, of which I was the president, entitled "The United States Doctrine of Citizenship and Expatriation." Later in the year I received, in consequence, a letter from Senator S. M. Cullom of Illinois, chairman of the Senate Committee on Foreign Relations, asking me to prepare material for amendments to legislation on this subject, which I did.

When Theodore Roosevelt became President of the United States through the lamentable death of William McKinley, one of my earliest relations with him was my being appointed by him as a member of the Permanent Court of Arbitration at The

---

* Reprinted from *Under Four Administrations,* Houghton Mifflin Company, Boston and New York, 1922, pp. 163–193.

Hague. Whether or not he acted herein in conformity with Mc-Kinley's intention, I cannot say. When McKinley was selecting the original members, he conferred with me and indicated that if agreeable to me, he would be pleased to appoint me as a member. Shortly afterward when the appointments were announced, my name was not among them. It was some time before I saw him again, and while I should never have mentioned it, he did. He said he was very sorry that through the pressure of duties he had quite forgotten his intention to name me when the time came to announce the appointments. I told him I thought perhaps I had been mistaken in understanding that he had offered me one of the appointments. He said I had not misunderstood, but that he would make amends should a vacancy occur while he was still President; he had wanted me as a member of the Court, not alone in recognition of the great services I had rendered, but because he regarded me as exceptionally qualified. He added that when he became ex-President he would like to be a member of that Court himself; it appealed to him more than any other office he could think of.

The vacancy in the membership of the Court occurred sooner than any one anticipated, by the death, in March, 1901, of ex-President Harrison; but by the decree of the gods McKinley himself was no longer with us when the time came to fill President Harrison's place. In fact I think the day we talked about the Court marked my last conference with him. He was always simple in manner and of charming personality. Together we enjoyed a good smoke that afternoon; he was fond of smoking and knew I enjoyed a good cigar, and he was wont to have me take one of his brand. I begged him not to concern himself further with the omission of my appointment at The Hague, that I was satisfied to know he thought me worthy of the selection.

It is possible that Roosevelt knew the circumstance and Mc-Kinley's intention, for he was Vice-President at the time it happened. At any rate, when the successor to President Harrison was chosen, I received the following appointment, somewhat different in form from most documents of the kind:

WHITE HOUSE
WASHINGTON, *January 8, 1902*

MY DEAR SIR:

Article XX of the Convention for the Pacific Settlement of International Disputes, signed July 29, 1899, by the Plenipotentiaries to the Hague Peace Conference, provides for the organization of a permanent Court of Arbitration, and Article XXIII of the same Convention provides for the selection by each of the signatory Powers of four persons at the most, as members of the Court, who are to be appointed for a term of six years.

It will give me pleasure to designate you as one of the four United States members if you will advise me that such action is agreeable to you.

Very Truly Yours,
THEODORE ROOSEVELT

HONORABLE OSCAR S. STRAUS
New York, N.Y.

Since then I have been reappointed three times: in 1908, again by Roosevelt, 1912 and 1920, by Wilson.

In April, 1902, there appeared in the press a dispatch to the effect that an expedition of twelve hundred men was to be sent to the southern Philippines to punish the Mohammedans there for killing one of our soldiers and wounding several others. I immediately wrote the President that I believed such a step would be unwise and would probably bring on a general uprising in that province. I called his attention to the negotiation I had had with the Sultan of Turkey regarding these people, and suggested that instead of the expedition a commission be sent to treat with them. The President asked me to come to Washington to confer with him in the matter, and after the Cabinet meeting I met him in his study. There were present also Mr. Taft, who had been appointed governor of the Philippines, Adjutant-General Corbin, and Mr. Sanger, acting Secretary of War. I presented my arguments more fully. The President had already telegraphed General Chaffee regarding the sending of a diplomatic mission, in accordance with my letter.

The result of our conference was that General Corbin was

directed to advise General Chaffee to use the office of the friendly datos to obtain the desired redress. It developed later that the soldier killed was laying a telegraph line, which procedure, not being understood by the Moros, was regarded by them as a device for their destruction. The slayers were surrendered and punished and the incident was satisfactorily adjusted.

At about this time disturbances in Rumania were being reflected in our country. Eleven years before, a committee of prominent Jews had brought before President Harrison the pitiable condition of the large number of Jews arriving in New York from Russia, and it was now necessary to take similar steps with regard to the Jews from Rumania.

In chapter IV I mentioned that Rumania disregarded the provisions of the Treaty of Berlin and placed restrictions upon her Jewish subjects. Into that treaty, by which Rumania was made an independent kingdom following the Russo-Turkish War, Article XLIV was inserted specially for the protection of the Jews, of whom there were about four hundred thousand in the new state. It provided that difference of religion should not be ground for exclusion in the participation of civil, political, or economic rights. In spite of this, however, the Jews in Rumania were being oppressed and discriminated against on the specious claim that they were foreigners, though they and their ancestors had been living in the land for generations. They were compelled to serve in the army, but not permitted to become officers; they were made subject to exceptional taxes; they were excluded from the professions and from owning and cultivating land. In every direction they were being throttled, and new laws were being promulgated to shut off every avenue of self-support.

The result was what had doubtless been the intention in putting into force these drastic measures: the Jews who could emigrated, and they left Rumania *en masse*. The obstacles in the way of their gaining admission into the countries of Western Europe were so great that few of them could settle there. The leading Jewish organizations of Great Britain and France, namely, the Jewish Colonization Association in London and the Alliance Israélite Universelle in Paris, laid the matter before their respective governments, but, on account of the disturbed conditions in the Balkans and the cross-currents of European politics, no pressure could be exerted through these governments.

The main stream of the Rumanian exodus was thus directed to America, and they arrived here in increasing numbers. The leading Jewish agencies of the country, particularly the B'nai B'rith Order under the presidency of Leo N. Levi, used their best efforts to distribute the immigrants over the country and to places where they were most likely to find employment. Later our very able commissioner of immigration at Ellis Island, Robert Watchorn, went over to Rumania for the special purpose of studying the situation and made a graphic report of what he learned. But to alleviate the situation action of a more official character was needed.

Jacob H. Schiff and I prepared a careful brief on conditions and presented it to President Roosevelt. The President said he was willing to take the matter in hand provided something could be done by our Government. Congressman Lucius N. Littauer also extended helpful cooperation. He had recently returned from Rumania and had first-hand knowledge of the question, which he took up in conferences with the President and with Secretary Hay.

Finally, in September, 1902, the President directed Secretary Hay to prepare his now famous Rumanian Note to the Powers signatory to the Treaty of Berlin. The note was sent to our diplomatic representatives in those countries with instructions to present it to the governments to which they were accredited. The occasion for sending it was found in connection with negotiations initiated by Rumania for the concluding of a naturalization treaty with our country. The note gave the reasons why, under the circumstances, we were unwilling to conclude such a treaty. After referring to the Treaty of Berlin and the obligations assumed by Rumania under it regarding the treatment of subject nationalities, the Secretary said:

The United States offers asylum to the oppressed of all lands. But its sympathy with them in no wise impairs its just liberty and right to weigh the acts of the oppressor in the light of their effects upon this country, and to judge accordingly.

Putting together the facts, now painfully brought home to this Government, during the past few years, that many of the inhabitants of Rumania are being forced by artificially adverse discriminations to quit their native country; that the hospitable asylum offered by this country is almost the only refuge left to them; that they come hither unfitted by the conditions of their exile to take part in the new life of this land under circumstances either profitable to themselves or beneficial to the community, and that they are objects of charity from the outset and for a long time—the right of remonstrance against the acts of the Rumanian Government is clearly established in favor of this Government. Whether consciously and of purpose or not, these helpless people, burdened and spurned by their native land, are forced by the sovereign power of Rumania upon the charity of the United States. This Government can not be a tacit party to such an international wrong. It is constrained to protest against the treatment to which the Jews of Rumania are subjected, not alone because it has unimpeachable ground to remonstrate against the resultant injury to itself, but in the name of humanity. The United States may not authoritatively appeal to the stipulations of the treaty of Berlin, to which it was not and can not become a signatory, but it does earnestly appeal to the principles consigned therein, because they are the principles of international law and eternal justice, advocating the broad toleration which that solemn compact enjoins and standing ready to lend its moral support to the fulfillment thereof by its cosignatories, for the act of Rumania itself has effectively joined the United States to them as an interested party in this regard.

One of the most valuable by-products of the Congress of Berlin was to bring into closer relations the autocratic with the liberal governments of Europe and cause the former to become more amenable to the enlightened conscience of the world. Hay's dispatch, while not pleasing to the Government of Rumania, yet, because of the world-wide publicity it received, had a measure of influence in modifying Rumania's indefensible proscriptions.

Another need for humanitarian diplomacy arose the following year. The attitude and proscriptions of the Rumanian authorities had doubtless encouraged anti-Semitic activity in Russia, and the latter Government, no longer contenting itself with the application of restrictions in the book of laws which compelled Jews to live in the Pale settlements, officially encouraged mobs to massacre and loot, culminating on April 19–20, 1903, with the outbreak in Kishinev, where forty-seven Jews were killed, ninety-two severely wounded, and some five hundred more slightly injured. In addition great material losses were inflicted: seven hundred houses were destroyed, six hundred stores pillaged, and thousands of families utterly ruined.

When these facts became known, they called forth an expression of indignation throughout the civilized world. In New York a mass meeting was called at Carnegie Hall by hundreds of the foremost New York Christians, in protest against the outrages upon the Jews in Russia and particularly against the Kishinev affair. The meeting was presided over by Paul D. Cravath, eminent lawyer, and the speakers were ex-President Cleveland, Mayor Seth Low, Jacob G. Schurman, president of Cornell, and Edward M. Shepard, well known for his unselfish devotion to the interests of the public. I have in my possession the manuscript of Cleveland's address on this occasion, which concludes:

In the meantime, let the people of the United States, gathered together in such assemblages as this in every part of the land, fearlessly speak to the civilized world—protesting against every pretense of civilization that permits medieval persecution, against every bigoted creed that forbids religious toleration and freedom of conscience, against all false enlightenment that excuses hatred and cruelty towards any race of men, and against all spurious forms of government protection, that withhold from any human being the right to live in safety, and toil in peace.

I will also quote part of the resolutions adopted that evening:

Resolved, that the people of the United States should exercise such influence with the Government of Russia as the ancient and unbroken friendship between the two nations may justify to stay the spirit of persecution, to redress the injuries inflicted upon the Jews of Kishinev, and to prevent the recurrence of outbreaks such as have amazed the civilized world.

A few weeks later a committee from the B'nai B'rith Order, consisting of Simon Wolf, Adolf Moses, Julius Bien, Jacob Furth, Solomon Sulzberger, and Joseph D. Coons, and headed by their president, Leo N. Levi, called upon Secretary Hay and presented to him a statement regarding the massacres in Russia together with a proposed petition which they wished forwarded to the Government of the Czar. The Secretary expressed great sympathy and the desire to do what might be possible in the matter. His reply to the committee, taken down in shorthand at the time, was published in full in the press, and from it I quote the concluding sentence:

All we know of the state of things in Russia tends to justify the hope that even out of the present terrible situation some good results may come; that He who watches over Israel does not slumber, and that the wrath of man now, as so often in the past, shall be made to praise Him.

The Secretary then accompanied the committee to the White House, where they met the President and presented to him an outline of the oppression of their co-religionists in Russia.

Early in July I received a telegram from the President's secretary to the effect that the President would like to have me lunch with him the day following at Oyster Bay, and that Simon Wolf of Washington, and Leo N. Levi also had been invited. When I arrived at Sagamore Hill there were present besides those named Dr. Albert Shaw of the *Review of Reviews*, and an English friend of his, Mr. Morris Sheldon Amos.

We discussed the Russian situation throughout lunch. The President suggested that a note be sent by the Secretary of State to John W. Riddle, our chargé at St. Petersburg, and that this note should embody the entire petition which Mr. Levi and his committee had drafted. Dr. Shaw observed that the embodying of the petition to the Czar and giving publicity to the note would have all the effects of a presentation even if the Czar should refuse to receive it, which was exactly what the President had in mind.

After luncheon we adjourned to the study, and Roosevelt said: "Now let's finish this thing up." Hay had been to see him the day before and had left a memorandum. Roosevelt at once drafted the note with his own pen, using part of Hay's memorandum. The note was to be sent as an open cable. It read as follows:

RIDDLE
St. Petersburg
You are instructed to ask an audience of the Minister of Foreign Affairs and to make him the following communication:

Excellency: The Secretary of State instructs me to inform you that the President has received from a large number of prominent citizens of the United States of all religious affiliations, and occupying the highest positions in both public and private life, a respectful petition addressed to his Majesty the Emperor relating to the condition of the Jews in Russia and running as follows:

[Here is set out the petition.]

I am instructed to ask whether the petition will be received by your Excellency to be submitted to the gracious consideration of his Majesty. In that case the petition will be at once forwarded to St. Petersburg.

Roosevelt wanted the cable to be sent at once and was in a hurry to get it to Washington. One of his reasons was that the late Russian ambassador, Cassini, had been dismissed and was on his way back to Russia, and he wanted the note to reach the Russian Government before Cassini arrived in St. Petersburg. Mr. Wolf, who lived in Washington, was to take the drafted cable to Secretary Hay; but as he could not return that night the President asked whether I could take it so that it might be dispatched next morning. By ten o'clock the following morning I placed the draft in the Secretary's hands and it was immediately put on the wire.

In planning the cable as he did, the President was right in his anticipation. Duly the American chargé at St. Petersburg informed the State Department that the Russian Government, through its Minister of Foreign Affairs, had declined to receive or consider the petition. Nevertheless, its purpose was accomplished. Official Russia was made to realize the aroused indignation and the public protests of the civilized world. This in turn had a decided influence in checking, for the time being at least, similar outbreaks threatened throughout the empire, besides bringing to trial and punishment some of the leaders of the massacres.

That afternoon at Sagamore Hill, after the Russian matter had been disposed of, the President was talking to Dr. Shaw and me about the Alaskan boundary question. He pulled out a map showing the disputed boundary, and explained that three commissioners from the United States and three from Great Britain and Canada would take up the dispute for investigation. He argued that they were not arbiters and he refused to sign an arbitral agreement; if they did not agree, he would take the matter into his own hands; that the whole trouble arose from the fact that the Canadians had shoved down the boundary line after the discovery of gold. "Suppose a man pitches a tent on my grounds and claims them, and I want him to get off; and he says he won't get off, but will arbitrate the matter!" Roosevelt exclaimed. Then, turning to me, he added: "Straus, you are a member of the Hague Tribunal; don't you think I'm right?"

I calmly replied that as a member of the Hague Tribunal I should first have to hear what the other side had to say and therefore must reserve my judgment. And we all had a good laugh.

During the Venezuela controversy in 1902, Venezuela on the one side and Great Britain and Germany on the other, Roosevelt was very much incensed that Germany, with the feeble backing of England, should undertake a blockade against Venezuela to make the latter carry out certain agreements, and he promptly took steps to prevent it. Thereupon there was a disposition on the part of Germany to ask Roosevelt to arbitrate. Secretary Hay, it seems, favored such a course, but I strongly advised against it.

At a luncheon to which I was invited by the President early in November, 1903, the conditions in Panama came up as the principal topic of conversation. There were present on this occasion, besides Mr. and Mrs. Roosevelt, Cornelius N. Bliss, former Secretary of the Interior; John Clark Davis, of the *Philadelphia Ledger*; H. H. Kohlsaat, of Chicago; Lawrence F. Abbot, of *The Outlook*; and the President's brother-in-law, Lieutenant-Commander Cowles, of the Navy. News had been received that Panama had separated from Colombia and we were about to recognize Panama. In his informal way, as was his custom at luncheons, the President began to discuss the situation, referring to the fact that our treaty of 1846 was with New Granada, which afterwards became the United States of Colombia and then the Republic of Colombia, and that in that treaty we had guaranteed to protect the transit route. One of the questions raised was whether the treaty still held us to that obligation, notwithstanding these several changes of sovereignty.

The President was directing his remarks toward me, which was his way of signifying the particular person from whom he wanted to draw comment. I answered that it seemed to me, as I recollected the terms of the treaty, which I had recently read, that the change of sovereignty did not affect either our obligations or our rights; that I regarded them in the nature of a "covenant running with the land."

"That's fine! Just the idea!" Roosevelt replied, and as soon as luncheon was over, he requested me to express that idea to Hay. He scratched a few lines on a correspondence card asking Secretary Hay to go over with me the suggestion I had made and to work into the treaty the "covenant running with the land" idea.

That evening I called on the Secretary. He seized the idea at once and said he would make use of it in a statement he was just preparing for the press detailing the whole situation. The following day there was reported in the papers of the country the fact that the President, following a meeting of the Cabinet, had decided to recognize the *de facto* government of Panama; and then the detailed statement by Secretary Hay regarding the terms of the treaty, the history of the negotiations, and the subsequent development, covered several newspaper columns. It contained this paragraph:

It must not be lost sight of that this treaty is not dependent for its efficacy on the personnel of the signers or the name of the territory it affects. It is a covenant, as lawyers say, that runs with the land. The name of New Granada has passed away; its territory has been divided. But as long as the isthmus endures, the great geographical fact keeps alive the solemn compact which binds the holders of the territory to grant us freedom of transit, and binds us in return to safeguard for the isthmus and the world the exercise of that inestimable privilege.

A few days thereafter I received a short note from the President reading: "Your 'covenant running with the land' idea worked admirably. I congratulate you on it." And from my friend John Bassett Moore I received an amusing letter:

So you had a finger in the pie! I find a good deal of amusement in reflecting on the end reached from the premise of my memorandum; and almost as much on the conclusion reached from your suggestion. Perhaps, however, it is only a question of words—that is to say, it is, indifferently, a question of the "covenant running with the land" or a question of the "covenant running (*away!*) with the land"!!

Those luncheons at the White House were always pleasant and interesting occasions. One met there all kinds of people, of every station in life, but always people who stood for something and who interested the President. At the table Roosevelt would speak without apparent reserve and free from all official restraint, and I doubt whether these confidences were ever abused. By this means, too, he received the frank, unreserved statements and criticisms of his guests.

As an illustration of the range of personalities one would meet at the Roosevelt luncheons, I remember one day when Seth Bullock, a former sheriff of the Black Hills district and an intimate friend of Roosevelt during his cowboy days, sat next to Seth Low at the table. And in his *Autobiography* Roosevelt himself says:

No guests were ever more welcome at the White House than these old friends of the cattle ranches and the cow camps—the men with whom I had ridden the long circle and eaten at the tail-board of a chuck-wagon—whenever they turned up at Washington during my Presidency. I remember one of them who appeared at Washington one day just before lunch, a huge, powerful man who, when I knew him, had been distinctly a fighting character. It happened that on that day another old friend, the British Ambassador, Mr. Bryce, was among those coming to lunch. Just before we went in I turned to my cowpuncher friend and said to him with great solemnity, "Remember, Jim, that if you shot at the feet of the British Ambassador to make him dance, it would be likely to cause international complications"; to which Jim responded, with unaffected horror, "Why, Colonel, I shouldn't think of it, I shouldn't think of it!"

Mrs. Roosevelt is a most charming and cultured woman, typically the wife and mother. Literary and intellectual matters appeal to her, though her dominant note is the domestic one. I am sure she would have been just as happy as the mistress of a private household as the leading lady of the land in the White House, despite her great tact, sweetness, and simple dignity in filling the latter position.

The President was an omnivorous reader. He could read faster and remember better than any one I have ever known. On one occasion he recommended to me Ferrero's *Greatness and Decline of Rome,* which he had just finished in the original Italian, and which had been brought out in English by the Putnam house. Subsequently, too, I met this author at the White House, where he and his wife were the guests of the President for several days.

In January, 1904, a large conference was held in Washington of representatives of the various peace societies and other persons prominently interested in the calling of an international peace congress. George F. Seward, of New York, was chairman, and others connected with it were the Reverend Edward Everett Hale and Robert Treat Paine, of Boston; Henry St. George Tucker, of Virginia, Andrew Carnegie, and myself. Resolutions were adopted recommending the negotiation of a treaty with Great Britain whereby all differences between us which might fail of adjustment through diplomatic channels were to be submitted for arbitration to the Permanent Court at The Hague. It was further recommended that we enter into like treaties with other powers as soon as practicable. We called on the President and the resolutions were presented by Mr. Tucker; Mr. Carnegie and I each made a few remarks, which the President in turn answered with a brief address. When he had finished and we were all standing around him, Mr. Carnegie said to him, "I have just been congratulating Mr. Straus on the compliments you paid him, and suggested that he get a copy of that portion of your remarks to preserve for his children and grandchildren." Roosevelt immediately turned to Mr. Loeb, his secretary, and instructed him to send to me that portion of his remarks, adding: "And I meant every word I said." I trust I may be pardoned for the egotism which prompts me to incorporate it in these memoirs:

I have had from Mr. Straus aid that I can not over-estimate, for which I can not too much express my gratitude, in so much of the diplomatic work that has arisen in this administration—aid by suggestion, aid by actual work in helping me to carry out the suggestions; and Mr. Straus was one of the two or three men who first set my mind, after I came in as President, in the direction of doing everything that could be done for the Hague Tribunal, as that seemed to be the best way to turn for arbitration.

At another pleasant luncheon there was present Alice, now the wife of Congressman Longworth, of Ohio, Roosevelt's daughter by his first wife. In the course of our discussion about the reciprocity treaty with Cuba and the making of more favorable tariff arrangements, I said: "We went to war with Spain for the liberation of Cuba, and now if we treat her step-motherly and starve her to death, what would the world say?" There was hearty laughter all round the table, and Miss Alice turned to me and said, in her naïve way and with a mischievous sparkle in her eyes: "Do I look starved?" The President had fairly exploded with laughter, and when I remarked that I had "put my foot into it," he added, amid another outburst, "Yes, both of them!"

The President did not smoke, but always served cigars and cigarettes to his guests. When I did not take one, he said, "Straus, you smoke."

"Yes," I answered, "but I certainly want to pay as much respect to you as I always did to the Sultan of Turkey. He did not drink, and I never took any when it was served."

"You go right ahead and smoke. If Root were here he would smoke and always does," replied Roosevelt.

After lunch that day, when the other guests had gone, he and I went into an adjoining room and had a general discussion— labor matters, the National Civic Federation, the Republican Party, etc., etc. He said he had received a number of requests to put into the Republican platform a plank protesting against the discrimination made by Russia against Americans of the Jewish faith. "You know," he said, "I am prepared to do anything that I can for all of our citizens regardless of race or creed, but unless we mean to do something further than simply protest it would look like an effort to catch votes, for such statements in the platform could not be regarded for any other purpose." He added he had in mind a diffeerent and more effective way of handling the subject when the time came. He said he remembered that I had never asked him to take action in this or any other question that was not justified on broad American principles, but that if anything arose which specially reflected upon the Jews he looked to me to bring it to his attention, and I was to regard that just as much my duty as the protection of American Christian interests in Turkey.

We spoke about the Russo-Japanese War, and I told him that some one had said that the Japs were yellow-skinned, but the Russians were yellow all the way through. This called forth a hearty laugh. Humor of any kind, provided it was clean, he always appreciated, and his own sense of it continually served, as it did for Lincoln, to lighten the seriousness of his duties.

Like Lincoln, too, Roosevelt combined with that balancing sense of humor an innate and always active sense of justice. Time and again in my relationship with him I have observed and admired it. I recall in this regard the case of an employee named Miller in the Government Printing Office, who was discharged because he did not belong to the union, and Roosevelt reinstated him. Mr. Gompers and several members of the Executive Committee of the American Federation of Labor thereupon called upon the President to protest against this reinstatement. They said his discharge was based on two points: that he was a non-union man, and also that he was an incapable worker. Roosevelt's answer was: "The question of his personal fitness is one to be settled in the routine of administrative detail, and cannot be allowed to conflict with or to complicate the larger question of governmental discrimination for or against him or any other man because he is or is not a member of a union. This is the only question now before me for decision; and as to this my decision is final."

As I was in constant touch with the President by correspondence and conferences, I wrote him telling of my gratification to find in his decision anent the Miller case such consonance in principle with his position regarding the anthracite coal strike, to which I received the following reply that brings out the point I have just made about his sense of justice:

WHITE HOUSE, WASHINGTON
October 1, 1903

MY DEAR MR. STRAUS:

I thank you heartily for your letter. When you can get on here I should like to tell you for your own information some of my experiences in connection with this Miller case. I feel exactly as you do—that my action was a complement to my action, for instance, in the anthracite coal strike, and that I could no more hesitate in the teeth of opposition from the labor unions in one case, than I could when the opposition came from the big monied men in the other case.

Sincerely yours
THEODORE ROOSEVELT

Perhaps no President has had a policy, with regard to labor, so wise and far-seeing as that of Roosevelt. Invariably he sought the counsel of labor leaders in matters affecting their interests, and always they were made to feel that redress for their just griev-ances, and their rights generally, were as much a concern of his and of his administration as any rights of the rich. In this con-nection I recall a remark of P. H. Morrissey, then head of the railroad train-men. We were seated in the Red Room of the White House for conference after dinner. There were present some thirty or more men prominently identified with labor, whom the President had invited to discuss labor legislation. Mor-rissey recalled one time several years before when he sat in front of the great fireplace in the Red Room waiting for the President; and he said he could not help reflecting what a long way it was from the cab of the locomotive engine to this stately room in the official residence of the President of the United States, an honor and a privilege that Roosevelt was the first President to give to men of labor.

On the same evening I saw in clear relief Roosevelt's wonder-ful tact, judgment, and understanding of men as I had never seen it displayed before. One or two of the labor leaders showed some bitterness in their criticism of certain legislation. Roosevelt showed frank approval of just complaints and allayed irritation in a most tactful way where the demand was unjust or unreason-able.

In the election of 1904 I took an active part and kept in close touch with Roosevelt. An unusual amount of bitterness charac-terized this campaign, though it was foreseen that Roosevelt would win by a large majority. In this connection I received a characteristic letter from him, dated at the White House October 15th:

I notice that various Democratic papers, including the *Evening Post,* have endeavored to show that I have appealed to the Jew vote, the Catholic vote, etc. Now the fact is that I have not appealed to any man as Jew, as Protestant, or as Catholic, but that I have as strongly as in me lies endeavored to make it evident that each is to have a square deal, no more and no less, without regard to his creed. I hope that this country will continue in substantially its present form of government for many centuries. If this is so it is reasonable to suppose that during that time there will be Presidents of Jewish faith, Presidents of Catholic faith. Now, my aim as President is to behave toward the Jew and the Catholic just as I should wish a Jewish or Catholic President to behave towards Protestants—in other words, to behave as a good American should behave toward all his fellow Americans, without regard to the several creeds they profess or the several lands from which their ancestors have sprung. Moreover, I am pleased at what Lebowich says at my not having a spirit of condescension or patronizing. I have enough of the old Adam in me to object almost as strongly to being patronized as to being wronged; and I do not intend knowingly to behave toward others in a manner which I should resent if it were adopted toward me.

These sentences bring to mind another and public statement of Roosevelt's in which he characterized Americanism; the occasion was an address at the unveiling of the Sheridan equestrian statue in Washington:

We should keep steadily before our minds the fact that Americanism is a question of principle, of purpose, of idealism, of character; that it is not a matter of birthplace, or creed, or line of descent.

Here in this country the representatives of many old-world races are being fused together into a new type, a type the main features of which are already determined, and were determined at the time of the Revolutionary War; for the crucible in which all the new types are melted into one was shaped from 1776 to 1789, and our nationality was definitely fixed in all its essentials by the men of Washington's day.

Soon after the election he invited me to come to the White House for dinner one evening and to spend the night; there were a number of things he wanted to talk over with me. When I arrived I found Dr. Lyman Abbott and his son Ernest had been similarly invited, and there were additional guests for dinner: Attorney-General Moody, Senator Knox, Secretary of War Taft, and James R. Garfield, chief of the Bureau of Corporations in the Department of Commerce and Labor.

At dinner the President announced that we had come together to do some business, and he produced from his pocket a slip of paper on which were noted several subjects he wished to consider with us, mainly things to be incorporated in his forthcoming Message to Congress. First there was the Negro question. The South had vilified him because he entertained Booker Washington and appointed Crum Collector of the Port of Charleston. When Congress assembled, one of the things he intended doing was to send in again the name of Crum for confirmation. "The Southerners either do not or do not wish to understand it," he said; adding that his position plainly was that he would do everything in his power for the white man South without, however, doing a wrong or an injustice to the colored man. He was sympathetic with the South, for he was half Southerner himself, his mother having come from Roswell, Georgia. His remarks on this topic were directed mainly to Dr. Abbott.

The conversation then turned to the recent election and became very general, every one joining and relating instances or experiences in connection with it. Mr. Taft, who had waged a vigorous campaign for the Administration, told a joke on himself: he had received a letter from Wayne MacVeagh saying that so far as he (MacVeagh) could see, Taft's speeches did not do any harm.

When the talk had gone along these general lines for a while, Roosevelt interjected with "Now we must get back to business," and proceeded to discuss the diplomatic service in relation to his Message. He thought civil service too strictly applied would be detrimental, as we had a great deal of old timber there that should be gotten rid of.

Next he took up a discussion of Panama. Mr. Taft with several others was to leave next day on a mission there to look into the difficulties between the native army and the President of Panama, and some one humorously suggested that he had better go down and take away the weapons from the army and let them muster as much as they wanted to without weapons.

After dinner we adjourned to the President's study on the floor above. He sat down at his desk and pulled open a drawer as he said: "I want to read to you incomplete drafts of portions of my Message which I should like to have you criticize, as on some of the subjects I have not yet fully made up my mind." The Message was in separate parts, each dealing with an important subject. He took up the part dealing with our foreign relations, in regard to Russia and Rumania, and addressed me, saying he would like me to pay special attention to that as he had consulted me all along concerning the action to be taken. He said our Government had been criticized as interfering with the internal affairs of other nations, and the statement had been repeatedly made that we should not like it if other nations took us to task for our Negro lynchings in the South; but he argued that the lynchings were comparatively few, and, though bad enough, were nothing compared to the wholesale murder in cold blood under official sanction and perhaps instigation, as in Kishinev. "My answer to all these criticisms is this," he said; "only a short time ago I received a remonstrance or petition from a society in Great Britain regarding the lynchings in this country. I did not reject it; on the contrary, I answered it most politely and expressed my great regret for these unlawful, unjustifiable acts, with which neither I nor the Government had any sympathy. On the contrary the Government does everything in its power to prevent these outrages and unlawful acts. And I authorize any one to make use of this information whenever the occasion presents itself."

To the labor question also he wanted me to pay special attention because of my experience with such matters and in the arbitration of labor disputes. He began with the statement that he was in favor of organized capital and organized labor. I asked him whether right at that point I might make a suggestion, which was that he begin with the general subject of capital and labor, because organized labor did not comprise more than fifteen per cent of the wage-earners of the country. This suggestion he accepted.

Roosevelt then expressed himself in favor of the eight-hour law. Messrs. Moody, Knox, Taft, and myself did not agree with his statement in the form he had it. We explained that there were several bills before Congress on the subject, some of which had passed the lower house, but were defeated in the Senate; that it was all right for the Government in its own yards to adopt an eight-hour day, but when it gave out contracts to other shops, while it had a right to say that the work upon that contract should be done by eight-hour days, it had no right to require work on other contracts to be done in eight-hour days. When we had discussed the subject quite thoroughly, it was agreed to omit it from the Message.

Next he took up the trust question. He said Mr. Garfield had several suggestions to offer for making the interstate commerce law effective. It was generally agreed that the law as originally passed fully provided the remedy that was intended, but it had been emasculated by the decisions of the Supreme Court. Messrs. Knox, Taft, and Moody referred to several of these decisions and pointed out that the railroads, under subterfuge of switches and free cars—cars that were furnished by such shippers as the beef trust—got completely around the law. They allowed a mileage charge for the supply of these cars in excess of what should be allowed, and under such cover it amounted to a rebate to those shippers and was a complete circumvention of the law. Garfield's suggestion was that the interstate commerce corporations be compelled to obtain a license or charter from the National Government to do business. We thoroughly discussed this, but it was disapproved as being an interference with the legal rights of States, and that therefore no such law could be passed by Congress. The President then turned to the legal members of our group and said, "Now here is a great wrong and you lawyers have always got a way of preventing us from reaching a remedy."

Knox created a laugh by replying, "The President wants us as usual to jump over the Supreme Court."

The work on the Message done, Roosevelt said it was his intention to go South and make a few speeches. He would begin at San Antonio and would visit Tuskegee and Sewanee Colleges, for he wanted his views in regard to the South and the Negro question fully understood. He read us a draft along the lines of thought he wanted to present, quoting much from Lincoln, which seemed highly to the point. When some one mentioned the curtailing of suffrage so as to have it based upon educational qualifications and property ownership, the President said it would not be wise to agitate that subject, and that herein Booker Washington agreed with him; but, he added, "There is something inherently wrong about a Southern member representing in some instances only a quarter of the number of votes that an Eastern member represents, and having an equal vote with him in Congress."

It was half after midnight when our little company separated. The President then suggested to Dr. Abbott and me that we meet at 8.15 breakfast, if we did not object to having this meal with him and the children. In the absence of Mrs. Roosevelt, who had gone to New York, the President next morning took the head of the table, and with the coffee urn before him served us each with our coffee, cream, and sugar. There were Teddy, Ethel, Kermit, Archie, and Quentin, the governess, the tutor, besides Dr. Abbott, his son, and myself. After the meal we strolled in the park back of the White House until 9.30, when the President left for his work-room in the new office building west of the White House.

I did not see Roosevelt again for several months. One day in May I took lunch with him upon his return from Chicago where he had had a conference with the representatives of the labor unions who were carrying on the teamster's strike that paralyzed the commerce of the city. He said he had received through his secretary my memorandum regarding an adjustment of the trouble, and that it was of great assistance to him in discussing the situation and coming to some equitable arrangement. He was preparing a Message for an extra session of Congress in October, and said he would send me parts of it, especially those referring to immigration and the Far East, for my advice and suggestion.

In 1905, when Roosevelt was busy with negotiations to bring peace between Russia and Japan, I received a letter from him stating that he had endeavored to get these two nations to go to The Hague, but Russia was most reluctant and Japan positively refused; nor would they go to either Paris or Chefoo, but they were both willing to come to Washington. In his own *Autobiography*, which I never tire of reading, Roosevelt gives an interesting sketch of his mediation between these two countries which finally brought about the conference and treaty at Portsmouth, New Hampshire.

Count Sergius Witte, head of the Russian mission to Portsmouth, was desirous of meeting some of the representative Jews of our country with a view to seeking what might practically be done to improve the condition of the Jews in the Russian Empire. While it was said that his wife was a Jewess, his interest in the Jewish question was perhaps primarily to improve the relations between Russia and the United States. The Russian massacres, with the resultant enforced emigration, the public meetings of protest in this country and the press comments, had seriously prejudiced public opinion here against Russia.

The Count therefore invited a committee to confer with him and Baron Rosen at Portsmouth. There were Jacob H. Schiff, Isaac N. Seligman, Adolph Kraus, Adolf Lewisohn, and myself. The Count admitted with much frankness the condition of the Jewish population of Russia, and that it was an injustice. He expressed his purpose to exert his best influence to remedy the just grievances of the oppressed Jews. We assured him that we asked for no special privileges for our co-religionists, but the same, and no greater, rights for them than were accorded other Russian subjects; that the granting of such rights would relieve Russia of the Jewish question and of the international ill-will to which this question naturally and rightly gave rise. Both the

Count and Baron Rosen agreed with us, but argued that it was not practicable to grant such complete emancipation, but that it should come about gradually. We told them, of course, that with that premise we could not and would not agree.

The Count was very much impressed with our presentation of the subject, and our statements were corroborated by his own observations later when he made a visit to the lower East Side of New York where he spoke with a number of the Russian-Jewish immigrants. He said that upon his return to Russia he would at once take up the problem with a view ultimately to secure equal rights for the Jewish subjects, that he realized the necessity for this not only from a humanitarian standpoint, but from the standpoint of Russia's best interests and of her relations with the leading nations of the world, particularly with the United States.

Before going to Portsmouth on Count Witte's invitation, I conferred with Roosevelt. He wanted me in an unofficial capacity to observe carefully the progress of the negotiations and keep him advised. Just at that time it looked as if the conference might break up, and before that stage was actually reached he wanted to be notified, for he would probably have a communication to make to the commissioners. On arriving at Portsmouth I had a confidential talk with Fedor Fedorovich Martens, the great Russian international jurist, who was one of my fellow members at the Hague Tribunal, and with whom I had been in personal touch on several previous occasions. He was legal adviser to the Russian delegation. I apprised him of what I knew to be the desire of the President, and he agreed that if a break became imminent, a communication such as the President would send would be likely to have the right influence, and he would see to it that, should the necessity arise for such a message, Roosevelt should be promptly informed. I advised the President of my understanding with Martens, but fortunately no rupture occurred and the terms of peace were agreed upon.

In his *Autobiography* Roosevelt says, with regard to these Portsmouth negotiations: "I had certainly tried my best to be the friend not only of the Japanese people but of the Russian people, and I believe that what I did was for the best interests of both and of the world at large." He refers with characteristic generosity to the help given him at St. Petersburg by our ambassador, George von Lengerke Meyer, who "rendered literally invaluable aid by insisting upon himself seeing the Czar at critical periods of the transaction, when it was no longer possible for me to act successfully through the representatives of the Czar, who were often at cross-purposes with one another."

And when the Portsmouth Conference was over, the President further took a deep interest in bringing about amelioration of the condition of the Jews in Russia. When Count Witte came to New York, Roosevelt wrote him the following letter, of which he sent me a copy:

OYSTER BAY, N.Y.
September 10, 1905

MY DEAR MR. WITTE:

. . . In furtherance of our conversation of last evening I beg you to consider the question of granting passports to reputable American citizens of Jewish faith. I feel that if this could be done it would remove the last cause of irritation between the two nations whose historic friendship for one another I wish to do my best to maintain. You could always refuse to give a passport to any American citizen, Jew or Gentile, unless you were thoroughly satisfied that no detriment would come to Russia in granting it. But if your Government could only see its way clear to allowing reputable American citizens of Jewish faith, as to whose intentions they are satisfied, to come to Russia, just as you do reputable American Christians, I feel it would be from every standpoint most fortunate.

Again assuring you of my high regard, and renewing my congratulations to you and to your country upon the peace that has been obtained, believe me,

Sincerely yours
THEODORE ROOSEVELT

Early in 1906, when the Algeciras Conference regarding Morocco was in session, and the press reported that it was likely to break up without an agreement on account of Germany's attitude, Carl Schurz, knowing of my close relationship with Roosevelt, wrote to me that the President could probably prevail upon the Powers concerned to refer the question to the Hague Tribunal. This letter I forwarded to Roosevelt; but although he was ever ready to vitalize the machinery of the Hague Tribunal, advice coming from Mr. Schurz at this time was not regarded with favor, possibly because of their previous differences. In his reply to me, however, the President showed what a clear and prophetic insight he had into Germany's attitude and purposes:

Modern Germany is alert, aggressive, military and industrial. It thinks it is a match for England and France combined in war, and would probably be less reluctant to fight both those powers together than they would be together to fight it. It despises the Hague Conference and the whole Hague idea. It respects the United States only in so far as it believes that our navy is efficient and that if sufficiently wronged or insulted we would fight. Now I like and respect Germany, but I am not blind to the fact that Germany does not reciprocate the feeling. I want us to do everything we can to stay on good terms with Germany, but I would be a fool if I were blind to the fact that Germany will not stay in with us if we betray weakness. As for this particular case, when I see you next I shall tell you all that I have done and you will see that I have been using my very best efforts for peace.

In all my relations with Roosevelt, even before I became a member of his Cabinet, I was more and more convinced that no consideration of political self-interest or partisan advantage ever entered his mind in determining his attitude or action in upholding the right or dethroning a wrong. He resented nothing more than when some politician or inconsiderate person made an appeal to him for action on the plea that it would be good politics. He was visioned, but not visionary; and withal highly practical, in that he understood the workings and tendencies of human forces. Just as he would read a book by absorbing a page at a glance, so he would instinctively appraise his fellow men; their qualities would impress him just as a brilliant paragraph in a book would arrest his instant attention.

Roosevelt would not make an idle gesture or even imply a threat which he did not purpose to carry into action. He was more abused by those whom he designated as "the interests," and better understood and trusted by the masses, than any President in our history with the exception of Lincoln. So it is always with real leaders, who seek to guide rather than pander to public opinion. The latter course appeals to weak though well-intentioned public men; the former requires not only clear vision but high courage, and these qualities Roosevelt possessed to an extraordinary degree.

JULIUS HABER

Julius Haber was born in Austrian Galicia in 1887. An active Zionist all of his life, Haber was one of that small army of dedicated men who attended Zionist meetings and conferences in the United States and abroad, and who were in contact with many of the important Jewish leaders of our time. He worked as a grocer, a tobacco planter in Palestine, and in the advertising business in the United States, to which he first came in 1903. He visited Palestine and Israel frequently, and had the satisfaction of seeing his children settle in Israel and contribute to its security and well-being. He died in 1966.

In his 70's, Haber wrote of his half-century experiences as a Zionist, describing the beginnings of American Zionism, in which he played a role of some significance. In The Odyssey of an American Zionist, *he reported on the great years in Zionist history, from his own attachment to the dream of Zion reborn in his little European village, up to and including the United Nations debates on the establishment of a Jewish State and, indeed, the creation of the State and its battle for survival and independence.*

Here we submit Mr. Haber's eye-witness experience on July 4, 1904, and the following day, when New York Jews mourned the death of Theodor Herzl, the father of political Zionism. Others have recalled the impact of Herzl's death, but Julius Haber, reminiscing across the decades, manages to convey the deep sense of sorrow and loss felt by Jews an ocean away, who realized that a giant had passed from their world.

Tribute to Herzl*

JULIUS HABER

IN THE TYPICALLY AMERICAN NEIGHBORHOOD where I lived at the time on Vanderbilt Avenue in Brooklyn, N.Y., the early morning of July 4, 1904 was a typical Independence Day—clear-skied, cheerful and already, at eight in the morning, more than a trifle warm, with a strong hint of humidity in the summer air that promised thundershowers before evening. Every house along the avenue flew its bright American flag; there was an air of easy, drowsy indolence about the entire neighborhood.

The sun was shining, the flags were flying on the lower East Side, too, when I arrived there later that morning. But the flags were draped with black. From several buildings which housed Zionist clubs, the blue and white flags of Zion, similarly somber-bordered, were at half-mast, and in windows everywhere, draped in mourning, were pictures of Theodor Herzl. I did not need the confirmation of black newspaper headlines to tell me that Herzl was no longer with us, that a chapter in the history of Zionism was irrevocably closed, with an ending that brooked no editing or author's revisions.

Word of Herzl's death had been received early that morning; already the Zionist clubrooms were crowded with people, some weeping openly, unashamedly; others were still too stunned for emotion. We had known for nearly a year that Herzl was ailing, that his great heart was running down under the continual strain of his dedicated task. We had known, from Dr. Wise's two-and-a-half month-old report, that Herzl was finally displaying alarming signs of illness and a vast fatigue. We had known—and yet, knowing that no human could long stand up under the burden of responsibility, the punishing task that Herzl had assumed, we

* Reprinted from *The Odyssey of an American Zionist*, Twayne Publishers, New York, 1956, pp. 36–43.

still had no prescience of tragedy, no sense of impending loss. For death comes only to mortals—and Herzl, in the seven brief years since the first Zionist Congress, had already achieved immortality. In his lifetime, he had become a legend—and legends do not die.

The newspapers that morning carried other news of triumph and tragedy; the *S.S. Norge,* en route from Sweden to New York, had gone down at sea with 700 passengers aboard, among them 200 Jewish immigrants from Russia. And the Russians, tasting the bitter dregs of defeat in the Russo-Japanese war, had agreed to surrender Port Arthur to victorious Japanese forces. But our sorrow over the disaster at sea, our elation at the downfall of a hated oppressor nation, were dwarfed by the somber shadow of our personal loss. Herzl was dead.

The United Zionist Societies, at that time an independent group not affiliated with the Federation of American Zionists, arranged a memorial meeting for the following evening, July 5th, at the Senier shul on the lower East Side. Dr. Joseph Bluestone, Rabbis Zisel Rubinstein and Moishe Zvi Rabinowitz addressed the throngs which crowded the synagogue. Outside, Montgomery Street was choked from wall to wall of the tenements that lined it, with thousands of grieving Jews.

Two days later on Thursday July 7th, the day when the funeral took place in Vienna, a similar meeting was held at the Rumania shul on Rivington and Orchard Streets, where Dr. David Blaustein, superintendent of the Educational Alliance, Rabbi Jacob Eskolsky, Abe Goldberg and Jacob de Haas, secretary of the Zionist Federation and a close friend of Dr. Herzl, paid tribute to the departed leader. And in the streets around the synagogue were countless young Zionists unable to gain admission to the meeting, straining their ears to catch a word, a phrase of the speeches that drifted distinctly through the open doors. Speculation already ran rife as to who would succeed Dr. Herzl. One name frequently mentioned was that of Oscar Straus, former United States Ambassador to Turkey and a member of the two man American delegation to the Peace Tribunal at The Hague, in the Netherlands. At the first mention of his name, many Zionists protested that he was not known to be active in the Zionist movement. "But he is a good Jew," came the reply; to which the young Zionists retorted, "Not good enough, or big enough to wear Theodor Herzl's mantle!" For Herzl, to them, was more than a mere ambassador; he was the Jewish President in the Diaspora and his capital was spiritual Zionism.

For days, the Yiddish press was filled with news, articles and special features on Theodor Herzl. The headline in the *Jewish Morning Journal* on July 5th read: "Zion in Mourning! Conference with von Plehve [Russian Minister of Interior at the time of the Kishinev pogrom] and Uganda Battle at Sixth Zionist Congress Hastened Herzl's Death."

Even the *Forward* put aside its prejudices in favor of accurate news reporting when it carried a special cable from Vienna, reporting that literally millions of Jews throughout Europe were weeping at Herzl's loss. His death, the cable continued, was a calamitous shock; for eight years, Jews everywhere had regarded Herzl as the most significant figure in modern Jewish life—and this, despite the fact that a decade earlier he had been virtually unknown to the Jewish world. He had given Zionism new meaning; he had brought it out of the ghetto and into the political arena of the world, attracting to the movement such men as the great Dr. Max Nordau, the famous Italian scholar Cesare Lombroso and the brilliant English novelist, Israel Zangwill. And though he had not been able to prevent the Zionist movement from creating many factions, according to the *Forward*, he had been able to guide it, to control it, to keep all factions directed toward the same objective. But his death, the article concluded, left a gaping void in Zionist ranks and there was none to fill it. Neither Nordau nor Zangwill nor anyone else, however capable, was endowed with the energy, the charm, the inspirational qualities that Herzl possessed.

These were strange words, coming from an avowed and active foe of Zionism. But several days later, the *Forward* in an editorial declared: "We respect leaders of new ideas, but we are sorry to see so much enthusiasm expended on such foolish ideas as Zionism." And yet, so overwhelming was Herzl's influence on Jewish thought at that time, so indelible was the stamp of his greatness, that even after this snide editoral comment, the *Forward* could not help conceding in closing the editoral that "the Zionists do not overestimate Herzl; he was a prominent leader in the Zionist movement, no matter what we Jewish Socialists think about it."

On Tuesday morning, July 5th, I had occasion to be on Cook Street, in a Jewish section of Brooklyn. People everywhere were wearing black-rimmed lapel buttons bearing Herzl's picture, mourning the great Zionist leader. I was amazed at this almost unanimous display of sentiment, and inquired of the friend I was visiting whether all these people belonged to the Zionist movement, or showed active Zionist sympathies. He replied that few, if any of them, would so much as buy a shekel or contribute to the Jewish National Fund, let alone a Zionist organization. Nevertheless, the news of Herzl's death had struck like a bolt of lightning; it had clutched at the hearts of Zionist and non-Zionist alike.

But people do not go on mourning forever. Within a week or two, both Herzl and Zionism had been banished from their minds, and it remained for the nucleus of the Zionist movement to carry on the battle for Jewish statehood.

Six weeks after Herzl's death, on Sunday August 17th, the Federation of American Zionists held a Herzl Memorial meeting at Carnegie Hall. The city poured forth its Jewish population for this solemn occasion; prominent Jews from many parts of the country came to New York to attend and some of them to speak at the meeting.

The famous Boy's Brigade, an early Zionist experiment in combatting juvenile delinquency among the youth of the lower East Side, turned out full force to march from Grand Army Hall, at the foot of Second Avenue, to Carnegie Hall, at 57th Street and Seventh Avenue. Dressed in their crisp, dark blue, brass-buttoned uniforms, they marched solemnly along bearing black-draped flags—an inspiring tribute to Zionism's constant preoccupation with youth and its problems.

For Zionism drew its strength from youth; to youth it owed its perpetual vitality in the face of seemingly insuperable obstacles. Today, in Israel, as for many years past, the rehabilitation of children, both from the war-torn countries of Europe and from the depressed areas of North Africa and the Middle East, is one of the country's major projects, and one of its most successful ones. It has evoked interested comment throughout the world, and yet in the Zionist scheme of things it is nothing new. Nearly half a century ago, the founders of the Boy's Brigade set out to accomplish virtually the same thing in the depressed areas of New York's slums.

It is almost a certainty that had it not been for this organization, founded by A. H. Fromenson, a prominent Zionist, many of the boys who joined the Brigade would have become special problems, living as they did, virtually on the streets, without guidance other than that casually administered by the public school of the time, and with no Hebrew education other than the reluctantly accepted preparations for Bar Mitzvah. It was this danger of abandonment of the higher values of Judaism that led Fromenson to fear for the future of the younger generation. At the same time, it was a similar fear, coupled with a horror of the inevitable repetition of the Kishinev massacre, that led such men as Dr. J. L. Magnes, the active honorary secretary of the Federation and years later Chancellor of the Hebrew University in Jerusalem, and Dr. Israel Friedlaender of the Jewish Theological Seminary who later became the first president of the Young Judea in the United States, to advocate the formation of Jewish self-defense units in Czarist Russia. It seems strange, however, in the light of their strongly conservative nature, to picture them as firebrands arousing Jewish America to contribute funds for the formation of these self-defense units, particularly in the case of Dr. Magnes who in his later years was as ardently pacifist as he had been militant after the pogroms.

As though it were only yesterday, I can recall Cyrus L. Sulzberger, slim and erect, dressed with an unobtrusive attention to conservative detail, as though he desired to remain as anonymous as possible, standing at attention as he reviewed the Boy's Brigade at that time. And I still carry vividly in my memory a recollection of that Carnegie Hall meeting in memory of Herzl. From Philadelphia had come Hyman Davidson, one of the staunchest supporters of the American Zionist movement, and one of the founders of the B'nai Zion. Dr. Harry Friedenwald, outstanding physician who had just been elected president of the Federation of American Zionists, had come up from Baltimore to address the gathering in English, as did Dr. David Blaustein, the Executive Director of the Educational Alliance. The Rev. Dr. Adolph Radin, though he was not understood by many, won a thunderous ovation when he chose to speak in Hebrew. The beloved Rev. Zvi Hirsch Masliansky, the most effective orator for Zion and teacher of Chaim Weizmann, spoke in Yiddish and reached the hearts of all those present with a deeply moving eulogy of Herzl. Another notable guest was the Rev. Dr. Joseph H. Hertz, then Chief Rabbi of the Union of South Africa and later Chief Rabbi of Great Britain, who was visiting the United States.

Despite the more imposing appearance and greater oratorical eloquence of other speakers, it was Cyrus L. Sulzberger, vice president of the Federation of American Zionists, who was most appreciated by his American followers. He had seen Dr. Herzl during the sixth World Zionist Congress at Basle the previous summer, had spent a great deal of time in the company of the departed Zionist leader, and his recollections of those precious hours, related without rhetoric and with simple dignity and restraint, constituted a more touching and deeply moving eulogy of Herzl than all the words uttered in his praise that day of August 17, 1904.

Mr. Sulzberger recalled a scene at the Basle synagogue where he had gone with Herzl to worship on a Saturday morning in the summer of 1903. After Herzl had been called to the Torah and the portion of the week had been read to him, Sulzberger told us, Herzl made an offering to the synagogue of 800 Swiss francs (at that time, about $160).

"Standing there at the desk where the Torah was read, wearing his *tallith* and silk hat, he was the very picture of Jewish manhood," Sulzberger said. "An artist might paint him thus, and without the slightest idealization, make an ideal picture. Tall, handsome, black-bearded, clear-eyed, erect in bearing, suave in manner, he looked as a Prince of Israel ought to look.

"Again, I met Herzl in his hotel, in the company of several important personalities, including Dr. Harry Friedenwald of Baltimore and Israel Zangwill. While Herzl spoke, Zangwill was sitting, as was his habit, with closed eyes. Herzl said, 'Don't go to sleep, Israel!' and quick as a flash came Zangwill's reply: 'The God of Israel slumbereth not, nor sleepeth—but Israel himself sometimes does!'

"The range of thought that evening was astounding," Sulzberger continued. "French, German and English literature, poetry and art, the drama—everything but Zionism. This latter fact rather puzzled me until we were returning to our hotel, when one of the Englishmen in the party explained the mystery. As we were entering the smoking room of the Trois Rois Hotel, a man attached himself to Herzl, taking him by the arm and accompanying him. Herzl introduced him to us as our very good friend, a Pasha, of Constantinople. This man, my friend informed me, was a Turkish spy sent by his government to ascertain what was being done and contemplated at the Congress, and it was owing to his presence that Zionism was not discussed at the gathering.

"Herzl asked me to speak before the Congress and give the American point of view on Zionism, which I did; afterwards, my remarks were translated into German for the delegates by Dr. Nordau. Finding a list of some thirty-five speakers who still remained to be heard, Herzl asked that their speeches be limited to five minutes each. At the conclusion, Herzl took the stand to reply. Such satire, such invective, such oratory I have never heard. He tore to shreds his opponents' arguments. Now convulsed with laughter, now storming with applause, he moved that Congress in a way impossible to describe. It was one of the most magnificent triumphs I have ever witnessed.

"A similar triumph was his," Sulzberger concluded, "on the night when the Russian delegates were about to secede, and it was his great personality which won them back. Upon whose shoulders his mantle will fall, and whether there be shoulders capable of carrying it, time alone can tell."

To the vast and solemn gathering that Sunday in August, 1904, it was apparent that Sulzberger had been particularly hard hit by Herzl's loss. With the death of the great Zionist leader, Sulzberger seemed to have lost some of the driving impulse, the compulsion to action that had marked his own efforts for the cause up till then. And though he remained an ardent Zionist, he was seen less and less at Zionist gatherings in the years that followed.

STEPHEN S. WISE

Rabbi Stephen S. Wise, one of the great rabbinical figures in American life, had a rich and varied career both on the Jewish and the American scene. He was born in Budapest in 1874 and was brought to the United States a year later. He died in New York in 1949. From 1893 to 1900 he was rabbi of the Madison Avenue Synagogue in New York, and then he accepted a pulpit at Temple Beth Israel in Portland, Oregon, where he served until 1906. In that year, he was called to Temple Emanu-El in New York City, and almost immediately was plunged into a controversy on the subject of freedom of the pulpit. This was a major debate in New York Jewish life at the time, and in the chapter included here from his autobiography, Challenging Years, *Rabbi Wise discusses this controversy and the establishment of The Free Synagogue in 1907.*

A great American-Zionist leader, Stephen Wise began his international Zionist career at the Second World Zionist Congress. He was a founder of the Zionist Organization of America in 1898, and was President of the Z.O.A. in 1917 and again from 1936 to 1938. He withdrew from the Zionist Organization together with Louis D. Brandeis and Julian Mack following a conflict with Dr. Chaim Weizmann, but later returned to play a major part in the movement. He was chairman of the American Zionist Emergency Committee for Zionist Affairs in the 1940's.

Wise was a founder of the American Jewish Congress and its President for many years. He also was an organizer and leader of the World Jewish Congress. In 1922, he founded the Jewish Institute of Religion.

Active in politics, Wise was a close friend of President Franklin D. Roosevelt. He organized boycotts against Nazis during the Hitler regime, and stood in the forefront in the fight for civil rights and civil liberties.

Founding the Free Synagogue*

STEPHEN S. WISE

AN EPISODE which changed the whole course of my life occurred in 1905 when I was still the youngish rabbi of Temple Beth Israel of Portland, Oregon. Out of a clear sky came the lightning of an invitation to give a number of sermons and addresses at Temple Emanu-El of New York, known as the Cathedral Synagogue of the country. Its pulpit was vacant after its long-time occupancy by two distinguished figures. The former of these was Dr. Samuel Adler, who had been called from Alzey, Germany, a most learned scholar. After Adler came my learned friend and teacher, Dr. Gustav Gottheil, who pioneered self-respectingly in the field of Christian-Jewish relations.

Leaving Oregon, I said to intimate friends, chief among them the former president of Oregon University, Dr. Chapman, and Richard Ward Montague, highest type of citizen and jurist, "I am going to New York to preach some trial sermons at the Cathedral Synagogue. They will call me to be their rabbi. I somehow feel that I will have to decline their call. If I decline it, as I believe I shall have to do, I will go back to New York from Oregon to found a Free Synagogue." That proved to be an accurate prediction of what was to happen.

One who preaches trial sermons lays himself open, as no man with self-respect should, to harassing experiences. After five years of free and independent preaching to a most friendly and indeed forbearing, as well as generously appreciative, congregation, I was greeted after preaching at Emanu-El by men and women, meaning to show their approval, with such exclamations as "We were very much impressed," "We were very well pleased," as if I had wished to please, when in truth I had sought solely to awaken. For the first time I came to understand the term trial

* Reprinted from *Challenging Years*, G. P. Putnam's Sons, New York, 1949, pp. 82–104.

sermons, as I had to listen to such expressions as "Doctor, it was a fine sermon." It was my soul that was tried; I had poured it out in earnest and unafraid appeal to these people to be single-minded and great-hearted Jews. They responded to me as if I had been delivering a high-school prize oration. I was chilled and disheartened to the last degree. Above all, it prepared my spirit for the great refusal, to which I was inexorably bound to rise after some days.

Negotiation began at once after my address by the president, James Seligman of the then famous banking firm. A committee consisting of a majority of the Board of Trustees of Emanu-El came to me. I name them for the record: James Seligman, M. H. Moses, Daniel Guggenheim, Isaac Spiegelberg, and Louis Marshall. Marshall, honorary secretary of the temple, was so much of a master or dictator in Emanu-El that Dr. Emil G. Hirsch, the greatest preacher of the American Jewish pulpit, once said, "Temple Emanu-El lives under *Marshall* law."

Marshall began by asking me with such geniality as he could muster for the performance of an uncongenial task, what would be my conditions in accepting the proposed call of Emanu-El to be its rabbi. I had carefully and self-searchingly considered what my reply would be to such an inevitable query. "Gentlemen, I name two minor conditions and one major. I must have part in the religious service, participation in which is precious to me, and I am accustomed to have the service of a private secretary." The answer was there could be no objection to these conditions, though both sounded novel to the committee, the congregation being accustomed to have the service chanted wholly by its cantor, and no previous rabbi at Emanu-El having asked for a secretary.

Thereupon I spoke in simple and earnest terms,"You are calling to me to be the rabbi of Emanu-El. I am not a preacher or scholar of note, but you have heard that I have gained for my temple, Beth Israel, my people throughout Oregon, and their rabbi, the respect and for the most part the good will of the entire Northwest community. If I have achieved that, it has been because in my inaugural sermon at Beth Israel, September, 1900, I declared: 'This pulpit must be free.' "

Mr. Marshall, perhaps to his credit be it said, without a moment's hesitation and without even the faintest pretense of consultation with his colleagues, said rather testily, as was his wont, "Dr. Wise, I must say to you at once that such condition cannot be complied with; the pulpit of Emanu-El has always been and is subject to and under the control of the Board of Trustees." My answer was clear, immediate, unequivocal: "If that be true, gentlemen, there is nothing more to say."

And that would have been the end had not one of Mr. Marshall's colleagues, all of whom seemed surprised by the finality of Mr. Marshall's statement and the immediacy of my reply, interposed the question, "What do you mean by a free pulpit?"

I replied fully and deliberately, putting my worst foot forward, "I have in Oregon been among the leaders of a civic-reform movement in my community. Mr. Moses, if it be true, as I have heard it rumored, that your nephew, Mr. Herman, is to be a Tammany Hall candidate for a Supreme Court judgeship, I would if I were Emanu-El's rabbi oppose his candidacy in and out of my pulpit." I continued, "Mr. Guggenheim, as a member of the Child Labor Commission of the State of Oregon, I must say to you that, if it ever came to be known that children were being employed in your mines," having reference to his presidency of the famous copper mines, "I would cry out against such wrong. Mr. Marshall, the press stated that you and your firm are to be counsel for Mr. Hyde of the Equitable Life Assurance Society. That may or may not be true, but, knowing that Charles Evans Hughes's investigation of insurance companies in New York has been a very great service, I would in and out of my pulpit speak in condemnation of the crimes committed by the insurance thieves."

I added that I could not and would not under any circumstances accept a call to be the rabbi of a congregation under such, as I saw it, humiliating conditions. The interview terminated though not before one of the deputation made clear, to Marshall's obvious irritation, that "any recommendation we may make with regard to your election as our rabbi would be accepted by the congregation." I arose, not however before saying for the last time, "If Mr. Marshall be correct, I would not under any conceivable circumstances accept the call of Emanu-El." The committee left. My mind was made up. My prediction seemed near to fulfillment. My wife, bravest and finest of spirits, waiting for me in the adjoining room, met me with a simple but infinitely heartening greeting: "You had no other choice."

But there was no finality. In the course of a week, before we could leave for Oregon, I had three visits, two of them from members of the committee that had come to extend the call, Messrs. Seligman and Guggenheim, president and treasurer respectively, who urged me most earnestly and generously to reconsider my decision, each maintaining that I was not to take Mr. Marshall's dogmatic assertions too seriously. A third and unexpected visitor was Jacob Schiff. After some talk, which was a renewal of the urging of the others, he asked me to accompany him as he walked to the Montefiore Home of which he was founder and president. Again and again he asked me to reconsider. When I complained of Louis Marshall's intolerable suggestion, Schiff said: "But he is like that—what the Germans call *ein Krakaeler*, the best possible rendering for which is a *forninster.*" Finally, in the course of the long and exhausting walk, I asked him point blank, "Would Dr. Parkhurst," and I named him because he was the outstanding clerical figure of New York in that day, "accept a call to a Christian church on the Marshall terms?" Mr. Schiff's answer made my decision final and unalterable: "That would be different. Dr. Parkhurst is a Christian minister and you are a rabbi." Nothing more could be said.

I hurried home and sought out Professor Felix Adler, whose father, Samuel Adler, as I have already pointed out, had been a rabbi of Emanu-El. Dr. Adler strongly supported my position, saying with real feeling what I later embodied in my epistle on the "Freedom of the Pulpit," that the position of Marshall was an insult to the memory of his father, who would never have consented to stand in such a muzzled pulpit. Professor Adler approved of a brief note which I sent to Mr. Marshall before leaving New York.

That might have been the end of the tale. But more happened. Rumors of the call to Emanu-El's pulpit had preceded my return to Portland. I preached on the first Sabbath eve thereafter, told the full story in unvarnished, withal strictly accurate, terms and announced that I would more than carry out the terms of my arrangement with the Congregation of Portland, remaining its rabbi till September, 1906, and then go to New York, there, in the largest Jewish community of history, to found a Free Synagogue.

The report of the sermon was telegraphed to New York, and Mr. Marshall at once saw fit, instead of dealing with the larger issue that had been raised, virtually to ignore it. He took refuge in what at best was a technicality, namely, that there had been no call and that there could not have been a call inasmuch as no congregational meeting had been held. How fair such quibble was it has become rather too late to debate. What alone troubled others and myself was that Mr. Marshall should have been willing to destroy the reputation of one as young as I then was and, what was even worse, that no member of the Board of Trustees, which had dealt with me, was ready to tell the truth and by so doing brave Mr. Marshall's wrath. Many years later, having invited Mr. Marshall to give an address before the Free Synagogue, I introduced and welcomed him as "the inspirer of the founder of the Free Synagogue," without evoking from him even a reluctant smile!

Assailed as I was, my veracity and integrity questioned, I prepared with utmost care the epistle on the freedom of the pulpit, and in this I had the help of two friends, Felix Adler and Richard Ward Montague, whom I have already named. It was carefully reasoned and clearly stated, remaining unanswered, and, I venture to believe, unanswerable, as a plea for pulpit freedom—not only the Jewish pulpit but the pulpit of religion! Few things in life have given me deeper satisfaction than to have ministers of Christian churches, as well as my rabbinical colleagues, throughout more than a generation speak gratefully of the battle I fought for the freedom of the pulpit.

Because this open letter marked the turning point of my life and served as the introduction to my ministry in New York, I include it here:

AN OPEN LETTER

PORTLAND, OREGON
JANUARY 5, 1906

TO THE PRESIDENT AND MEMBERS OF TEMPLE EMANU-EL,
NEW YORK, N. Y.

GENTLEMEN:

On the first of December I received a communication from Mr. Louis Marshall, chairman of a committee of the board of trustees of Temple Emanu-El.

NEW YORK, DECEMBER 1, 1905

DEAR DOCTOR:

At your request, I am formulating the substance of what was said to you last evening by the committee of inquiry appointed by the Board of Trustees of Congregation Emanu-El.

The committee waited upon you, for the purpose of ascertaining whether or not, in the event that it should be concluded by the board of trustees and the congregation, to extend to you a call to occupy our pulpit, in conjunction with its present incumbent, Rev. Joseph Silverman, such call would be accepted.

In making this inquiry it was stated to you by the committee, in view of the traditions of the congregation, and out of consideration of the church polity which had always prevailed therein, was considered as a necessary condition, applicable to any incumbent of the office of rabbi in the congregation, that the pulpit should always be subject to and under control of the board of trustees. This was considered to be particularly important, in view of the circumstances, that the requirements of the congregation were such as to render it essential that there should be two incumbents of its pulpit, of equal rank and performing identical functions.

It is fair to say, that this announcement of our congregational law is not a mere figure of speech or an empty formula, although in the past it has never led to any friction between our rabbis and our board of trustees. It does not mean that the board of trustees will call upon any incumbent of our pulpit to sacrifice or surrender his principles or convictions.

The converse of the proposition is equally important—that the board of trustees shall not, and will not, sacrifice or surrender the principles or the convictions which it officially represents. The logical consequence of a conflict of irreconcilable views between the rabbi and the board of trustees is that one or the other must give way. Naturally, it must be the rabbi. It goes without saying, therefore, that at such a juncture, he should have the privileges of resigning. His failure to exercise that option necessarily implies an acquiescence by him in the views of the board of trustees.

Our insistence upon the phraseology which I have employed, and which is a mere adoption of the terms in which the unwritten law of the congregation is couched, is based upon the idea, that it is but fair to the rabbi and to the congregation that both shall understand at the outset the nature of the contract which exists between them, and that the former shall enter into the pact with his eyes open, so that he may never have occasion to complain, should a difference ever arise, that he was placed in the position of either sacrificing his principles, or of becoming a martyr to what he may possibly describe as the intolerance of the board of trustees.

The committee likewise believes that, without in any way detracting from the dignity of the rabbis or of the congregation, both of co-equal importance, whatever understanding is reached between them should be perpetuated by some form of writing, whether it be by correspondence, memorandum or formal agreement. The very fact that in our several conferences there has arisen the necessity of defining the language used by the respective conferees indicates the wisdom of such a course.

With best regards, I am very truly yours,

LOUIS MARSHALL.

Dr. Stephen S. Wise.

On December third I addressed to him the following reply:

Mr. Louis Marshall,
    CHAIRMAN OF COMMITTEE OF BOARD OF TRUSTEES,
        TEMPLE EMANU-EL.

DEAR SIR:

If your letter of December first be expressive of the thought of the board of trustees of Temple Emanu-El, I beg to say that no self-respecting minister of religion, in my opinion, could

consider a call to a pulpit which, in the language of your communication, shall always be subject to, and under the control of,
the board of trustees. I am,

YOURS VERY TRULY,
STEPHEN S. WISE

While my position in the matter under question is thus explained in unmistakable terms, I feel that it is become my duty
to address this open letter to you on the question of the freedom
of the Jewish pulpit.

I write to you because I believe that a question of super-
eminent importance has been raised, the question whether the
pulpit shall be free or whether the pulpit shall not be free, and,
by reason of its loss of freedom, reft of its power for good. The
whole position of the churches is involved in this question, for
the steadily waning influence of church and synagogue is due in
no small part, I hold, to the widespread belief that the pulpit is
not free, and that it is "subject to and under the control" of
those officers and members of the church or synagogue who, for
any reason, are powerful in its councils. The question, therefore,
"Shall the pulpit be free or shall it not be free?" is of infinitely
greater moment than the question of the occupancy of your
pulpit by any man whosoever, and it is the deep conviction that
this is so that has impelled me, now that any thought of a direct
relation between us is definitely set aside, to address you in
earnest language as men equally concerned with myself in the
well-being and increasing power of our beloved religion.

When a committee of five, constituting a majority of the board
of trustees of the congregation, came to me, for the purpose of
ascertaining whether a call to occupy your pulpit would be accepted, and, if accepted, upon what terms, I stated that I had
but one stipulation to make with respect to the terms of such call,
and that I was ready to leave everything else to the judgment of
the board of trustees and the members of the congregation,
merely adding that a written contract ought not to be deemed
necessary between a congregation and its minister. The one
stipulation I made in the following words: "If I am to accept a
call to the pulpit of Temple Emanu-El, I do so with the understanding that I am to be free, and that my pulpit is not to be
muzzled." I made no other stipulation; upon this I insisted.

Counsels of prudence, which were urged upon me, suggested
that I should have taken this freedom for granted, but viewing
the manner in which my stipulation was met by the members of
the committee, I deem it most fortunate that I anticipated the
situation which has arisen. . . . It was indeed held by some members of the committee that the phrase, "the pulpit shall always
be subject to and under the control of the board of trustees," was
"an empty formula," or "a mere figure of speech," which interpretation, however, the chairman of the committee at once emphatically disavowed. Even though this phrase were admitted to
be an empty formula, I would still be under the moral necessity
of refusing to maintain a fiction, of making a compact in terms
of falsehood to teach in a place dedicated to truth. But how can
a form of words so threatening to the liberty of a minister of
religion be regarded as a mere figure of speech? The very fact
that it was insisted upon is evidence that it was not intended as
a formula, and, if it be intended seriously, as it clearly is, I have
only to repeat that no self-respecting minister of religion could
consider a call to the pulpit of a church or synagogue on such
terms. Such a formula, taken under any construction that may be
put upon it, is not chiefly humiliating to me, who unequivocally
reject its terms, but much more humiliating to the congregation
in the name of which such terms are offered. . . .

It is not said that in the event of a conflict of irreconcilable
views between the rabbi and a majority of the members of the
congregation the rabbi must give way, but that the acceptance of
the terms "the pulpit shall always be subject to, and under the
control of, the board of trustees," implies acquiescence on the
part of the rabbi in the views of the board of trustees in the event
of a conflict of irreconcilable views between him and them, or the
necessity of exercising the "option" or "privilege" of resigning.
The board of trustees thus assert for themselves in the last analysis the custodianship of the spiritual convictions of the congregation. . . . Stated more simply, the rabbi, whose whole life is given
to the study of and preoccupation with religion and morals, must
always hold his views subject to revision or ratification at the
hands of the board of trustees, or of any number, howsoever
small, of the members of the congregation having sufficiently
formidable influence with the board of trustees. In other words,
the mere fact that a certain number, not necessarily a majority,

of the members of the congregation or certain members of the board of trustees, might object to his views is to compel retraction, silence or resignation, without the slightest guarantee that reason and right are on the side of the objectors. The mere statement of the case is its own severest condemnation. . . .

The chief office of the minister, I take it, is not to represent the views of the congregation, but to proclaim the truth as he sees it. How can he serve a congregation as a teacher save as he quickens the minds of his hearers by the vitality and independence of his utterances? But how can a man be vital and independent and helpful, if he be tethered and muzzled? A free pulpit, worthily filled, must command respect and influence; a pulpit that is not free, howsoever filled, is sure to be without potency and honor. A free pulpit will sometimes stumble into error; a pulpit that is not free can never powerfully plead for truth and righteousness. In the pursuit of the duties of his office, the minister may from time to time be under the necessity of giving expression to views at variance with the views of some, or even many, members of the congregation. Far from such difference proving the pulpit to be in the wrong, it may be, and oftimes is, found to signify that the pulpit has done its duty in calling evil evil and good good, in abhorring the moral wrong of putting light for darkness and darkness for light, and in scorning to limit itself to the utterance of what the prophet has styled "smooth things," lest variance of views arise. Too great a dread there may be of secession on the part of some members of a congregation, for, after all, difference and disquiet, even schism at the worst, are not so much to be feared as that attitude of the pulpit which never provokes dissent because it is cautious rather than courageous, peace-loving rather than prophetic, time-serving rather than right-serving. The minister is not to be the spokesman of the congregation, not the message-bearer of the congregation, but the bearer of a message to the congregation. What the contents of that message shall be, must be left to the conscience and understanding and loyalty of him in whom a congregation places sufficient confidence to elect him to minister to it.

In the course of the conferences held between the committee and the writer, it was urged that the pulpit has no right to demand exemption from criticism. The minister in Israel does not regard his utterance as infallible. No minister will refuse to correct an opinion—though he will take the utmost pains to achieve correctness in substance and form before speaking—when reasons are advanced to convince him of his error. Nor will he fail to welcome criticism and invite difference of opinion to the end that truth may be subserved. . . . To declare that in the event of a conflict of irreconcilable views between the minister and the board of trustees, it is the minister who must yield and not the board, is to assert the right not to criticize the pulpit, but to silence its occupant, and, above all, to imply that the board of trustees are always sure to be in the right, or else that the convictions of the board of trustees shall stand, whether right or wrong, and that the minister must acquiesce in these convictions, right or wrong, or else exercise the "option" and "privilege" of resigning.

The Jewish minister, I repeat, does not speak *ex cathedra*, and his views are not supposed to have a binding force upon the congregation to which he ministers. He is to express his convictions on any subject that comes within the purview of religion and ethics, but these convictions do not purport to constitute a creed or dogma to which a congregation must in whole or in part subscribe. But the board of trustees asserts the right to define and to formulate the views in which the rabbi must acquiesce, or failing to acquiesce therein, resign. . . . Not only is the rabbi expected to sign away his present independence, but to mortgage his intellectual and moral liberty for the future. Stated in briefest possible terms, the rabbi is asked to subscribe to a statement of present and future convictions of the board of trustees. The demand is put forth that he subscribe to a blank page the contents of which are to be determined, not on the basis of his understanding of and loyalty to the teachings of his religion, but by "the views of the board of trustees." This is indeed to attempt to rob the pulpit of every vestige of freedom and independence. I am asked to point the way, and my hands are tied; I am asked to go before and my feet are fettered. . . .

If I could bring myself to accept a call to the pulpit of Temple Emanu-El upon such terms, and this is unthinkable, the board of trustees would never find it necessary to call upon me to surrender my convictions, for assent on my part to the stipulation, "the pulpit shall always be subject to, and under the control of, the board of trustees," would involve such a sacrifice of principles as would leave me no convictions worthy of the name to surrender at any subsequent behest of the board of trustees. It is equally meaningless to declare that "in the past this has never led to any friction between our rabbis and our board of trustees." Where a rabbi is reduced to the choice of acquiescence in views, right or wrong, because held by the board of trustees or of silence, friction is impossible. The absence of friction in the past between the rabbis and the board of trustees of Temple Emanu-El proves that either the pulpit has been circumspect or that it has been so effectually muzzled that even protest was impossible on the part of an occupant who had subscribed to such conditions. A third possibility obtains—that the board of trustees has had the forbearance of the angels with the occupants of the pulpit insofar as they have not abused the power which they claim as their own. As for the forbearance of angels, which has possibly been theirs, I wish to make clear that I would not deliver my conscience into the keeping of the angels. My conscience is my own.

Finally, to hold that the subjection of the pulpit to, and its control by, the board of trustees is a written or unwritten law of the congregation is to maintain that the pulpit of Emanu-El never has been free, and this, I am sure, does not accord with the memories that still remain alive in me and in others of high-minded, independent, revered teachers who have occupied that pulpit. One of the former occupants I have intimately known, and were he living today he would repudiate the claim that he had for many years been the occupant of a pulpit which was not free.

I have sought to do you the justice of helping you to realize the seriousness of the situation which you face. This situation, I believe, you have not planned; into it you have, however, permitted yourselves to drift. That this appeal to the spirit of my people at its highest shall not have been made in vain is my hope, for the sake of our religion, which a free pulpit alone can truly serve.

I am,

FAITHFULLY YOURS,
STEPHEN S. WISE

Only two things remained, in a sense equally difficult: To take leave of Oregon with all its precious associations and memories was the first. That was most difficult, for in the six years of residence in Oregon I had come to love the state and its people. The second was to move on to New York. This I did in order to establish the Free Synagogue, which some months ago celebrated the forty-second anniversary of its founding.

A somewhat amusing postscript remains to be added. Twenty years later, the houses adjacent to the synagogue were occupied by that excellent pioneering, progressive Walden School. The little children were wont to play upon a second-story roof near my study in the adjoining house. One day they were particularly boisterous.

I called down, "Children, would you try to be just a little less noisy? I have a meeting in my study." The noise subsided slightly. A few moments passed, and the children were a little more noisy than before. I went to the window overlooking the playground and called down, not too sternly, "Boys and girls, I beg you to be a little more quiet at your play."

Suddenly a girlish voice cried out, "My grandfather could not muzzle you, and you are not going to muzzle us." I was startled by the reminiscence of an incident of long ago. Sometime later, the child's father, the distinguished lawyer and educator James Marshall, elder son of Louis Marshall, said to me, "The little girl who called out to you, 'You are not going to muzzle us,' was my daughter." Thus again out of the mouths of babes and sucklings!

Thus far I have dealt only with the outward circumstances which marked the founding of the Free Synagogue in 1906–1907. I had half resolved to found a Free Synagogue even before my series of "trial sermons" before the Temple Emanu-El. The task proved more difficult than I had forseen. I soon found myself facing a rather wide, if not deep-seated, hostility on the part of temple and synagogue groups within the community. The hostility sometimes verged upon the vulgarity of abuse, as in the case of one of the so-called leading rabbis of New York, who described the Free Synagogue in its earliest days as "a hall, with an orator, an audience, and a pitcher of ice water." Orator was meant to be a contemptuous substitute for preacher. Hall it really was, first in fact the Hudson Theatre by the kindness of its owner, Henry B. Harris, and after that the Universalist Church of our Father on West 81st Street for two years. Thereafter we entered into and for thirty years, 1910–1940, occupied Carnegie Hall in succession to Felix Adler, who with the Society for Ethical Culture, had been its tenant from its erection in 1892 until 1910.

An unexpectedly hospitable response greeted my first addresses or lectures. Some supporters, I do not doubt after all these years, were attracted by the mere novelty of the undertaking—David, challenging, without wishing to slay, the Goliath (of a synagogue) of the Philistines. Perhaps the daring of a still young rabbi (of thirty-two years) to found single-handed, a synagogue organization awakened some admiration for the proposal and its author.

Among these supporters were such as were appealed to by the vitality and freshness of the venture, seeing that there had been nothing new and vital in American synagogue life for a generation. Many of them wondered at the vigor and directness of my Jewish affirmations and my still more Jewish self-affirmation. I made clear beyond all doubt that the Free Synagogue would never become a retreat or asylum for fainthearted and pusillanimous Jews, that it was to be wholly, unequivocally a Jewish adventure, that it would be deeply, unreservedly, and even rejoicingly Jewish. In my first address delivered in January 1907, I asked the question: What is a Free Synagogue, and answered:

A Jewish society, for I am a Jew, a Jewish teacher. The Free Synagogue is not to be an indirect or circuitous avenue of approach to Unitarianism; it is not to be a society for the gradual conversion of Jewish men or women to any form of Christianity. We mean to be vitally, intensely, unequivocally Jewish. Jews who would not be Jews, will find no place in the Free Synagogue, for we, its founders, wish to be not less Jewish but more Jewish in the highest and noblest sense of the term.

Underlying, in truth inspiring, the liberalism of the Free Synagogue lay my own deep protest against the lifelessness of what had once been a great and living Jewish movement, the lifeblood of which had been pressed out as witnessed by the smugness characterizing New York temple Judaism. This had ceased to be Reform Judaism without even ever having become liberal. Its strength, such as it was, lay merely in its opposition to equally unvital Jewish Orthodoxy.

It was the pulseless, meagerly attended Sabbath service that moved me to establish within the Free Synagogue in the fall of 1907 a Sunday-morning service. This was not meant to replace the traditional Sabbath service but to supplement it for those who could not take part in the seventh-day Sabbath service. We did not seek to disestablish the Jewish Sabbath, as Emil Hirsch had frankly, even militantly, moved Chicago's Sinai to do. What we sought was to substitute the living voice of the Hebrew Prophets for the little-understood reading of the Hebrew Pentateuchal or Torah Scroll.

Herein we erred, for, as I have long seen, even the form of the Torah, the Scroll of the Law, had become too precious to the tradition of the synagogue to be lightly, indeed on any account, abolished. For years its use has become a part of traditional Sabbath and Holy Day services. I made a further mistake in taking it for granted that my unchanging Zionist position was fully understood by those who flocked to the services, not that I for a single moment concealed or minimized my Zionist loyalty. But I failed to make clear, as I ought to have done, the duality of my faith in liberalism as the (religious) expression of the Jewish spiritual genius and in Zionism as the faith and hope for the future of the Jewish people. I must frankly add that my sabbatical year, which came in 1913, meant my first visit to Palestine and resulted in the final and irrevocable decision that there was no other way than to rebuild the land and the people—land and people, people and land, reacting reciprocally, the land rebuilding the people, the people recreating the land.

To return to the persons and groups warmest and eagerest in welcoming the Free Synagogue, the largest number of its adherents was made up of such as had not only been estranged but actually had come to feel repelled by the unvital character of temple and synagogue institutionalism and were trembling on the edge of come-outism. It was such Jews, quite a few members of the secular, withal spiritual, Society for Ethical Culture, whom the prophetic mood of the Free Synagogue recalled and regained for positive relation once again to the faith of their fathers.

Many of these were not merely flirting with but closely approaching the Ethical Society. This was true because of the great appeal of Felix Adler, who was the one prophetic Jewish voice in the life of the city, though even he seemed to fail to understand that in truth he was in his own generation in the authentic line of the Hebrew Prophets—Emerson in form, but his spirit that of Isaiah.

One further group was halted in its exit, those Jews who felt that the Unitarian Church, too, was monotheistic. That feeling was vastly reinforced by the attractive personality of a group of noted preachers of religion over two generations in the Unitarian pulpit of New York—Collyer, Wright, Williams, Slicer, Chadwick, Savage, Chapin, Hall, and most notably in my own day the second Theodore Parker of his own Communion, bravest of teachers, noblest among men, John Haynes Holmes.

To such as these, my clear and uncompromising Jewishness made appeal, plus the adventurous tale of a young, little-known rabbi out of the West, remembered if at all only as a Zionist protagonist, who had dared to refuse the premier Jewish pulpit of America.

Perhaps I have not thus far made wholly clear the principle on which the Free Synagogue rested or was to rest. It was the principle, as I saw it, of pulpit freedom, which, according to Mr. Marshall, had uniformly been denied to the men who stood in Emanu-El's pulpit. This denial had done most to make the American Jewish pulpit without significance save in the fewest of instances—Hirsch in Chicago—Sinai, and before him the most prophetic figure who has stood in an American Jewish pulpit—David Einhorn. He had been almost alone among American rabbis in braving the wrath of slavery's defenders in an almost wholly Southern community, Baltimore. My first and last words alike in my Portland congregation were the demand that its pulpit must remain free, and in truth its freedom had given me the strength to battle though a number of critical situations that had arisen during my six Oregon years. What I had named as the *sine qua non* of my acceptance of the Emanu-El pulpit was merely a restatement of my experience in the Far West congregation of Beth Israel.

One of the deepest satisfactions of my life has been to see that the Jewish pulpit is become free, that is to say as free as the men who stand in it will it to be, and that many younger men in the Christian ministry have generously acknowledged that they owe the freedom of their pulpits in part to the battle I once waged when I declared that a pulpit that is not free is without moral and spiritual meaning.

My second and not minor plea was that the synagogue must again become democratically managed and that there could be no synagogue democracy as long as the pews and dues system obtained. Both together introduced into what should have been the democratic fellowship of religious communion all the unlovely differentiations of the outer world—pews occupied by and reserved solely for their owners, and definite sums exacted from those who chose to be affiliated with synagogue or temple. Pews in a religious assembly thus became a purchasable and taxable commodity, and the best places—what ought to have been the places of honor—reserved for the possessing, never for those in humbler circumstances. We therefore introduced the system of unassigned pews, to which we added the concept and practice of voluntary and free contributions. Beyond all this, we sought to introduce the mood and manners of democracy into the traditional but almost forgotten democracy of the synagogue.

Not only was the pulpit to be free and unfettered and the pew untaxed and voluntary in its support but something more important than these, the synagogue was to be inwardly free, free in its innermost ideals and aspirations, free to follow the high traditions of its prophetic genius. This was the beginning of my never ending revolt against that Reform which had become formal and lifeless, which, after having long fought Orthodoxy, had with the years become no less unvital than Orthodoxy, without evoking the loyalty that the rich and traditional beauty of the Synagogue at its best was still capable of commanding.

I felt and feel that neither conformity nor reformism is the secret of Synagogue power, but solely its right to develop with such freedom as is the guardian and guarantee of the strength of progress. The synagogue can never forswear or forfeit that free development and unhindered growth that, apart from and above Reform and Orthodoxy, has been the quintessence of its genius. If I have a regret in relation to the launching of the Free Synagogue, it is that its earliest appeal rested too much on unessential aspects of its progran, the Sunday service, the substitution of English and voluntary prayers for the Hebrew liturgy with its undeniable majesty somewhat marred, alas, by repetitiousness.

Yet another aspect of the Free Synagogue movement became of high importance. I had felt from the beginning that a synagogue should be more than a gathering of divine worshipers and that within the synagogue's life worship should be translated into collective and organized human service. I could not abide the reproach that in most synagogues social service is left to the sisterhoods when these do not limit themselves to the meeting of mortgage interest, as if the wise and true care of the needy bore no relation to brotherhood and brotherliness.

I called Rabbi Sidney E. Goldstein, then the assistant superintendent of Mt. Sinai Hospital, to become the head of the Social Service Division of the synagogue. He shared my views and we proceeded to put them into practice, beginning with the service of our volunteer synagogue members among Jewish patients at Bellevue Hospital and later Lebanon. This formula was continued throughout forty fruitful years. Notable among the contributions of the Social Service Division throughout a generation was the service among the tuberculous of Bellevue and later Montefiore, out of which, with our help, there grew the factory for the tuberculous with its opportunity for part-time employment under medical supervision and our very special and socially enlightened service in the field of mental hygiene at Bellevue.

From the beginning, our plans with relation to social service as a part of the synagogue life had met with the approval of the social-service leaders, such as Dr. Lee K. Frankel, Homer Folks, happily still among the living, then and up to recently secretary of the State Charities Aid Association, and later Frankel's successor, Dr. Solomon Loewenstein. The Social Service Division formally began its work and among those to speed it on its way was Jacob Schiff, who said:

The word of God heard in the Synagogue becomes of value only if it is carried into everyday life. This is so well understood that it sounds like a commonplace to repeat it. And still how few in daily life practice this! How few stop to consider how egotistical are their lives, and that most of their acts, unknown to themselves, are done for their own personal comfort.

There is, perhaps, no more cruel principle, even though it be inexorable, than that upon which, as Herbert Spencer has expressed it, the world rests, "the survival of the fittest." Because of this we should feel that duty calls us to step in and be of help to those who are left behind in the race by reason of this inexorable rule. These we meet everywhere—in our families, among our acquaintances, in the pursuit of our daily vocations, and we so often pass them without taking notice.

In this large community how many need us, to how many can we be useful! It need not only be the sick and the needy who perhaps more readily excite our compassion, to whom service can be rendered in many forms. To every one of our fellow-citizens, through work for the municipality, to the dependent classes, through cooperation in movements for the benefit of the dwellers in tenements, to the immigrant, to the delinquent, to numberless others who need us and to whom we can become of service.

Social Service is service to the very society of which we form an integral part, to which we owe a constant duty and in rendering service of value to society, we bestow the greatest benefit upon ourselves. It is in this spirit of benefiting all who need you, that I wish you Godspeed in the work of Social Service which you are about to inaugurate. If you achieve success therein, as I doubt not you will, you will only the more largely increase the claim for recognition of the movement which your self-sacrificing leader has taken up with so much inspiring enthusiasm.

But the story of the founding of the Free Synagogue does not tell the whole tale. Within a year thereafter many requests came to me to found a Free Synagogue branch on the East Side. These requests were fortified by a meeting held at the Henry Street

Settlement, suggested, if not called, by Lillian Wald, a meeting for the most part of young people under Henry Street Settlement inspiration. That meeting did much to convince me that it was my duty as well as privilege to bring the teaching and influence of the Free Synagogue not only to the favored and possessing groups but to the masses, who had not forsaken their Orthodox Jewish moorings and yet were eager in the midst of their humbler milieu to hear the word and the message of an intensely loyal Jewish liberal. We found a meeting place, namely, Clinton Hall near Grand Street, for Sabbath Eve services, and we conjoined with this a religious school to provide a pleasant and friendly meeting place for young people, who were all but compelled to find their social life amid places unfit for the young intellectuals of the East Side.

Here a difficulty arose that was bound up with the generous spirit and good will of Mr. Schiff. It was he who, soon after I returned to New York from Oregon, made the proposal that instead of founding a synagogue in the center of the city I go to the crowded East Side Jewish district and there establish and conduct a Downtown East Side Free Synagogue. For two reasons I found it necessary to decline the offer, which included a budget large enough to maintain a planned program of such synagogue activities as I visioned, without calling on me to perform the painful task of securing the needed funds.

First, I knew that the East Side Jews had in no wise been taken into the counsel of the New York Jewish community. East Siders were still regarded, a full generation after their fathers' arrival in this country, as beneficiaries, whom "uptown" and its charities had once served and might again be called upon to serve. East Side Jewry was in no real sense consulted with respect to Jewish problems, great or small. Counsel was given, asked or unasked; decisions were taken; consultation there was practically none. I felt at once that I would place myself in an intolerable, indeed inexplicable, situation if I preached and conducted religious services exclusively for the masses, the ill-to-do. This would be doubly true if it were known, as I would insist that it should be known, that the services were subventioned by the well-to-do, even though the subsidy should come from one of large substance who was a man of deep, traditional Jewish piety. Mr. Schiff, whose judgment was rarely questioned, whose generosity was still more rarely rejected, agreed with some reluctance.

The East Side services were held regularly on the Sabbath Eve with a crowded attendance, made up for the most part of the sons and daughters of Conservative and Orthodox families, who probably looked a little askance at a service conducted in English by a rabbi quite frankly liberal, who did not wear the traditional cap. As for that cap, it would have been the part of wisdom and conciliatoriness to have worn it. To have done so would have violated no personal conviction; not to wear it offended many of the older generation, whose children in that case attended the service without the approval of their parents.

No man could have preached to a more finely intelligent group, deeply concerned about Jewish and general problems, religious, racial, political. Some years later it was suggested to me that the Downtown Branch of the work was unnecessary. I frankly placed the question before the Executive Committee of the East Side Free Synagogue. Their response was reassuring and heartwarming not only to me but to my associates in this pioneer work:

NEW YORK, MARCH 23, 1915

DEAR DR. WISE:

It is our earnest hope and wish that the Free Synagogue will continue its work on the East Side. A very wide gap would be left here if the Free Synagogue should remove its beauty and inspiration from the life of the Downtown people. More people than we can even imagine have come under the influence of the Free Synagogue, although these people are not consciously aware of it their lives have been filled with beauty and kindliness toward their fellowmen as a result of this influence. We hope and pray that the Free Synagogue may long continue its beneficent work, doing true Social Service Work, not merely almsgiving. . . .

We, who have been interested in the work from the very beginning, feel that the Free Synagogue is constantly appealing to a larger number of people Downtown day by day. The results of such work as you are doing cannot be felt definitely within a year or two or three, but need years to build it up and show something really tangible in results obtained. But the influence is constantly at work, and will bring the results aimed for surely.

Sincerely yours,

[signed] Celia Hentel

To this day, after nearly forty years, I meet in every part of the country with men and women who tell me of regular attendance at the Clinton Hall services of the Free Synagogue of long ago. Among these are some of the Jewish leaders and scholars, of our time—to name only one among them, the learned, the brilliant Dr. Solomon Goldman of Chicago.

SAMUEL CHOTZINOFF

Samuel Chotzinoff was born in Russia in 1889 and had a distin-guished career in music in the United States, where he died in 1964. An excellent pianist, he was the accompanist for the vio-linists, Efrem Zimbalist and Jascha Heifetz, and the concert singer Alma Gluck. He was a music critic on the New York World *and the* New York Post, *a consultant to the National Broadcasting System, and its General Music Director for radio and television. He played an important role in organizing the NBC Symphony Orchestra, and persuaded his close friend, Arturo Toscanini, to accept the post of conductor of the Orchestra.*

Chotzinoff married Pauline Heifetz, the sister of the noted violinist.

In A Lost Paradise, *he describes the first sixteen years of his life—in Russia, England and New York.*

The chapter that follows describes how, in 1910, the young Chotzinoff became Americanized and adjusted himself to the New York school system.

Life on Stanton Street*

SAMUEL CHOTZINOFF

THE *St. Paul* made a record run of less than seven days from Liverpool to New York. The trip was smooth and pleasant, though our quarters, which we shared with about two dozen other passengers, were somewhat cramped. This room, in which we could do little but sleep, was designed like a large egg crate, with three tiers of cubicles for bunks and with just enough room in the center to move about before climbing in and out of our beds. The ship featured a kosher kitchen for the Orthodox Jewish passengers, but my father had doubts about its authenticity, and both he and my mother subsisted on oranges and the *kuchlech* my mother had baked in preparation for the journey. As a result of earnest representations by my mother, the children were permitted by paternal dispensation to eat the ship's food if they chose. But the dining-saloon was stuffy and airless, and the only food we could keep down comfortably was raw herring and bread. Besides, our parents' show of super-Orthodoxy gave us, notwithstanding their sanction, an uncomfortable feeling of guilt, and we debated among ourselves the possibility of being overtaken by divine retribution on the Day of Atonement. Although it was a good ten weeks to Yom Kippur, it was not to be supposed that God would fail to remember our semi-transgression on the day when He decides the fate of every living soul.

The voyage introduced us to an olfactory phenomenon known to all transatlantic travelers of those days as the smell of "ship." This pervasive, insidious odor, a distillation of bilge and a number of less identifiable putrescences, settled on one's person, clothes, and luggage and stayed there forever, impervious to changes of habitat, clothing, and the cleansing agent available to

* Reprinted from *A Lost Paradise*, Alfred A. Knopf, New York, 1955, pp. 68–79.

the poor. It was many years before I realized that only steerage passengers smelled of "ship." Until then I assumed that all persons, rich or poor, traveling on ships became, as a matter of course, victims of this affliction. And, like all afflictions that are protracted, it lost its terrors through familiarity. One *expected* arrivals from Europe to smell of "ship." So much so that on visits to the homes of neighbors, one could tell at once by the pervading smell of "ship" that they were entertaining guests from abroad.

Smells, in general, played an important part in our lives. Not an unpleasant part, I recall, but one that in its way made life a little easier, serving for identification of persons, their habits and social position, perhaps as clues to character and occupation. Everything and everybody had a smell. Some smells were generic and impersonal, others particular, like the leitmotifs in the music dramas of Richard Wagner. And just as the introduction of a leitmotif warns the listener that the personage it represents is about to appear, so the insinuation of a smell in a room usually heralded the approach of the person who had become identified with it. Immigrants, however, could not so be identified individually for at least a year or two after their arrival, as their own odors were overpowered by and absorbed into the more exigent smell of "ship."

Old people had, in general, an acrid smell, and old men invariably smelled of snuff. Young people and children merely smelled unwashed. We knew that we too would smell of snuff when we grew old. That was in the nature of things. Life was stern and realistic, and the conditions it imposed were not subject to question or criticism. After taking snuff it was quite proper for people to blow their noses without the interposition of a handkerchief. In rooms not graced with spittoons, what was more natural than to spit on the floor! It was natural, though not desirable, for children to have lice in their hair and for grown-ups to harbor them in the seams of their clothing and underwear. Beds and bedding and all overstuffed furniture were infested with bedbugs. The pests were periodically hunted and exterminated; but their presence was not considered a disgrace, and they shared with

poverty and disease the status of divine visitation. "What brand
of bedbug powder do you use?" was a natural query when housewives met on the street or entertained one another with tea and
kuchlech. Presumably the question was also asked by housewives
on the West Side. The world was most probably the same for
everybody. We knew that rich people had more rooms, better
food and clothing, and easier lives than the poor; but we had no
reason to believe that their lot was otherwise different, or that
they were exempt from what we believed to be universal afflictions. On the visible world, half of which we knew first-hand, and
the other half of which we could only imagine, there were, for us,
certain unchangeable phenomena: children were dirty and were
obliged to scratch their heads; mothers were unkempt and slat-
ternly; everybody, old and young, had teeth pulled regularly, so
that middle-aged and old people had few if any teeth; a great
many children died young; everybody slept in underwear; parents always quarreled; mothers were generally indulgent to their
children, but fathers either kept aloof or were brutal to them.
And, of course, everyone over fourteen years of age was employed
in gainful labor. Not before the age of fourteen could one obtain
one's working papers. It took a considerable amount of experience in the realm of what is now called "the underprivileged"
before I could collate these observations, draw my conclusions,
and, by extension, relate the picture thus built up to that part of
the world which lay outside my knowledge and beyond my reach.

When the *St. Paul* reached New York, we were met by my
father's second cousin, the junk-dealer. This kinsman's name was
Gold. It had been Goldstein, but on his arrival in America he
had thus shortened it at the friendly suggestion of an immigration officer who was passing on the fitness of arriving aliens to
enter the United States. Now, on the pier, our cousin urged my
father to perform a similar operation on our own "useless"
family name, as he termed it, suggesting "Chot" as a desirable
abbreviation. My father rejected the idea on the ground that he
failed to see the need for any alteration of any name. In an effort
to convince him, Mr. Gold recalled how he, too, had resisted at
first, but had been unable to deny the appositeness of the immi-

gration officer's question: "What good is Stein to you?" He now demanded to be told what possible good the last two syllables of our name could be to us in a country so dynamic and so impatient of nonessentials as America. "For here," Mr. Gold said triumphantly—and we heard enunciated for the first time the then celebrated and popular slogan—"Time is money." My father, however, remained unconvinced, and, much to Mr. Gold's displeasure, we retained what he always regarded as an impossible, noncommercial name. Many years later my three brothers arrived independently at the junk-dealer's philosophy of nomenclature. Indeed, they went farther than Mr. Gold by discarding altogether our family name, each one adopting a terse, one-syllable, indigenous, respectable, and consequently absolutely commercial surname. Louis, the youngest of the three, chose White; Solomon, the next in age, adopted Chase; and Albert, the eldest, who all his life meticulously observed the entire ritual of Jewish Orthodoxy, selected the name of Church.

Although Passaic fell short of being the Eden that Mr. Gold had promised in his letters to my father, it proved to be a lively town, with horse-cars, interesting shops, and sidewalks paved with tar, which had a pleasant smell, and became so soft on very hot days that one's heels sank into it. Our cousin lived on the outskirts of the city in an area inhabited only by Jews. He occupied one floor of a two-story frame house. On the second floor there were two vacant rooms, which, with one room in Mr. Gold's apartment, were assigned to us. I do not recall in what manner the ten of us were disposed in this arrangement, but not many days elapsed before Mrs. Gold's exuberant show of hospitality was replaced by an impatience with our presence which could not be lost on any of us. On the other hand, there was no visible alteration in Mr. Gold's interest in us and in his solicitude for our future, though it soon was evident that he was unable to fulfill his promises of work for my brothers and sisters and a teaching position in a *cheder* for my father. To the end of our stay he kept reiterating his faith in the commercial possibilities of "Birdie Kahndie," his exotic mispronunciation of Bergen County. His pride in this region was immense, and he would prophesy that in ten years' time "Birdie Kahndie" would out-strip in population and wealth any territory of its size in the United States.

He seemed oblivious of the rancid smells of the long stretches of milky swampland in the vicinity of his home, and impervious to the bite of the large mosquitoes that filled the air the moment the sun went down. But I was not. And soon after we settled in "Birdie Kahndie" I developed malaria and walked about weakly, feeling queasy and running slight but uncomfortable tempera-tures. Mr. Gold took me to a dispensary in Passaic, where a doctor prescribed quinine and a change of climate. As there was nothing now to keep us in Passaic except Mr. Gold's unconvinc-ing prognostications of a speedy change for the better in our fortunes, my health became a consideration of importance. And in a council held by the heads of both families it was decided—with Mr. Gold dissenting—that we should try the climate of New York as an antidote to my malaria, at the same time testing the reputation of the metropolis as a place of great opportunity for the enterprising alien.

Enthusiastically shepherded by Mrs. Gold, my mother jour-neyed to New York and rented a suitable apartment in Stanton Street, on the lower East Side, one block from the Bowery. Into this we moved one very hot morning in late August. Right in front of our house a large black horse lay dead in the gutter. He must have been there for some time, for the stench was dreadful, and flies, large and small, covered every inch of the carcass and hovered in swarms over it. Later in the day I looked out the window and saw several small boys astride the animal, engaged in skinning it with their pocket knives. Their sport was presently interrupted, however, by the arrival of a large van for the re-moval of the horse. This complicated operation attracted all the children in the neighborhood, who watched the departure of the beast with regret.

My health improved slowly in Stanton Street. Once a week I walked to a dispensary at Second Avenue and Fourteenth Street and received, gratis, a dose of quinine. My mother accompanied me there, for she, too, was unwell, frequently announcing in a dramatic tone of voice that her heart had stopped beating. I was not unduly alarmed, for I was at the time unaware of the crucial function of this organ. Nor did the doctor at the dispensary regard my mother's condition with the seriousness she thought it demanded. He would laugh at her extravagant claims and prescribe Hoffmann's drops. A few drops of this magic liquid on a lump of sugar had the effect of instantly reviving my mother's dormant heart.

The public schools opened in September. I was to enter the second grade of the school nearest my home, a large red-brick building on Houston Street. Preparations for the fall term could be observed everywhere. The shops on Stanton Street were displaying every necessity for the resumption of learning. All manner of boys' clothing, including ravishing sailor suits with whistle attached and smart brown knee-length gabardine overcoats, were on view behind the plate-glass windows. The candy stores had the most interesting display of articles used in the classroom. The number and variety of pencil boxes alone took one's breath away. There seemed to be no limit to the complexity of pencil boxes. Beginning with the simple oblong box, plain or lacquered, they evolved into two- and three-storied structures with secret compartments. Prices ranged from seven cents to the fantastic sum of a dollar. The pencil box was, admittedly, a necessity; but a box costing more than ten cents became a symbol of social superiority. The very few who could afford dollar boxes became the acknowledged leaders of their classes. A highly prized peek into the lavish interiors of their pencil boxes was vouchsafed only as a reward for services promised or performed.

It was out of the question for me to begin school without a pencil box and some other less important "supplies" that beckoned through the window of the candy store on our block. Those others ranged from plain and colored blotters to school bags in the shape of knapsacks. Though I pleaded hard for a two-storied pencil box costing a quarter, my mother bought me a plain, oblong casket with a sliding top for ten cents. When our shopping was done, my supplies consisted of the pencil box, four writing pads at a penny each, and a set of colored blotters costing a nickel, the last wrung from my reluctant parent after I had conjured up a classroom crisis in which the teacher would call for a show of blotters and I would be the only pupil unable to produce any. My mother had a horror of nonconformity, a failing I early spotted and often exploited.

On the first Monday in September my mother took me and my scanty supplies to school, where I was enrolled and given a desk and a seat in a large classroom. The teacher, a gray-haired, middle-aged lady, told us to call her Miss Murphy. I wondered if she meant to imply that this was to be her name in class and that at home she was called something else. The name sounded alien and therefore forbidding, and might have been chosen to emphasize the natural barrier between teacher and pupil. She was obviously a pagan—a *Chreestch*—our name for any non-Jew. Miss Murphy read out our last names from a long paper in front of her, and we raised our hands to signify our presence. She was severely distant, and her impersonal attitude, added to the formality of being called by our last names, cast a chill on the classroom. Soon one began to long for the sound of one's first name as for an endearment that would, at a stroke, establish a human relationship between oneself and Miss Murphy. But it was not to be. By the following morning Miss Murphy, having already memorized the surnames of her entire class, called the roll without once referring to her paper.

She then went to the blackboard and in beautiful script wrote "Catt" and, looking over the sea of heads in front of her, said: "Something is wrong with the spelling of this word. Katzenelenbogen, stand up and tell me what is wrong." A small, skinny boy rose in the back of the room and said something in an indistinct voice. "Speak up, Katzenelenbogen!" Miss Murphy sharply commanded. My heart went out to Katzenelenbogen in his ordeal. I was conscious of the disparity between the long and important-sounding name and the frailty and insignificance of its possessor. Miss Murphy, however, could not be blamed for adhering to a long-established practice in all public schools. Even in kindergarten, I learned, four- and five-year-olds were called by their last names. The practice was inevitably adopted by the children among themselves in their out-of-school hours, of course with suitable abbreviations of the longer names, and often with prefatory, highly descriptive adjectives.

Notwithstanding Miss Murphy's frigidity, she soon commanded our interest and respect, and we made good progress in reading and spelling. For some mysterious reason, we were more interested in spelling outside the classroom than in it. In the classroom we were content to plod along with the elementary vocabulary of *McGuffey's Eclectic Second Reader*. But at recess time in the yard, and on the street on our way home, we challenged one another to spell long and complicated words whose meaning we didn't know and never dreamt to inquire. Words such as "combustible" and "Mississippi" were somehow in the air. How the craze got started I never knew. But walking home one afternoon, I accidentally collided with a boy I didn't know. Instead of the usual, belligerent "Hey! Can't you look where you're going?" I was peremptorily commanded to spell "combustible." I couldn't, never having heard the word before; whereupon the boy rattled off "co-mb-us-ti-bl-e" with incredible speed and triumphantly went on his way. It was not long before I, too, learned to spell the fascinating word and others equally difficult and provocative. Soon I could rattle off "M-i-double-ess-i-double-ess-i-double-p-i" as rapidly as any child in the neighborhood.

The words in *McGuffey's*, though simpler, lacked the lovely sibilance and long, musical line of those we challenged one another with on the streets. In consequence, they were more difficult to spell. But they did have the advantage of intelligibility, and as strung together in *McGuffey's Reader* they told connected, highly interesting stories. *McGuffey's* took the reader into town and country, but I was delighted to discover that, like myself, it had a strong bias for the latter. I was much taken with a story in the reader called "The Town Mouse and the Country Mouse," which presented a dialogue between two rodents residing respectively in a metropolis and and on a farm. The city dweller, who spoke first, advanced apparently incontrovertible arguments on behalf of urban life, stressing especially the prevalence of food left carelessly lying around by humans and the plenitude of holes and crevices and other avenues of escape from cats and destructive agents in general. But when he confidently rested his case, the country mouse, a timid and gentle creature, spoke up, painting an idyllic picture of life in the open, gently emphasizing the delicious leftovers in the country kitchen, the sweet smell of hay in the barn, the coziness of attics in the winter, the feeling of space and freedom, and, above all, the security offered by fields and forests. The issue was settled after the country mouse had returned home, when the town mouse, overconfident of urban security, fell a prey to the machinations of a cat, who devoured him with the sophisticated relish peculiar to city felines. Miss Murphy, who read aloud to us, appeared neither interested in nor moved by the *McGuffey* stories. She read without nuances and exhibited no emotion. Completely indifferent to the music of poetry, she would recite a line like the exquisite "How would I like to go up in a Swing, Up in the air so blue!" in a cold, earthbound voice, look up from her book, and say: "Plotkin, spell 'swing.' " Yet she was an excellent disciplinarian, and our class speedily gained a reputation for good spelling.

She also conceived and put into effect a new system for the handling of hats and overcoats which saved time and enabled us to begin our studies in the mornings a few minutes after nine and to be out on the street soon after the bell rang at three. The system was simplicity itself. As each boy entered the class, he deposited his hat and coat on a designated spot on the floor on either side of the blackboard. At nine o'clock, at noon, at one, and at three two boys selected for their strength and stamina would station themselves in front of the class to right and left of the room. Each of the two would pick up a hat and coat from the heap in front of him, hold it aloft for recognition. The owner would then announce his name and open wide his arms to receive the garments flung in his direction. For a few minutes the air would be filled with hurtling coats, scarves, hats, and, on rainy or snowy days, rubbers and rubber boots. But it offered the pleasures of a humorous game, what with the uncertain aim of the throwers and the possibility of being knocked over by a too speedily propelled overcoat. For this innovation and her general efficiency, Miss Murphy was soon liked and even admired.

Miss Murphy lived in Brooklyn, an hour's journey by the Grand Street horse-car to the East River, the ferry to cross it, and another horse-car on the other side. She therefore always brought her lunch with her. This consisted, much to our surprise, of one sandwich of jam, the bread remarkably white and of the texture of cotton, and one thin slice of sponge cake, each wrapped in tissue paper, and both done up in brown wrapping paper and tied with cord, It seemed to all of us rather meager nourishment for a strong-minded, powerful woman. But I had heard it said that Christians in general ate sparingly, the women especially showing a marked distaste for food. The men, on the other hand, were partial to drink, as could be verified by visiting the Bowery around the corner from the street I lived on. When she dismissed her class at noon, Miss Murphy would ask one of her pupils to run and buy her a bottle of milk, and we soon began to regard this errand as a privilege and a special mark of favor. Yet she was careful to rotate us, and by the end of the term every boy in the class had bought her a bottle of milk. She had a way of saying: "Would you hand me my *puhss?*" which we thought elegant. When the pocketbook was handed her, she would extract a coin from it delicately with her thumb and forefinger, the little finger stretched out as if she was about to bring forth something precious or highly dangerous. She ate her lunch privately, seated at her desk. Even with no one to see her, one could be sure that she ate her jam sandwich with the decorum of Chaucer's "Nonne, a Prioresse," and "let no morsel from her lippes falle." Incidentally, the sandwich was responsible for my first demerit in class, the morning when Miss Murphy taught us to sing "Columbia, the jam of the ocean." I thought of Miss Murphy's sandwich and could not repress a giggle when we sang the opening line with its stress on the word "jam." Sometimes Miss Murphy would bring a bunch of violets, which she would place in a glass of water on her desk. She looked stylish at all times, her hair in a pompadour, a gold watch pinned on her blouse, a large, black patent-leather belt around her waist. She was immaculate. At least twice each day she would remove the flowers, dip the tips of her fingers in the glass of water, and wipe them with her handkerchief. So conscious did the class become of Miss Murphy's fastidiousness that for Christmas most of her pupils gave her a cake of soap.

Stanton Street was an exciting place in which to live. It was the shopping center of the neighborhood, and in men's clothing it rivaled Hester Street. Perhaps in volume of sales Hester Street stood supreme; but its garments were in the main second-hand, while Stanton Street's were quite new. Furthermore, samples of the clothes on Stanton Street could be seen in all their chic and splendor on marvelous, lifelike dummies in the shop windows. One window that held me spellbound displayed a father with an elaborate mustache, surrounded by his five sons, ranging in size from an infant to a young man almost as tall as his parent. Each child wore the clothes suited to his age. I yearned for the blue sailor suit with whistle attached on the fourth son, a child of about my own age. It occupied my thoughts and even dreams for years.

Stanton Street had other attractions besides shop windows. Organ-grinders with monkeys would appear at all hours and play a varied assortment of music. Through them I learned many popular songs, but the only one I can now recall is *Sweet Rosie O'Grady*. I found it a sweet ballad and a tender declaration of love, notwithstanding its waltz-like rhythm. The organ-grinders played other tunes of a more serious character, which, through repetition, I learned to sing, though it was years before I discovered their identity. Among them were the *"Miserere"* from *Il Trovatore* and *"Addio del passato"* from *La Traviata*, both of which brought tears to my eyes. Often I would follow an organ-grinder through many streets and so hear the *"Miserere"* perhaps a dozen times over, never failing to respond to the somber, inexpressibly said minor chords at the beginning and the noble but equally doleful melody in major which comes soon after. I have since wondered at Verdi's predilection for the major mode to convey sadness, and his success in doing the opposite of what all other composers before and after him did.

Stanton Street ended at the Bowery, a block away from the house in which I lived. The Bowery was in bad odor with all the parents of the neighborhood for a great many reasons, all of them concerned with the welfare of the children. The street was the habitat of drunks and criminals, the latter so bold and vicious that they were often more than a match for the policemen who attempted to restrain them. Nevertheless, the temptation to explore for oneself so infamous a street was too strong to resist. In company with a playmate or two for protection in case of assault, I frequently roamed the Bowery as far north as Eighth Street and south to Chatham Square. It is true that nothing noteworthy ever happened, but the din of the elevated trains passing overhead, their engines belching smoke and sending showers of sparks and cinders down on the wagons and pedestrians below, the noise coming through the swinging doors of the many saloons, the spectacle of drunkards swaying and teetering and talking loudly to themselves, combined to give us a delicious feeling of daring and fear. Sometimes the Bowery invaded Stanton Street in the persons of derelict women we called "Mary Sugar Bums." The poor, dirty, ragged creatures would come reeling into our block, cursing and swearing, and we would run after them, calling out "Mary Sugar Bum! Mary Sugar Bum!" and they would threaten us grotesquely with their fists and lunge at us futilely when we came too close.

There was always excitement on Stanton Street from the time school let out until supper time, and for an hour or two between that meal and bedtime. Something was always happening, and our attention was continually being shifted from one excitement to another. "What's-a-matter?" was a perpetual query as we were attracted by a sudden frantic exodus from a tenement, the clang of an ambulance as it drew up in front of a house, a person desperately running, pursued by a crowd, a runaway horse and wagon, a policeman forcibly propelling a drunk and twisting his arm until the wretch screamed with pain, an altercation through open windows between next-door neighbors. Occasionally there was the excitement of a Western Union messenger trying to deliver a telegram and asking the children playing on the street on what floor its recipient might live, for there were no bells or letter boxes in the entrance corridors of the tenements on Stanton Street. The mailman blew a whistle in the downstairs hall and called out names in a voice loud enough to be heard even on the fifth floor, and the people would come running downstairs to get their letters.

The arrival of a telegram was a most serious occurrence. Everybody knew that telegrams were dispatched only to announce the death of a relative or friend or, at the very least, a serious illness; and the appearance of the fateful, gray-clad messenger was sure to draw a crowd. On hearing the name of the addressee, the people would speculate aloud on the identity of the deceased, and some neighbor might offer to precede the messenger and tactfully and mercifully prepare the bereaved for the tidings to follow. "Something *terrible* has happened—Mrs. Cohen just got a telegram!"

Every day after supper I would beg to be allowed to play for a while in front of the house, where I could be seen from our windows and, at the proper time, summoned to bed. Between sundown and evening, on fair days, Stanton Street had an enchantment of its own. The dying sun benevolently lacquered the garish red-brick buildings, softly highlighting a window, a cornice, or a doorway. We would play on the sidewalks and in the gutter until the air grew dark and we could barely tell who was who. Then the lamplighter would emerge from the Bowery, carrying his lighted stick in one hand and a small ladder in the other. In the light of the gas lamps we played leapfrog over the empty milk cans in front of the grocery store. Each of us would vault over a single can and then, if successful, augment the hazard by adding a can for the next leap. Some of us learned to vault over as many as seven cans! Or we would play hide-and-go-seek in the dim vestibules of the tenement houses. We very rarely left off our play to return home voluntarily. Those of us who were sought out and induced to go home by mothers or sisters were fortunate, for the appearance of one's father on the scene carried with it the certainty of punishment. Fathers, with few exceptions, were insensitive, brutal, and quick to resort to force in obtaining obedience.

Mothers, too, frequently resorted to force, but only after they had exhausted all peaceful means. I would sometimes try my mother's patience to a degree that drove her to the retaliatory use of what sounded like curse words. I suspected they were not actual words, though, spoken passionately, they sounded authentic enough. They must have been inventions that would have the force but not the connotation of curses one could properly call down on persons one didn't love or wasn't related to, for no one else ever used them and I never discovered their meaning. "You can go tar-tar-ar-ee!" my mother would shout wildly at me, as if she were consigning me to the devil. The effect, for the moment, was the same. For the most part, however, my mother found relief in rhetorical queries addressed to the heavens, like "What does he want of me? Does he wish to shorten my life?" Or she would hurl an epithet and cannily negate it in the same breath, like "The cholera should seize him—not!" My father wasted no time with me when by chance he came into the room at such critical moments. "Let *me* handle him," he would say grimly as he placed himself between us. "Skinning *alive,* that's what he needs," and he would undo his belt preparatory to carrying out what he thought I needed. My mother would then interfere and make excuses for me and the half-withdrawn belt would be reluctantly returned to its place. But on one occasion the two acted in concert against me, thus bringing about the first great disillusionment of my life.

I had disobeyed strict orders not to go outdoors barefoot on a cold rainy afternoon. I returned several hours later with every expectation of being scolded by my mother or punished by my father if he happened to be home. I found both of them at home, but my apprehensions vanished when I saw no anger or resentment in their faces. On the contrary, my father asked me in a pleasant way if I had had a good time, the while he busied himself undoing the knots in a clothesline. I said I had and went to the window to signal my friends on the street that everything was all right, when suddenly I was seized from behind and felt my mother's arms hard around me. A second later my father had bound my legs and hands with the clothesline and dragged me with—shame to tell!—my mother's help into the kitchen, where he tied me fast to a leg of the sink. My father's deceptive behavior did not surprise me; I could expect it of him. But my mother's perfidy shattered in one instant my previously unquestioned trust in her love for me. My refuge and security were gone. My world had toppled around me. If such things could be, my only wish was to die. An hour later I was released, but my freedom, while physically gratifying, could not restore the faith I had lost. It was weeks before I would permit my mother to touch me.

We lived in Stanton Street for about a year. My father, not having the capital to open a *cheder* of his own, taught Hebrew to a few boys in their homes. This brought in very little money. Besides, the inattention of the pupils, who could not keep their eyes on the Bible, but kept staring out of the window, brought on my father's old headaches. Furthermore, he came up against a newfangled idea among parents that teachers were not to administer corporal punishment. It had not been so in the old country. And my father would rather give up a pupil than relinquish so necessary and important a prerogative. My mother reminded him that beggars could not be choosers, but he insisted that they *could*; they could choose starvation! At any rate, *he* required nothing, or very little, for himself. All he needed, he said, was a piece of bread and herring and a roof over his head.

Nevertheless, he usually ate what we all did. Friday nights he would expect and plainly relish a full ceremonial dinner of several courses, beginning with a stuffed fish, the head of which was reserved for him, and of which he ate all but the eyes and the more resistant bones. There would then follow sweet and sour meat roasted to a point of delicious disintegration and flanked by roast potatoes saturated in gravy, and limp, candied carrots. Soup would come last, and my father would help himself to two brimful plates from the large bowl placed in the center of the table. He was inordinately fond of calf's-foot jelly, which my mother would cook on Fridays and put out on the fire escape to cool. On Saturday after *Mincha* (late afternoon prayers) it would be served, preceded by a little whisky, as a delicate collation for him and a fellow worshiper he generally brought home with him.

All in all, he ate so very well that it was difficult to believe his declarations of austerity.

My oldest brother, Albert, had married and had gone to live in Waterbury, Connecticut, where he practiced carpentry and undertook small repair jobs. He had talked my brother Solomon, next to him in age, into going with him, with a view to their forming a partnership as builders and contractors. My brother Louis, aged fourteen, got himself a job as a presser's assistant in a tailor shop in the vicinity of Stanton Street. My three older sisters found work in a cigarette factory. My younger sister hadn't yet reached the kindergarten age. She played around the house and got in my mother's way, and when sent to play in the street, frequently fell down the stairs. Neighbors would pick her up and carry her upstairs, and my mother would have to drop her work and apply poultices and bandages and still her cries, thus defeating the purpose for which she had been relegated to the streets. After school hours I would help out my mother for an hour or so by "minding" the unstable child.

Though most of our family were employed, their aggregate earnings provided the barest subsistence for us. It is true that on Friday nights we invariably had a feast, but that repast was made possible only by economy and deprivation during the rest of the week. I was generally hungry, and I always invested the penny I infrequently got from my mother in "broken cake" at the grocery store. Sweet biscuits in that era were sold, on the East Side at any rate, from large barrels, and "broken cake" was the name for the bits and splinters of biscuits remaining in the bottom when all of the unfractured dainties had been removed. We longed, of course, for the biscuits in their original unharmed condition. Yet "broken cake" had a flavor of its own, owing to the very circumstance that caused its degradation. Lying crushed and chipped under the weight of its unharmed fellows above, it assimilated a variety of aromas, so that the flavor of a piece of "broken cake" offered a concentration of all the flavors of *all* the biscuits in the barrel. I preferred "broken cake" to candy at "Cheap Charlie's," where one could buy ten chocolate-coated walnuts for a penny.

Every street had a "Cheap Charlie." I used to wonder at the

singularity of the candy-store business being exclusively in the hands of men of the same name. These candy stores had an extraordinary attraction for children because of the personal attitude of Charlie to his young customers. This was an even more potent lure than the advertised cheapness of Charlie's wares, which we accepted on faith without inquiry or comparison. Charlie was human and understanding, and was not above entering into the problems of his patrons. Thus it was possible, when one did not happen to have a penny at the moment, to confide in Charlie and, on a promise to pay up at the first opportunity, to leave the store with the chocolate-covered walnuts in a paper bag. The groceryman was less understanding. I suspected that my mother was responsible for his insistence on prompt payment for "broken cake." Nor did I have the heart to blame her. Her own relations with the man were often delicate. I myself had witnessed humiliating scenes in which he categorically refused to give her further credit. But my mother always managed to persuade him to change his mind, alleging an imminent favorable turn of events for us which would promptly take care of all our financial indebtedness.

In school the time for promotion drew near and a great uneasiness swept the class. The fear of being "left back" gripped all but a very few boys who were obviously so brilliant that it was early conceded by the rest of us, as well as by themselves, that there would be no question about *their* promotion. Being "left back" was definitely a dishonor. But not because it was a reflection on one's scholarship. Scholarship was, in fact, suspect, and the "smart" boys who got A's or "stars" became the objects of ribbing and were likely to suffer ostracism. Being "left back" doomed one to loneliness, the sudden disruption of friendships, and a separation from the intrigues, scandals, pleasantries, and feeling of solidarity of a long-established class. Long before the dreaded day arrived we could see Miss Murphy working on the "promotion list" during our study periods. We tried hard to guess at the names she so carefully wrote out by watching the movements of her pen. The crossing of a "t" or the dotting of an "i" could be a clue in that it ruled out a great many names that did not contain those letters. The boys who occupied desks in the first row were sometimes able to catch a name she was writing: a boy would raise his hand for permission to "leave the room," as our trips to the water closets were politely called, and in making for the door would sidle near Miss Murphy's desk and attempt a swift look at the promotion list. But Miss Murphy was aware of these stratagems and did what she could to defeat them. When she left the room, even for a moment, she would lock the list in her desk.

On promotion day the class arrived all scrubbed and neat, with hair combed and definitely parted, the labor of mothers who cherished a wild hope that in case of doubt an extra bit of cleanliness might tip the scales. Miss Murphy gave no indication that she was aware of anything unusual in our appearance. Neither by word nor by look did she indicate that she had sealed the fate of fifty boys in the document that now reposed in her desk. Tense, nervous, and dispirited, we went through our usual morning routine. At ten o'clock the monitors left their seats and opened the windows halfway with long poles while the class rose and exercised their arms and heads with Miss Murphy leading and commanding "Inspire!—Expire!" the class noisily breathing in and out in response. At a quarter to twelve the room suddenly became unaccountably still. Miss Murphy seated herself by her desk, opened it, and drew out the promotion list. I could see the red line down the middle of the page, looking like a thin blood barrier, which separated the names on either side. Miss Murphy, before addressing herself to the list, was exasperatingly deliberate in tidying the top of her desk, arranging her pencils in a row, and moving the water glass with its little bouquet of flowers to one side. At last she was ready.

"I shall now read the promotion list," she announced. "As your name is called, rise and stand in the aisle. Those whose names are not called will remain seated." This seemed to foreshadow doom for many. Classes were known to have been promoted en masse. Clearly ours would not be one of these. The class held its breath as Miss Murphy again gave her attention to the list. "Abramowitz," Miss Murphy intoned, and Abramowitz got to this feet precipitately and stood in the aisle. "Abrams, Abramson, Askenasy." The B's seemed endless, but at last Miss Murphy said: "Chasmanovitch." There was a pause. "Chisel" followed "Chasmanovitch" in the daily roll call. What about Chisel? Chisel's fate did not concern me. Ordinarily I would have wished him well. But if Chisel was not on the list my name should come next. Why did Miss Murphy pause? What could the hesitation portend for me? I waited for the blow. Should Miss Murphy now pronounce the name of Cohen, then both Chisel and I had been "left back." My eyes isolated Miss Murphy's lips as they began to form a name. "Chisel!" Miss Murphy pronounced, and the wretch (his desk was in front of mine), who had slumped down in his seat in despair, now looked about him incredulously, like a criminal who had received a last-minute reprieve. Slowly he got up and shifted over into the aisle. I continued to stare at Miss Murphy's lips. There was another pause, and then I heard my name, clear and loud. I stepped into the aisle in a daze and stood there for a long time, experiencing no sensations of any kind. It was like the suspension of consciousness. Then all at once I was aware of many boys standing in the aisles and Miss Murphy was calling out "Rabinowitz, Redin, Rickin, Sokolov, Spingold, Steinberg, Teitelbaum, Ulansky, Wissotzky, Yarmolovsky, Zeitlin." It was all over. Three wretched boys still sat: Katzenelenbogen, Gershowitz, and Vlacheck. Katzenelenbogen had covered his face with his hands and was crying softly. Gershowitz, his face white, stared straight in front of him. Vlacheck alone showed no signs of defeat. He had been "left back" twice before, and he smiled and leered as if he had expected nothing else and rather gloried in continuing to belong to a minority.

We promoted boys, at a command from Miss Murphy, closed ranks and were marched into an adjacent classroom, where we found four dejected boys, the leftovers of our new grade. Miss Murphy made us a formal farewell address and turned us over to Miss Applebaum, our new teacher. Then the bell rang and we marched into the street and scattered quickly to our homes, for once not loitering to talk and plan, in our eagerness to carry the good news to our families.

I was now a third-grader. My promotion had given me a new confidence in myself, and I looked forward to an interesting term with my old schoolmates under the tutelage of Miss Applebaum. But before a week had passed, my parents decided, most unaccountably, I thought, to leave Stanton Street and move to distant East Broadway, a neighborhood I had never even seen. In consequence, I obtained a transfer to P.S. No. 2 on Henry, between Rutgers and Market Streets. Except for the fact that I was assigned to the third grade in the new school, I was in all other respects in the position of a Katzenelenbogen, Gershowitz, or Vlacheck, for my classmates were all new to me and I had to set about making new friends.

East Broadway was a wide thoroughfare. Our apartment on the third floor of a house on the corner of Rutgers Street overlooked a large square, or rather oblong, adorned by a large black marble fountain, rising in several tiers. I could sense the possibilities of the neighborhood. For, besides the fountain, all the buildings on the west side of East Broadway, extending from Essex to Jefferson streets, had been razed for the eventual construction of a park, and the debris offered the very terrain for possible war games, with rival armies marching and countermarching and striving to gain certain desirable heights. It would be at least a year before the place could be cleared and the park begun, and I foresaw many late afternoons and evenings, not to speak of Sundays, devoted to maneuvers, with myself in some kind of leading role, perhaps as captain of a powerful striking force. The potentialities of the place were innumerable. Looking up Rutgers Street toward the east, there was the river in the distance, with boats of every description plying up and down. Huge warehouses near the water's edge were forever discharging crates and barrels with mysterious contents, and at night one could sit on the large empty trucks parked on the wharves and watch the river and the lights from Brooklyn across it.

Within walking distance were splendors like Brooklyn Bridge, the City Hall, and the Post Office. The mysterious alleys of Chinatown were no more than half a mile away. Certainly East Broadway, at its meeting with Rutgers Square, was the center of the universe, and I looked forward to an exciting and fruitful existence on it. But the prospect of a strange school, a new teacher, and new schoolmates was unpleasant, and I would gladly have relinquished the future delights of East Broadway for the old routine and associations of Stanton Street.

NORBERT WIENER

Norbert Wiener was one of the most remarkable men of the twentieth century. He was a brilliant mathematician, a writer of both fiction and philosophy, and a scientist whose work had a major influence in the contemporary world.

Dr. Wiener became world famous in 1948, when he published a book called Cybernetics. *The word "cybernetics," which was his own invention, derives from the Greek word for "steersman." Wiener used the term cybernetics to define a field that "combines under one heading the study of what in a human context is sometimes loosely described as thinking, and in engineering is known as control and communication." His work in this book and in others helped accelerate the development of computers and automation. During World War II, he made major contributions to the development of radar, tracking, and gun-aiming devices.*

Wiener was born in 1894 in Columbia, Mo. His father, Leo, was Harvard's first professor of Slavonic languages, and the author of A History of Yiddish Literature.

A child prodigy, Norbert Wiener knew the alphabet at the age of eighteen months, could read and write when he was three, and had mastered arithmetic, algebra and geometry at the age of six. When he was fourteen he earned a Bachelor of Arts degree from Tufts College; and he received his Ph.D. from Harvard at 19. He was a member of the faculty of the Massachusetts Institute of Technology for forty-two years, up to the time of his death at the age of 69 in 1964.

Although his father had a deep interest in Yiddish literature, the young Wiener was not aware of his Jewishness until he was sixteen years old. In the selection that follows, drawn from his autobiography, Ex-Prodigy, *he relates some of his achievements as a student, and the shock of his discovery of his Jewish identity.*

Disinherited*

NORBERT WIENER

I HAD WON a scholarship at Cornell. Father was to accompany me to Ithaca, and at the end of the summer we had to decide how to get there. This was still in the days before the inter-urban trolley had been superseded by the bus and the coach. Father and I decided on a romantic trolley jaunt to central New York and Ithaca. There we called on Professor Thilly and made plans for the ensuing academic year. It was decided that I was to have the free run of the Thilly house, and to confide my youthful troubles and perplexities to Professor Thilly and his wife.

My father and Professor Thilly had a long evening talk together about the old days at the University of Missouri and about many other matters. In the course of the rather miscellaneous discussion, Thilly casually mentioned to Father that he remembered an allusion many years ago to a much earlier philosopher in the family, Maimonides. Father admitted hearing of rumors, perhaps not authentic but depending on old documents that my grandfather had lost, to the effect that we were descended from Maimonides.

I had not previously heard of the tradition, nor even of the name of Maimonides. Naturally I did not delay long before I had recourse to the encyclopedia. I found there that Maimonides, or Rabbi Moses ben Maimon, known as Rambam according to the conventional Jewish use of initials, was a native of Cordova domiciled in Cairo, and the body physician to the vizier of the Sultan Saladin. I learned that he was the head of the Jewish community of Egypt and a great Aristotelian and that his most famous book is known as *Moreh Nebukim,* or the *Guide of the Perplexed.*

* Reprinted from *Ex-Prodigy. My Childhood and Youth,* Simon and Schuster, New York, 1953, pp. 143–163.

I was naturally interested to have such an important figure on which to hang our family pride, but the implications of the legend came to me with a profound shock. For the first time, I knew that I was Jewish, at least on my father's side. You may ask how it was possible for an intelligent boy like me to have any doubts about this when my grandmother Wiener as far back as I could remember had received a newspaper printed in what I knew to be Hebrew characters. I can only answer that the world is complex, with ramifications not very understandable to an adolescent, and that it still seemed possible to me that there might be non-Jewish people in eastern Europe who used the Jewish characters. Furthermore, my cousin Olga had once told me that we were Jews; but my mother had contradicted this at a time when I had not yet learned to question the word of my parents.

At that time the social disadvantage of belonging to the Jewish group was considerably greater than it is now, and there was definitely something to be said for allowing children to grow up through their early lives without consciousness of the social stigma of belonging to an unfavored group. I do not say categorically that this was the right thing to do; I merely say that it was a defensible thing to do and could be motivated—in fact, it was actually motivated—by a desire for the protection of the children. The moral responsibility of a policy like this is great. It is done nobly or it is done basely.

To put the best possible light on this course of action, it would be necessary that the children brought up in ignorance of the fact that they historically originated from the Jewish group be also brought up with an attitude of understanding. They should be made to see that the disadvantage on the part of others of belonging to such an unfavored minority group is an unmerited burden which they should at least abstain from intensifying. Such an attitude should be carried throughout the whole of life and should be directed equally against the unjust stigmatization of Jews, of Irishmen, of recent immigrants, and of Negroes, et cetera. Of course, the best thing and indeed the only one that would be thoroughly justifiable from a moral point of view would be to excite in the child a resistance, if not hostility, to all forms of belittling prejudice, no matter what the objects might be. However, short of this, every word by which the child's prejudice may be excited or intensified is a blow against his moral integrity, and ultimately a blow against his confidence and belief in himself when he should come to know, as he inevitably must, the truth of his own origin. The burden of the consciousness of Original Sin is hard enough to bear in any form; but a particularly insidious form of it is the knowledge that one belongs to a group that he has been taught to depreciate and to despise.

The responsibility for keeping the fact of my Jewishness secret was largely my mother's. My father was involved in all this only secondarily and by implication. I believe that he had originally intended not to burden us by the consciousness of belonging to an undervalued group, while at the same time he wished to preserve intact our respect for that group and our potential self-respect. He had written a number of articles on Jewish themes as well as a *History of Yiddish Literature*. He was also the first person to bring the name of Morris Rosenfeld to the attention of the non-Jewish public. Father had been engaged in various negotiations with the Jewish Publication Society and with other similar Jewish organizations, and I gather these had involved considerable friction. Later I found that Father always claimed that the friction was the result of an arrogant insistence on the part of the Jewish organizations that a Jew was a Jew before he was a man, and that he owed inalienable allegiance to his own group before humanity itself. My father was always an individual, and was the last man in the world to stand pressure of this kind.

My mother's attitude toward the Jews and all unpopular groups was different. Scarcely a day went by in which we did not hear some remark about the gluttony of the Jews or the bigotry of the Irish or the laziness of the Negroes. It is easy enough to understand how these sops to the prevailing narrow-mindedness of that epoch were thrown out by one who had experienced the disadvantages of belonging to an unfavored group; but though one can understand the motives leading to this conformist spurning of one's own origins, and can even forgive it in the sense in which the religious man hopes that his sin will be forgiven him, one cannot help regretting it and being ashamed of it. He who asks for equity must do equity, and it is not good for the children of a Jewish family, whether they know they are Jewish or not, to hear another Jewish family spoken of contemptuously for making the same efforts to pass over that their own parents have been making.

The maintenance of a family silence such as that which my parents maintained, even if it might be considered advisable, is much more difficult than it appears at first glance. If there is agreement that such a silence shall be maintained, what can one partner do when the other makes disparaging remarks about the race before the children? He can either terminate the secret, or he can be a silent and unwilling observer of a course of conduct that can lead to nothing but delayed emotional catastrophe on the part of the child. The vital danger of even the whitest of lies is that if it is to be maintained it must lead to a whole policy of disingenuousness of which the end is not to be seen. The wounds inflicted by the truth are likely to be clean cuts which heal easily, but the bludgeoned wounds of a lie draw and fester.

In offering the maximum apology which I can for the course of conduct adopted by my parents, I do not wish to justify it as a whole or to condemn it. I do mean to affirm that it had serious consequences for me. I was led very quickly into a rebellion against my parents and to an acceptance of their disfavor. Who was I, simply because I was the son of my mother and father, to take advantage of a license to pass myself off as a Gentile, which was not granted to other people whom I knew? If being a Jew was something to invite a shrug of the shoulders and a contemptuous sniff, then I must either despise myself, or despise the attitude by which I was invited to weigh myself with one balance and the rest of the world with another. My protection may have been well intentioned, but it was a protection that I could not accept if I were to keep my integrity.

If the maintenance of my identity as a Jew had not been forced on me as an act of integrity, and if the fact that I was of Jewish origin had been known to me, but surrounded by no family-imposed aura of emotional conflict, I could and would have accepted it as a normal fact of my existence, of no exceptional importance either to myself or to anyone else. Probably some conflict would have been excited by the actual external anti-Semitism which I found to belong to the times, and which would sooner or later have hit me one way or another. Nevertheless unless there had been an ambiguity in the family attitude, this would not have hit me where it really hurt, in the matter of my own internal spiritual security. Thus the effect of an injudicious attempt to conceal from me my factual Jewish origin, combined with the wounds which I suffered from Jewish anti-Semitism within the family, contributed to make the Jewish issue more rather than less important in my life

I say these things with the very clear and explicit intent to help prevent those who may be tempted to repeat this mistake of starting the child into the hurly-burly of life with this unnecessary sense of frustration and damnation.

Thus, when I became aware of my Jewish origin, I was shocked. Later, when I looked up my mother's maiden name and found that Kahn is merely a variant of Cohen, I was doubly shocked. I was not able to defend myself by the divided personality which allowed my mother's family to weigh strangers and their own kinsmen with different weights. As I reasoned it out to myself, I was a Jew, and if the Jews were marked by those characteristics which my mother found so hateful, why I must have those characteristics myself, and share them with all those dear to me. I looked in the mirror and there was no mistake: the bulging myopic eyes, the slightly everted nostrils, the dark, wavy hair, the thick lips. They were all there, the marks of the Armenoid type. I looked at my sister's photograph, and although she was a pretty girl in my eyes, she most certainly looked like a pretty Jewish girl. She had features not unlike those of a Jewish boy who happened to be my fellow lodger in my Cornell boardinghouse. He was a member of a recent immigrant family and appeared very foreign against the background of his Anglo-Saxon classmates. My snobbishness prevented me from accepting him fully as a friend, and the meaning of this was clear to me: I could not accept myself as a person of any value.

In this emotional and intellectual dilemma, I did what most youngsters do—I accepted the worst of both sides. It humiliates me to think of it even at the present day, but I alternated between a phase of cowardly self-abasement and a phase of cowardly assertion, in which I was even more anti-Semitic than my mother. Add this to the problems of an undeveloped and socially inept boy, spending his first long visit away from home, to the release from the immediate educational pressure of my father before I had developed independent working habits, and you have the material of which misery is made.

For I was miserable. I had no proper idea of personal cleanliness and personal neatness, and I myself never knew when I was to blurt out some unpardonable rudeness or *double entendre*. I was ill at ease with my associates in the middle twenties, and there were no youngsters of my own age to replace them. The habits of vegetarianism inculcated in me by my father had increased the difficulty of a social life away from home, and together with other people. Yet I was greatly under his spell, and because of my upbringing, even the remote threat of his powers made me loath to abandon these habits as my sisters were later to do.

My studies at home had always been under the close inspection of my father. This made it hard for me to develop good independent habits of study. I know that Father claimed to have always been in favor of my intellectual independence, and to have wished me to stand firmly on my own feet; yet whatever he purported to wish, the pattern of our life together worked in exactly the opposite direction. I had grown to depend on his support, and even on the support of his severity. To pass from this shelter to the full responsibility of a man among men was too much for me.

I took a rather diverse series of courses during my year at Cornell. I read Plato's *Republic* in Greek with Hammond and found that I had not lost too much of my Greek fluency in my Harvard year. I also attended the psychological laboratory and took a course with Albee on the English classical philosophers of the seventeenth and eighteenth centuries. Albee's course was dry but instructive, and I believe that there is an element still in my literary style which I owe to the rapid perusal of a large amount of seventeenth-century material.

I tried to take a mathematical course under Hutchinson on the theory of functions of a complex variable, but I found that it was beyond me. Part of the difficulty came from my own immaturity, but another part—to my way of thinking—from the fact that the course did not cover an adequate approach to the real logical difficulties of the subject. It was only later at Cambridge, when I found these difficulties faced boldly by Hardy instead of left to the student with an attitude of "Proceed and faith will come," that I began to find myself at home in function theory.

I did not fall down so badly in the Plato course, for this was but the continuation of my father's teaching under another preceptor. In my metaphysical and ethical courses I suffered from a new and vague adolescent religiosity (which did not last very long), and it needed a sharp logic to keep me from diffuse sentimentality.

I had to write essays for Albee on the seventeenth- and eighteenth-century philosophers. I was cramped by a boyish style, together with a physical awkwardness with the pen. My essays wound up in compact knots of words, so at variance with the norms of the English language that I was more than once asked whether my first language had not been German.

Cornell University had a philosophical periodical of its own, and one of the duties of the Sage Fellows was to write brief abstracts of articles in other philosophical journals to be included in a special section devoted to the purpose. The original languages were English, French, and German; and the exercise of translation familiarized us both with the philosophical vocabulary of these languages and with the ideas current in the world. I cannot vouch for the quality of our translations, but I have a very profound impression of the intellectual value of the work to ourselves.

There were some reliefs in this black year of my life. Although I could not fully share the companionship of my fellow students, the picnics up a neighboring creek and the winter sleigh rides which took place there after the fall of the snow were very pleasant indeed. There were one or two undergraduates in my boardinghouse with whom I had good times and bull sessions, and they used to play childish pranks on me and on one another. The scenery of the campus was gorgeous and later, when spring came around, the plantations of flowering quince were beautiful beyond anything I had seen on the Tufts College campus or elsewhere. There were sailboat rides on Cayuga Lake and tramps to neighboring waterfalls, where we swam and bathed under the plunging masses of water.

I have carried down to the present day the friendship of more than one of my fellow students. Christian Ruckmich, a gaunt, Lincoln-like figure, was my partner in many of my walks and in the psychological laboratory. I have heard from him from Abyssinia within the last few years. He has been engaged there in reforming the educational system of the country, and his boy has taken up aviation.

There was also Tsanoff, the Bulgarian, whom I have seen within the last year or two at the Rice Institute, still teaching philosophy. There was a delightful couple by the name of Schaub with whom I often lunched. Schaub taught a course on comparative religion, and his discussion of the Old Testament fitted in very well with the philological interest which I had acquired from my father, from Professor Wade at Tufts, and from browsing around our library.

As the year went on, it began to appear that I had not earned a renewal of the fellowship which had taken me to Ithaca, or at any rate if I were to receive it again, it would be by special grace. I felt oppressed, not only by my indifferent success in my courses, but by that sense of adolescent guilt that accompanies the internal sexual development of almost every normal young person. My sense of guilt led me to avoid the Thillys, and this alienation ended in a quarrel between my father and Professor Thilly. It was almost impossible to make my father believe that one of his family could be at fault. It was even more impossible for me to stand up to the withering stream of invective which a discussion was bound to bring down upon my head.

Before the end of the year there was other news from home. I had a new brother, a sickly child, who scarcely lived out the year. With the bad news from Cornell, my father snatched me out of the Sage School and forced me to transfer to the Department of Philosophy of the Harvard Graduate School. I know that the responsibility of my family made it difficult for my father to back a doubtful bet, but I nevertheless wish that as a young man I had received the opportunity to redeem an error in the place in which I had made it. The result of Father's policy of transferring me was to increase my lack of self-confidence, which was already great enough. My blunders became a menacing sequence of dead years never to be undone. Meanwhile I did not have the opportunity to learn the arts and techniques of independence, and the future was for me a turbid and depressing pool.

I had time after I came home to take stock of my moral situation. My achievement of independence during the year at Cornell had been incalculably retarded by the confused mass of feelings of resentment, despair, and rejection which had followed early in the year upon the discovery of my Jewishness.

Some of my friends have asked me to render more specific the discussion of the shock which I experienced and the subsequent adjustment which it was necessary for me to go through in order to be reasonably at peace with myself. Manifestly to be at once a Jew and to have had inculcated in me by certain of my mentors hostile or depreciating attitudes to the Jews was a morally impossible position. It might have led me into a continued Jewish anti-Semitism or, on the other hand, to a flight into Abraham's bosom.

In fact, neither of these escapes was possible for me. I had received too strong a lesson in intellectual and moral integrity from my father to be willing to accept one brand of justice for myself and my near kinsfolk and another brand of justice for the outer world. I had heard enough harsh remarks at home concerning other university families of Jewish origin who had tried to escape from Judaism to realize that there were those close to me who weighed the Wiener family with one scale and the rest of the world with a very different one. Quite crassly, even if I myself

and some of my immediate family had been willing to deny my
Jewish origin, this denial would not pass current one foot beyond
our doorstep.

In short, I had neither the possibility nor the wish to live a lie.
Any anti-Semitism on my part must be self-hatred, nothing less.
A man who hates himself has an enemy whom he can never
escape. This way there lay only discouragement, disillusionment,
and in the end madness.

Yet it was equally impossible for me to come into the fold of
Judaism. I had never been there, and in my entire earlier education I had seen the Jewish community only from the outside and
had the very vaguest idea of its rites and customs, its permissions
and obligations. The break with Orthodox Judaism had indeed
begun in my grandfather's time; in pursuit of his desire to Ger-
manize the eastern Jews and to replace Yiddish by High German,
my father had been sent in part at least to a Lutheran school.
Thus a return to Judaism on my own part would not be a true
return, but a fresh conversion and conviction. For better or
worse, I do not regard conversions of any sort with very favorable
eyes, nor did my father. There is something against the grain in
the attitude of abnegation and of denial of personal judgment in
the wholesale acceptance of any creed, whether in religion, in
science, or in politics. The attitude of the scholar is to reserve the
right to change his opinion at any time on the basis of evidence
produced, and I was born and bred to the scholar's trade.

This training of mine went very deep into my nature. I have
never had the impulse to gregariousness in my thinking and
feeling despite all my very deep respect for man as man, whether
he be a scholar or not. It was emotionally impossible for me to
hide myself in the great majority as a fugitive from Judaism; but
it was equally impossible for me to hide myself and be consoled
in a restrictedly Jewish community. I could not believe in the old-
line New Englanders as a Chosen People: but not even the vast
weight of the Jewish tradition could persuade me to believe in
Israel as a Chosen People. The one thing that I had known about
my father's relation to Judaism was that he had been an assimilationist, rather than Zionist, and that he had had many arguments

with Zangwill and others on this issue. This was a position which I approved not only because he was my father but also because I thought he had seized the stick by the right end.

Thus I was powerfully moved by the discovery of my Jewishness, but I could see no way out in anti-Semitism or in ultra-Judaism. What, then, could I do?

I cannot tell when I arrived at an answer to my problems, for the solution occurred step by step and was not reasonably complete until after my marriage. Yet one thing became clear very early: that anti-Jewish prejudice was not alone in the world but stood among the many forms in which a group in power sought, whether consciously or unconsciously, to keep the good things of the world for itself and to push down those other people who desired the same good things. I had read enough of Kipling to know the English imperialist attitude, and I already had enough Hindu friends to realize how bitterly this attitude was resented. My Chinese friends spoke with me very frankly concerning the aggressions of the Western nations in China, and I had only to use my eyes and ears to know something of the situation of the Negro in this country, particularly if he aspires to be something more than a farm hand or an unskilled worker. I was quite adequately informed concerning the mutual bitterness between the old Bostonian and the rising Irish group which demanded its own share of power in the community and took a very liberal view of what that share should be when other immigrants and minor groups came into question.

The net result was that I could only feel at peace with myself if I hated anti-Jewish prejudice as prejudice without having the first emphasis on the fact that it was directed against the group to which I belonged. I felt anything less than this as a demand for special privilege by myself and by those about me. But in resisting prejudice against the Oriental, prejudice against the Catholic, prejudice against the immigrant, prejudice against the Negro, I felt that I had a sound basis on which to resist prejudice against the Jew as well. For a long time I had been interested in my fellow students from the Orient and from other foreign countries, and I now saw their problems as parallel to my own and, in many cases, far deeper and more difficult.

Moreover, when I heard of our reputed descent from Maimonides, I realized that even deeper than our simple Jewishness, in a sense the Orient was part of our own family tradition. Who was I, a man whose proudest ancestor had led a life in a Moslem community, to identify myself exclusively with the West against the East? Thus I came to study and to observe parallelisms between the intellectual development of the Jews, especially in that interesting period of transition which began with Moses Mendelssohn and led to the integration of Jewish learning with European learning in general, with similar phenomena taking place before my eyes among the non-European men of learning. This came to an even sharper focus later on when I spent part of a year assisting Professor Hattori, a Japanese professor at Harvard, in the routine work of his course on Chinese philosophy.

This covers the intimate personal side of my reaction to my discovery that I was of Jewish origin. It may be well, however, to add a few facts concerning anti-Semitic prejudice and its history in those communities in which I have lived since my childhood. It is fairly clear from the history of those Jewish families who came to the United States before the middle of the last century that anti-Semitic prejudice was not a considerable factor in their lives. As a matter of fact, the dominating Protestants in the United States were more than ready to acknowledge the extent to which they had drawn upon the Old Testament in their writings and thought and to see in the Jewish immigrant a reflection of their own traditions. I have been told that even the "Know Nothing Movement" was not particularly anti-Semitic and, further, that some of the leaders of this unsavory episode in our history were drawn from the Jews themselves. Be that as it may, the beginning of the twentieth century saw the blunting of our national resistance to anti-Semitism as it was the blunting of New England's traditional friendship for the Negro and of many other of the broader attitudes of earlier days. The Gilded Age had already come to an end and had left as its heir the Varnished Age.

That summer we spent at a farmhouse not far from Bridgewater, New Hampshire. There was only one small mountain in the immediate neighborhood, and it was too rough and trailless for my father to permit me to climb it. I tramped the roads of the neighboring countryside in search of summer camps where I might earn a little money as a teacher, and find a little companionship in the bargain, but my services were not in demand. I pitched hay in a local field and fell desperately ill under an allergy to haydust. I read back numbers of *Harper's* and *Scribner's Magazine* and *The Century,* and I longed for the beginning of term to relieve me from the boredom which came from a family living too close together and driven in upon itself.

My father's revolutionary theories of education were confirmed in his eyes by the success which, with all my shortcomings, I had already found in intellectual work. It soon became clear that my sisters, although very clever girls by any ordinary standard, were not responding to my father's training as I had. And in part, my father did not expect as much of them. This was laid to their being girls, unable to stand up to the severe discipline to which I had been subjected.

Our family portioned out the fates of the family members in advance. The expectation that my sister Constance was to be the artistic one made my parents assign music, painting, and literature to be her field. To prevent any contretemps, they were to be strictly eschewed by the rest of us.

Thus Constance, and, in a similar way but later, my sister Bertha too, was removed from the sphere of intellectual competition into which I had been initiated. Occasionally I indulged in a certain envy of their easier fates, and there were times when I would have considered it a privilege to be born a girl and to be faced no longer with a need for the hard work of intellectual effort, and the ultimate requirement of standing alone in a world I felt to be hostile.

The case of my brother Fritz was of course a very different matter from that of my sisters. It was not until I was a graduate student at Harvard that he had reached the age where his education severely impinged upon us. He was destined by my parents for the same career of scholarship as I. This time there was no question of weaker demands on the weaker sex, and my father's educational theories had to be faced in their full significance. My father had reiterated that my success, if indeed I had had any genuine success, was not so much a result of any superior ability on my part as of his training. This opinion he had expressed in print in various articles and interviews.[1] He claimed that I was a most average boy who had been brought to a high level of accomplishment by the merit of his teaching and by that merit alone. When this was written down in ineffaceable printer's ink, it had a devastating effect on me. It declared to the public that my failures were my own but my successes were my father's.

Now that my brother had come of school age, there was a second Wiener candidate for fame and distinction, and for the upholding of the judgment of my father. It was inevitable, and it had been made publicly inevitable, that my father should try to duplicate with his younger boy what he had already accomplished with me. It became almost as inevitable that the anticipation of Fritz's success was to be thrown in my face in order to deflate me and to exalt the authority of my father.

I never agreed with Father in his estimate of me as a boy of average abilities, which I always felt had been adopted to curb my self-conceit and cut me down to family size. It was not fair to expect a priori that Fritz could do what I had done. Furthermore, Father did not take into consideration the fact that although I was a nervous and difficult youngster, I had plenty of stamina, and could absorb without utter destruction a punishment far greater than that which the average child could take. Thus when my brother turned out to be a somewhat frail child, endowed with what I believe to be good average ability but without any exceptional powers, the scene was set for trouble.

The bickering about Fritz's education lasted for well over

[1] An article entitled "New Ideas in Child Training" by H. Addington Bruce, published in *The American Magazine* in July, 1911, quoted my father directly:

I am convinced that it is the training to which we must attribute the results secured with them. It is nonsense to say, as some people do, that Norbert and Constance and Bertha are unusually gifted children. They are nothing of the sort. If they know more than other children of their age, it is because they have been trained differently.

twenty years. I resented as unfair the extra weight which my parents threw into the scales to equalize the balance between my brother and me. I was also very much displeased with the role that I was given at sixteen as my younger brother's mentor and nursemaid, taking him to primary school every morning before beginning a full day's work. I was expected to display to him a companionship rarely to be shown by a lumbering adolescent to a mere child eleven years younger. This age difference was critical. When I was sixteen, he was five; when I was twenty-five, he was still only fourteen.

In defense of my parents' expectations of my relationship with Fritz, it is necessary to remember that the world was changing even during that period before World War I when I was growing up. When I and my older sister had been young children, not even the relative poverty of the family had kept my mother from having the assistance of at least two servants, one of whom had been cook and the other generally an excellent nursemaid. The changes of the century had already begun to dry up the stream of immigrant household labor, and wages had risen sharply. Not even our greater prosperity could make up for the new conditions and re-create a class of labor that had almost ceased to exist. Thus the care of the younger child fell on the older one.

Looking back on the matter from my present point of view, I cannot blame my parents for passing on to me a responsibility which they had taken so readily in the care of the elder children, yet the circumstances of my responsibility were not fair to me. My duty to Fritz was a deputized one, completely unaccompanied by authority. Fritz was tiresome under my tutelage, and if I took any measure, no matter how mild, to make him behave, he had only to complain to our parents. Whatever step I might have taken was inexcusable to them. Furthermore, I was a confused, socially inept adolescent, who by any reasonable standard had been overworked for years and who needed every available moment to develop his social contacts and his social poise.

It will be no surprise that my companions, whether boys and girls, whether men and women, were judged more critically by my parents according to whether they accepted or did not accept

Fritz than on any other point whatsoever. This, too, was unfair
to me. It is too much to ask young people to take as a friend
another youngster who always has an infant brother toddling
after him, particularly when he has no authority over his brother
and the child knows this. Thus there is plenty of explanation, if
not excuse, for the fact that I was often harsh if not cruel to my
brother. Irony and sarcasm are the weapons for those who have
no other weapons; and these I did not spare. The difficult situation grew even more difficult.

To a certain extent, too, I was given the responsibility but not
the authority for Fritz's education. Fritz rapidly developed a
vocabulary of the intellectual, far beyond his understanding. In
the competition within the family, he tried to hold his own by
asking questions of a learned sort, with answers he did not fully
understand and in which he had no deep interest. I was told that
I was to answer these questions in detail, even when they had
ceased to have an interest to Fritz and when his mind was wandering elsewhere. When the family went to the theater together,
I was supposed to offer a commentary on whatever features of the
show had excited my brother's desire to display his intelligence,
and I did not have a decent opportunity for the reflections on it
which belonged to me for myself and for discussions with my true
intellectual contemporaries.

Of course, in all this I am going well beyond the period of my
history that I have made the subject of this chapter and I am
giving an account of a festering sore which continued to infect
our family life. During a considerable part of this period I was
living at home, either as a minor or as an adult paying his
contributions to the family fund. It may be asked why I did not
leave the family to take lodging somewhere for myself, perhaps
even in Cambridge. Many times I was on the point of doing so,
and many times my parents indicated that if I continued my
course of conduct, this would be the inevitable result. However,
it was made clear, particularly by my mother, that the separation
would be held against me for all eternity, as a sign of my ultimate failure, and would mean the complete and final collapse of
family relations.

During the earlier period of my life at home, I was made aware that I was completely dependent on the family bounty, and that such sums as I gained by scholarships were only a partial offset against this. Later, when I had acquired the ability to earn my own living, I had still not acquired any circle of friends outside the family. Thus, while separation from the family might have been desirable, exile from the family was exile into outer darkness.

Those who read further in this book will see that my summers were marked by long mountain excursions for many years before my marriage. Later on, these excursions were replaced to some extent by trips to Europe, often together with my sisters. These gave some alleviation of the pressure of family life, and in particular of my forced custodianship of my brother, and were absolutely essential to my well-being. However, my parents made every attempt to compel me to accept Fritz as a companion on my mountain hikes. This was inequitable, and represented a demand that I could not accept.

This had not been the first time that the rather patriarchal structure of the family had disturbed me. Once, in my youth, my father had planned to join with me in making a museum collection of the fauna and flora of the Old Mill Farm neighborhood and had proposed that we spend a large part of our spare time in maintaining this collection. Once he had spoken of his intention, when Constance and I had grown up, to devote the rest of his life to the conducting of a children's school on his own principles, in which my sister and I were to be teachers. More than once he had talked of returning to the romantic adventure of his youth, and of crossing the continent with us in a covered wagon. All these projects were admirable as indications of his youthful spirit, and would have been most charming suggestions of paternal love and family interest in a household less strictly under parental control. As things were, they represented another turn of the screw.

The summer always found us raising a garden, and I was relegated to the tasks of weeding, thinning asparagus, picking peaches, and the like. These were light tasks, and would have been most agreeable if they had not represented a simple outdoor extension of the regime of my filial servitude. I was clumsy and I was inefficient and I was lazy; and I had to hear these faults ding-donged into me hour after hour as I worked by my father's side in the fields. I was quite as unsatisfactory a farmhand as my father indicated, and I certainly developed a repugnance for work in the fields. This has lasted to the present day, and has hampered me at a time when my diminishing stock of muscular vigor would otherwise make me welcome light garden work as a still admissible form of bodily activity. Nevertheless, so long as my father's mentorship continued to dictate my way of life all winter, it was intolerable that the summer, which I needed badly for recuperation and the formation of new social contacts, should merely be an extension of the winter regime.

Indeed, at a later period after World War I, when Father had sold the Sparks Street house as too large for a family no longer needing growing space, he put the money not only into a smaller and older house on Buckingham Street, but into an apple farm in the town of Groton, Massachusetts. He had hoped that the whole family would co-operate in this work, at least during the apple-picking season, and that the place would furnish in return a cool summer for the married children and the expected grand-children. The scheme was bound to fail from the beginning. Young people in their early twenties have to consider the press-ing necessity of their own social life, and cannot long be denied the opportunity for seeking and meeting their prospective mates.

HARRY GOLDEN

Harry Golden is a phenomenon on the American cultural scene. As an author, editor, publisher and columnist, he became famous and influential in the 1950's. His books, Only in America, For 2¢ Plain, Enjoy! Enjoy!, You're Entitle!, *and* So What Else is New?, *culled from* The Carolina Israelite, *a paper he founded and edits, won for him a reputation as an American Jewish thinker and humorist on a popular level.*

Born in 1903 in Mikulince, Galicia, Harry Golden was brought to America in 1905. He was the son of a part-time journalist and part-time cantor. He moved to Charlotte, North Carolina in 1939, where he established The Carolina Israelite *two years later.*

Upon its publication in 1958, his first book, Only in America, *became a national best seller, and helped transform him from a modest journalist into a nationally syndicated columnist, a television and radio personality, a popular campus lecturer, and a "specialist" on Jewish affairs.*

In all of his work Golden shows an interest in American problems relating to minority groups. Although living in the South, he is an eloquent foe of segregation, and espouses the cause of civil rights for the American Negro.

In this excerpt, drawn from a longer essay contributed to a volume entitled Five Boyhoods, *the author recalls his childhood on the East Side during the first decade of the present century.*

East Side Memoir, 1910's*

HARRY GOLDEN

EVERYBODY SAID I was the handsomest kid on the block. By Old World standards, of course. It simply meant that I was a fat kid with black curly hair. And you were never considered too fat, not even the female folks. I had a middle-aged aunt who was still looking for a husband, and I remember the time my mother taught her a sitting posture that would convey the idea that she had a double chin. Our whole family life centered around the dining-room table. You could be ten years old and already weigh one hundred and seventeen pounds and if one time you dawdled over your food, your mother would say, "Look at him—nothing but skin and bones." We were poor and there was poverty all around us, but there was always plenty to eat. In all the homes I knew as a boy on the Lower East Side of New York, the tables literally creaked under the weight of the food on the Sabbath and on all the other holidays.

When an unthinking neighbor commented on my handsome looks, my mother began the elaborate ritual of warding off the Evil Eye. (The widespread superstition was that the Evil Eye was particularly interested in children and the way to attract its attention was to single out a child for special praise. The moment after anyone had praised me or my sisters, my mother muttered some prayers, turned a glass upside down, and made a fig—the thumb placed between the first two fingers; at the end of this ritual my mother placed her hand on my head and said solemnly, *"Zul deir gurnisht shottn"*—may nothing bad ever happen to you.)

I became a dividend for the neighborhood. Neighbors used to beg my mother to send me around to do chores after school. Like

* Reprinted from *Five Boyhoods*, edited by Martin Levin, Doubleday & Co., New York, 1962, pp. 37–48.

most parents, my mother had no idea of how much I, a child of ten, really knew. I knew the neighbor was pregnant and that she wanted me around the house in the sympathetic hope that if she kept looking at me the child she was about to bear would also be handsome—a fat kid with black curly hair.

I became Americanized quickly enough to begin to worry about being too fat. But my mother consoled me; "In America, my son, the fat man is always the boss and the skinny fellow is always the bookkeeper."

At age ten I knew many of the secrets of life. In fact I was almost casual when Moe Yasser led me behind the alley to the rear of Katz's Turkish Baths on First Avenue and Second Street one day. It was Wednesday—ladies' day in the baths—and Moe had found a peephole through which we kept turns looking inside. I remember Moe, in deep disappointment, telling me; "Aw, you can't see nothing but the hair."

Two years later I took this same Moe Yasser into St. Patrick's Cathedral on Fifth Avenue when we were out of school because of a Jewish holiday and after we had spent a half hour there in one of the pews, I said, "Moe, you are now a Christian." Moe spent a miserable afternoon, afraid to go home, and I walked with him until nine o'clock when, mustering our courage, we decided to ask my father about it. My father listened to our story. He was quite serious at hearing us out because we saw he kept stroking his beard. But as we neared the end, when Moe confessed his unwitting conversion, my father suddenly laughed aloud and sent Moe home, but poor Moe was never the same after that.

Neither my handsomeness nor my fears of conversion by exposure were naive assumptions, not in the immigrant section in which I lived, the Lower East Side of New York City, which, when we immigrant Jews first moved in, was as absolutely parochial as any Jewish village or Pale of Settlement in Eastern Europe. It is true we Jews were not the first occupants of this ghetto. The Germans were first, followed by the Irish, followed by the Jews, the Poles, and the Italians, (now the Negroes and the Puerto Ricans) and each of us who lived there populated these city blocks with our own separate myths and held to our own separate values. Each of these groups left a deposit before they moved on. Because they left this deposit, the Lower East Side of New York City plays an important part in the history of the United States. The deposit we found was that the promise of America did come true. It is in terms of realizing that promise that I would like to write about the three and a half million immigrants who settled on the Lower East Side betwen 1880 and 1920.

The Lower East Side was not only a voluntary ghetto, but six or seven smaller ghettos within the one large one. Geographically, the main ghetto of New York was about a square mile below East Fourteenth Street between the two rivers, the East River and the Hudson. Those blocks bordering on the East River were populated by the Italians and across Manhattan along the Hudson River lived the Irish. Thus no Jewish boys learned to swim. With the Italians and the Irish holding the river fronts we Jews were landlocked. Instead we devoted our energies to basketball, which we played in the settlement houses, in the basements, and on the tenement roofs.

Soon the Italians began to overflow into the Jewish section and even in my day they were already living on Chrystie Street, the first street eastward from the Bowery. As the Italians moved in, the Jews continued to move on and after the Williamsburg Bridge was completed on Delancey Street, the Jews by the thousands moved across the river into the Williamsburg section of Brooklyn. Throughout the section there were whole tenements of Poles who we were led to believe were natural-born anti-Semites. Most of the stories I heard as a boy about anti-Semitism in Europe were in terms of the Polish peasant class and it is interesting to note that when the Poles came to America, with the entire continent open to them, so many thousands of them settled right down there among the Jews again.

We were surrounded by Poles and Italians but it was the Irish and the Irish alone we admired. It wasn't that the Irish were prior immigrants. Indeed not. But we identified the Irishman not only with the English language but also with what an American should look like. Although the immigrant Jew and the New York Irish did not get along well, these Irish were the figures the Jewish immigrants wanted to emulate. I saw Orthodox Jewish women literally jump for joy at the birth of a grandson, and say: "He looks just like an Irishman."

It was the Irish who instructed us in one part of the legacy of the East Side. The legacy was that we could proceed outward as had they. For by the time we occupied the tenements that soared to meet us, many of the Irish had moved inland to the Bronx, to New Jersey, to Chicago and points west. They were already policemen, brokers, politicians, and ballplayers. The other part of the legacy we brought from the old country. This was our Jewishness, the fact positive that we were immigrants. In one sense or another, Jews are always "immigrants," they are the eternal "alien," and this confers upon them a special vigor, an intellectual vigor which might well be the key to Jewish survival through twenty centuries. Immigrants came off the gangplank at Ellis Island, looked at the faces of passing Americans, and said, "When will I be like him?" The reason for the Jew's everlasting vitality is that even after a fifth generation he's still striving "to be like him," and he dare not relax in his effort.

My family lived in the heart of the Lower East Side—the "Times Square" of the ghetto—at 171 Eldridge Street, between Rivington and Delancey Streets. In those days, one tenement fronted another. The two tenements were separated by a back yard about twenty feet wide. The rent "in the back" was considerably less than the twenty-two dollars we paid for four rooms in the front on the top floor. The toilets for both tenements were located in the yard between them. There were five of them, each about the size of a telephone booth. If you lifted the board in one of these, the boards in all of them came up which led to a constant argument always echoing from one booth to the other. Once a month, Poles in hip boots came and cleaned these privies.

It was with a tenant "in the back" that I made my first contact with death. A man in one of the rear tenements died when his coal stove poisoned him during the night. He was a ragpicker. I had seen him every day carrying huge sacks on his back and I could see him at night, sitting in his flat "in the back" sorting the rags he had collected into a dozen different piles, according to size, quality, and color. Each of these piles was bundled and he sold them somewhere.

Sociologists have written much about "the need" Jews have had to be self-employed, to go into business for themselves. They have said that sometimes the Jew is "unemployable" and sometimes they have intimated that the Jew is more "aggressive." But I have never heard a sociologist say that one of the reasons for a Jew's self-employment was his wish to observe in all its particulars the Jewish Sabbath. The ragpickers and the peddlers who lived "in the back" were self-employed because they believed that was the only way they could observe the Sabbath which began on Friday afternoon. If they entered the open society, they were afraid their employers would not forgive the necessary hours from sundown Friday until sundown Saturday, to say nothing of at least a dozen other observances during the year.

The ambulance came and some attendants carried this ragpicker out. There was a policeman there writing down names and the man's daughter came screaming from another tenement a few blocks away. Her father was dead and her grief and hysteria were profound and finally the policeman went and fetched a rabbi and some of her other relatives. I can still remember that ragpicker. He had a big black beard and I thought of him as an old man, like the other old men who went daily to the synagogue. I was puzzled later that evening when I heard my father tell my mother that the ragpicker was thirty-nine years old. After school that afternoon I accompanied my mother to the synagogue. I saw her weave from left to right in apparent anguish at the death of this ragpicker and she moved her lips in prayer. Actually, there were few women who went to the synagogue as often as my mother, which meant there were few boys who went as often as I did. Women were rarely seen at a synagogue except on the Sabbath or on holidays. My mother couldn't read or write and I am sure the prayers she said that afternoon she knew by repetition and by rote, but every occasion of death sent her to the synagogue in anguish and prayer, in the same spirit that prompted John Donne to write, "Every man's death diminishes me." Very often she was the only woman in the balcony reserved for wives and daughters.

Whenever I went with her to the synagogue we usually passed the Catholic church on Second Avenue and Second Street, where the late Cardinal Hayes once served as pastor, and invariably as we passed it my mother would spit and say, "Oh, what memories!" Once when someone came toward us and it would have embarrassed her to spit, she refused to miss the opportunity. She held me by the hand until the man passed by us, then she proceeded and gave a quick spit and a fast, "Oh, what memories," and went on. I escaped the burden of the Middle Ages of Europe. The Catholic Church never frightened me. I married an Irish Catholic girl in the vestry of one.

For us it all began in the year 1905, around Passover time, when my mother, born Anna Klein, my two older sisters, Clara and Matilda, and I arrived at Ellis Island on the Hamburg-American liner, the S.S. *Graf Waldersee* out of Hamburg. Clara was nine, Matilda was seven, I was two, and my mother was thirty-eight. We had journeyed overland from the most eastern corner of the Austro-Hungarian Empire, the town of Mikulince on the river Sereth in Kaiser Franz Josef's province of Galicia.

Thousands of Jews from Russia, Poland, Rumania, and Hungary embarked at Hamburg. But at Hamburg there was always a wait; inspections, documents, examinations, and the posting of the ship's schedule. While these immigrants waited, the German Jews took over. They had established a free clinic and a hostel, and provided gifts of money if a family did not have enough, or had been robbed on the overland trip as frequently happened. Sometimes a family was separated: a child developed an illness or a parent was found to have trachoma and in these emergencies the German Jews took charge. They sent the family on its way and nursed the separated member back to health and arranged for him to sail as soon as they were sure he could pass the physical requirements at Ellis Island.

The radicals on the Lower East Side always said the German Jews were so kind because they wanted to keep us moving and not cause them embarrassment in their native German father-land. But the radicals would have had a hard time proving this. It is much easier to prove they did all of these things for us be-cause they were innately generous and because they were Jews, a most fantastic and interesting fraternity to belong to.

My father, Leib Goldhirsch (1860) and my brother Jacob (1888) had preceded us to America a year earlier. This was the normal pattern, and that is why ninety percent of all the Jewish immigrants from Eastern Europe between 1890 and 1920 were males, married men, or single boys who came to America and began to save enough money from their earnings to send for their wives, children, parents, fiancées, and other relatives.

My father became a Hebrew teacher and my brother Jacob took to peddling. Jacob was already sixteen years old but he registered in night school which he attended for the next ten years, completing both the grammar and high-school courses. The immigrants did not call it Evening Grammar School, which it was. It was more dignified for grown men (some of them with beards) to say they were going to "night school."

In the Jewish household the father was a figure of authority, the boss. This meant that no one sat down to the dinner table until he came home from work and that we did not speak until he spoke first or until he had asked us a question. Jews call this *derekh eretz*, a phrase literally translated as the "custom of the land." In actual usage it means respect for elders and particu-larly for parents. Mother made all the decisions but she was always obedient to the idea of *derekh eretz*. Alone, she would tell my father, "I found a new apartment on Ludlow Street. I paid a deposit and I've asked the moving van to come Monday." That evening at the dinner table during a lull she would say, "Chil-dren, pay attention. Papa has something very important to say to you." Father would proceed to describe the move next Monday and Mother would listen through the whole process as though hearing it for the first time, even congratulating him afterward on his excellent judgment.

The idea of *derekh eretz* was so profound that the most effec-tive discipline in the family was *the look*. If you forgot yourself and started roughhousing with your brothers, your father suddenly raised his head and gave you *the look*. He simply stared at you as a warning of displeasure. It shamed you. You stopped. No words exchanged. Many a boy said he would rather submit to a whipping than suffer *the look* from his father. Occasionally, however, Mother herself employed *the look* and against your father when she thought he was unfair. This too was silent communication. The mother stared at the father but her face had a new tension. She opened her eyes wide and raised her chin and, as articulate as any sentence, her look said, "Why don't you leave the kid alone?"

My father became a citizen in 1910. He and a group of other Galitizianers studied the American Constitution, the Declaration of Independence, and the laws of the State of New York and went down to a Manhattan courthouse where a sober, dignified, white-haired Irish judge questioned them about American history and American legal and political processes. They raised their right hands and forswore allegiance to Emperor Franz-Josef and pledged themselves to the American destiny. After the oath, the judge said, "Now you are all American citizens." Lowering his voice, he continued, "And don't forget to vote the straight Democratic ticket." My father told this story about Tammany for the rest of his life and he always said that he was not only made a citizen that day but completely Americanized.

How long does it take to become an American? Not as long as one would think. Arrive from Mikulince in 1905 and five years later you are the "king" in a school pageant parading down Fifth Avenue, a participant in the Hudson-Fulton celebration of 1909, and how much more American can you be? My "queen" was a little girl whose parents ran the hand laundry in the basement of 171 Eldridge Street. Their name was Cohen and the older sister had a big red birthmark on her face. This kept her indoors and whenever she did venture into the streets she held her hand against this blemish. We called her "red nose" and this cruelty gives me shivers every time I think of it.

Yes, how long does it take to become an American? Not long, for each group brings with it its own unique contribution. The

English brought the law, the Scandinavians the log cabin, the Germans commerce, and the Jews an intellectual vitality that has had no parallel in the history of our country. I remember distinctly as a boy that the Board of Education ordered the public schools of the Lower East Side to remain open during the evening hours because there were not enough rooms in the settlement houses and public halls to accommodate all of the debating societies, study groups, and a thousand and one other political and intellectual organizations. I also remember that immigrant Jews at the Neighborhood Playhouse on the East Side produced plays by Shaw, Ibsen, and Sudermann, some of them for the first time in America.

MARIE SYRKIN

In the biography of the Socialist Zionist theoretician and philosopher Nachman Syrkin, his daughter Marie Syrkin has written an interesting memoir not only of her father's life in America but of her own. Writing of the period around 1910, Miss Syrkin recalls her own experiences as a child in New York while living with her father.

Nachman Syrkin participated in the first Zionist Congress, and broke away from the Zionist movement for a short period, during which he espoused the cause of territorialism. Later, however, he rejoined the Zionist movement, and in 1907 settled in the United States. During World War I, he helped to found the American Jewish Congress.

Miss Syrkin was born in Switzerland in 1900 and was brought to the United States as a child. She was educated in New York, and was graduated from Cornell University. She has been a school teacher, and has written an important book on the American public school system entitled Your School, Your Children.

Following World War II, she visited Palestine, interviewed Jewish survivors of the Hitler years, and wrote Blessed Is the Match, *a moving and emotional narrative about Jewish heroes and heroines who resisted the Germans to the very end. She has written a biography of Golda Meir, Foreign Minister of Israel,* Woman of Valor, *and another version of Golda Meir's life. Miss Syrkin has been for many years editor of* Jewish Frontier, *the influential Labor Zionist monthly. She is on the faculty of Brandeis University.*

In New York*

MARIE SYRKIN

OUR FIRST NEW YORK HOME was a four-room apartment on Charlotte Street in the Bronx. It had such improvements as gaslight in every room and central heating. Furniture, of course, was purchased on the installment plan. I was sent to a neighboring public school to begin my formal education outside the home, and life in the United States seemed hopefully launched.

For a few months I thought it suitable to prate about American "materialism" in the fashion of my elders and to mourn for Paris, but Americanization came easily. My linguistic accomplishments found ready appreciation in school; it was not long before I could chatter in English with the children on the block who proved well disposed though they would ask embarrassing questions. The chief of these was, "What kind of a doctor is your father?" I would be forced to admit that though my father was addressed as "Dr. Syrkin," he was no healer: there was no point in seeking advice about an upset stomach or a fever. My confession that he was a doctor of "philosophy" would be met with ill-disguised skepticism by my inquisitors, especially as I found it impossible to make clear just what kind of a doctor that was. There was a suggestion of fraud about the title and though I knew that my father was an innocent man, I found myself wishing that there were less to explain to Mabel, aged nine. Nobody had ever challenged me in Vilna or Paris.

In some respects life was unchanged. Papa still went to the "library" and meetings. Old friends kept reappearing for the familiar hour-long discussions. Many comrades from the Berlin or Vilna days arriving in America found their way to our house. And periodically I would sleep on an improvised bed made of

* Reprinted from *Nachman Syrkin: Socialist Zionist, A Biographical Memoir*, Herzl Press and Sharon Books, New York, 1961, pp. 135–156.

four chairs while the impecunious comrade searched for living quarters. Just as in other circles it was taken for granted that relatives or "landsmen" should be housed by those who had preceded them to America, in our midst the bond was ideology. I always knew that the four chairs meant a night of long talk, much tea and obscure excitement.

It is hard to disentangle the mature men and women, acquaintances of my adult life, from the delightful companions of those childhood years: big, hearty Baruch Zuckerman, who sang Yiddish folk songs so resonantly and his beautiful young wife, Nina; tall, thin "Davidovitch" to whom we revealed the marvel of oatmeal with sugar and of grapefruit, and whom I was to meet later as the impeccably elegant Lvowitch of the Ort; irrepressible young Auerbach whose career as a streetcar conductor was interrupted because he could not bear to collect fares from the indigent, just as his subsequent profession as a dentist was to suffer from a plethora of non-paying comradely clients of whom I was to be one; wonderfully blonde Sonia Kamenetsky and dark, brooding Chaika Cohen—all from the Vilna days. The brilliant, suave Zhitlovsky would be a welcome visitor even though he and my father differed heatedly on most issues. Sholem Asch, moody and self-centered, already with an air of grandeur though not yet internationally famous, would put in an occasional appearance. The Yiddish writer Liessin lived near us. I mention those that I happen to remember but there were many more. All the active intellectual and political currents in the Jewish life of the period touched our home at some point.

Outside diversions, too, had a heavy ideological cast. We went for boat trips up the Hudson organized by the Poale Zion. There would be "balls" bearing no resemblance to any type of function usually designated by the name except that speeches would be followed by dancing and refreshments of tea and sandwiches—an obvious hangover from the student "balls" of Russia and Switzerland, each of which was dedicated to a "cause." One might meet Alexander Berkman and Emma Goldman unaccountably turning up at a social-democratic ball despite their anarchism. And there were endless public meetings lasting late into the night to which one had to go. Baby-sitters were an unheard of institution as far as I can judge; in any case, the cost would have been prohibitive. Besides, I believe my parents felt that a bright ten-year old should be able to appreciate political discourse at any hour.

But the worm turned. I recall confiding to the guest of honor who asked how I had enjoyed his address on one such occasion that everyone in the audience had been wishing for him to conclude because he spoke much too long. I was not being smart or rude; the truth was sacred and that was the truth. When I met my parents' subsequent remonstrances with this argument I felt beyond reproach and they were both uneasy: could they risk infecting their child's probity by inoculation with some of the whiter lies? The problem was to recur.

Our family finances, despite my father's public acclaim, remained at a low ebb. Paying the rent was always postponed to the last possible day; the landlord turned out to be an admirer of my father's and was prepared to be as elastic as possible in his construction of what date constituted that last day. The grocery storekeeper was apparently a less zealous reader of the Yiddish press. These difficulties were new only in that I was developing a greater awareness of them, though by no means a painful one. What changed the situation was my mother's decision to find work in a factory.

It sounds simple enough today. Why not? One must reconstruct the state of mind of these European intellectuals of middle-class origin to appreciate that for both my father and mother, despite their socialism and "proletarian" ideology, this represented social decline.

To be a hungry student or a chronically indigent intellectual was proper and vaguely praiseworthy, but for my mother to seek work in a factory was as great a loss of caste as if my father had become a petty shopkeeper. To have become a peasant or farmer might have been in the *narodnik* or Tolstoyan tradition and tolerable as such. This was different. For the first time I was told to keep a secret. Our friends were not to know.

My mother's only training was that received in two years of

medical school before her marriage, but she was a clever needle-woman, as her intrepid insistence on making black alpaca suits for my father in Paris attested. She applied for work in a milli-nery factory on the East Side—under an assumed name for fear that some erudite foreman would recognize Syrkin's wife and provide a bit of unwelcome publicity. After a few fumbling days she learned how to stitch the straw but though the few dollars she earned were badly needed, my father was so depressed by our solvency that the experiment was abandoned after a few weeks.

It was to be resumed once more in my father's absence. The party may not have had money for its editor and foremost ideol-ogist, but there was no question that once back in the Socialist-Zionist fold he had to be sent to the Zionist Congress held in Germany in 1909. I don't know what arrangements for his fam-ily's support had been made but they rapidly collapsed. Shortly after my father left, my mother pledged me once more to secrecy —I was to write none of this to papa. Being "experienced" she got another job at "hats." I was left with the apartment key and, when I returned from school, would wait till she came home. At night I would dream of the wonderful gifts my father would bring from the Congress. In each letter I would add to the list of the things I wanted; it never occurred to me that my father could come back from a long journey without many packages of presents. He always brought me something—sometimes my mother chided him for extravagance—and surely this occasion would be very special.

He returned during the day while my mother was at the fac-tory. When I came from school I found him waiting on the street, deeply disturbed because my mother had not come to meet him and he had found no one at home. I explained quickly that mamma was working, and then I demanded my presents. He gave me a little rotogravure print and asked when mamma would be back. I could not conceal my disappointment and though he assured me that he would soon buy me many, many lovely things, for the first time I was dubious.

But my father's natural buoyancy quickly erased the bleakness of the homecoming. My mother again abandoned solvency via the factory and her secret proletarianizing came to an end.

My father too had a secret. Something had happened at the Congress of which he was unwilling to speak until forced by persistent reports in the Yiddish and Zionist press. He had had a fight with Nordau—not the usual verbal variety but slaps had been exchanged.

An eyewitness of the incident, Ernst Calmus, has left the following account: "As chairman of the local Zionist Organization in Hamburg I was a member of the Executive Committee. We decided together with Nordau and Wolffsohn to send a telegram of greeting to the Kaiser in the name of the Congress in accordance with the usual custom. To avoid an open debate we had decided to publicize the content of the telegram only after an answer had been received. But the matter leaked out and Syrkin learned of it. His deepest feelings were outraged and he stormily demanded an explanation from Nordau, the chairman of the Congress. Later, he got into a serious argument with Nordau in the lobby. Two political antipodes stood opposed to each other— each stubborn, each mercilessly consistent, and each equally critical of the other. Both men of flaming temperament and perhaps for this reason extremely antagonistic to each other. It is said that they came to blows. A court of honor hushed the matter up so that it should not be made public. When it came to tyrants, Syrkin understood no trifling."

My father's version, told with great reluctance and with unusual embarrassment, was somewhat different. In the course of the argument Nordau said something my father found offensive. He slapped Nordau. After they were separated by horrified delegates, Nordau challenged my father to a duel. "As a socialist, I, of course, refused," explained my father.

I remember thinking then that the life of a socialist was full of unexpected disadvantages. It would have been more gallant to duel like D'Artagnan whatever the ethical objections to the practice. My father's obvious and uncharacteristic unwillingness to describe the incident circumstantially and with gusto makes me wonder whether he too had shame-faced yearnings for swordplay. Perhaps valor on the field of honor might have been preferable to rationalist scruples.

A childhood friend of my father's, Dr. I. Lourie, appeared on the scene, to my father's delight. Old attachments, any bonds with Minsk or Mohilev became increasingly precious to my father as he grew older. The Lourie family were practically our only personal friends in the sense that the relationship stemmed neither from comradeship in the "movement," nor from the teacher-disciple relationship so common in my father's circle.

Dr. Lourie, in addition to a medical practice, owned some apartment houses in Flatbush, and probably in view of our perennial difficulties with callous commercial landlords, we moved to Flatbush from the Bronx. We had a five-room apartment on Gravesend Avenue, more spacious than the Bronx flat but there were a few disadvantages. There was no furniture for the additional room and the apartment had no central heating. Our furniture was concentrated in rooms directly adjoining the kitchen with its coal stove—the only source of warmth for the apartment. Consequently, the living room at the other end of the railroad flat was bare except for a piano which had been bought on the installment plan so that I should get music lessons. On one occasion, Sholem Asch, then himself a poor man, visited our partly furnished apartment and I recall this honest appreciation of our uncluttered space. The only trouble was that winter days were cold.

There is another circumstance about that apartment which I now find puzzling. Of the two bedrooms only one had a window. The other was a windowless corridor between the dining room and the icy living room. Naturally, I was given the light room while my parents slept in the dark, airless chamber. Both my parents had studied medicine; they were aware of my mother's tubercular history. Why were they so heedless?

The family finances did not grow more brilliant. My father left daily for the Astor Library, which served him as research center and office. Any crank or lunatic who wanted to find him—and the tribe was numerous—knew that he could discover Syrkin either at work in the Jewish Room or pacing meditatively up and down the corridor. To save the cost of lunch my mother would give him a sandwich cut into bite-size pieces which he would keep in his pocket and eat while reading. She would also

dole out the exact change for carfare because papa was danger-
ously extravagant and if he had an extra quarter would be likely
to spend it on some delicacy for me, or part with it to one of the
hapless cranks who besieged him.

This period coincided with the height of my father's enthusiasm for the cooperative movement. He was writing and lecturing
not only about the general idea but about specific cooperative
projects. In 1910 the Central Committee of the Poale Zion had
devoted several meetings to a study of a plan for the cooperative
colonization of Palestine prepared by Syrkin and favorable resolutions for the future were adopted. But now the cooperative
fever extended to the American scene. For a brief period my
father became a paid professional worker expounding the merits
of a cooperative hat store. It was the first time in his life that he
enjoyed what is called a "regular" job. His salary was $15.00 a
week and he felt like a millionaire. My mother of course had to
keep watch lest a good part of this sum be expended on "luxuries" for the family on pay day, but she was not always successful.
Papa would come home with forbidden fruit, gay and careless of
the morrow, and sensible remonstrances would provoke a scene.
But the corruption of wealth lasted only a few months and
penury, less jolly as time went on and I could understand its
effects, was restored.

I must be careful not to leave a false impression. As a child it
would never have occurred to me to think of our family as
"poor." My father's constant intellectual excitement, his marvel-
lous exuberance, set the tone of the house. And always there was
the proud sense that any material lack was a voluntary surrender
on our part rather than a deprivation. On some days, with no
sense of self-pity, I would walk a good twenty minutes to Borough Park because three cents would buy four rolls there and
only three rolls on Gravesend Avenue. How my mother managed
to maintain this atmosphere amazes me now—it seemed natural
then. I remember only two occasions when she weakened. Once,
when I was twelve, she bought me high-heeled shoes at a sale and
I squealed with delight at the unaccustomed high heels. My
mother's eyes filled with tears and she said gently, "These are not

the shoes I would buy you, if I had my choice." Another time she gave me a bottle of beet soup which she had made and sent me to a friend's house with it. As I left she added, "Perhaps they will invite you for supper." I understood that there was nothing to eat in the house except that soup but it did not occur to me then to wonder what she ate that evening because she had been careful to smile as she sent me off.

Occasionally even my father's genius for dwelling in another sphere would crack. One Sunday I had asked him for five cents for an ice cream soda—the current price—and he grandly handed me the coin. When my mother objected to the extravagance, he burst into a wild rage. All his formidable forensic talents entered into his denunciation of the "forces" that were crushing him. The attack, though delivered in Russian, was not directed against my mother but against an anonymous "they." When he had spent himself, he was penitent, but my mother wept and I never forgot that ill-fated strawberry ice cream soda.

My mother made one more attempt to supplement the family income. Since her experience in the hat factory she had begun to make hats for herself and for me. She had something of a flair for millinery and she decided that in America, the land of business, perhaps she, too, should become an entrepreneur. Going into business meant investing in straw and ribbon for exactly two hats placed in the window of the living room, which faced the street, as a sign that she was ready to create bonnets for anyone who would ring the bell. Whereas this venture could not be kept absolutely secret, it was given the minimum of publicity. Our friends, who might possibly have become patrons, were not informed. On the contrary, visitors to our house carefully pretended not to notice the two hats and no mention of their purport was ever made. These middle-class intellectuals were as ashamed of trade as of labor. It is difficult for anyone brought up in the United States to understand these European delicacies. Needless to say the hats remained in the window for a couple of months gathering dust. Two women once rang the bell but did not develop into customers. One hat was finally given to a second cousin and the other was reserved for family use. It was much simpler and pleasanter to have the hats out of the window. So much for trade.

It was at this time, too, that my father gave me my first and unforgettable lesson concerning the sanctity of public funds. My sixth-grade class in P.S. 130 had decided to have a party. Ten cents a head was collected for refreshments and a committee of three, of whom I was one, set out one afternoon to buy candy and favors. After we had finished shopping, prudently and economically, we had six cents left. As the exhausted committee pondered the disposition of this excess sum, too small to divide among our classmates, we had an inspiration. It flashed on us that we had enough for a glass of cherry soda apiece. It seemed a reasonable reward for our efforts.

When I unwittingly gave an account of the day's events to my parents that evening, my father went into a fury. I had witnessed the phenomenon before and though I could never be sure what apparently innocent act might precipitate his indignation I was never left long in doubt. This time it seemed I was an embezzler; my graceless committee and I had betrayed a sacred trust. We had used public money for private pleasure. This put a new light on the cherry soda. My father gave me six cents which, much abashed, I gave to the teacher the following morning with a complete confession. After restitution had been made I tried to collect four cents from the other members of the committee but they had no spare cash and had endured no equivalent moral qualms.

My father's anger was all the more impressive because, hot-tempered though he was, he was an adoring parent, more likely to embarrass me with extravagant praise than to reprove me. But in any question of principle he made no allowances for inexperience, age, or circumstances. Two cents misappropriated at the age of eleven from the public treasury was a breach of trust and had to be dealt with as such. The lesson remained and proved costly. It took me years before I learned to dine as well as a lecturer merited when an organization was paying, and I have never been able to pad an expense account intelligently.

Since my father's reactions were often extreme and unpredict-

able, I developed a certain wholesome wariness even in childhood. A year after the embezzlement scandal I was to graduate
from elementary school as class valedictorian. The theme for the
valedictory oration which I was to compose had been assigned by
the teacher: I had to expound Julius Caesar's utterance, *Veni,
vidi, vici*. I embellished my composition with all the fancy adjectives and big words I could think of—then a happy thought
occurred to me. An idea that I was struggling to express had been
aptly phrased by Walter Scott in a passage I happened to read. It
was just the sentence I needed and it seemed silly not to make
use of my discovery. I don't know why quotation marks did not
occur to me. I must have had some doubts because I consulted
my mother who seemed to think that one useful sentence from
Scott could be innocently incorporated into my address. The
significant thing about the episode is that I did not approach my
father who was the logical person for advice on the problems of
writer or speaker. Deep in my heart I knew that the lovely sentence from Walter Scott would never get quietly embedded into
my speech if I asked papa. How my teachers failed to detect this
bit of arrant plagiarism puzzles me to this day; Scott's elegant
period stuck out like a flagpole. And when my father listened to
me on graduation day he was too busy adoring his little daughter
to take note of the text. Besides, this was English, a language in
which his sense of style was unsure.

A passionate man like my father, full of enthusiasms and in-
dignations, never on an even keel, was not easy to live with. Our
friends considered him and ideal husband and father because all
the personal feeling of which he was capable was rapturously
concentrated on his wife and child. There were no deviations, no
side attachments. But my father's temperament, together with
unremitting economic hardship, developed stresses which could
not escape me as I grew older, no matter how hard my parents
tried to keep them from me. The last year before my graduation
from elementary school was a stormy one. My father's delight in
life, his humor—I have never heard anyone laugh as wholeheartedly as my father—was as keen as ever, but he was developing an
increasing and furious impatience with every effort to pluck him

momentarily from the cloud on which he dwelt. And there would be scenes whose intensity bore no apparent relationship to what had provoked them.

No doubt the kind of pressures cheerfully accepted at twenty or thirty became harder to bear at forty. But the tension, whatever its causes, came to an end abruptly. My mother began to cough again. It was not an ordinary cold. Badly frightened, my father insisted that we move to a centrally heated apartment in the Bronx a month before my graduation; I finished the term living with the family of Dr. Lourie.

Once more we were back in the Bronx, on the same Charlotte Street to which we had come four years earlier on our arrival in the United States. For a while the situation appeared to mend. I enrolled in Morris High School for the February term. My mother's health seemed to improve and my father's unquenchable optimism reasserted itself. He was again irrepressible, full of exact, clear-cut plans for his abiding visions. But the spring of my thirteenth year was to be the last in which my family was whole.

As I entered into adolescence my view of my father became increasingly critical. The atmosphere of incense and gunpowder which always enveloped him—he was being either worshipped by his followers or attacked by his opponents—had ceased to impress me. I knew better. I knew about his sudden rages, and I knew that he could be selfish. Once he had gotten two tickets for the opera—one for "Madame Butterfly" and one for "Gotterdammerung." The financing of this coup eludes me now. But what I never forgave was his insistence on going to "Gotterdammerung" —he was a fervent Wagnerian—and sending my mother to "Madame Butterfly" though he had seen the whole Ring cycle before and my mother had not. This piece of injustice rankled and though papa smiled guiltily when I protested, he went to "Gotterdammerung."

In addition, his public behavior was often outrageous. He had a number of weird pet names for me, among which *Pililee* and *Katiolochka* were among the more euphonious. It was barely tolerable to be addressed by these endearments in the privacy of our home, but my father had a disconcerting habit of sticking his head out of the window if I happened to be taking the air with friends on Charlotte Street, and calling resoundingly, *"Pililee, come home."* The tactful silence of my best friends, the snickers of more distant cronies, were hard to endure. But no remonstrances helped. The dreadful summons would be repeated. What was wrong with an affectionate *Pililee* anyhow? Why be such a timid conformist?, papa would ask. Sometimes, to tease me, he would threaten to burst into song in the most unlikely places. Though endowed with neither a good voice nor a good ear, he was particularly fond of singing snatches from operatic arias—particularly Wagner. He would chant a *leitmotif* whenever and wherever so impelled. Knowing my cowardly nature, he would choose horribly public places like a crowded subway train to whisper to me: "Now I will sing, *Nothung, mein schwert"* (the theme from Siegfried). To do him justice, he never did more than hum the melody quietly, but my anguish would be extreme. And he would be both puzzled and amused at my reaction.

He was disconcerting in other ways. As a man of forty-three he was short, stocky. The lean, taut air of his youthful photographs was gone, though his gray eyes were as intense as ever. His tie, a ready-made affair which hooked on to the collar—the model is, I believe, extinct—was generally askew, and one could never be too sure that his socks matched in color. He was a great believer in the virtues of water; if he noticed a stain on his suit he would douse the approximate locality generously with water and rub the spot with vigor. The operation completed he would emerge a shade more rumpled but confident that all essential measures had been taken.

At this time he wore a beard which would vary from an imposing square one *a la* Marx to a pointed one like Poincaré. Once, richly bearded, he was walking with me on a Bronx street. Aroused by the beard, a boy yelled "kike" and started to run. My father, obviously unable to overtake the boy, imperiously stopped a young man who was passing by, pointed to the running boy scampering away, and demanded of the stranger, "Catch him for me." The innocent passerby walked away bewildered, indicating that he was not inclined to catch local hoodlums.

Even I realized that the young man would not run after the boy. It was not his business and my father's demand was ridiculous, but there was to be no age at which my father would understand that one might walk by and see injustice done, without involvement, be the matter small or great. He was always getting involved and trying to involve others with results that would prove embarrassing to a self-conscious teen-ager. But it was impossible to instruct papa in proper behavior. If one said severely, "Why should that young man run after a boy who insulted you?" he would look at you with such blazing amazement that the question would shrivel in the asking.

The second Charlotte Street dwelling proved no more durable than the first. Before the spring term was over I came home one day to find my parents waiting for me. They had something to tell me. My mother told me, gently and smiling, that the old disease had returned. It was not much but the doctor advised a change of climate. She would leave as soon as possible for the Denver Jewish Hospital for Consumptives.

I know now that she should not have been torn away from her family and sent away to Colorado. But that seemed the wise course then. My mother was afraid of infecting her child, and the physicians my father consulted favored a radical change of environment. The distance from home was described as an advantage. There would be less temptation to return before a total cure had been effected. Besides, my father was assured that his wife would receive preferential treatment in any Jewish institution even though he had no money to pay.

The arguments seemed good and my mother left. I was to keep house with my father.

We had one stroke of good fortune that summer. We made friends with the family of David Ludins, a Russian Jewish intellectual of my father's ilk. His wife Olga looked after me like a second mother, and the daughters, Tima and Ryah, became my lifelong friends. Though our apartment was in my charge and I tried to clean and cook, my father had the assurance that on the many nights when he came home late from a meeting, I could wait for him at the warm Ludins' home.

My housekeeping was not of the most accomplished. Many girls of thirteen would have done better, but there had been little occasion in my wandering childhood to learn the domestic arts. If friends came to tea and I had no clean white tablecloth, I would spread a clean bedsheet—white material was white material. My father did not notice the difference.

Strangely enough, I felt my father's dejection more than my mother's absence. She sent resolutely hopeful letters and I expected that she would be back soon, at last strong and well. But my father's sadness was contrary to nature and troubled me as such. Soon another decision had to be made. As the summer drew to an end, it became clear that the house would have to be broken up. During the winter my father was away a good deal on lecture tours; furthermore, when the school term started a more efficient housekeeper than myself should be in charge. An arrangement had to be made whereby my father could come and go without feeling that his daughter was alone. We would have to room with some suitable family.

Again there was the question of disposing of the simple household effects gathered together and paid for with such effort. Some acquaintances took the bookcases, our chief asset; my mother's hand-run Singer Sewing Machine was handed over to someone else. Our unpaid-for piano returned to its owner. Whatever else seemed desirable was looked over and distributed. These treasures were to be given back—"when your mother gets better." There remained a hard core of furniture—bedroom and dining room—which nobody wanted to "storage." Some woman in the neighborhood learned that there was second-hand furniture for sale in our apartment. She looked appraisingly at the beds, the table, the chairs, the bureau; then she glanced at my father and made her offer for the lot: five dollars. I don't know whether she expected him to bargain with her. I shall never forget the anguished bitterness with which he answered, "All right. Take it away." That was the end of my mother's American household. I sometimes wondered about the whereabouts of the Singer Sewing Machine but no one remembered who had taken it.

The next years were to be the darkest in my father's life. My mother did not get better. On the contrary she grew rapidly worse in Colorado—whether because of the enforced separation from her family, the climate or the inevitable course of the disease. Since Italy had helped her a decade earlier, it was decided to try a sanitarium nearer New York and preferably in the South. Her brother, Minai Osnos, who had made a brilliant career as an electrical engineer in Berlin and held many patents with *Telefunken*, sent her money regularly to make possible a stay in a private sanitarium. There began a heartrending search for a place which would agree with her—Liberty, Lakewood, a town in the South—all were tried in a grim journeying to find health and quiet breathing.

During the summer we were reunited at a farm in the Catskills and my mother knew a brief respite from solitude if not from illness. By then I understood what a price she had paid for her life of dedicated hardship. She should have been given ease and comfort. But as a girl she had declared, in words that might have come from Lermontov, "I would rather live a short time like an eagle than a long time like a crow." Now in her mid-thirties, haggard and wasted, she said to me, "I would rather have lived this way with your father than a long time with an ordinary man."

At last she returned to New York, to the Montefiore Hospital in the Bronx. The search for healing was over: she would be near her husband and child. I used to visit her several times a week after school. One December afternoon she looked at her fifteen-year old daughter in a transport of maternal love, and said, "You are just the kind of daughter I dreamt of having"—apparently she had forgotten the boy who was to look like Herzl. That was the last time I saw her. Two days later she took an unexpected turn for the worse; pneumonia developed. All day the hospital authorities tried to reach my father who was somewhere at a meeting. By the time they located him, late in the afternoon, she was dead. She had died alone on December 19, 1915, at the age of thirty-six.

Now we became lodgers in earnest with no expectation of a

family home again. A small hall bedroom for my father and a somewhat larger one for me in the apartments of kindly, impoverished ladies who offered room and board to paying guests was to be home for my father till his remarriage six years later. It was a lonely and unhappy time, made endurable only by the unflagging intensity of his intellectual absorptions. Whatever his inner griefs the pattern of his life remained unchanged. He would leave for the 42nd Street Library and come back in the evening, usually after a meeting. He had eaten alone in some cafeteria; if it were not too late he would come into my room for a report of the day's doings.

His zeal for my intellectual progress was high but unsustained. I had been a precocious child and my father was not likely to be less enthusiastic about his daughter than about other matters which engaged his emotions. But I cannot say that his instruction was methodical. Periodically he would start a reading and study project. Three books were the *bêtes noires* of my early adolescence: the Bible in Hebrew; *Das Kapital* in German; and Spinoza's *Ethics* in Latin. Every once in a while, on a Saturday or Sunday when I was not in school and he was free, he would sit me down for an hour of learning; however, the interruptions were so many, the lapses between one lesson and the next so long, that I never seemed to get beyond the first chapter of these volumes. In addition, by the age of fifteen, I had developed a passion for the English romantic poets and my father was dismayed at my frivolity in preferring Shelley to Spinoza.

In other respects, too, he found the education of a young girl trying. He had fed me the complete idealistic pablum of his generation: the freedom of women, the equality of the sexes, the absurdity of conventions, the innate goodness of man. To the pure all things are pure and the inner light is a maiden's best guide. Very fine, but by the time his daughter was fifteen he disclosed a troublesome inconsistency. A nice young man who invited me to a concert was informed that I might go provided a chaperon accompanied us to Carnegie Hall—to the discomfort of all three in the party. Another nice young man who wanted to call had to be informed by me that my father, forgetting about the equality of sexes, had decided that distinctions existed and that he considered me too young for callers; the young man could write letters. So all that spring, the young man dwelling in Brooklyn wrote me long, formal letters to the Bronx, chiefly about Henri Bergson. Since I knew nothing about Bergson, I delighted my father temporarily by my unexpected interest in the French philosopher. After a while, however, it dawned on him that my leading questions were designed to extract replies likely to impress my Brooklyn correspondent.

Yet after behaving briefly like a Victorian ogre he capitulated completely. Our debates on his bourgeois deviations from principle, plus counsel from Mrs. Katz, the unwilling chaperon who thought he was too strict, plus pointed reminders of what Mr. Barrett did to Elizabeth, proved too much. As usual, there were no half-measures. Since the Strunskys, friends of his, owned the Atlantic Hotel in Belmar, New Jersey, he decided that the seashore would be an appropriate place for me to get fresh air and improve my mind. Besides, the Strunskys, knowing his circumstances, were generous enough to give him reduced rates. My independent career, as well as my troubles with my father, had begun.

The Atlantic Hotel was a delightful place at that time—a favorite resort for the Jewish intelligentsia. One evening one might see Sholem Aleichem, tiny and twinkling in a corner. Or Sholem Asch might appear, soulful and lumbering. Ossip Dymov, too, was a habitué and other familiar names. My father, too, came once or twice for a week-end to observe my progress, always inadequate. He was torn by his natural pleasure in his daughter and his sense that she was failing the destiny he had set for her. Once, Pinchas Rutenberg, a warm friend, walked over to my father as we were sitting on the veranda facing the sea—I can't remember whether it was Marx or Spinoza this time—and chided my father: "Syrkin, what are you doing? Let her go dancing." Papa smiled a little wistfully; he was no longer sure.

But whatever his personal tragedy as a widower and his problems as a father, the tempo of his public involvements showed no slackening. As a small child I used to ask him—since I was sure that he loved me more than anything in the world—hypothetical questions dear to children: "What would you do if . . .?" One of the questions tells a good deal about the man questioned: "If you had to choose between me and the Jewish people which would you choose?" Those had been the two poles of love in my father's life as I perceived them at the age of seven, and he would answer, kissing me, "the Jewish people." Ten years later I asked no such silly questions, but whenever my heart would hurt at the sight of my father's stricken eyes in an hour of anguish, there would be the relief of knowing that the hours at his desk or the exaltation at a meeting were as keen as the pain.

Perhaps this is the place to indicate that as I grew into womanhood many personal conflicts were to arise between my father and me. In his relationship to his daughter he was as dramatic, self-willed and sure of his rightness as in all other aspects of his life. But the difficulty of that struggle is as much mine as his and its details, since they involve others still alive, must be omitted.

LOUIS WALDMAN

Louis Waldman was born in Russia in 1892. After emigrating to the United States from the small town of Yancherudnia, he worked his way through engineering school and law school. While still a law student, he was elected to the New York State Legislature. Mr. Waldman was a member of the New York State Assembly in 1917 and in 1919. In 1933, he was a member of the New York State Convention to repeal the Eighteenth Amendment, and four years later was named to the New York State Constitutional Convention Committee by Governor Herbert H. Lehman.

Waldman introduced the first social insurance bill in the New York State Legislature, and was a fighter in many fields of social interest. From 1928 to 1941, he was the New York State Chairman of the Socialist Party and the Socialist Democratic Federation. He was also the Socialist candidate for Governor of New York in three campaigns, and was a founder of the American Labor Party, which he left in 1940, when he charged that it had fallen under Communist control.

Louis Waldman's autobiography, Labor Lawyer, *is a fascinating account of his career. In the section included here, he tells the story of his early "lessons in labor relations," of his Socialist beginnings, and gives an eye-witness account of the tragic Triangle fire, which eventually led to many labor reforms.*

Lessons in Labor Relations*

LOUIS WALDMAN

Without ever having seen a large city in Russia, although Kiev and Zhitomir were not far from Yancherudnia, I was now on my way across the world to America. I was young, I was hopeful, and for the first time in my life I had seventy-five dollars in ready cash in my pocket. My tickets were paid for in advance, my practical father having made all the arrangements through a travel agent.

The first detour I met on my highroad to adventure occurred at a frontier town in Germany where I discovered that, unaccountably, my railway ticket to Rotterdam had not yet arrived. But, refusing to let that little setback dampen my spirits, I settled down to wait and enjoy my new role as world traveler.

This way station was a clearing center for the hordes of emigrants pouring out of the Ukraine and Russia. While I waited for my tickets I wandered among them and was moved to pity when I found that hundreds were stranded there, defrauded by unscrupulous travel agents. Whole families were completely without funds and without means of continuing the journey. My heart went out to these poor unfortunates and, with a youngster's serene unconcern with money matters, I distributed my wealth lavishly among them.

The days stretched into weeks, until one day I realized that all my money was gone. It was only then that it finally dawned on me that I, the great benefactor, was in the same boat as the other stranded emigrants. My ticket never made its appearance, nor did the disreputable travel agent.

I rallied quickly from this blow, however. A mere lack of money was not going to keep me from America, after I had got

* Reprinted from *Labor Lawyer*, E. P. Dutton and Company, Inc., New York, 1944, pp. 19–38.

that far. Boldly I sought out the head of a travelers' aid organization and told him of my plight. I must have presented a heart-rending spectacle, for I walked out of his office generously supplied with money for a ticket—which was all that I, with characteristic improvidence, had asked for.

I had absolutely no money for food on the trip. Somehow I had managed to obtain some bread before I left and this, with unlimited quantities of water, served to keep me alive on the three day train journey from eastern Germany to Holland. I saw absolutely nothing of the cities or countryside through which we passed. I was chained to my seat in the train by weakness and my complete lack of money. When I arrived at the steamship office in Rotterdam I fell into a dead faint. By some miracle, I found the steamship ticket waiting for me.

I traveled steerage to America—and I marvel at the equanimity with which I write these words. Crossing the Atlantic in steerage thirty-odd years ago was a terrifying and nauseating experience. There were some forty or fifty men, women, and children crowded into one room with absolutely no ventilation other than that provided by the hatchway through which we had entered. Cots were set up in tiers with just enough space between the sets of bunks for one person to squeeze through with difficulty. The odors were indescribable, and breathing was far from a reflex activity; it required actual effort. Baggage had to be kept either on the floor or beneath the cot or on the cot itself. People were constantly stumbling over stray bags and packages.

We ate at long tables and from large bowls into which the entire meal, except for liquids, was dumped. But the foul odors of the ship and of unwashed bodies packed into close quarters were not conducive to hearty eating. In a way this was fortunate because there was not enough food for all. It was only after seasickness began to take its toll that those who could eat had enough food. After starving my way across Europe, at first I attacked the ship's victuals ravenously. But I could not stomach them for long and spent the rest of the trip detesting food and longing for an end to this tormenting journey.

Wasted, unsteady on my feet, but still hopeful, I arrived at

Battery Park, New York, on September 17, 1909. Behind me was the bustling harbor with its innumerable boats, the sight of which made me seasick all over again. Facing me, beyond the open spaces of the park, were the tall buildings of lower Manhattan, buildings which were more magnificent and higher than any I had ever imagined, even in my wildest dreams of this metropolis of the new world.

No one had come to meet me, for no one knew precisely when I was to arrive. And there I stood in Battery Park in my tight pants and round hat, with my knowledge of the Talmud, Yiddish, and Ukrainian, but in abysmal ignorance of English. I wandered around the park for some time, trying to find someone who could understand my language and direct me to 118 Orchard Street, where my sister Cecilia lived. After enduring the blank stares of several park bench idlers I at last discovered someone who understood me, and I was off via horse-car in the direction of the lower East Side.

When I got to the Orchard Street address I had to climb five flights of rickety and malodorous stairs to my sister's tenement flat. It was the first day of Rosh Hashanah and all my four sisters were there, seated around a festive table. They were at the same time overjoyed and alarmed when I walked in, for I was pale and gaunt from hunger and from the days I had spent below decks. They had known, of course, that I was coming, but my difficulties with the fraudulent travel agent and the delay in Rotterdam had confused them as to the exact day and hour of my arrival.

First on the order of business for the new immigrant was a visit to a clothing store.

"You think you can walk around like that, looking as green as grass?" my sister Anna said. "Why, no one, not even a peddler, will give you a job!"

And so it was that I parted forever with my tight pants, my round hat, and my high, creaking Ukrainian boots.

My American store clothes became a sort of passport which gave me the right to walk the streets as an equal of anyone and to consider myself as belonging to this vast city. This cheap, ready-to-wear East Side suit bridged the first gap, a sartorial gap, to be sure, between my past and my present.

However, while my new suit put me more at ease in the streets, my ignorance of English made me envious of other immigrants who spoke even a few halting words of the new language. Above all, if I wanted to become a real American, I realized, it was necessary for me to speak the language of Americans. And so, within a week after my arrival I enrolled in an East Side night school and set about the task of learning to read and speak the language of my adopted land.

Soon the entire neighborhood in which I lived became a school room, so to speak. As I walked in the streets I would pronouce aloud the words I saw written on signs, on billboards, or street corners. "Butcher shop," I slowly spelled out. "Gayety Burlesque" (what a strange word!), "Shoes Repaired Here," "Uneeda Biscuit." Mumbling to myself I would stand before some store window struggling with a strange unintelligible word until an irate shopkeeper told me to move on. I did move on but only to take up my post at another establishment, for I was determined to learn to speak my adopted language fluently even if the entire East Side had to listen painfully to my lessons.

One of the first things I learned was that if I were ultimately to study law I would first have to find a job. In the house in which I lived everyone worked, men, women, and even children, and before long I joined their ranks.

Getting a job in those days had a certain directness about it which is lacking in our larger American cities today. My sisters told me where the various factories were located and all I had to do was to go from door to door to find out whether anyone could use my services.

Finally I stumbled across a chandelier factory on Canal Street which proclaimed on a crudely painted sign—but in three languages—that a "hand" was wanted inside. I walked up several flights of stairs and finally spoke to the foreman. He looked me over, and made careful note of my husky appearance, and told me I could start working. My salary was to be two dollars a week,

but he added: "Don't worry, there's room for advancement."
Five months later when I quit I was still getting two dollars a
week.

I was not asked whether I had done this type of work before or
whether I had a union or apprenticeship card, nor was there any
labor organization to represent my interests and to see that I
received a fair wage for my work. I was hired, I was shown the
machine I was expected to operate, and then, after a few brief
instructions, I set to work.

I worked at a press which bent a strip of metal into a ring. My
job was to keep feeding my hungry, clattering machine strip after
strip of metal. The tempo of work was set with complete disre-
gard to myself. I had no control over the speed with which the
press came down. If I failed to feed it at the rate to which it was
regulated, this fact immediately became known, for if the metal
was not inserted in time the press descended with a loud, hollow
telltale clang which could be heard throughout the shop. The
foreman checked on our work by continually passing along the
row of machines and closely watching the size and pile of rings
which accumulated at the side of each press.

There were about one hundred men and women who worked
in this hot, noisy loft. And we worked from seven in the morning
until six at night with half an hour off for lunch. But this ten-
and-a-half-hour day seemed much longer than it really was because of the monotonous clang of the machine and the unvarying
routine of my work.

I paid my sister Cecilia one dollar a week for my room and
board and I shared a narrow, almost cell-like room with another
boarder. My lunches usually cost me two or three cents; one cent
for a sizable hunk of rye bread and another cent for an apple or a
half of a salt herring, and since I invariably walked to work I
found myself with a small surplus at the end of the week.

Yet, despite the monotony of the work and the low pay and
despite the fact that my fingers soon became sore, bruised, and
swollen from the constant handling of the metal, I was reasonably
happy. The working conditions, though onerous, were acceptable
to me because I did not know that factory work might be easier or

that my pay might be greater. It was all very different from the farm and outdoor work which I had hitherto known, but I assumed that the monotony, the heat, and the unpleasantness of it all were part of any city job.

At the machine next to me there was an Irish-American girl called Mary Bolan. Since I could not talk English and Mary could not talk Ukrainian or Yiddish, we smiled at each other above the clattering din of the chandelier factory. We smiled and smiled—and understood each other.

Months of work at the same task had given Mary Bolan speed and skill. Her nervous hands moved rapidly and deftly under the constant threat of mutilation by her machine. Unable to express myself to this delightful Irish-American girl other than through a wholly inadequate smile, I spent hours at my machine dreaming of the day when I would master both English and my natural timidity and summon courage to ask her to go for a walk with me some evening after work.

Absorbed in this pleasant daydreaming late one afternoon, I was startled out of it by a girl's scream. At once, all machines in the shop came to a halt. Looking up in alarm, I saw Mary Bolan lying on the floor at the side of her machine, blood streaming from the fingers of her right hand. The hovering threat had become actual.

I leaped from my place and ran to her side. She was unconscious and was bleeding profusely. I tore a strip from my shirt and made vain efforts to staunch the flow of blood. Workers gathered around the prostrate girl, some frightened, some giving expression to anger.

"It's those God-damned machines."

"It's cut off two of her fingers."

"Why the hell haven't they got guards on these machines?"

The foreman pushed his way through the crowd angrily, shouting: "Come on! Back to your machines, get back to your machines!"

We went back to work but somehow there was some difficulty getting the power started again. We sat silently in that dark loft, each man holding his own fear.

A little later we heard the clang of an ambulance in the street outside. Two orderlies carried the unconscious girl out of the factory. Then, once again, the stamping machines began their incessant clatter.

That night and for many nights thereafter I kept thinking of Mary Bolan. Her right hand had been mutilated, made useless, gone forever. Who would take care of Mary Bolan now? Owners of factories wanted strong healthy workers, workers with ten, not eight, fingers.

The day after the accident a man with a black portfolio came into the shop and, together with the foreman, started to make the rounds of the workers. Those who had seen the accident were asked to sign a certain paper. The man with the portfolio came over to my machine and shoved the paper under my face and asked me to sign.

"What is it?" I asked.

"We simply want you to sign saying that it was her fault. It's just a formality."

The word was a strange one to me.

"What," I asked in my broken English, "is this formality?"

"Never mind," the man with the portfolio said abruptly, "just sign!"

I hesitated.

"Go ahead, sign the paper," the foreman ordered.

"But it wasn't her fault," I objected.

"Then say it was the fault of the boy who brings the metal to the machines. He must have pushed her accidentally."

"I don't know anything about that," I replied.

The foreman spoke up sharply: "Listen, you! Don't you want to work here?"

"No," I answered.

Most of the workers, intimidated by the foreman and the man with the porfolio, signed. A few of us, however, refused and were discharged on the spot. I made fruitless inquiries about where Mary had been taken but no one seemed to know. I never saw her again.

I had received my first lesson in labor relations.

When I arrived home that evening, friends and neighbors gathered around to hear the story of my rebelliousness and to offer sage advice.

"You should have signed the paper, Louis."

"You will get nowhere in America by fighting the bosses."

"You see, there were some to be found who signed it anyway. And now you are without a job."

My sisters held solemn conclaves about my future and finally, after much discussion, they came to the conclusion that I should apply for work in the shop in which they worked and where one Benjamin Hirshorn was boss.

"When you apply for the job," one of my sisters said, "don't tell Hirshorn anything about refusing to sign any papers. Say that the work was too hard or that the pay was too low."

"If you don't get into fights with your employers and if you do as you're told, some day you will be a cutter."

While my sisters talked and argued, plotting the chart of my future, I sat by, silent and a little amused. For I had another plan which, for the time being, I kept secret. I still held fast to the ambition that one day I might become a lawyer.

Night after night I went to the neighborhood night school and hungrily devoured instruction. And because it was an utter impossibility to study in the wrangling, noisy intimacy of my family, I decided to perform a domestic surgical operation. Astonishingly enough, even on the two dollars a week I had been earning at the chandelier factory, I was able to save fifty or sixty cents a week, so that now, after several months of work, I had accumulated a nest egg of thirteen dollars. With this fortune I was determined to leave the noisy shelter of Cecilia's flat and move out into the world and find a room where I could have solitude and peace in which to continue my studies.

The immigrant's world in New York in those years was limited by the boundaries of the lower East Side. New York might be a vast sprawling city with several boroughs and wide spacious suburbs, but for those of us who were trapped by poverty, the East Side was all that we knew.

I found a room on Allen Street which by comparison made the

one on Orchard Street seem a paradise. I lived in a six-story tenement where families were doubled up in small apartments and where each family kept its quota of boarders to help meet the monthly rent. Some slept by day and others by night and very frequently, except on Sunday, the beds never had an opportunity to be aired. Each floor had a community toilet and a water tap in the hall and in some of the houses on Allen Street sanitary facilities were located in the back yard.

At night, when the gas light consumed the little air that managed to come through the halls and narrow windows, my room was stifling, and I suffered from headaches, dizziness, and nervous irritation. But I was alone, my time in the evenings was my own and I could study whenever the spirit moved me, which was often. I still recall vividly that curious, congested, miserable, yet fascinating life. I see Allen Street with its elevated structure whose trains avalanched between rows of houses. I see the gloom of the street where the sunlight never penetrated. I see the small shops, shops which somehow never achieved the dignity of selling anything new, but specialized in old furniture, old clothes, old dishes. It was a street which dealt in castoff merchandise. Even the pale children who played on Allen Street seemed old, second hand, not wanted. This street I now called home.

My room looked out on a dark air shaft blackened by dirt and time. My studies were continually carried on to the accompaniment of bedlam: screams of babies, the ceaseless loud-voiced wrangling of neighbors, and occasionally a snatch of song. There I would sit of a night studying American history, reading of its great figures: Jefferson, Paine, Washington, reading of the great nation they had founded and wondering whether my lot in it would always be confined to a cell-like room on Allen Street.

It was at times such as these that I thought of the openness and freedom of my life in Yancherudnia, of the pond behind our house and the forest encircling our little Ukrainian village. On a hot summer's night when breathing was almost impossible, when all the East Side odors seemed to come down the air shaft and into my room, I lay on my bed and in my imagination breathed deep drafts of the sweet-smelling air of the forest where I had played and worked as a boy.

My rent was four dollars a month. As for food, there were weeks and even months when I somehow managed to live on three to four cents a day. A fifth of a sizable loaf of rye bread cost me one cent. The endless rows of pushcarts on Orchard, Delancey and Allen Streets offered a variety of fruits and vegetables all at astonishingly low prices. Sometimes when I felt in a particularly spendthrift mood, I would buy one or two cents' worth of *halvah*, an Eastern European confection which is made of crushed sesame seeds, honey, nuts and albumen. But of course I had *halvah* only on special festive occasions. For the rest, my fare was simple, usually monotonous, but nourishing.

Finally, through the efforts of my sisters, in March 1910, I was given an opportunity to become an apprentice to a cutter of ladies' garments. I worked six weeks without pay but this was considered a privilege, for cutters in the garment industry were the aristocrats of the needle trades. I learned my work quickly and on the whole rather enjoyed it; in addition, my prospects for increased pay were greatly enhanced.

This routine of factory work from eight in the morning until six at night, followed by evenings in the classroom or study at home continued pleasantly until it was interrupted by the great cloakmakers' strike of 1910. Without hesitation I walked out with the rest of the workers, and, since I was now on strike, I joined the union. Our grievances were many and just and included an upward revision of the wage scale, the shortening of the work day, and improvement of sanitary conditions, and called for an investigation into possible fire hazards as well as demands for the abolition of the sweatshop system. More than fifty thousand cloakmakers answered the strike call.

I found the tense, exciting union meetings far more interesting than evenings spent at home studying, and I was soon drawn into the maelstrom of union activity. The cutters on the whole were an intelligent, literate group of men and our meetings were filled with lively discussion and debate. I enjoyed these debates both for the content and for the opportunities which they offered for putting my limited English to use.

It did not take very long, however, for me to become painfully aware that being on strike was more than a matter of picket-line heroics or thundering rhetoric. We received no strike benefits and this, quite, naturally, meant that we had to live on savings, friends, or, as was the case with many of us, on miracles. I could not turn to my sisters for help because they too were on strike. I had no savings. The few dollars I had accumulated as a result of my work in the chandelier factory had been used up during my six weeks' apprenticeship without pay. True, my activities in those days were largely confined to the picket-line and the picketing committee saw that all pickets were more or less adequately fed. But I did not picket continually, and on picket-less days I went hungry.

Still, there was a certain compensation for not working. When I was through with my day's activity on the picket line, which was usually fairly early in the morning, I ran off to the library to lose myself in reading and studying.

On the second day of the strike, as we approached our factory, we found several toughs strolling nonchalantly back and forth before the entrance. The older and more experienced workers looked at each other and whispered: *"Shtarke!"* I had heard the expression before. These *"shtarke"* were in reality strong-arm men, gangsters, hired by the employers to help break the strike. As we proceeded to march up and down before the building, not only peacefully but timidly as well, the strong-arm men soon began to walk at our sides pretending to be ordinary pedestrians. Now and then one would brutally push a picket off the sidewalk, sending him flying into the gutter, at the same time muttering to the stunned picket: "Quit pushing!" If the picket stood firm the gangster would then, in "self-defense," knock him down.

All day long this brutal game went on, but the pickets stuck it out. And the police, I observed, were nowhere to be seen while the thugs were at work. This state of affairs called for the special attention of the cutters. They were the most Americanized group in the union, while the tailors had the customary timidity of immigrants, fearful to strike out in defense of their rights. The cutters were thus obliged to act as an emergency squad, subject to the call of the tailors wherever the going was toughest. They pitted their courage and bare hands against the blackjacks and lead pipes of the gangsters.

Since the days of the great cloakmakers' strike, I have heard many fulminations against racketeering in the American labor movement. But I know today, on the basis of what I witnessed in 1910, that strike-breaking was the door through which gangsterism entered the American labor movement.

In the early days of the strike, several prominent and public-spirited citizens interested themselves in the plight of the workers. These included the late Justice Louis D. Brandeis and the late Louis Marshall, who made efforts to bring about peace between the manufacturers and the workers. After the strike, the ladies' garment industry, then one of the most backward and disorganized in America, adopted what has since been described as the most advanced and enlightened code of labor relations in the form of a collective agreement which was known as "the perpetual protocol of peace."

This document became famous in American labor history. Its findings and provisions were the basis of surveys and investigations by the departments of labor in many states and by the Federal Government. The protocol was, in fact, a remarkable instrument and went beyond the usual economic conditions in most labor agreements. As a means of eradicating the sweatshops a joint board was set up, composed of representatives of employers, workers and the public, with elaborate machinery for periodical inspection of factories and lofts and the abatement of unsanitary conditions. The protocol also made provision against harsh treatment of workers and their summary dismissal from employment.

The strike had lasted eleven weeks and now I was back at work as a lining cutter. I also had special responsibilities toward the union which included "police" duties. There was a provision in the protocol which called for protection against chiseling, and so, on one occasion when I observed that the agreement was being violated, I promptly reported this to the union. And just as promptly my employer discharged me.

Officials of the union wanted to call a strike on my account but I insisted that I could take care of myself and get a job elsewhere. However, my optimism was short-lived. I soon discovered that I was on a black list. My employer had informed the industry that I was a troublemaker and there was no one in the industry, the protocol notwithstanding, who wanted to hire me.

This was my second lesson in labor relations, a process that was to continue for several years.

And so once again I found myself without work and again I led a precarious existence. Unable to find work in the garment industry, I became a peddler, going from house to house with a basket of ribbons, but apparently I was unsuited for commerce even on this modest scale and I later took a job in a paper-box factory. After three months of this I found work as a cutter in a millinery factory. The work was hard, the pay was low, and, worst of all, the hours were long. But after two periods of unemployment, following each other in rapid succession, I clung desperately to the job because, while it offered me only the barest of livings, it enabled me to continue my studies.

When I was eighteen-and-a-half years old, that is to say, after I had been in the United States for nearly a year, I was graduated into high school. It is true that it was an evening high school, but it was high school nevertheless. We were an eager, intense lot to whom free education was more than something to be taken for granted. We worked assiduously, and among these immigrant high school students the cutting of classes and other student pranks were unknown things. Education represented to us the only avenue of freedom from long hours, hard work, poverty, and the thralldom of the East Side slums. Classes consisted of youngsters and middle-aged people of both sexes. A list of the graduates of my class, if it were compiled, would constitute a minor *Who's Who* in art, business, and the professions of New York today.

I finished my course in the East Side Evening High School in 1911 and during the summer of that year, in order to make up for a few deficiencies in my curriculum and to prepare for the regents examinations, I took several courses in the Eron Preparatory School—the Groton of the East Side—then located on East Broadway. I was determined to pursue some professional study, preferably law, but here the problem of finances beame paramount. To say that I had no money is a gross understatement. I was literally penniless, living from day to day on my meager, inadequate earnings.

It is true that there were colleges such as the College of the City of New York which required no tuition fee, but what I wanted was professional training, which City College did not then provide. I made inquiries at Columbia, New York University, and the New York Law School but found that the basic requisite of study was the payment of tuition fees and expenses which amounted to about $200 a year. My chances of earning $200 a year in those days, let alone saving that amount for tuition, were as remote from possibility as anything I could imagine. I talked this situation over with Dr. Shipley at the East Side Evening High School and he persuaded me to enter Cooper Union and take up engineering, for which no tuition fee was required. And so by force of circumstance and lack of funds, a boyhood ambition came to be realized in the fall of 1911 when I entered Cooper Union. Immigrant, semi-skilled worker, one-time aspirant for the law, I now bent all my energies toward becoming a civil engineer.

My life at this time was a continuous routine of factory during the day and school in the evening, and, because I had no money to spend on amusement and since my social life was virtually nonexistent, all my free time was spent in a near-by library.

One Saturday afternoon in March of that year—March 25, to be precise—I was sitting at one of the reading tables in the old Astor Library, now the building of the Hebrew Immigrant Aid Society on Lafayette Street. It was a raw, unpleasant day and the comfortable reading room seemed a delightful place to spend the remaining few hours until the library closed. I was deeply engrossed in my book when I became aware of the sounds of fire engines racing past the building. By this time I was sufficiently Americanized to be fascinated by the sound of fire engines. Along with several others in the library, I ran out to see what was happening, and followed crowds of people to the scene of the fire.

A few blocks away, the Asch Building at the corner of Washington Place and Greene Street was ablaze. When we arrived at the scene, the police had thrown a cordon around the area and the firemen were helplessly fighting the blaze. The eighth, ninth, and tenth stories of the building were now an enormous roaring cornice of flames.

Word had spread through the East Side, by some magic of terror, that the plant of the Triangle Waist Company was on fire and that several hundred workers were trapped. Horrified and helpless, the crowds—I among them—looked up at the burning building, saw girl after girl appear at the reddened windows, pause for a terrified moment, and then leap to the pavement below, to land as mangled, bloody pulp. This went on for what seemed a ghastly eternity. Occasionally a girl who had hesitated too long was licked by pursuing flames and, screaming with clothing and hair ablaze, plunged like a living torch to the street. Life nets held by the firemen were torn by the impact of the falling bodies.

The emotions of the crowd were indescribable. Women were hysterical, scores fainted; men wept as, in paroxysms of frenzy, they hurled themselves against the police lines. As darkness came on, the fire was brought under control and by word of mouth the details of the dreadful story spread through the East Side.

The Triangle Waist Company, owned by Max Blanck and Isaac Harris, was a non-union shop which the previous year had stubbornly held out against the equitable demands of the Waistmakers' Union. One of the conditions which the union had won during the strike called for a half-day's work on Saturdays. And so while all other waist factories in New York were closed that afternoon, the Triangle factory was open with a full shift of about 850 workers, most of them young girls.

The factory had woefully inadequate sanitary facilities, so that it was necessary for the workers to leave the plant in order to reach the toilets. As a precaution against what the employer called "interruption of work" the heavy steel door which led to the hall and stairway had been locked. Piles of oil-soaked waste lay under the sewing machines. A carelessly tossed cigarette or match had ignited these piles of waste material and the fires leaped from machine to machine, converting the overcrowded plant into a roaring holocaust. The girls, sitting at the machines, were packed in tightly, row upon row, chairs back to back. In the face of such crowding, escape was virtually impossible, and panic must have been instantaneous.

One of the owners of the Triangle Waist Company who was in the building at the outbreak of the fire left it hurriedly without unlocking the exits, thus dooming the girls inside. Nor had the girls ever been permitted to use the passenger elevators, due to the owners' fear that they might carry out stolen material.

When the fire was over the toll of the Triangle disaster was 147 killed and burned to death and several hundred suffering from serious burns. Police and firemen on entering the charred building discovered bodies literally burned to the bone. Blackened skeletons were found bending over machines. In one of the narrow elevator shafts of the building they found lifeless bodies piled six stories high.

A few days later the Waistmakers' Union arranged for a mass funeral of the dead, since most of the victims had been burned or mangled beyond recognition. City officals prohibited any demonstration, but the plans for the funeral were carried out nevertheless. More than one hundred thousand workers marched in a silent cortege behind the flower-laden hearses. The streets through which the sad procession passed were draped in black and purple; East Side places of business were closed for the day.

Together with thousands of others I stood on the sidewalk and watched the funeral procession go by. A mass emotion of sorrow and despair was felt everywhere on the East Side that day. But in the weeks that followed these emotions gave way to angry questioning and a determination that a similar tragedy must never take place in New York again. We all felt that the workers who had died in the plant of the Triangle Waist Company were not so much the victims of a holocaust of flame as they were the victims of stupid greed and criminal exploitation.

Shortly after the mass funeral, a crowded meeting was held at Cooper Union to consider the tragedy and its meaning for the working people of New York. The historic basement auditorium of Cooper Union was jammed long before the meeting was scheduled to open. I have been to many a meeting in that auditorium since and I have addressed many meetings there myself, but never have I witnessed anything remotely comparable to that one. The audience was silent. There was none of the friendly chatter which is usually heard before a meeting starts. There were no greetings, no one smiled.

The families of the Triangle victims were there, reminding us, if any of us needed reminding, of the recent tragedy. The finest orators of the New York labor movement were there, among them, of course, Meyer London, later to become the first Socialist congressman from New York City. But more memorable, indeed unforgettable, was another speaker whose oratorical powers and great personal charm impressed me as perhaps no other man has impressed me since. He commanded the breathless attention of the audience with his first few words. His thought was clear, logical, and every sentence which he spoke was uttered with a purity of diction which transformed everything he said into literature.

Quietly, out of the memory of the days when he himself had been a factory worker, the speaker recounted life in the factories: the long hours, unsanitary conditions, fire hazards, unguarded and dangerous machines. And sitting there in that packed auditorium we all felt that this man was the spokesman of our unexpressed thoughts, a voice for the voiceless. It is thirty-two years since the night of that meeting and I still recall vividly every word he spoke, remembering it as though it were yesterday.

He spoke of the law of the sea by which the master of a vessel is always the last to leave a sinking ship. But the masters of industry, he said, were bound by no such honorable code. The masters of the Triangle Waist Company had locked the steel doors of the factory, had locked them and left the women and children, the crew of the factory, to their dreadful fate. The Triangle fire was simply a dramatic demonstration of what was constantly happening in the lives of workers, it was the epitome of a thousand similar, if smaller, tragedies which had occurred over a period of many years. The life of the worker was constantly attended by fire, disease, mutilation under machines without safety devices. And now, as a result of the Triangle tragedy we must make the cause of New York's workers known to everyone, to other workers, to city officials, to the legislators in Albany, to the country at large. . . .

America would listen to us if only we could find the voice with which to declare our wrongs and the will to declare them earnestly and constantly. Sympathetic editorials in the newspapers were good, but not enough. The governor must act, the legislature must live up to its reputed function of truly representing the people. The speaker ended with these words: "The greatest monument we can raise to the memory of our 147 dead is a system of legislation which will make such deaths hereafter impossible."

Never in all my life had I been held and fascinated as I was by this speaker. A few days before, we had stood sorrowful and helpless on the sidewalks of the East Side as the funeral cortege slowly passed by; but now there was a firm determination that the victims of the Triangle fire should not have died in vain. I felt that I was now ready to follow wherever this speaker led. The audience stood and cheered when he concluded, and since I had not caught his name when he was introduced I turned to my neighbor and asked who the orator might be.

Incredulously, the man replied: "Do you mean to tell me you've never heard Morris Hillquit before?"

Hillquit had been an immigrant factory worker, coming to America as a young man and working in the sweatshops of New York and, like so many other American emancipators, determined to get out and speak for those who could only stammer or remain silent.

And all through his life, wasted by the tuberculosis he had contracted in the New York factories, he spoke at meetings, planned for the people, argued before judges and legislatures.

*Worker, attorney, orator, theoretician, historian, Hillquit spoke
and pleaded for a future where people would not be mutilated
by machines, where girls would not leap to their deaths on
bloody pavements, where money would not be superior to
human lives, no matter how humble or obscure. . . .*

*He called this future society Socialism; others had called
it the Kingdom of God or the Brotherhood of Man. But it all
amounted to the same thing. This world of which Hillquit
dreamed, and for which he constantly worked, was a world in
which we would cease thinking of our fellows as Catholic or
Protestant, Jew or Gentile, white or black, Caucasian or Asiatic,
but rather as creators or destroyers. For in the last analysis, he
realized that this is the only test of a man. Does a man (or a
nation) build and create so that the world may become a more
humane place in which to live? Or does he (or it) destroy, lay
waste and ruin everything to which he (or it) puts his hands? He
realized, together with all the Socialistic thinkers who preceded
him, that we may build with enlightened progressive laws, with
an easel or a palette or a typewriter, as well as with a slide rule.
He realized that we may destroy with international cartels as
well as with artillery and bombing planes. He knew that society
lived in a sort of idiotic planlessness for which it had found high-
sounding names. He knew there was excitement and tension in
the world through which he passed, but that the excitement was
the excitement of men hunting each other for game, and that the
tension was the tension of madness. He knew that unless men
realized that they must live together in harmonious creativeness
and in a mutual helpfulness they would perish from the face of
the earth. . . .*

*In 1933, his body ravaged by tuberculosis contracted in a
sweatshop, he died after forty years of service in the American
labor movement. . . .*

Others at that meeting at Cooper Union might have stirred the
audience with demagogic oratory into an angry destructive mob
whose actions might have been spectacular but fleeting. Hillquit,
however, galvanized us all into public energy ready to work.

Committees were appointed to bring our problem before the public and before the proper officials. Everyone's service was enlisted in one way or another. Some of us were instructed to distribute leaflets, others to undertake the letter-writing campaign to the governor, still others to arrange for street corner meetings throughout the city. I, who had never taken part in any political activity, was placed on a local committee to assist in arranging meetings in the neighborhood in which I lived. The fight for more humane labor legislation was launched and in the weeks and years that followed I knew that the mutilation of Mary Bolan was not to be a forgotten individual tragedy or the deaths of the 147 girls in the Triangle fire an utterly meaningless catastrophe.

MRS. GUSTAVE HARTMAN

Born May Weisser on New York's lower East Side in 1900, she became the helpmate and wife of Judge Gustave Hartman, and it is as Mrs. Gustave Hartman that she has told the story of her husband's (and her own) philanthopic work on behalf of orphan children. In I Gave My Heart, *Mrs. Hartman tells of the first 37 years of her life. She was a lively hard-working girl when she began to work for Judge Hartman as a bookeeper for the Israel Orphan Asylum which he founded.*

At this time, in 1920, Gustave Hartman was a popular communal and civic personality in New York. A Republican, he was a Municipal Justice, then the first Republican elected to the City Court in New York City. May Weisser admired him and worked closely with him for eight years before they were married in 1928. By this time, Mrs. Hartman had become the Superintendent of the Israel Orphan Asylum and, together with her husband, devoted all her time to the orphans, to the raising of money and to the establishment of an All-Star show at Madison Square Garden in behalf of the Asylum.

The Hartmans had two children, and when the eldest was only two years old, Judge Hartman died of a heart attack in 1936. His widow carried on their work and in her autobiography, which is the story of two unusual people, she reveals how men and women from all walks of life aided in their humanitarian efforts.

My First Job*

MRS. GUSTAVE HARTMAN

INTO THE LOWER EAST SIDE swarmed not only Jewish immigrants but Italian immigrants, who lived in the tenements on First Avenue and along Thirteenth and Fourteenth Streets from Second Avenue to Avenue B. They had their markets and pushcarts all along these streets.

Many families of German Christian origin lived along Avenue A. On the extreme East near the river were Irish immigrants. The lower West Side of Manhattan was Italian and Irish.

The immigrants, who had come to these shores to find the freedom and opportunity denied them in the lands of their birth, had these things in common—an intense love for the land of their adoption and a deep sense of responsibility towards their coreligionists.

Churches, synagogues, hospitals and welfare agencies sprang up everywhere, supported by men and women of very modest means. They had understanding and compassion in their hearts and sought to help each other out. When one of them contributed fifty cents or a dollar to a charity, it was a real sacrifice, and in some instances the denial of a meal.

After a long, hard day's work in a factory, or a store, or at home raising a large family, these men and women would go out to raise funds for charity. They would climb steep flights of stairs to upper-floor assembly halls, to make appeals at lodge and society meetings. When such an evening's effort resulted in a collection of a few dollars, there was elation.

The Orthodox Jews collected funds for hospitals and homes for the aged, and for orphanages where kosher food could be served and other religious customs of their forefathers observed. The Hebrew Immigrant Aid Society, Beth Israel Hospital, and the

* Reprinted from *I Gave My Heart*, Citadel Press, New York, 1960.

Home of the Daughters of Jacob were among many East Side institutions that were to become famous.

Bessarabia, a Rumanian-speaking province of Russia, was the birthplace of my parents. The Bessarabian Verband Association was composed of many lodges and societies, organized by immigrants from the little towns of Bessarabia.

There was a crying need for a home where orphan boys, between the ages of six and fourteen, could be raised in the Orthodox tenets of the Faith, and the Bessarabian Verband started the organization which was to become the Hebrew National Orphan Home.

My parents were among the founders and much of their activity took place in our home. My mother helped organize the first Ladies Auxiliary and my sisters Sally and Minnie started the Young Folks Auxiliary.

The Verband purchased and renovated a fine brownstone house for the orphans at 37 East 7th Street, between First and Second Avenues, on the lower East Side. It had been the home of Rabbi Philip Klein, who was famous on the East Side. A charter was obtained from the State Board of Charities.

The official opening was scheduled for June 7, 1914, with a celebration to last an entire week. This would be a fund-raising event.

For several months, the Board and Auxiliaries had been selling raffle tickets and collecting thousands of prizes from merchants and manufacturers. Tickets of admission to the celebration were fifty cents each and entitled the owner to a prize, according to his luck when he pulled a number.

I volunteered my services and at the age of fourteen I started, at the beginning of June, to work in the Home.

My plan for the handling of the prizes had proved so successful that the Board and Auxiliary members turned over all sorts of jobs to me.

This certainly was not going to be any permanent job for me, I thought, but there was so much to do that I stayed on way beyond the summer. Then I found the work so fascinating and stimulating, especially when the children began arriving, that I continued to stay on.

The first to be admitted were four pitiful little brothers, parentless and neglected, who were brought in by a very sick grandmother. Since no house staff had yet been hired, the women of the Auxiliary took turns looking after the children.

Each day one would bring in the meals prepared in her own kitchen. Another stayed with the children during the day, until another relieved her in the evening. They rendered this service with love and earnestness.

When I could slip out of the office, I would play with the little boys in the backyard; and I always came around on Saturday to be with them.

On Sundays our office was like a beehive, with directors and members all over the place.

With the arrival of more children a superintendent was engaged. Soon a medical staff was set up and we had a complete organization to look after the children.

The Superintendent distrusted me at first because of my closeness to the directors and their wives, but he overcame his prejudice when he realized that I never carried tales or sought information or favors, but was only interested in doing a good job. I became his right hand.

The Superintendent was a very able man. He knew how to make people cry when he made a speech, because he was sincere in his own feelings. This made him a good fund-raiser, which, of course, is necessary for running a charitable institution. He also was able to recruit volunteer workers.

From him, I learned my first lessons in public relations.

There were now three of us on the office staff and my salary, which I had just started receiving, was raised from five to six dollars a week.

Though only fifteen, I was in charge of the office and handled all the funds. Besides, I was secretary to the Board of Directors and to all committees. I worked every evening, except Friday.

At meetings, I not only took notes but participated in the discussions.

During a House Committee meeting on which my mother served, the chairman suddenly turned to her and said, "You'll see, someday your daughter May will be the president of a great institution." All the members nodded their heads in agreement.

My mother was pleased and proud, but to me it sounded very farfetched.

So accustomed was I to being sent on errands that I wasn't surprised when the Chairman of Finance said to me, "May, I want you to go over to Rabbi Philip Klein. Tell him we are short of funds and unable right now to meet the interest on the mortgage. Ask him for an extension of time."

I had never met Rabbi Klein, from whom the orphanage building had been purchased. I had heard that he was a great spiritual leader and a learned scholar and that he was of Hungarian origin.

He received me very kindly. I was impressed with his distinguished appearance and courtly manner.

He listened to me earnestly, and then said, "How come that they send a child to ask me this?"

In all innocence, I answered, "I suppose they were too embarrassed to come themselves." A smile flitted across his handsome face and he answered, "All right, my child, you can go back and tell them that you accomplished your mission. I'll wait until they have the funds."

He then asked me about our work and was pleased that the children were being well cared for, and especially that we were adhering to the rules of Orthodoxy.

I was sent on a similar errand to the Bank of the United States at the Delancey Street Branch, when a note, that we were unable to meet, fell due. I walked in and asked for Mr. Joseph Marcus, the President.

A stocky, gray-haired, little gentleman, wearing a frock coat and striped pants, came forth. He received me courteously and, after listening to me, inquired just as Rabbi Klein had done, why the directors had sent me on this important errand.

I gave him the same answer I had given the Rabbi.

He threw his head back and chuckled, "You know, you are a very smart and nice little girl. I wish I had someone like you in my bank. Tell the committee that I will extend the note for three months."

A secretary of one of the lodges gave me a check to be used as a deposit on a purchase. After a few moments' reflection, he said, "I think it would be a good idea if you went over to the bank and asked them to 'satisfy this check.' "

I looked at him in bewilderment and said, "What shall I ask?"

He repeated, "To satisfy this check." When I asked a third time he showed his annoyance and made me feel stupid.

I approached the teller in the bank and in a faint hesitant voice said, "I would like to have this check satisfied."

"What?"

I repeated my request.

He walked over to an officer of the bank, then came back with a big grin on his homely face and said, "Here is your satisfied, I mean *certified*, check."

I blushed to the roots of my hair.

When I returned to the office, I said to the secretary, "Here is your certified check," and unable to control my indignation, I hissed, "Not satisfied."

He shrugged his shoulders and calmly replied, "When that stamp is on a check, everyone is satisfied."

LUDWIG LEWISOHN

Ludwig Lewisohn was perhaps the most important Jewish writer in the English language in twentieth-century America. Born in Berlin (1882–1955), he was brought to the United States at the age of eight. His family settled in Charleston, South Carolina, where young Ludwig attended Christian schools and "accepted Jesus as my personal Saviour." But before he was twenty years of age, he was confronted by anti-Semitism and he eventually became one of the most eloquent spokesmen among American Jews in the fight against assimilation and the battle for Jewish identification.

Lewisohn taught German at the University of Wisconsin and Ohio State University, and then left the academic life to become a full-time magazine contributor, literary critic and author. He became drama critic for The Nation, *and translated from German into English the work of such men as Gerhart Hauptmann, Jacob Wassermann, and other classic German writers.*

Most of his later work was Jewish in content. His novel, The Island Within, *which dealt with intermarriage, was an international success. His autobiographical works,* Up Stream *and* Mid-Channel, *and a number of his other books, were concerned with his personal problems as a Jew, and with issues that faced all sensitive Jews.*

Lewisohn was the author of more than forty books, although he had a busy public career as editor of The New Palestine, *the official organ of the Zionist Organization of America, and as a professor at Brandeis University.*

Ludwig Lewisohn died in 1955. His reputation as a major Jewish literary figure remains secure. The selection here, taken from Up Stream, *describes the author's first encounter with anti-Semitism in his attempts to obtain a teaching appointment while at Columbia University.*

The Making of an Anglo-American*

LUDWIG LEWISOHN

MY GRADUATION was made a notable event in our small circles. All the leading citizens of the town are alumni of the college and are proud of its work and its traditions. So they had followed my writings in the magazine and in the papers, and when I took two degrees and delivered a commencement oration which, for once, made some concessions in manner to the more florid type of Southern oratory, they had a moment of enthusiasm over me. This enthusiasm was shared by the press of Queenshaven and by my class-mates. I was a bit more of a hero than the youth who wins a series of important football games for his university. It was a very great day for me and an even greater day for my parents: the happiest they had known in years, the happiest they were ever to know again. Under the influence of this wave of communal approbation a board of Episcopal clergymen elected me to the chair of English in a local academy. But the aged clergyman to whom the school really belonged arose from a bed of illness and removed the trustees he had himself appointed for electing a person distasteful to him. He used this expression quite openly in a letter to the *Courier*. The gentlemen on the board, however, wrote me apologetic letters and my friends and parents agreed that it wasn't, after all, my ambition to teach in a denominational school. Besides, I was only just nineteen and the world seemed all before me where to choose. . . . By Ferris' advice I registered in several teachers' agencies and sent my master's thesis to a scholarly journal by which it was duly accepted for publication.

The long summer weeks dragged on and nothing happened. One New England teachers' agency did, indeed, suggest a place

* Reprinted from *Up Stream*, Boni and Liveright, New York, 1922, pp. 99–126.

or two but nothing came of my applications. Ferris assured me by letter that this lack of success was due to my youth and inexperience. Since he had counseled me from the first to apply for a fellowship or scholarship in one of the large graduate schools of the East, I accepted his explanation for these happenings as well as for other experiences that came when I applied for school positions within the state. His advice was that I should stay at home for a year, pursue my studies and write a few more scholarly papers to submit with my fellowship applications the following spring. My father, ever the soul of unworldliness in money matters, agreed heartily to this plan and my mother was glad that she could have me with her for another year.

That year stands out in my memory as a pleasant one. I saw little of any one except Ferris, but I was quite free to devote myself to the cultivation of my tastes. And I wrote my first extensive piece of work: an essay in biography and criticism about fifty thousands words in length. Ferris pronounced it well-grounded and well-written—a notable piece of work for a mere youth. So when April came I applied for fellowships at Harvard and Columbia and both Ferris and I were hopeful of the results. From both universities, however, I received only pleasant acknowledgements of the work I had sent in support of my applications, an invitation to pursue my graduate studies and regrets that neither a fellowship nor a scholarship were available. This was a hard blow. It was obvious that I could not go on living on my father's kindness. On the contrary, I was passionately anxious to help him and my mother to free themselves from the bonds of their Queenshaven life. I did not speak of this, for I did not want to render their consciousness of it more acute. But it weighed on me heavily. I thought and thought and came to a resolve which many American youths take lightly enough, but which cost me infinite hesitation and pain: I would borrow money. The notion of working my way through the graduate course never occurred to me. For I was not concerned with textbooks or, primarily, with degrees, but with a life to be lived, an absorption and dedication to be accomplished. And this never presented itself to my mind as possible upon any terms but those of a complete release from sordid preoccupations.

Unhappily for me the wealthy Jewish physician of my Methodist days had recently died. Had he been alive my way would have been easier. I felt close to him and he was kind and generous. As it was, I had to go to other prominent citizens and alumni of the college. These men had all liked me and made much of me for years; I felt quite at home with them in all essential matters and yet it was a terrible struggle. I put off my errand from day to day; I went to the door of some office and hadn't the courage to enter. A sensation of physical nausea and of burning shame overwhelmed me. . . . I have never been able to feel differently. If I must ask for something, however clear my right to make the demand or the request, the old, sickening misery comes over me and I am helpless, stupid, stammering, absurd. For the sake of others I have had to ask things since then. For myself I would never have the strength to face that sense of spiritual nakedness and abasement. Perhaps it is from this native feeling that there has grown my passion for justice. The more just we are to our fellowmen, the less need we wound and degrade them with our wretched mercy. True justice—I do not mean the tribal terrors or capitalistic voracities of our legal and moral codes—true justice need not be tempered by mercy. It excludes the necessity for mercy. You do not need to be merciful until you have ceased to be just . . .!

The Queenshaven gentlemen, it is but fair to add, made my dreadful task comparatively easy. Several of them met to discuss the matter and made up for me a loan of three hundred and fifty dollars. I had really wanted six hundred to see me through the year at Columbia, since the tuition alone was a hundred and fifty. But wild horses, in the vivid old phrase, could have dragged no further begging from my lips. I thanked them with what grace I could master and proceeded to get ready for my great adventure.

Let any one who has an unclouded vision of our American life, and not least of the academic part of it, consider my undertaking. How often since have I reflected on it, sometimes in a mood of bitterness, sometimes in one of irony. I had lived utterly for the things of the mind and the emotions. I was twenty years old and knew less of practical matters than many a child of ten. I had no social adroitness but the most quivering sensitiveness and pride. I was passionately Anglo-American in all my sympathies, I wanted above all things to be a poet in the English tongue, and my name and physiognomy were characteristically Jewish. I had ill-cut, provincial clothes and just money enough to get through one semester. Such was my inner and outer equipment for pursuing in a metropolitan graduate school the course which was to lead to a college appointment to teach English. No one warned me, no one discouraged me. It seems incredible that Ferris had no inkling of the quality of my undertaking. But he, too, kept silent. So I faced the future with a steady hopefulness. Only when I sought to grasp what separation from my mother would mean to her and me did my heart sink. We tried to comfort each other, she and I, by dwelling upon the certainty of a successful career for myself. But during the last days we gave up these feeble and hollow efforts and fell quite silent before our unavertible fate.

I

In those days the steamers from the South landed at piers on the North River. I was too deeply preoccupied with that first, tremendous, lonely plunge into the world to watch the harbor or the sky-line of New York. I stood on deck, grasping my valise tightly, holding my hat. The sharp wind was full of scurries of rain. It was almost dark when we passengers trickled across the plank into the appalling mud of the streets. The lower West Side is, I still think, the dismallest port of the city. On that day, coming from the bland and familiar South and from a life that touched reality so feebly, it seemed brutal, ferocious, stark. . . . An indifferent acquaintance met me and hustled me to the nearest station of the Ninth Avenue "L." We climbed the iron staircase, scrambled for tickets and were jammed into a car. It was the evening rush hour and we had barely standing room. The train rattled on its way to Harlem. At One Hundred and Sixteenth

Street we slid down in the elevator to the street, frantically dodged people and vehicles across Eighth Avenue, turned south and west and stood presently before one of a row of three story houses wedged in between huge, dark buildings. My guide introduced me to the boarding-house keeper, a hard-featured, heavily rouged woman who seemed in pain and in a hurry. They led me to a hall bedroom on the third floor, lit a whirring gas-jet and, in another minute, were gone. I put down my valise and took off my overcoat and stood still, quite still, between the bed and the chiffonier. I could touch one with either hand. I was in New York. I was alone.

At such moments one's intentions to conquer the world avail little. Especially if one is twenty. I heard the far away roar of New York like the roar of a sinister and soulless machine that drags men in and crunches them between its implacable wheels. It seemed to me that I would never be able to face it. I huddled in that small, cold room in an old traveling robe of my father's and bit my lips. But I had the manhood not to write home in that mood. Indeed my old stoicism had not deserted me and my parents never learned of the grinding misery of my first weeks in New York.

In the morning the October sun shone. At breakfast the landlady seemed not nearly so menacing. I may add at once that she was an intelligent and courageous woman who had suffered much and undeservedly and that we became great friends. She gave me on that first day what simple directions I needed. I left the house, walked to the corner and turned my face toward the west. Morningside Heights with its many poplars rose sheer against a sparkling autumn sky. The beauty of it seemed much colder to me that day than it does now. But it was beauty—something to dwell with, to calm and to console the mind. I took heart at once and climbed the heights and presently came upon the approach to the University library. The river shone still farther to the west, with the russet Palisades beyond. But I hastened across the quadrangle, eager for some human contact in this new world full of cold power and forbidding brilliance.

Professor Brent of the department of English, with whom I

had had some correspondence, received me with a winning kindliness. We had a talk the other day and I observed him and remembered the old days. He has grown grayer. Otherwise he is the same—the lank, unathletic but not graceless form, the oblong head lengthened by a pointed beard, the pleasant, humorous but powerful glance, the easy pose, tilted back in his chair, the eternal cigarette between his long, bony, sensitive fingers. A scholarly and poetic figure, languid enough, but capable of a steady tenacity at the urge of some noble passion of the mind. That he was a trenchant and intrepid thinker I always knew. How magnificently he would stand the ultimate intellectual test of this, or perhaps any age, I was to learn much later. . . . He introduced me to Brewer, secretary of the department, a pale, hesitant, chill-eyed New Englander with a thin strain of rhetorical skill and literary taste.

German was to be my second "minor," largely because it would be easy and would give me more time for my English studies. And so I went to present myself to Professor Richard who had also written me a pleasant letter. I found him tall, erect, frugal and incisive of speech, a spirit of great rectitude, of a purity almost too intense to grasp the concrete forces and passions of the fevered world; clear, high-souled, a little passionless, but all that without effort or priggishness. His intellectual and artistic sympathies were, of course, limited. But within its limits his was an admirable and a manly mind.

The qualities of Brent and Richard did not, of course, reveal themselves to me at once. Nor, indeed, for long thereafter and then in private interviews and at club-meetings. The lectures of these excellent professors were dull and dispiriting to me. I found in them no living sustenance of any sort. For years I sought to grasp the reasons for this fact. I do not think I grasped them wholly until I myself began to lecture to graduate students and to have such students in my own seminar. I came to the university with the reading I have described. I knew all the books that one was required to know in the various lecture courses. What I wanted was ideas, interpretative, critical, aesthetic, philosophical, with which to vivify, to organize, to deepen my knowledge, on which to nourish and develop my intellectual self. And my friends, the professors, ladled out information. Poor men, how could they help it? I thought in those days that all graduate students knew what I and a small group of my friends knew. I am aware now of the literally incredible ignorance of the average bachelors of our colleges. . . . I cannot, of course, absolve the professors entirely, though only the rigorous veracity that gives its meaning to this narrative can force me to admit even so much of friends who have stood by me so long and so wholeheartedly as Brent and Richard. They did not give themselves enough, nor freely enough. They did not realize that, the elementary tools of knowledge once gained, there is but one thing that can teach men and that is the play of a large and an incisive personality. In a word, I was an ardent disciple and I found no master. So I drifted and occasionally "cut" lectures and wrote my reports and passed creditable examinations without doing a page of the required reading. I had done it all! I read for myself in entirely new directions—books that changed the whole tenor of my inner life—and struggled to make a living and wrote verses and walked and talked and sat in bar-rooms and cheap eating-houses with my friend Ellard—my friend of friends, whom I found at this time and who is still *animae dimidium meae.*

II

It was a grey, windy November forenoon that we first talked on the steps of Fayerwether Hall. He was tall and lank and thin to emaciation. An almost ragged overcoat fluttered behind him, a shapeless, discolored hat tilted a little on his head. His delicate nostrils seemed always about to quiver, his lips to be set in a half-petulant, half-scornful determination. From under the hat shone two of the most eloquent eyes—fiery and penetrating, gloomy and full of laughter in turn—that were ever set in a human head. He spoke with large, loose, expressive gestures and with a strange, abrupt way of ending his sentences. I felt drawn to him at once. Freedom and nobility seemed to clothe him and a stoic wildness. A young eagle with plumage ruffled by the storm. . . .! I asked him, I don't know why, whether he wrote verse. And when he said that he did I knew instinctively that his verses were better than mine, far better, and curiously enough I was not sorry but glad and, in a way, elated. I cannot tell at this distance of time how rapidly our friendship ripened, but I know that we soon saw a great deal of each other.

He lived in a small, crowded room up four flights of stairs. A large kerosene lamp stood on his study table. A sharp, triangular shadow lay steadily across bed and wall. He was tormented by poverty and love and by the intellectual bleakness that was all about us. For two years he had been at Bonn and though by blood a New England Brahmin of the purest strain, the sunny comradeship and spiritual freedom of the Rhineland city had entered into his very being. I see him standing there in the blue cloud of our cigarette-smoke chanting me his verses. I had never met a poet before and poetry meant everything to me in those days. A lovely or a noble line, a sonorous or a troubling turn of rhythm could enchant me for days. So that I was wholly carried away by my friend and his poems. And we both felt ourselves to be in some sort exiles and wandered the streets as the fall deepened into winter, engaged in infinite talk. We watched as evening came the bursting of the fiery blooms of light over the city and again, late at night, met in some eating-house or bar-room on Amsterdam Avenue where the belated, frozen car men watched us with heavy curiosity. We found ourselves then, as we have found ourselves ever since, in complete harmony as to the deeper things in life. That that harmony has become, if anything, more entire during the past seven crucial years of the world's history, I account as one of the few sustaining factors in my life and to it I attach, not foolishly I think, an almost mystical significance. . . .

I have been re-reading his poetry. I can detach it quite coldly now from the romance of our early comradeship, from the comforts of our maturer friendship. Nor am I as easily stirred as I was once. It is inferior to no poetry that has been written on this continent. At its best it is at least equal to the noblest passages of Emerson and it is far less fragmentary, far more sustained upon an extraordinary level of intellectual incisiveness, moral freedom and untraditional beauty. And there are many lines and passages that in their imagination and passion and wisdom cleave so deeply to the tragic core of life that they might bring tears to the eyes of grave and disillusioned men. . . . What has it availed him? His volumes scarcely sell; the manuscript of his third one is being hawked about from publisher to publisher. His verse is handicapped by its intellectual severity and its disdain of fashion—the poetic fashion of either yesterday or to-day. But it has the accent of greatness and that is bound to tell in the long run.

Other friendships there were for me at the university, pleasant enough at that time, but all impermanent save one more. I still count George Fredericks, sober-minded, virile, generous, among my chosen comrades. And I still think, with much kindness, of G., now a college professor in the East, a fine, pure spirit, a New Englander like Ellard, but unlike him striving quite in vain to transcend the moral and intellectual parochialism of his section and his blood. But, indeed, I sought no companionship, taking only such as came my way. For mean anxieties soon beset me as my slender borrowings came to an end and I tramped the streets in search of tutoring. A crowd of queer and colorful and comic scenes—sorrowful and humiliating enough at that time—floats into my mind. In a gorgeous palace near Central Park the footman eyed me contemptuously and an elderly woman tried to hire me to conduct her evidently rowdy boys to and from school. I refused curtly to do a nurse-maid's work. But walking across the rich carpet to the door I heard my torn shoes make a squdgy sound and almost repented. In another elaborate establishment I gave, in a very ready-made Louis XV room, a single lesson to the young daughter of the house. Next day a note came dispensing with my services. I wasn't surprised. The girl was pretty and I was hungry for charm and love and she had evidently not disliked me. . . . At last I got a couple of boys to tutor (one a deaf-mute) and lessons in scientific German to give to the staff of one of the city institutions. Two evenings a week I was ferried across Hellgate in the icy wind to give this instruction. It was a bleak and tiresome business, but it paid room and board and tobacco and an occasional glass of beer.

III

Meanwhile I read the nights away. Fascinating hints had come to me in Queenshaven, despite my whole-souled absorption in English literature, of certain modern German plays and poems and novels which seemed, by all reports, to differ wonderfully from both Schiller and Heine, the two German poets whom I knew best, and also from such popular mid-century writers as Scheffel and Heyse. But very few German books ever made their way to Queenshaven. Here, in the University library, I found them all and I read them all.

I read them with joy, with a sense of liberation, with a feeling that no other books in the world had ever given me. I struggled against that feeling; I seemed to myself almost disloyal to the modern English masters, to the very speech that I loved and which I hoped to write notably some day. But a conviction came upon me after some months with irresistible force. All or nearly all English books since Fielding were literature. This was life. All or nearly all the English literature by which our generation lives is, in substance, rigidly bounded within certain intellectual and ethical categories. This was freedom. I now understood my old, instinctive love for the prosemen of the eighteenth century. They had the sense for life—a life remote from ours, to be sure—but their sense of it was manly and incorruptible. In Wordsworth and in Tennyson I found substantially the same elevated sentiments. Except in the narrow field of the religious emotions, they and their contemporaries had no sense for reality at all, only for pseudo-nobility. And in English fiction, in 1904, all the people really held the same elevated sentiments, sentiments which were mostly false and unnecessary, and of course couldn't and didn't live up to them. They were all like poor Byron who half believed that one ought to be a Christian and a church-going householder and who was romantically desperate over his own wicked nature. Or they were like the slim, pale-eyed son of my old Sunday school superintendent. The lad had an excellent tenor voice and joined a small opera company. On one of his visits home he said to me with a troubled look in his eyes: "I don't see why I should be this

way. My father's such a good man." . . . Of course I'm stating the
case crassly and unjustly as one always does and must for the sake
of emphasis. And, of course, I shall be held, whatever I say, to be
approving a drifting with the passions of human life—like that
of Burns—instead of an understanding and use and mastery of
them. But it will not be denied by any really honest and penetrating thinker that English literature from Fielding until quite
recently was curiously remote from life, curiously helpless and
unhelpful and yet arrogant in the face of it. Such books as
Moore's *Esther Waters,* which I hadn't read, and Wells' *The
Passionate Friends,* which hadn't yet been written, have introduced into English letters an entirely new element of spiritual
veracity and moral freedom. And these were the qualities which I
found so pervasively and overwhelmingly present (yet with no
lack of beauty and music in structure and style) in modern German literature. If in these books there was a noble sentiment it
was there because it had grown inevitably from the sweat and
tears, the yearning and the aspiration of our mortal fate—it was
never set down because it was a correct sentiment to which
human nature must be made to conform. I understood
very fully now the saying of that character in one of Henry
James' stories: "When I read a novel, it's usually a French one.
You get so much more life for your money." I read French books,
too. But compared to the German ones they seemed, as they are,
rather hard and monotonous and lacking in spiritual delicacy. . . .
Someone gave me a copy of Hans Benzmann's anthology of the
modern German lyric. I found there an immediate rendering of
life into art, not mere isolated elements of it selected according to
a tradition of pseudo-nobility and then fixed in the forms of post-
Renaissance culture. The pangs and aspirations of my own heart
—and of all hearts, if men would but be honest among us—were
here, the haunting echoes of my inner life, the deep things, the
true things of which I had been ashamed and which I had tried
to transmute into the correct sentiments of my Anglo-American
environment—I found them all in the lyrical charm of these
poets, in their music, which is the very music of the mind, in
their words, which are the very words of life. They spoke my

thoughts, they felt my conflicts; they dared to be themselves—
these modern men and women who were impassioned and troubled like myself, who had not snared the universe in barren
formulae, but who were seekers and strivers! They didn't know
the whole duty of man; they didn't try to huddle out of sight the
eternal things that make us what we are; they hadn't reduced the
moral and spiritual life of the race to a series of gestures of more
than Egyptian rigidity. They made me free; they set me on the
road of trying to be not what was thought correct without reference to reality, but what I was naturally meant to be. They
taught me, not directly, but by the luminous implications of
their works, the complete spiritual unveracity in which I had
been living and in which most of my Anglo-American friends
seemed to be living. . . . This whole process was, of course, very
gradual on its practical or outer side. Within me, too, the old
ready-made formulae would often arise to inhibit or torment me.
And from this conflict and turbidness of feeling and vision there
sprang some grave errors of action. But that was because my
freedom was not yet a rational freedom, nor one corrected by a
power of rational experience. My youth had been passed amid so
much falseness that my mastery of fact was quite inadequate for
the practice of a real moral freedom. I had no way at all of seeing
things as they really are, no power of measuring the origin and
direction of the forces that rule men and the world. I was like
someone to whom is offered the freedom of a great library, but
who had been deliberately mistaught the meaning of the symbols
in which the books are written. I knew that it was my duty now
to read for myself. I didn't know how to read. I am struggling
to express a difficult and momentous truth: The young creators
of new values come to grief so often not because their values are
wrong, nor because their rebellion is not of the very breath of the
world's better life. They come to grief because they have no
mastery of fact, because they carry with them the false old inter-
pretations and conventional idealizations of man, and nature,
and human life. . . . Nevertheless the world now opened itself to
me in a new guise. I had been accustomed, as I had been taught,
to approve and to disapprove. Now for the first time I watched

life honestly and lost myself in it and became part of it with my soul and my sympathies, detached only in the citadel of the analytic and recording, never more of the judging mind. I became aware of faces—the faces of people on the streets, in the cars, in the subway. And I no longer thought of people as good and bad or desirable or undesirable, but I saw in all faces the struggle and the passion and the sorrow, sometimes ugly, unheroic enough always by the old, foolish tests, but full of endless fascination. . . .

To a modern Continental, French or German or Italian, this whole matter will seem primitive and absurd. He may be sure that I am touching on the central weakness of the Anglo-American mind—its moral illusionism. That mind is generally quite sincere. It really arranges its own impulses and the impulses of other men in a rigid hierarchy of fixed norms. It has surrendered the right and the power of examining the contents of such concepts as "right," "wrong," "pure," "democracy," "liberty," "progress," or of bringing these conventionalized gestures of the mind to the test of experience. It has not, indeed, ever naively experienced anything. For it holds the examination of an experience in itself, and without reference to an anterior and quite rigid norm to be a "sin." It hides the edges of the sea of life with a board-walk of ethical concepts and sits there, hoping that no one will hear the thunder of the surf of human passions on the rocks below. . . .

IV

A face, a voice, a gesture that seemed strange and unheard of arose before me and I was stricken by a blind and morbid passion. All the repressions of my tormented adolescence, all the false inhibitions in thought and deed now went toward the nourishing of this hectic bloom. It was winter. A white and silent winter. Playing with curious fancies we called our passion roses in the snow. I committed every extravagance and every folly. I knew nothing of life, nothing of human nature. I knew ethical formulae which, obviously, didn't apply—that were, at best, vicious half-truths. Thus all the defenses of my soul broke down. I had never been taught a sane self-direction. The repetition of tribal charms which were quite external had been deemed a sufficient safeguard. Happily, though my passion was morbid enough and caused me untold suffering, it was blended with the love of letters and with a keen though unwholesome romance. There was nothing in it of baseness, nothing of degradation. I am not proud of it but I am not ashamed of it. I look back upon it and it blends, in strange tones, into the inevitable music of life— neither good nor evil, neither right nor wrong. We are both married now and meet in pleasant friendship and remember half-humorously that long ago—so long ago, it seems a fairy-tale—we caused each other delights and pangs and tears. . . .

But if I had a son I should say to him: "Dismiss from your mind all the cant you hear on the subject of sex. The passion of love is the central passion of human life. It should be humanized; it should be made beautiful. It should never be debased by a sense that it is in itself sinful, for that is to make the whole of life sinful and to corrupt our human experience at its very source. Love is not to be condemned and so degraded, but to be exercised and mastered. If you are of a cool temper and continence leaves your mind serene and your imagination unbesmirched, very well. But let not your soul, if it is ardent, become contaminated and disordered by false shames and a false sense of sin. Love in itself is the source of loveliness and wisdom if it is gratified without falsehood and without abandoning the sterner elements of life. Natural things are made sinful only by a mistaken notion that they are so. Account love, then, as inevitable and lovely, but remain master to your soul and of yourself and of the larger purposes which you were born to fulfill."

To me, as to every American youth, it had been said: "Passion, except within marriage, is the most degrading of sins. Within marriage it is forgiven but never mentioned as being, even there, unmentionable. This is the law." Meantime all the men and youths I knew slunk into the dark alleys of Queenshaven whither I did not follow them. And curiously, in that very act, they still believed the follies they proclaimed. They were simply moral men sinning against their own convictions. That astonishing ethical dualism of the English mind— (so truly and so moderately set forth by George Gissing in the memorable twentieth chapter of the third book of *The Private Papers of Henry Ryecroft)*—that ethical duality of conscience I hold the chief and most corrupting danger of our life as a people. It must be fought without ceasing and without mercy. . . .

Of that duality there was nothing in my being. I was bound or I was free. But having been a slave so long I ran amuck in my freedom and in the recoil came almost to utter grief. I was saved and made steadfast only by the thought of those two watchers in the distant South. However absorbed in that most passionate adventure, I never missed an opportunity of going home at Christmas or even at Easter—planned for it, saved for it, and always my mother's hand in mine and her eyes upon me made me well again.

Also I could now conquer many moods and free myself from them by fixing them in art. My verse was no longer the echo of a sonorous tradition. It grew no longer out of the love of poetry but out of the pain of life. And from my modern Germans as well as from a new and powerful movement in our English verse I learned to write directly and truly. Somehow, in Queenshaven, I had missed a poem which is not, of course, the greatest, but assuredly the most important English poem of the third quarter of the nineteenth century: Meredith's "Modern Love." The application of English poetic art to the actual, the contemporary and the real had there been inaugurated. In addition I now read Henley and Housman's "A Shropshire Lad" and "The Love Sonnets of Proteus" and, above all, I found the two-volume edition of the poems of Arthur Symons. Granting the hostile critic his monotony of mood (but is not Shelley's mood quite as monotonous in a different spiritual key?), and his morbidness (though what *is* morbidness, after all?) and there remains in his work the creation of a new style, a new method, a new power. The conventional taste of his generation still lags behind his method, but in it is one of the essential forces of the future of English poetry.

V

The various experiences which I have set down so briefly extended over two years. At the end of the first year I duly took my master's degree and applied for a fellowship. Among the group of students to which I belonged it was taken for granted that, since Ellard had completed his studies for the doctorate, I would undoubtedly be chosen. I record this, heaven knows, not from motives of vanity but as part of the subtler purpose of this story. The faculty elected my friend G. I went, with a heavy heart, to interview Professor Brewer, not to push my claims to anything, but because I was at my wits' end. I dreaded another year of tutoring and of living wretchedly from hand to mouth, without proper clothes, without books. Brewer leaned back in his chair, pipe in hand, with a cool and kindly smile. "It seemed to us," he stuttered, "that the university hadn't had its full influence on you." He suggested their disappointment in me and, by the subtlest of stresses, their sorrow over this disappointment. I said that I had been struggling for a livelihood and that, nevertheless, my examinations had uniformly received high grades and my papers, quite as uniformly, the public approval of Brent and himself. He avoided a direct answer by explaining that the department had recommended me for a scholarship the following year. The truth is, I think, that Brewer, excessively mediocre as he was, had a very keen tribal instinct of the self-protective sort and felt in me—what I was hardly yet consciously—the implacable foe of the New England dominance over our national life. I wasn't unaware of his hostility, but I had no way of provoking a franker explanation.

I forgot my troubles in three beautiful months at home—three months seemed so long then—or, rather, I crowded these troubles from my field of consciousness. I wouldn't even permit the fact that I wasn't elected to a scholarship to depress me. Brewer wrote a letter of regret and encouragement that was very kindly in tone. The pleasant implication of that letter was, of course, a spiritual falsehood of the crassest. He knew then precisely what he knew and finally told me ten months later. But his kind has a dread of the bleak weather of the world of truth, and approaches it gingerly, gradually, with a mincing gait. He, poor man, was probably unconscious of all that. In him, as in all like him, the corruption of the mental life is such that the boundaries between the true and the false are wholly obliterated.

In the passionate cries of the second year I often walked as in a dream. And I was encouraged by the fact that the department arranged a loan for my tuition. In truth, I was deeply touched by so unusual a kindness and I feel sure that the suggestion came from Brent. If so, Brewer again did me a fatal injury by not preventing that kindness. For he had then, I must emphasize, the knowledge he communicated to me later—the knowledge that held the grim upshot of my university career.

Spring came and with it the scramble for jobs among the second year men. My friends were called in to conferences with Brewer; I was not. They discussed vacancies, chances here and there. It wasn't the chagrin that hurt so; it wasn't any fear for myself. After all I was only twenty-two and I was careless of material things. I thought of my father and my mother in the cruel sunshine of Queenshaven. Their hope and dream and consolation were at stake. I could see them, not only by day, but in the evening, beside their solitary lamps, looking up from their quiet books, thinking of me and of the future. . . . I remembered how my father had believed in certain implications of American democracy. I remembered . . . I was but a lad, after all. I couldn't face Brewer's cool and careless smile. I wrote him a letter—a letter which, in its very earnestness and passionate veracity must have struck like a discord upon the careful arrangements of his safe and proper nature. For in it I spoke of grave things gravely, not jestingly, as one should to be a New England gentleman: I spoke of need and aspiration and justice. His answer lies before me now and I copy that astonishingly smooth and chilly document verbatim: "It is very sensible of you to look so carefully into your plans at this juncture, because I do not at all believe in the wisdom of your scheme. A recent experience has shown me how terribly hard it is for a man of Jewish birth to get a good position. I had always suspected that it was a matter worth considering, but I had not known how wide-spread and strong it was. While we shall be glad to do anything we can for you, therefore, I cannot help feeling that the chances are going to be greatly against you."

I sat in my boarding-house room playing with this letter. I seemed to have no feeling at all for the moment. By the light of a sunbeam that fell in I saw that the picture of my parents on the mantelpiece was very dusty. I got up and wiped the dust off carefully. Gradually an eerie, lost feeling came over me. I took my hat and walked out and up Amsterdam Avenue, farther and farther to High Bridge and stood on the bridge and watched the swift, tiny tandems on the Speedway below and the skiffs gliding up and down the Harlem River. A numbness held my soul and mutely I watched life, like a dream pageant, float by me. . . . I ate nothing till evening when I went into a bakery and, catching sight of myself in a mirror, noted with dull objectivity my dark hair, my melancholy eyes, my unmistakably Semitic nose. . . . An outcast. . . . A sentence arose in my mind which I have remembered and used ever since. So long as there is discrimination, there is exile. And for the first time in my life my heart turned with grief and remorse to the thought of my brethren in exile all over the world. . . .

VI

The subconscious self has a tough instinct of self-preservation. It thrusts from the field of vision, as Freud has shown, the painful and the hostile things of life. Thus I had forgotten, except at moments of searching reflection, the social fate of my father and mother, my failure to be elected to the fraternity at college, and other subtler hints and warnings. I had believed the assertion and made it myself that equality of opportunity was implicit in the very spiritual foundations of the Republic. This is what I wanted to believe, what I needed to believe in order to go about the business of my life at all. I had listened with a correct American scorn to stories of how some distant kinsman in Germany, many years ago, had had to receive Christian baptism in order to enter the consular service of his country. At one blow now all these delusions were swept away and the facts stood out in the sharp light of my dismay. Discrimination there was everywhere. But a definite and public discrimination is, at least, an enemy in the open. In pre-war Germany, for instance, no Jew could be prevented from entering the academic profession. Unless he was very brilliant and productive his promotion was less rapid than that of his Gentile colleagues. He knew that and reckoned with it. He knew, too, for instance, that he could not become senior professor of German at Berlin (only associate professor like the late R. M. Meyer), nor Kultusminister, but he could become a full professor of Latin or philosophy, and, of course, of all the sciences. I am not defending these restrictions and I think the argument for them—that the German state was based upon an ethnic homogeneity which corresponds to a spiritual oneness— quite specious. I am contrasting these conditions with our own. We boast our equality and freedom and call it Americanism and speak of other countries with disdain. And so one is unwarned, encouraged and flung into the street. With exquisite courtesy, I admit. And the consciousness of that personal courtesy soothes the minds of our Gentile friends. . . . It will be replied that there are a number of Jewish scholars in American colleges and univer- sities. There are. The older men got in because nativistic anti- Semitism was not nearly as strong twenty-five years ago as it is today. Faint remnants of the ideals of the early Republic still lingered in American life. But in regard to the younger men I dare to assert that in each case they were appointed through personal friendship, family or financial prestige or some other abnormal relenting of the iron prejudice which is the rule. But that prejudice has not, to my knowledge, relented in a single instance in regard to the teaching of English. So that our guard- ianship of the native tongue is far fiercer than it is in an, after all, racially homogeneous state like Germany. Presidents, deans and departmental heads deny this fact or gloss it over in public. Among themselves it is admitted as a matter of course.

I have not touched the deeper and finer issues, though I have written in vain if they are not clear. My purest energy and passion, my best human aspirations have been dedicated from my earliest years to a given end. It was far more than a question of bread and butter, though it was that too. I didn't know how to go on living a reasonable and reasonably harmonious inner life. I could take no refuge in the spirit and traditions of my own people. I knew little of them. My psychical life was Aryan through and through. Slowly, in the course of the years, I have discovered traits in me which I sometimes call Jewish. But that interpretation is open to grave doubt. I can, in reality, find no difference between my own inner life of thought and impulse and that of my very close friends whether American or German. So that the picture of a young man disappointed because he can't get the kind of job he wants, doesn't exhaust, barely indeed touches the dilemma. I didn't know what to do with my life or with myself.

In this matter of freedom and equality and democratic justice, then, I found in my Anglo-American world precisely that same strange dualism of conscience which I had discovered there in the life of sex. The Brewers in the academic world do truly believe that our society is free and democratic. When they proclaim that belief at public banquets a genuine emotion fills their hearts. Just as a genuine emotion filled the hearts of my Southern friends (who used Mulatto harlots) when in the interest of purity and the home they refused to sanction the enactment of any divorce law in their native state.

I do not wish to speak bitterly or flippantly. I am approaching the analysis of thoughts and events beside which my personal fate is less than nothing. And I need but think of my Queenshaven youth or of some passage of Milton or Arnold, or of those tried friendships that are so large a part of the unalterable good of life, or of the bright hair and gray English eyes of my own wife to know that I can never speak as an enemy of the Anglo-Saxon race. But unless that race abandons its duality of conscience, unless it learns to honor and practice a stricter spiritual veracity, it will either destroy civilization through disasters yet unheard of or sink into a memory and into the shadow of a name.

BORIS D. BOGEN

*An educator and a prominent social worker, Boris D. Bogen
was born in Russia in 1869 and died in California in 1930. His
autobiography,* Born a Jew, *was published posthumously.*

*Bogen was an instructor at the Baron de Hirsch Trade School
and at the Hebrew Technical Institute. He also served as Superintendent at the Baron de Hirsch Agricultural School in Woodbine, N.J. He was Director of the United Jewish Charities in
Cincinnati, and field agent of the National Conference of Jewish
Social Service. He served as Director-General of the Joint Distribution Committee in World War I, and traveled with the
Hoover Mission and organized the distribution of funds contributed for relief by American Jewry. Active in the B'nai B'rith,
Bogen was international secretary of B'nai B'rith from 1925 until
his death in 1930, and Managing Editor of the* B'nai B'rith
Magazine.

*His autobiography is especially valuable as a contribution to
the history of Jewish social work, and in the chapter that follows
he writes with authority and knowledge of the important labors
in which he was engaged.*

Born a Jew*

BORIS D. BOGEN

MY WIFE'S UNCLE took us to the East Side. Tall brick walls of houses hemmed us in. The dingy discomfort of the steerage, the tremulous march up the gangplank, our terror before the admitting officers . . . these things belonged to another life. We were in America.

The people who hurried past us or stood in groups before doorways were not strange to us. The dark beards, the dusty caftans, and the animated gesticulation were bewilderingly familiar. The shops bore Yiddish signs, and Jewish newspapers and books were displayed on stands. Tradesmen, huddling beside market carts, called out their wares in the singsong Yiddish of the Pale. Only the heavy shadows of the elevated trains thundering above us spoke of another world.

Was this the America we had sought? Or was it, after all, only a circle that we had traveled, with *Zariadie,* the Jewish Ghetto in Moscow, at its beginning and its end?

The proprietor of the "immigrants' hotel" operated a saloon on the ground floor, and it was from behind the bar that he came to greet us and lead us to our room. It was five flights up; by a peculiar sense of the fitness of things, he set the price at five dollars a day. His fat, unpleasant body, his bright, bulging eyes, and the grim complacency with which he left us in the little stuffy room gave him a striking resemblance to a spider. We hastened to close the door after him to shut off the smell of stale beer that seeped up the stairways.

From my first exploration tour of the street, I returned with a big and cheerful watermelon. But as I started to mount the stairs with it, picturing to myself Lisa's pleasure at the familiar and

* Reprinted from *Born A Jew,* The Macmillan Company, New York, 1930, pp. 36–81.

luscious object, the Spider pounced upon me. What? Was I mad? Watermelon . . . just after getting off the boat? It would make us deathly sick, if in fact it did not finish us altogether. And with this benevolent warning, he relieved me of my treasure and re- tired behind the bar, while amused snickers testified to the ap- preciation of his audience.

The next morning we were awakened by the sound of can- nonading. It was the Fourth of July. Proud of our knowledge of the holiday we came down in our best attire. Children hurled explosives at our feet and passed on calmly, while we shrank in horror from the spurt of flame and the clatter of shot.

That evening we watched the celebrating street from our door- way. The sound of shooting increased. Great streaks of flame lit up the strip of sky that loomed between the roofs. Bonfires blazed in the roadway and men and boys rushed by us, dragging boxes, barrels, and boards to feed the flames. Somewhere in the distance martial music sounded. A red light flared up from the sidewalk and illuminated the bunting at a window. Lisa, my wife, lifted the baby, so that it could see the flag which we regarded as ours.

A passing boy pulled the tail of my frock coat and his compan- ions nudged each other and laughed. Their derisive call echoed after them—"Greener."

The food and the price at the Spider's drove us to look for another room. We finally found one in a "dumb-bell" tenement, whose solid walls of masonry, extending through the block, were separated from adjoining buildings only by the central shafts upon which the windows of the inside rooms opened. But our room was on the top floor, where we had light and air that could never penetrate to the lower floors.

The poverty, the discomfort, the squalor of the Ghetto settled upon us like a dark cloud. We became used to the communism of tenement life, to the sound of family quarrels that floated in from adjoining rooms, to the sight of sickness and old age and tears. The houses were dark and dirty and hot; the street noisy and relentless. At a street-crossing stood a gigantic figure in blue and brass whom we invariably passed in a great hurry and with averted eyes, for our neighbors had told us stories about the brutality of the policeman. And he was an American.

One morning the sound of children singing brought us to a corner where an old man, with a red-jacketed monkey on his shoulder, turned the crank of a decrepit organ. The children flocked from all directions, danced and sang. The bright summer sky, the happy, dancing children, the lively strains of the music seemed of another world. Here was America at last. We listened, rapt. "On the Bowery" sang the children. "The American song" we said to one another, and felt that our initiation as Americans had begun.

The process of becoming Americans absorbed us. I hastened to have my beard removed, for I had noticed the smooth faces of the Americans, whose independent swagger I had come to recognize. I searched the neighborhood for a place where I might learn English, and was thrilled to discover the Hebrew Institute, which we knew as the Immigrants' Palace. But when I came to an English class there, I learned to my dismay that the language of instruction was Yiddish which I should first have to learn. Then I was attracted by signs announcing immigrants' classes in other places, but my very first inquiries made it clear that these were simply a mask for missionary activities.

It was during that first week in America that I tried to use my scant knowledge of English. We had already learned to endure the sultry nights by climbing to the roof to sleep. These roofs, divided only by the ridges and chimneys of the buildings, stretched off on all sides like a battlefield, except that so many of the bodies lying there huddled in sleep were children, and women with babies at their breasts. We lay beneath the stars, with all the city beneath us, and the hot, tired bodies of strangers all about us.

So we lay one night, tossing, trying to forget the heat and the whimpering of the children and the coughing near by, when a shout from below startled me: "Fire!" And we were seven floors up. With a frantic cry I seized the baby and hurried Lisa down to shout a hoarse warning to those near me. Whether my Russian phrase meant nothing to them, or whether they slumbered too sweetly, I do not know, but none followed me and I was too much in a hurry to contemplate that fact. We rushed frantically down the steep, dark stairs. Voices came from behind us. I did not stop until we had reached street level where I excitedly asked where the fire was. Only then did I realize that the sounds behind me had been laughter.

"Fire?" I asked. Where was it? The people laughed.

It wasn't "fire!" I heard but "fight!" There was a fight in the house and some one had shouted through the window . . . for reinforcements, I suppose. One old woman took pity on us and scolded the others for laughing at us.

"Go back to bed," she said to us in a curious mixture of Russian and Yiddish, and then she added gently in English: "Greener."

"*Djid,*" that malignant Russian sneer, had been left behind us. We had become members of another group. It was not hated; it was not despised. But it was laughed at, joked about, pitied. Greener!

My new friends gave me careful directions about reaching the office of Mr. Worth, the American with whom I had become friendly when he visited Moscow. The imposing stonefront building, with its scrubbed steps and carpeted vestibule, was a far cry from the tenement. And, sure enough, there was the row of bell buttons, with a name printed beneath each. Suppose I should make a mistake and press the wrong button? But I could not hesitate; some one might notice me and if I should be addressed in English, what should I do? So I pressed the button. It was just as they had said; a strange clicking noise sounded and the door unlocked itself. This, thought I, with elation, is American progress, and I went in.

Up two flights of stairs, in a little office whose shelves were lined with books, I came face to face with the man whose visit to Moscow had encouraged me to leave for America. Now he sat before a desk loaded with papers and magazines, busily engaged with a manuscript. But he put it aside as I entered and greeted me warmly.

"Tell me," Mr. Worth said, "what are your plans for earning a living here?" I told him I wanted to be a teacher. He gazed upon me with evident sympathy and amusement.

"Forget it," he advised me. "An immigrant, and a Jew to boot, has no chance here for anything like that. You will have to begin like every one else . . . in a tailor shop or as a peddler."

And he went on to tell me of the hardships that he had had to endure upon his arrival in America. He told me of others who had gone through similar and even harder experiences. Still, he continued, he would do what he could for me. In fact it was quite possible that he could place me, for he was about to establish a Russian newspaper.

I left his office, treading on air.

Mr. Worth was as good as his word and within a few weeks we were started on the new enterprise. I was to manage the printing of the sheet, he told me, and I gladly consented to go to work in a printing shop to learn details of my task. For I was not merely an employee; I was a full-fledged partner in the concern, and it had seemed quite right that, in exchange for Mr. Worth's services as editor and his experience and connections, I should furnish the cash capital, which amounted to exactly the sum we had brought with us, about $500. Mr. Worth's business acumen aroused our admiration. A basement floor was rented for our purposes and, to avoid waste of space, we took up our living quarters in the rear cell, while the two front compartments were devoted to our business.

How the days dragged by until we could begin actual publication! There was no Russian type to be had and, after frantic searching, we found a man who could make the type for us, cutting out the molds and pouring lead by hand. He was assisted by his nine-year-old son; he had gotten as far as "r" when the child died, and then we had to wait days and days until he found an assistant. At last the type was completed, the material for our first issue was lined up, and I started to set the type.

The Russian Review was made up mostly of a review of news, culled from the newspapers received from Russia, and of reprints and translations lifted from the Yiddish press. We all shared in the preparation of manuscript; Mr. Worth handled the editorials; I spent weary hours scanning old newspapers and magazines for possible material; Lisa prepared excerpts of Russian articles. We had an advertising department, too, and it was my job to solicit ads and to set them up as well.

The advertisements were my Waterloo. I set them up most carefully. But I did not pay particular attention to the addresses of the advertisers; I knew their locations by sight, for I had gone myself to solicit the ad and I would know where to call for payment. But when the first issue appeared, with streets and numbers most strangely confused, the storm broke. Advertisers came in, furious. They shook angry fists. They assured us that, far from paying for the advertisements, they intended to sue for damaging their business. All I could do was to make myself as small and inoffensive looking as possible and wait for the excitement to subside. And like all things, it passed in time, but it took uncomfortably long.

The Russian Review began to look important. Jacob Gordin consented to act as contributing editor, and his tall, proud figure, so completely the Russian intellectual, came and went in our dimly lighted rooms. Other literary lights in the Jewish world began to pay attention to us.

But profits were slow in manifesting themselves and the newspaper demanded constant expenditures. Mr. Worth expressed his regret that he could not advance any money to me; he pointed out that since Lisa knew how to sew, it might not be a bad idea to get work for her from some jobber so that we might eke out an income that way. He himself found a jobber who sent in materials to be made into neckties. So, in the gray dusk of the room, Lisa bent over a board table piled high with ties and I sweated over the presses, and we both counted the days when the paper would begin to get on its feet.

I began to discover that Mr. Worth was not so important a person as we had believed at the time of his visit to Moscow and as his office had suggested. The books that lined the walls had been his stock in trade; he was trying to earn a living by running a bookstore. He was a teacher in the evening school for immigrants, receiving a small wage for his service. He secured his main income by working as an agent for a life insurance company. He was, in short, a poor man, struggling for an existence for himself and his family, and bending every effort to establish himself on a safe basis. As all this became clear to me I felt drawn closer and closer to him, though troubled at the thought that my patron was less formidable than I had thought and hoped.

And then I learned that arrangements were being made to sell *The Rusian Review,* that Mr. Worth represented himself as sole publisher and owner, and that the paper itself, bearing his name as editor, bore no indication of my share in it. And while I demanded justice of my erstwhile protector, and he, suddenly indifferent and unfriendly, became more and more annoyed at my protestations, the purchasers of the plant prepared to take possession.

That night some friends forgathered in our little back room to discuss our plight. They decided to seize the bull by the horns and, going into the press room, proceeded to remove as much of the equipment as they thought should constitute my share of the enterprise. Suddenly the front door flew open and, like a miniature tornado, Mr. Worth came upon us. At the time, some one was lifting a type form with the next issue of the paper set up. Mr. Worth's hand came down upon his arm, the form crashed to the floor and completely pied, the type scattering in all directions.

And then reinforcements from both sides proceeded to settle the matter among themselves.

When morning came, Lisa and I tied up our bundles and left our dream behind. I was richer, far richer, in experience; but our friend and protector had become our enemy, and our money was gone. We must continue our struggle empty-handed.

It was terrible for me and my wife to realize that we were penniless in a strange land. I tried to find work. My halting English, my lack of experience in any trade, my bewildered look that betrayed the greenhorn, seemed to shut all doors against me. Our friends gathered about us, a generous, eager little group.

But they, too, had only recently come from Moscow (it was this that had drawn us to them) and they were poor people—peddlers, needle workers, and "hands" in factories and shops. They tried to cheer us, they invited us to share their congested rooms; and there they had to stop. New York, whose very strangeness and bigness had thrilled us, assumed a sinister, fearful aspect.

And then came a letter from my wife's uncle. He had gone to Baltimore and had a good job in a furniture factory. But he, being almost American, could easily get another job, he wrote. In fact, he intended leaving the factory anyway. Would I care to try my hand at it? The pay was good; I would be able to send for my wife, Lisa, and the child, and in Baltimore people could live comfortably. In the meantime Lisa could keep up her sewing; soon I would be able to send money from my wages. I went to Baltimore.

"When you go for the job," cautioned Uncle Matvey, "don't whatever you do, act like a greenhorn. Say you are experienced in this line. That is bluff. In America one gets along like that." So I assured the foreman at the furniture factory that I was an experienced furniture finisher; Matvey's departure had left an opening and I got the job.

They took me down to the basement and pointed to a newly built sideboard; I was to take it up to the second floor and there apply varnish. I seized the object in my arms and, staggering, tugging, and pushing, got it upstairs. I reached the first landing exhausted, but triumphant. But I dared not rest; some one with an air of authority was regarding me curiously. Panting, I took hold of the monster once more and resumed the climb. At last I reached the top. Looking down, I could not repress a shudder at the steepness of those stairs. I must have relaxed my grip. At any rate, my burden slipped from me and crashed down the stairs. I ran after it, with some desperate notion of beating it to the bottom and breaking its fall. The race ended in a tie; the sideboard was wrecked; I was terrified.

The boss expressed himself to the effect that as a furniture finisher I was finished. Before he was through speaking, I found myself on the sidewalk, departing rather rapidly. For want of something more profitable to do, I continued walking. As I walked, I resolved that I would postpone further bluffing until I had become more of an American and had improved my technique. I knew something about printing; I would look for work in a printing plant.

The supply of printing hands in Baltimore appeared discouragingly adequate, but my search was finally rewarded by a card bearing the legend "Boy Wanted," tacked upon a door. Since the loss of my beard I had several times been taken for less than twenty-three years; perhaps I might now turn my boyish appearance to good account. Of course the pay was correspondingly small, but I was only too happy to be on any payroll.

I was stationed beneath a machine that poured out squares of paper destined to cover packages of cigarettes. It was my task to dip a small brush into gilt and, as the papers fell in rapid succession, to gild each sheet and place it to one side before the next sheet fell. I worked in desperate haste. The man at the machine above me, amused at my terror, would speed up that relentless mechanism. My day's work became a veritable nightmare of dip, brush, lift, and place . . . dip, brush, lift, and place . . . all in a blind furious rush to keep up with that swift procession of papers. This was not the precise, logical task of setting type and working a press . . . this was a terrible contest, my untrained hand pitted against the devilish skill of the machine.

There was one other Jew working there, a husky, swarthy fellow, whose task it was to set type for a Hungarian newspaper printed in our shop. At the stroke of twelve, when the men would drop their work and draw out their greasy parcels of lunch, Herman's voice would boom at me. "Boy," he shouted, and I had to go to him. Carelessly he would hand me a can and a coin and order me to fetch beer from the near-by saloon. Always, when I received the can over the bar, it would be foaming and running over; but always, no matter how I hurried by the time I handed the can to its owner, the foam had subsided to a mere scum and the can was not full. Then Herman would fall into a mock rage, calling upon all present to witness how the greenhorn was robbing him by drinking half of the beer. In vain I protested. The joke was too good to pass.

But night brought me into another life. I discovered the existence of an evening school for immigrants. The teacher was Henrietta Szold, a quiet, earnest young woman, absorbed in her work with an almost painful intensity. My eagerness in class and my perhaps conscious tendency to introduce philosophic and learned subjects into my compositions won her interest. When I told her about my life in Russia, and about our circle there, she asked me whether I would speak on Russia at an evening entertainment to be given for the benefit of the school.

At last the evening arrived. I dressed myself in my cherished frock coat and hastened to the hall. At the doorway, collecting the admission fees, stood Herman! I had been told that I would be admitted free of charge upon announcing myself, but I could not resist the opportunity to pause before my erstwhile tormentor and hand him my dime. And though I passed on without a backward look, I could feel the bewildered stare that followed me.

I must have done passably well with my lecture. At any rate, Miss Szold told me I did, and the chairman of the evening invited me to visit his home. So I spent a blissful hour in the luxurious home of an American Jew and returned to my drab room, my brain filled with a confused, dazzling picture of velvet curtains, mirror-like floors, and the thoughtful, kind face of my host. Pervading all, I felt the glorious freedom and security of those lives I had touched.

It seemed fantastic to go to work the next morning as if nothing had happened, to take up once more the wearying round of dip, brush, lift, place . . . dip, brush, lift, place. I wondered how Herman felt about last evening's encounter; I tried to picture his dark, coarse face rapt in thought, but I rejected the idea with a rueful smile. A shout called my attention to the heap of papers piling up before me, smeared with gilt from the one at the bottom which I had painted. The noisy, dirty reality closed in on me. I pushed the ruined sheets to the floor and resumed the dizzying contest.

Noon came. The men dropped their work and drew out their greasy parcels. Herman seemed slow in calling me today; I essayed a sidelong glance in his direction. He was not there, and with a sigh of relief I settled down to my own lunch. I ate, and as I ate, considered the curious state of things that bound me to Herman despite myself, that made me feel that I stood with him, as apart from the others in that place; for Herman was a Jew, too.

"Boy!" Herman's deep voice boomed through the loft. I jumped. The men about me snickered. The Jew had come in and was sitting in his familiar place, with the familiar can beside him. Puzzled, I came up to him.

He motioned to the can; evidently some one else, perhaps he himself, had made the trip to the bar, for the foam was settling within the vessel. I glanced up at Herman's face. The roughly chiseled features were stolid, brutelike as ever; but the eyes held a startling expression. They were proud, tender, wistful. They spoke of pride in respect for learning; they spoke of brooding tenderness over the scholar, even a scholar as meager as I; they spoke of wistful yearning to feel kinship with him. A Jew can look like that.

He lifted the can, held it out to me, and asked me to drink.

A few days later Matvey came around at noon, brandishing a letter. His friend Dave, up in Connecticut, sent good news. He had a fine position as a weaver in a woolen mill; wages were high, living was cheap, the work was pleasant and not hard to learn. Matvey, himself, was entirely satisfied with his job, but how about me? My wages barely covered my living expenses; the time when I could send for my little family was as far off as ever. Certainly anything else was worth trying.

He told me about the Jewish charity organization; sometimes they would get you a railroad ticket for half-price, providing you really left the city. So I went to the office of the charities and sat in a room with forlorn, frightened men and women, until I was called into the inner sanctum. I suppose they treated me rather decently, because I don't remember anything about it. I got my ticket and left for Dogville.

Matvey's friend met me at the station. We went to his boarding house. I was plunged into a sea of noise and confusion and hurry, and felt as if I were drowning. Yet this was a tiny town, laughably so in comparison with New York's East Side. I could not understand what every one was shouting, and for one terrible hour I thought I had learned some other language instead of English, by mistake. Then Dave told me that the crowd was speaking French; this town was a sort of French-Canadian colony and most of the weavers spoke no English among themselves.

They are all greenhorns here, I thought. I am as good as they. But at the mill next morning I was placed under the supervision of a young woman with snapping eyes and a clicking tongue. She was assigned to teach me how to weave and she seemed far from delighted with her task. Her disgusted look spoke volumes of scorn for the unskilled worker and I tried to fight against the sense of inferiority her glance evoked. My English was as good as hers. But I was a "greener," nevertheless.

Her hands flashed across the loom while she directed at me a rapid flow of mingled English and French that left me dazed. Then she stepped aside and I took her place; almost instantly the threads and spindles were a tangled mass in my fingers, and I called for help. Again and again her swift hands leaped across the loom; again and again my fumbling fingers tried to follow those quick movements. Just as I began to feel a glow of achievement as the threads shot through in rhythmic lines, the young weaver gave me up as a bad job and sent me to the boss for another assignment. And so ended the first day.

From that time on I was an ordinary mill hand. I carried great bales of rags from a barge on the river into a room at the mill. I spread the rags in layers on the floors, with oil between them, and then fed the slippery mass into a great gin that chewed it into fibrous piles. Then it went to the spinners to be made into yarn for the weaving of "shoddy." But I stayed with the rags and the gin.

Each morning at the boarding house we were aroused by a piercing yell. The noise of the awakening household was almost deafening. The clatter of crockery, the shrill talk, and the shouts of laughter mingled in a great roar over the long breakfast tables. The great platters of bacon and eggs, griddle cakes, and fried potatoes, all reeking with grease, and the tanks of steaming porridge appeared singularly unappetizing.

One night Dave remarked that there was a Jewish family a mile or so up the road. He was surprised and puzzled at my eager insistence to visit them that very evening. As we came up the road, the lighted windows of the little farmhouse seemed strangely alluring.

The head of the house greeted us jovially. He was a plaintive, bearded little Jew, who clung to his farm with grim determination. His wife and stepladder series of children shared in the farm work, tended chickens, gathered vegetables for the town stores, and milked cows. Real peasants, they seemed. The little man clutched at us when we rose to go . . . it was good to see a Jewish face and hear a Jewish voice.

It was arranged that we should board at the farmhouse. Each morning we trudged the two miles to the mill and, wearily, each evening we plodded home. Dave grumbled over the distance, but I knew that nothing could make him move back to town. The house had become our home.

So far, America wanted only my hand; beyond that, I must prove myself. I had seen some Russian magazines which, I had been given to understand, paid money for contributions.

I carried my lamp to my bedside and wrote, and wrote. I did not write of the America I knew. I wrote of the fair land conjured by my dreams and by the fleeting glimpses of happiness I had caught. I wove vivid phrases about the beautiful houses I had seen, the great spreading lawns of the villages I had viewed from train windows, the eloquent brilliance of billboards extolling patent medicines and cheap tobacco. I wrote with an air of calm authority. I mailed my manuscripts to several of the leading Russian magazines. I tried not to hope.

Passover was approaching and, despite my old indifference to the holiday, I wanted to have my family with me when it came. The farmer fed me well and cheaply and I hoarded my dollars. At last I could write Lisa to sell our few bits of household furniture and come to me. She should leave as soon as she got my letter; there was a through train direct to the town and I would meet her at the station. We would have our first day for ourselves, for it would be Sunday.

The mill seemed a kindly, familiar place to me now. I worked almost automatically, forking up the rags and feeding them into the great gin. I thought of my wife and baby soon to be with me, and of the happy times we would have together out in the country. I was earning twelve dollars every week; we could live quite nicely on seven of them. That meant I would be able to save five dollars a week. I would keep my job until I had saved enough for at least one year at the university. Then, after a year of study in America, I would be in position to put my training in pedagogy to advantage. . . .

A terrible, rending roar crashed in upon me. The gin trembled, and then stopped. A piece of iron had become mixed with the rags and I had fed it to the gin. The machine was wrecked.

The mill rose as one man and swooped down upon me. The stopping of the gin meant there would be no material for the spinners, for the weavers, in our section. The machine could not be fixed until Monday, and this meant that they must lose the rest of Saturday's pay. I gathered all this from the imprecations hurled at me, from the furious shouts, from the raised fists and menacing eyes of the men who drove me from the building. I was running toward the station, and they were still at my heels, I felt, but I did not dare turn to look. I suppose I got into a train. But to me it seemed as if I had run all the way to New York.

I dragged my dusty feet down East Broadway, exhausted, desperate, masked in the grease and lint of the mills. Lisa and the baby were somewhere en route to Dogville.

Lisa had missed the train to Dogville. For some time she stood in the station, the child tugging at her skirt and her bundles still clutched in her arms, staring down the tracks toward where the cars had disappeared. Then she turned and wearily made her way back to the Ghetto. She trudged along, hoping that no one she knew would see her . . . tired . . . disappointed . . . but above all, ashamed that she was so much a greenhorn as to miss the train. Finally a friend did meet her and found her shelter for the night, promising faithfully to disclose her whereabouts to no one. Let them think she had taken the train; she would go the next day anyway.

So it was that when I reached New York, exhausted, grimebespattered, and still terrified by my escape from Dogville, I could at first find no trace of my little family. My friends insisted that they had bade Lisa farewell that very morning; she must surely be in Dogville by now. I implored them to help me get back my wife and baby. The news of my frantic plight spread, until at last it reached Lisa herself. My failure to establish my family in the country of whose beauties I had so glowingly written, the fact that we were without the simplest household necessities, that there were no means of livelihood in sight, were forgotten in the relief and joy of reunion.

Our friends helped us to establish the semblance of a home. One brought a teakettle, another a few dishes, a third a saucepan. I tramped the streets, climbed stairways wearily, sought out dark-cellar workshops, looking for work. I could find nothing. We learned that the bread of charity, though it be the genial charity of friends, is bitter fare.

We could not go on this way much longer. Our little circle came together to consider a way out for us. It seemed clear that I was not adapted for the struggle of life in America. Surely existence here could bring us only more hardships and repeated dissillusionment and disappointment. They came to the conclusion that we must return to Russia. They agreed to collect among themselvess the sum necessary for our passage to Moscow.

I did not even consider this solution. I could not give up my dream of a free life in America. I could not bear the thought of taking up once more the cramped, furtive existence of the Jew in Russia. I went out into the streets to take up the dreary round once more.

At Salvation Army headquarters, the "Help Wanted" columns from a newspaper were tacked up in a doorway. I studied them carefully, reading every word of each item, spelling them out desperately, hopelessly.

"Typesetter wanted. Temporary work." I copied down the address and started to hope again.

I did not sleep that night. It was still pitch dark when I started out the next morning, for my destination was Brooklyn and I had no money for carfare. The skies began to grow light just as I crossed the bridge. I remembered that there had been much talk about several recent suicides who had leaped from this bridge into the murky blackness below and I reflected, conscious of the drama of it, that if I did not get the job, I would come back this way and end it all in the popular manner. Luckily I was not compelled to put my determination to the test. I was the first in line when the shop opened, and I got the job.

I was setting up type for a placard when I was brought to a full stop by the word "Temmany." I was positive that the second letter was intended to be an "a" and, with considerable trepidation, I pointed out the error to the boss. He praised my alertness and his voice had all the sweetness of a heavenly chorister, for this was the first time since I had come to America that my work had gained an approving word.

Noon came. I remained at my task, trying to ignore the appetite I had no means of satisfying. The boss strolled over and asked why I did not go to lunch. I reluctantly explained; he tossed me a quarter and told me to go ahead. If one is hungry enough, he is not proud.

I made straight for a saloon. I realized my mistake as soon as I had passed through those swinging doors, for the counter was bare of aught but mugs and bottles. This particular saloon was apparently in the fortunate situation of being able to attract customers without the bait of free lunch. I thought of slipping out again, but dared not venture it. Suppose the man at the bar would ask what I meant by walking in and out without buying anything. So I shoved my worldly wealth across the bar and received a foaming mug in return. There seemed to be no question of change. The astute bartender assumed that I expected none and when I had managed to finish the beer, he pushed a glass of something else toward me. I was glad to make good my escape and get back to the shop.

At the end of the day's work the boss handed me a dollar. He said I seemed to be a hard worker and he was sorry he had no more work for me; this was merely a rush job that he had had to finish.

I studied my dollar carefully, debating my next step. If I

walked home, I would have the whole of it to show to Lisa; but it would take me hours to get there and meanwhile there was not a scrap of food in the house and no money to buy it with. And Lisa and the little one had been hungry when I left in the morning. If I took the street car, it would cut into my dollar; but it would bring me home so much sooner. I was tired, and hungry besides. I took the car.

My heart was light as I reached our tenement and I took the last flight two stairs at a time. Absorbed in preparing the little speech with which to present my earning, I hardly noticed voices and laughter that drifted down the hall. I threw open the door to our room with a flourish—and stood blinking in the lamplight.

It was our landlady's best lamp that stood in the center of the table, its light reflected in the amber gleams of steaming glasses of tea. Great loaves of bread and platters of sliced meats proclaimed that nothing short of a feast was in progress. And Lisa sat feasting in the midst of our friends, quite certainly the hostess of them all.

They let her tell me the great news. A letter had come from one of the Russian papers to which I had sent an article while I was in Dogville; they accepted it and wanted more like it. They engaged me as their American correspondent at a monthly salary of fifty rubles and they enclosed the first month's allowance, to seal the bargain and pay for my first article. Of course, it was not much money, but I was to receive a regular income (only later events proved it to be not so regular, after all) and, above all, I was a writer, a man of thought. Was it not only proper that we should celebrate this victory of mine with a party? It was.

For me this stroke of good fortune meant just one thing. It would pay for a roof over our heads and something to eat now and then. It would give me a little breathing space . . . I would be able to learn English. I would lift myself, once and for all, from the tragedy of the unskilled laborer in a strange land.

I knew that the various schools teaching English to foreigners were not popular. The teachers had no special preparation for dealing with adults, and their attempts to treat us as children in the first grades of school, teaching us to read childish sentences and spell out little rhymes merely annoyed us. And I knew, too, that as soon as any one could afford it, even by sacrificing actual necessities of life, he left those classes and arranged to take private lessons, usually from a former immigrant who spoke his own language. This was my opportunity. I studied frantically to master a working knowledge of English. When I considered myself able to use the language without confusion, I made it known that I would give private lessons to those desiring to learn. I actually did get a pupil now and then and although the pay was small and irregular, it gave me confidence in my new role. I decided to try for a regular position in one of the schools. But one had to pass an examination in order to become a candidate, and the preparation consumed precious weeks; the remittance from Russia arrived late and it became necessary to get money and get it quickly.

It was just as hard as ever to find work of any kind. I haunted printing plants and now and then managed to get some temporary work in one of them. This seemed the nearest to anything for which I had had special training and somehow farthest from the terrible drive of the labor machine. One of my temporary jobs was in a cigar factory. Later when I took the teacher's examination I was painfully conscious of the reek of tobacco emanating from me. But I passed the examination and shortly thereafter secured a position in a private school conducting English classes in the evening for immigrants.

About this time I renewed my acquaintance with young Rosenberg, in whose father's printing shop I had secured my first introduction to the trade. The youth was now a student at New York University. I confided to him that I was rather pressed for material to embody in my articles upon fantasy and imagination. He promptly suggested that I could get all the material I could possibly use out of the encyclopedia, which I could buy on monthly installments. It so happened that he was selling this very set of volumes to pay his way at college. The thing seemed reasonable enough; I got the books, he got the commission, and every one was satisfied. After that my contributions to the Russian paper were at least authoritative.

My friend held the job of assistant to the professor in chemistry at the university and so he naturally felt a sort of proprietary interest in the institution as well as in me. He urged me to enter the university; he himself would see to the admission formalities and now, with the funds from Russia and the pay for my work in the night school, I should be able to get along. He looked over my credentials; my studies in Russia had not covered all of the required subjects.

Then he came across a letter from Count Tolstoy; with this, and a record of my pedagogical studies in Moscow, he laid siege to the admissions office. Russian pedagogical methods and Russian innovations in manual training happened to be of particular interest to American educators just then. At any rate, they made much of my possible knowledge in these matters and, on the strength of this, and my acquaintance with Tolstoy, I was admitted to the university's School of Pedagogy.

A door that I had despaired of ever beholding had opened to me. But it was not as a Jew that I entered the university; they looked upon me as a Russian and it was as a Russian student that I embarked upon my studies. Troubled, I tried to find my setting among the Jewish students. I saw several of them in my classes and found occasion to draw them aside and ask them about our status. They looked about apprehensively, fearful lest we be overheard. Why should we go out of our way to make ourselves known as Jews? Why make our work in class all the harder for ourselves? Why run chances of being held back because of prejudice on the part of this or that professor? Why cripple one's opportunity to secure a position, after graduation, especially if one meant to go into teaching? They shrugged their shoulders almost resentfully.

At the university I came to know well and to love Professor Dubs Shimer who was humanitarian as well as teacher, a double identity that should be, but is not always, found in all teachers. From him shone the first genuine sympathy I was to see in America. Another like him was Dr. Saul Badanes who was a teacher at the Hebrew Technical School and who led my feet to a social-service career; for it was he who obtained for me the position of custodian of the reading room of the Hebrew Institute.

But an adventuring young man needs stern masters as well as kind friends and it fell to me to have as master, in the Hebrew Institute, a benevolent tyrant, Dr. Henry M. Leipziger. He was like those good fathers who know how to use the rod judiciously and who, if they are not loved, are vastly respected, and thanked in later years.

If the ways of Dr. Leipziger were almost cruel at times, one came to understand afterward that his harsh discipline had the kindliest of purposes. Roughly enough, he kept pushing his subordinates toward higher endeavors.

"How long do you intend to remain on this job?" he would say to us. "Why don't you try for a higher position? This place is not a lifetime berth. There are other deserving young men who need a start. Why don't you vacate it?"

He understood immigrants and treated them as individuals and not as a crowd. The rich benefactors of the immigrants thought of them as a mass to be thrown into a melting pot and made over into Americans.

These philanthropists were of German immigration and in them was all the wealth of Jewry. They were proud Americans who thought the way to assimilate Europeans was to strip them of their inheritance of language and custom and bedeck them in a ready-made suit of Americanism. Yiddish must be stricken from the tongues of Jewish immigrants, though these protested, saying, "Is this America, where we may not speak our mother tongue? Even in Russia they permitted us to speak Yiddish."

Upon non-Jews who had immigrated to America, there was no such high-pressure Americanism inflicted by their countrymen who were already here, and even in the second generation German-Americans were speaking German in their homes, and they were proud of their *Männerchor* which sang German songs with resounding voices in public places, while in the Civil War there had been several regiments of German immigrants to whom commands were given in the German language.

I looked about the queer reading room, thrilled to feel that I, but recently an immigrant, was already part of the great force for the Americanization of my people. Here, in the Hebrew Institute, one spoke English if one could—and if not, there were English classes available. American flags, American pictures, adorned the walls. American holidays were celebrated with a fervent gesture. American ladies and gentlemen, zealous in behalf of the newcomer, exhorted the children to love this new land of theirs, and to join the classes and clubs at the Institute. This great, stately building seemed of another world than that of the seething, clamoring, steaming street. I was impressed by the order, the beauty, the quiet of it all.

Then, suddenly, the quiet struck me as strange. The reading room was almost deserted, its well-stacked shelves undisturbed. Where were the eager immigrants, yearning for knowledge? Now and then some one drifted in, gazed about—and drifted out again. A member of the Board of Directors passed through and stopped to inquire about my work; in so crowded a neighborhood, and with people in the building all the time, there seemed no reason why the library should not be crowded; I looked at him helplessly. The well-bred voice, the faultless American attire, the cool, appraising glance, made me feel uncouth, barbaric. A queer loneliness oppressed me; I almost wished that I, too, could tiptoe from the room with the other immigrants.

To-day I can smile at the furious mixture of emotions aroused in me at that early encounter with a director. Humility, distrust, resentment—a faint glimmer of understanding. Here was an American gentleman whose forbears perhaps hailed not from the misery of the Pale, but from urbane West Europe. And he was established here, an American. He wanted to help us, to make us like himself, to have us shed our foreign speech, our old customs, our dark memories, as one might shed an outworn coat. And I, who had so longed to forsake that past, who had dreamed only of becoming part and parcel of this new world, somehow resented that proffered help. I wanted to voice my resentment. I wanted to tell this fine gentleman that I, too, did not come bare and empty-handed.

But instead I decided to wait for an opportune moment to suggest the addition of Yiddish and Russian newspapers and periodicals to the reading room; I was thrilled when, shortly thereafter, this suggestion was put into effect and workingmen and students began to come in, to study and to read. This was not Americanization, perhaps, but it was bringing the people into the building and must not this, after all, be the first step?

I found a friend and kindred spirit in Isaac Spectorsky, who was superintendent of the Institute. He disagreed thoroughly with the inflexible Americanization policy laid down by the Board. I was won over completely by his disarming sincerity and earnestness. Within the narrow latitude permitted him, he was attempting to draw the immigrants into the Institute through interests and activities of their own choice. It could not compel the neighborhood to reflect its American spirit and culture; it must itself reflect the life and interests of the ghetto. And here, in this palace of the immigrants, they would come to know the real America, the America of freedom, of tolerance, of justice. So, while the directorate attempted to emphasize the pure American- ism of the Institute by eliminating the religious implication in its name, transforming it into the "Educational Alliance," it grudg- ingly consented to the use of Yiddish in its adults' groups.

Mr. Spectorsky was respected and loved in the neighborhood. His office was a small room under a stairway, his records were not tabulated with that perfection that social workers to-day consider so vital, and he was perhaps lacking in modern technique.

My work at the university taxed my energies. I was doing rather well, not setting the world on fire—struggling to grasp the often rapidly spoken classroom lectures, wondering, the while, how we could make ends meet. I tried to eke out my salary from the reading room by giving private lessons in English. I scanned the newspapers, burrowed deep into my encyclopedia, and dogged the footsteps of notables to secure material for my Rus- sian press correspondence. Somehow we must struggle along until I could qualify as an educator. I was no longer fearful of such a career, for I now realized that my future would lie among my own people.

The rich, older Jews were quite upset by the strange mixture that was pouring in upon them from Eastern Europe and which by a generous giving of money they were trying to make American. There were Socialists of several varieties who, far from consenting to be made over, were resolved to help make America over. When one Sunday I offered to a group of them a lecture on the need of Jewish education, terrible was the reproach that fell upon my head. I was denounced by various members of my audience. I was only an echo from a dead past. I was seeking to revive an institution which their superior minds had long ago rejected. I should not have been permitted to speak, they said.

These Socialists were most embarrassing to the bountiful German Jews who believed that the best interest of Jewry demanded that these new Jews be brought up to cherish the regular parties instead of bringing heterodox political doctrine to the new land. What would the neighbors say?

The shades of Jewish radicalism tapered to the deepest red of the Anarchists who were fond of scandalizing Orthodox Jews on the Day of Atonement. If for the Orthodox this was a day for fasting, for the Anarchists it was a day for feasting and dancing. They made their rendezvous in a restaurant on Division Street and on the day before a certain Yom Kippur they advertised that the restaurant would be open for the feeding of all freethinkers on the holy day.

And though there is no day in the Jewish calendar holier than Yom Kippur and though the time of pious Jews should be spent altogether in the synagogue on that day, many of the Orthodox Jews went to serve Jehovah as pickets before the Division Street restaurant. And whatever Jew attempted to enter was severely beaten, and the police sent reserves to quell the tumult of outraged Jewry.

Hearing of this, I hastened to the restaurant and persuaded the proprietor to close it; but mine was the unhappy lot of the peacemaker, for when I emerged from the restaurant, there were shouts of "Anarchist! Anarchist!" and the mob fell upon me and belabored me and it was only with the aid of the police that I escaped with my life.

The New York ghetto was a comparatively new thing then and the hundreds of thousands were yet to be put into it, and the

problem of what to do for the inhabitants had become a vitaliz-
ing factor in American Judiasm. The American Jews of Reform
persuasion made contributions of money for the welfare of these
immigrants and the immigrants in turn made contributions of
new Jewish life and provided their benefactors with causes for
new Jewish devotions.

While the rich patrons of Jewish charity were trying to make
them over into Americans, these perverse immigrants insisted on
living their own lives in their own way. Every night they were
filling their theaters to see the plays of Jacob Gordin who was
turning out new dramas at high speed. He had brought new
ideals to the Jewish stage, which had fallen to a low estate in the
United States. Gordin, tall, imposing, austere, was more Russian
than Jew and loomed in the streets of the East Side above the
heads of the multitude of undersized men.

It was disgust with the Jewish stage he found in America that
prompted him to write plays of his own, and his success was
almost instantaneous. He wrote in three days plays that live and
are revived from time to time even to this day, and in a few years
he had produced sixty of them. He was no steady worker, but in
a few hours of inspiration his genius conceived and wrote a play
for which a less gifted mind would have consumed months.

More amazing is the fact that Yiddish was not a familiar language on his tongue when he came here, for his speech was Russian; he mastered Yiddish and in his plays polished it to the
elegance of a classic tongue.

Israel Zangwill came to the United States and there was an
occasion when he and Gordin were thrown together in a certain
place of Jewish resort. Being told that Gordin was in the room,
Zangwill desired to meet him.

"Gordin," I said, "Zangwill wants to meet you."

"I, the father of eleven children, should go to meet him!"
exclaimed the whimsical Gordin. "It is he who should come to
meet me—the father of eleven children."

Upon receiving this message, Zangwill straightway went to
Gordin.

"You should have come to me," Zangwill said reproachfully.

"You have only eleven children? Well, I have 'The Children of the Ghetto.' "

Never before had I seen the nimble-witted Gordin caught without a ready retort. He could only laugh.

Gordin gave release to Jewish life wretched in foul tenements. But with all its miseries, Jewish life in New York slums was more endurable than the life of the non-Jewish neighbors in the same environment. Jewish life had, at least, the comfort of Jewish tradition which was the only riches it had brought from Europe; it established Hebrew schools for the children and in the basements of synagogues old men studied the Talmud the livelong day. Saturday was still honored as the day of rest, and Zionists were in force, dreaming the timeless dream.

To me opportunities for educational work through the various groups seemed inviting. The Socialists had established their own school for workers; I was permitted to teach a class in English there. Abraham Cahan, leonine, unrelenting in his scorn of the unbeliever, was already a popular figure. I had met him first in his editorial room where I went to interview him for material for an article on the Jewish press in America. When he learned that I was not a Socialist he refused to be interviewed. But then we became close friends and spent long evenings together.

Having graduated from the university, I became instructor of English in the Baron de Hirsch Trade School, and one of my duties was to hunt for pupils, and difficult they were to pursue. Once in Brownsville we called a meeting to which no one came save a few leaders of Jewry. Then I went into the street to entice an audience by subterfuge, saying that men were needed for a *minyan*—the ten men without whom there can be no Jewish religious service. And where the cause of technical education had not served to inspire any, now many flocked to the meeting to partake of the *mitzvah* of prayer.

The school had a rather dubious reputation, and pupils were few, and so I was glad to receive appointment in the Hebrew Technical Institute which, besides being a better field, offered more lucrative employment.

Now among the dreams of those who looked for a better life for the new immigrants was Woodbine. Woodbine, in New Jersey, was founded in 1891 by the Baron de Hirsch Fund, as a Jewish agricultural colony, on five thousand, three hundred acres of land which had been bought for seven dollars an acre. This was sold to colonists on terms by which a mortgage would be paid off within five years—provided the colonist had the capacity to pay.

There was a flaming spirit at the head of Woodbine, Professor H. L. Sabsovich, a Russian Jew educated for agriculture in Switzerland, who had been an agricultural chemist in the University of Odessa, and, establishing himself in the United States, had become a teacher of agricultural chemistry in the Colorado State Agricultural College.

The East Side of New York knew him well, for he was no cloistered scientist, content among test tubes. He was a sort of prophet who liked to journey frequently from the sylvan shades of Woodbine to the East Side in order to impart a portion of his spirit to the ghetto. With him was often Dr. Paul Kaplan, a warm-hearted, kindly fanatic who carried a dream of settling Jews upon the soil. They gathered groups of us about them in some East Side café and the night through they lectured us on the beauty of the outdoors and on the good promise of the soil where, they said, the manifest destiny of the immigrant Jew lay.

Dr. Sabsovich's dreams ran far ahead of reality at Woodbine, where the land was covered with a dense growth of scrub oak and pine and where settlers were housed in a temporary shack and where backs that had bent over sewing machines were almost broken struggling with a difficult soil. So before the end of the first year many of the colonists had deserted, while those who remained earned only the meagerest living.

Then it was suggested that if there were industries at Woodbine, its farmers would have wages to eke out the small yield of their acres. And so there was brought to Woodbine a garment factory and later a knitting mill which were protected against loss by liberal subventions. And there came to Woodbine also a machine shop and a hat factory. And now Jews settled Woodbine in numbers again to work in the factories, and it seemed Woodbine might become an industrial community instead of a farm colony. For the work of the factories which was done with swift machines was far less laborious than digging an obstinate soil.

Then it was said, "If we cannot make farmers of the old ones, let us work with the new generation," and an agricultural school was established for the children of the inhabitants of Woodbine as well as for others.

So five years passed, and, despite its difficulties, Woodbine had made a little progress as an industrial if not an agricultural community. The wheels of the mills turned swiftly, but the soil was stingy. Now the time had come when the pioneers of Woodbine, of whom there were few left, must pay their indebtedness for their farms to the Baron de Hirsch Fund.

And great was the shock in the East Side of New York when the mortgages of some of them were foreclosed and the farmers evicted. I was dispatched by the *Jewish Forward* as correspondent to investigate, and reported that the land was unfit for farming and it was not to be expected of the farmers to pay their debts. And the result was that the evicted farmers were permitted to return to their lands.

This was the beginning of my association with Woodbine, for not long afterward I was sent there to settle a strike in the Baron de Hirsch Agricultural School and remained there as principal.

There had come to my hands the materials with which I might help to create a new Jewish life in the New World. The feet of Jewish youth were to be turned toward a new destiny, leaving behind the peddler's packs and the sweatshops and the slums of their fathers.

The earth which was our laboratory was sandy and stingy, but the devoted spirits of our students wrung from it a rather good reward. They were elevated by the consciousness of a mission. They thought of themselves as pioneers blazing new trails for a people.

There was that first graduation when some thirty youths went forth to labor on farms, to suffer the discouragements of the beginning, to water with their sweat the acres of others before they could hope to have their own. But they were illuminated by a sense of being bearers of a new calling for their people. It had been said of the Jews that they were a non-productive people; these youths thrilled with the consciousness of being flaming messengers proclaiming to men, "Behold, the Jew is a worker!" Alas for Jewish dreams that must meet the facts of Jewish character!

It was not that we thought only of making things grow in the soil; even more we were concerned with planting a good Jewish life. If the farms could not give good harvests, we could establish here a wholesome and lovely Jewry. There came to join us devoted teachers and workers, bringing ideals. There was Bernard Palitz, who was the manager of Temple College in Philadelphia, a man oppressed by the world-wide tragedy of his people and looking for light in the darkness. There was Mrs. Steinberg, who became the matron and was more than matron, and who remains a beloved memory in Woodbine. There was Mr. Hillier, a Christian, a former minister, whose soul embraced the good of all religions and who found himself at home in our synagogue even. To him Judaism was one of a number of good ways of life and in it a Christian might walk and even lead with a good heart.

The school had grown from a most unpretentious beginning to a large institution that the Paris International Exposition and the Exposition at Buffalo delighted to honor.

The inhabitants of Woodbine numbered some two thousand, all Jews, with few exceptions. Out of this waste land there had sprung a community with all the aspects of a good town—factories, stores, schools, and social life. We made the school the social center for the community. We linked the life of the agricultural school to the life of the community, hoping that the inspirations of the school would illuminate the town. For life was hard and work was not always to be had; periods of unemployment were getting longer and there were strikes against the injustice of employers.

Nor did civic virtue stand godlike in Woodbine, for some of its voting inhabitants were not averse to being corrupted on election days. So we thought of separating Woodbine from the hands of the surrounding politicians and making of it an independent political unit. As a self-governing community Woodbine would become conscious of its civic responsibilities and there would be a proud citizenship scorning the corrupter. It would no longer be dependent for its school system on the beneficence of the neighboring politicians and would maintain itself by a tax system instead of by the philantrophy of the Baron de Hirsch Fund.

And notable was that day when the Borough of Woodbine was established—the first all-Jewish political unit in America and, for that matter, in the world—and from New York and Philadelphia Jews came to celebrate the occasion, among them Jacob Gordin and Abraham Cahan and Joseph Barondess; and sociologists and social reformers and soul-savers came to see this experiment, and among these were General Booth and Booker T. Washington and Edward Steiner.

The banner of political purity was forthwith raised, and only a few of the pioneers who, by reason of being old inhabitants, had enjoyed the prestige and the perquisites of political leadership were unhappy. There was the solemn day of election when the politically untutored Jew proved he was as good as any in all the technique of politics, save that he conducted this election with clean hands.

And so there was installed a Jewish administration in the borough government. A lawyer was engaged to instruct the officials in the rules of parliamentary procedure and to teach them the basic laws under which they functioned. A rather pretentious city hall was built and streets were paved, and a fire department organized, and the erection of a new schoolhouse begun. Thus Woodbine quickly acquired all the conveniences of an American city and soon, also, it became afflicted with those civic vices without which no American city was complete. For privilege seekers came to get what they wanted.

It was proposed by a promoter to build an electric tram line through Woodbine, offering opposition to the existing transportation system, and bitter was the strife between the two as they went about with substantial persuasions to win this leader or that to their respective sides. And Civic Virtue, being young in Woodbine and still pure, became sick at the sight.

Then that corrupter, the liquor traffic, came to Woodbine for privileges. Woodbine had beeen in dry territory, by local option. Now, being an independent political unit, it might determine for itself whether it wanted saloons. The agents of the brewers and the distillers massed in force in Woodbine, raising hopeful banners.

"Bring the saloon to Woodbine and wake up the town."

"An open town is a live town."

"The saloon will bring prosperity."

We argued with the people: What good would the saloon be? Why should a new community like Woodbine embrace the curse that afflicted other cities? But the population had become politically independent and no longer need lean on philanthropic advisors. So Woodbine, which was to have presented to the eyes of America a model of social and civic purity, went wet, and three saloons quickly were established. And with the saloon came all the attending evils.

But who might point scorn at Woodbine? Its civic weaknesses were the weaknesses of all American cities of that time when corruption reeked in every community large and small. It was the time of the Crokers and the Coxes, when the saloon was the source of American politics. Who might say "Shame!" to these immigrants when there was no exemplar of civic righteousness even in the cities whose foundations reached deep into the history of the land?

If we entertained dreams of a contented Jewish peasantry, we were soon disillusioned. In our school we were graduating young men who did not want to remain toilers of the field in all their days. Being Jews they could not be classified by a mere dictum: "You must be forever diggers of the soil."

After working a due period as laborers in the fields, our graduates began to look beyond the horizon, and reached for the less laborious stations of the agricultural industry. They went to agricultural laboratories, they entered higher institutions of agricultural learning, they sought positions in the Department of Agriculture at Washington; some deserted agriculture altogether.

Our directors were distressed. This had not been their plan.

They had thought of a contented Jewry working in the fields, tilling the acres of others and, eventually, their own. They suggested, perhaps, our method of education was all wrong. We had put visions in the eyes of these boys and, as soon as they could, they lifted their eyes from the ground to follow these visions. There must be a change in the program.

They said we must simplify the course to avoid the false ideas which had entered the heads of the boys and were leading them to pursue ambitions far from the soil. Our course was three years long; we must cut it to one year. Our course was scientific; we must no longer expose the students to higher educational and social influences. Thereafter the work of education must be altogether in the field where they would become inured to the lot of the humble toiler and be content, not knowing any better. Thus we would bring up a toiling class.

Such a program was based on the social philosophy of a great many philanthropically inclined people in that time. The immigrant was a child who must be carefully kept in his place. His benefactors knew better than he what was good for him. These benefactors had made substantial business successes and, therefore, felt they were the competent guardians of the new-comers. These immigrants were distant relatives whom one must look after carefully lest they do things that might bring the family to shame. From their lofty elevations their benefactors looked down upon them and built settlements for them; but in the end they were to settle their problems for themselves.

To shut out light and to curb ambition is not the function of a teacher. My relations with my superior officers became strained. There were other discouragements as well. My young dream of a righteous American community had come to disillusion. My efforts to make the school a decent influence in the life of the community of Woodbine did not always receive that warm embrace that my enthusiasm thought they deserved. I resigned.

Disconsolate, I went home, and there the week's issue of the *American Hebrew*, just arrived from New York, awaited me. My eye fell on a conspicuous advertisement: "United Jewish Charities of Cincinnati, Ohio, wants a superintendent. Opportunity for the development of educational activities, etc." The opportunity for educational activity prompted me to try my fortune.

On the impulse I wrote a letter of application and forthwith mailed it, but as I slipped it into the mailbox I felt as one throwing a pebble into bottomless space from which no echo would ever come.

And in the meantime peaceful relations were resumed at the Woodbine school, and I was asked to withdraw my resignation. But an echo did come after a few days in a telegram requesting me to visit Cincinnati that I might be looked over.

Cincinnati! Amid the tenements of a congested portion of this city lies a small burial ground in which sleep the pioneers of Cincinnati Jewry, and some of the tombstones were carved a hundred years ago. Its oldest temple has passed the century mark. It was a seasoned and well-rooted Jewry that I found in this mid-Western city. The leaders spoke English with a decided German accent and the prominence and prestige of Cincinnati Jewry were in their hands. The Jews of the Russian immigration were still weak, for the most part peddlers and tailors, and even the renowned Manischewitz was baking matzos in a small structure in a back yard.

The German stock of Jewry had come to Cincinnati years before, often with peddlers' packs, and by integrity and diligence had prospered enormously and had established great jobbing houses and clothing industries and distilleries. The American-born generation of them were already entering middle age and shortly the son of one of them, Julius Fleischmann, was to become the mayor of the city. And twenty-five years later another of their sons, Murray Seasongood, was to lead a sweeping political reform that was to elevate him to chief executive of the city.

Even in that time, when generous giving had not yet become a universal habit among the rich, the generosity of the German Jews was proverbial in Cincinnati, and they were the pillars of philanthropies and of the arts.

To Cincinnati Rabbi Isaac M. Wise had come in the fifties with the torch of Reform and here he had founded the Hebrew

Union College, the first of the Jewish theological seminaries of which there are so many now in the United States. Here was born the Union of American Hebrew Congregations, the source of Reform propaganda, and here served one of Dr. Wise's pupils, Rabbi David Philipson, who emphasized a strictly American Judaism, and who is the *bête-noir* of all good Zionists unto this day.

To Cincinnati there had been coming since the early eighties a rather steady stream of Russian immigration that was adjusting its early pieties to the new conditions. But there were a few of the older Orthodox families that were pointed to with something of awe, for they had been faithful in all things. Outstanding among these were the Isaacs.

This was an amazing American-born family that in the third generation carried on a European Orthodox life. The first of these Isaacs in America was Schachne, who had come here far in advance of the East European stream. By reason of piety and learning he came to be known as Reb Schachne, and many years there stood a synagogue called Reb Schachne's schul, and the small cemetery in which he sleeps is Reb Schachne's. By occupation he was a merchant. His sons were Moses and Abraham, who were born in the United States, and they followed the path of stern Orthodox tradition in which their father led them. Moses was childless, but the sons of Abraham Isaacs were no less observant than their grandfather, and though they rose to high places in their professions the service of the faith always came before any temporal duty.

Cincinnati Jewry looked up to the Isaacs as to courageous men standing on a summit unattainable to all others. There shone about them an aura of aristocracy which seemed far finer and rarer than the aristocracy of the richer German Jews.

When the Orthodox young went to the university and commenced to break away from the teachings of their fathers, their unhappy parents pointed to the sons of Abraham Isaacs: "See those Isaacs boys. They, too, are in the university and excel every one in scholarship and yet they are faithful. What a pleasure it is to see all the Isaacs boys sitting in the schul with their father on the Sabbath!"

At the time when I arrived in Cincinnati a portion of Cincinnati Jewry was feasting its eyes on a certain glamorous young figure—Judah Leon Magnes, who had graduated from the Hebrew
Union College and was a teacher there. He was a sort of heretic
in Reform Judaism, for he was preaching Zionism even though
he had been brought up in the Hebrew Union College. The German Jewish leaders were quite sure he was ruining his career,
while the Orthodox thought of him as a brand plucked from the
burning and made much of him. Zionism then was scarcely more
than an ache of the heart which people relieved by singing "Hatikvah," and even the best of the dreamers would not have dared
to fancy this young Magnes sitting in time as chancellor of a Hebrew University in a Jerusalem that was the capital of a Jewish
homeland.

In this citadel of Reform, Zionism was an enemy held in no
respect. The Reform Jews were sure that to be a Jew was to be a
member of a religious communion and nothing else. To suggest
that to be a Jew was any sort of national distinction was altogether un-American; this had always been taught at the Hebrew
Union College.

Being a Jew had to do only with membership in a temple, of
which there were two, and with social service which was represented by the Jewish charities. Indeed, in Cincinnati Jewry there
had developed a technique of social service which years later was
to be accepted universally and be known as the community chest.

In this mid-western community the problem was not so dis-
tressful as in New York. Here were no slums. A few years before
the older Jewry had begun to move out of its comfortable brick
houses that stood row on row in that part of the town that was
called the West End; to these houses came the later immigration,
not crowding. The three-story house that had contained one of
the old families now was the habitation of two or three of the
new ones. Later we were to see the newer Jewry following the
older to the suburbs, and it was to come to pass even that the
newer Jews would be the neighbors of the older ones, occupying
mansions as lovely as theirs, and lo! building great apartment
houses for their comfort.

And so, as I went about that first day in Cincinnati, I saw that in this mid-western town there were no such depths of misery to plumb as in New York. The homes of this ghetto lacked many comforts, but most of them were, at least, habitable.

My guide was Max Senior. He was the prophet of Jewish social service in Cincinnati; not a professional worker, but a business man whose feet were on solid ground and his eyes in the stars. We shall meet him more intimately farther along in these adventures. He charmed me; his depth was something of which one was always conscious in his presence.

To be looked over informally I was taken to the offices of the United Jewish Charities where a number of the community leaders were awaiting me for that purpose. They impressed me as a very devoted group of people, but I was conscious that they were sizing me up, and I did not like that. One of the ladies, Mrs. Moses Isaacs, however, attracted me. She seemed so kind and earnest and enthusiastic, albeit very reserved. She uttered a few Yiddish words and that made me feel at home.

Besides the scrutiny of the laymen there were also upon me the expert eyes of Dr. Solomon Lowenstein, the retiring superintendent who was going to New York to become assistant to Dr. Lee K. Frankel in the management of the Jewish charities there.

Nor was I soon released from this inspection. In the evening I must visit the homes of various of the directors who lived in the suburbs and were lavish with hospitality. And on the second day there took place that formal inquisition which was to determine whether I or one of the number of other candidates was to be the superintendent of the United Jewish Charities of Cincinnati.

This took place in the Federal Building office of Bernard Bettman, the revenue collector for Southern Ohio and chairman of the board of the United Jewish Charities. And clever and meaningless questions were put and clever and meaningless answers were given, and after an hour of this I was dismissed and the next candidate admitted.

I left Cincinnati distressed by many doubts. If this place were offered, ought I take it? It meant more than turning over a new leaf; it was starting a new book. I had been a teacher; this was a new profession for me. But doubt quickly changed to decision when a telegram from Cincinnati notified me that I had been chosen. I accepted and left Woodbine after five years.

I went to New York to sit for two weeks under the tutelage of Dr. Frankel, to attend meetings of his committees, to go with case workers in the field, to study in the National Desertion Bureau and the Industrial Removal office. A group of my friends gave a farewell dinner in a Grand Street restaurant. They were rather sorry for me. They were sure I would not long remain in an institution of charity. They had no use for charity. "You, who were cut out to be a teacher, to go into charity!"

I departed with the blessing of Dr. Frankel.

"Do not hurry to introduce innovations or changes," he said. "Just do as your predecessor did. When you are absolutely certain that you have convinced at least a majority of your board that you measure up to their standards, then and then only begin slowly and cautiously to introduce your own ideas. I should say the first six months not a single new idea, not a single new measure, not a single change."

Now that the opportunity had presented itself, it seemed to me a logical and infinitely desirable one. My personal Jewish question no longer troubled me. My material needs, even with a growing family to provide for, were met, modestly. A full spiritual satisfaction arose from the fact that my work involved service to others and from the fascination of contact with youth.

I felt that, in entering the field of social work, I would find happiness and self-fulfillment for myself and my family.

Relief was the best part of our work in Cincinnati. We gave our afflicted bread, but our effort chiefly was to enable them to earn their bread, and so for this one we bought a horse and wagon that he might go about peddling, and for that one we established a small store.

When the public-health service in the city still was in a most elementary state, we were conducting a clinic for our people and providing visiting nurses. We went into the field of education to establish a manual-training school for our boys because manual training was then lacking in the public schools. By reason of a corrupt gang the public schools had fallen into neglect, and the newspaper that championed righteous government pointed to us, saying: "Because of the failure of the government, a private group must perform one of the functions of the government," and this was true; no sooner was manual-training in the public schools than our own school was closed.

We treated tuberculosis as a social disease, providing adequate relief not only for the patient but also for his family, and the Cincinnati Jewish community was the first to serve in this beneficent way.

The patient was not compelled to separate from his family; if he was sent to a sanitorium, the family was established in the city where the sanitorium was located. If he remained in Cincinnati, a comfortable home was secured for the entire family in a sparsely settled suburb. In any case, an adequate allowance would be provided and, as soon as the patient was in condition to undertake efforts at self-support, steps were taken to assist the family re-establish itself on a self-supporting basis in the place that had proved itself beneficial to the stricken one.

We experimented also with the "treatment" of deserted families, working on the asumption that Jewish family desertion has unique features. Any man may desert his family for love of drink, or of another woman, or out of plain good-for-nothingness. But when a Jew leaves his family it is apt to be because the endless struggle to make ends meet and the miserable surroundings have become more than even loyal devotion can bear; if he leaves, the family will be looked after by charity—they will be better off without him.

So we would refuse to give aid to a deserted family, allowing the non-Jewish relief agencies to handle the case. The wandering husband was notified through the press that, unless he was heard from, the family would be broken up; the Jewish Charities would not concern itself where the father himself was indifferent. In the meantime the National Desertion Bureau would conduct the search.

In most cases the man would return quickly and anxiously; we

would take up his problem with him, and would try to find a
way out of the material hopelessness. Desertion might be a way
out for the father; it was no way out for the family. This was the
thesis of the Cincinnati method of treating desertion. Within a
few years family desertion had decreased almost to the vanishing
point.

This determination to treat the family as the unit of our social-
service thinking guided us in dealing with Jewish orphans. In an
age of enthusiasm for bigger and better orphan asylums, we tried
to provide for dependent children by placing them in supervised
boarding homes. When one hundred and twenty-five pogrom
orphans were brought to America for adoption into Jewish
homes, the Cincinnati community accepted eight of them, only to
discover that they were all of one family, brothers and sisters.
True to Jewish tradition and Cincinnati policy, we determined to
keep the entire family intact by boarding out all eight in one
home. Finding the home was not, however, a simple task. Finally
my wife and I agreed to add them to our own six youngsters.
Overwhelming though the experience might have been, it certainly provided a laboratory in which to work out our own social
experiments.

In addition to the work at the relief office, I shortly took over
the direction of the Settlement House, which was located a little
farther uptown, where the ghetto was retreating before the invasion of Negro settlers.

The non-Jews in the neighborhood represented many lands
and walks of life. There were Italian immigrants, old German
settlers, "poor whites" who had wandered up from the South and
secured a precarious foothold; poverty, the saloon, neglect, flourished unashamed. Here was a task for the Settlement; whatever
might happen later on, it was important that in these surroundings the Jewish youth should be kept from assimilation with the
cheapening influences of tenement life.

We must emphasize Jewishness as something worth while; we
must encourage activities that might strengthen the tie of
sympathy between the old generation and the new, bridging over
the widening gap between them. In the midst of plans for club

activities, organization of classes, promotion of entertainments and lectures, I sought continually for means of emphasizing this Jewish note. Jewish movements of all kinds were encouraged to make the Settlement their center. Jewish holidays were celebrated by community gatherings and festivities; at the seder table in the Settlement auditorium, families reserved places year after year and the neighborhood girls joined hands with the women of our board in serving the guests; at Purim the children's clubs conducted a public presentation of gifts to parents.

One year we staged a "Jews of Many Lands Exposition." The entire building was utilized for booths, each one representing the settlement of Jews in another land, and each presided over by men and women in the picturesque costume of that land. For months in advance the neighborhood had been preparing for the Exposition; family chests were ransacked for clothes brought over from the old country; young folks met to paste letters on charts showing the story of Jewish settlement and life in different places; children's clubs conducted imaginary travel tours; Jewish homes loaned ceremonial objects for the special ceremonial exhibit which was an important feature of the Exposition; Jewish housewives prepared delicacies famed in their birthlands.

It was the pride of this Cincinnati Jewry to be known as the exemplar of social service for the eyes of all other Jewries, and everywhere Jewish charities were being federated as ours was.

Social service was par excellence the medium of religion in the Reform Jewry of Cincinnati; it was religion. In the Hebrew Union College there was established a social-service course for the instruction of the embryonic rabbis and I was the teacher. This was a new thing in theological seminaries; since then social service has been put into the curricula of most seminaries, non-Jewish and Jewish as well.

That the devoted hands of Jewry would have enough work to do for many, many years to come in serving the immigrant was never questioned. Each year brought more of them to our shores, and our mid-western city was getting a good share. The Russian pogroms were driving our brethren to us in vast numbers and our favorite altars were not in the temples so much as at their feet; and we made no end of serving them.

We could forecast quite accurately how many of them each year would bring to us; at that time immigration restriction was the vague aspiration of a few irresponsible organizations and it was a thing not to be thought of by politicians, since millions of the voters were of recent immigration and their American-born children were soon to be of voting age.

We had no international problems of Jewry on our hands, save that which had to do with the passport matter in Russia. Jews of whatever nationality were not admitted to Russia, though they carried the passports of their governments. This, however, was an academic issue, since so few Jews sought the pleasure of touring in Russia. Dr. Gotthard Deutsch of the Hebrew Union College, Cincinnati, who loved liberty as much as he loved Jewish history, brought it to the conscience of the nation when he demanded of the Russian consul at Chicago a visa for a passport that the American government had issued to him. This was in due course refused and Dr. Deutsch made thunderous protest to the government in behalf of American Jewry.

But our chief concern was not to get Jews into Russia but to get them out and make a good life for them here; and this we did well. We were not then burdened with the worry of perpetuating Judaism in America, nor did we hear much of Jewish education. We knew that as long as these Jews from Europe came to us, Jewish life would not only be perpetuated but also enriched. These we would serve and in the serving our Jewish consciousness would remain vivid and alert. And we were sure that there would be no end of their coming to us; we never thought otherwise. In that time America still was cherishing the good tradition: it was the refuge of the oppressed of all the world.

So my work was cast in good fields during the Cincinnati years, and the horizon of my tasks stretched, for one may not be an active Jew in one place without touching Jewish life in many places; we are always divided but we are like the head, the heart, and the hands that continued to yearn for each other after they were severed and separated and carried to far corners. For though the head and the heart and the hands had often quarreled they secretly loved one another.

IRMA L. LINDHEIM

Irma Lindheim, who served as President of Hadassah, the women's Zionist organization, was born in New York City in 1886. She has enjoyed a distinguished public service career and has led an unusual life, as her autobiography, Parallel Quest, testifies.

The selection in this book, drawn from Parallel Quest, describes how Mrs. Lindheim, who was born into an assimilated German-Jewish family and anti-Zionist as well, became a dedicated and active Zionist.

She was trained in the field of child study and social service. During World War I, Mrs. Lindheim served as a first lieutenant in the Motor Corps of America. Following the Balfour Declaration, she became interested in the Zionist cause and in 1919 was elected President of the Seventh District of the Zionist Organization in New York. Three years later she became a student at the Jewish Institute of Religion, where she was accepted as a candidate for a rabbinical degree, but did not, of course, become a rabbi.

She visited Palestine and was inspired by the life of the pioneers and, upon her return to the United States, became the second President of Hadassah, following in the footsteps of Henrietta Szold.

In 1928, when her husband died, Mrs. Lindheim decided to tear herself away from Hadassah leadership and to find herself anew. Within a few years, she and her five children went to settle in Palestine. She joined the kibbutz Mishmar Ha'emek, and has been living there ever since. It was in this kibbutz that she wrote her moving and illuminating autobiography—the story of a brave woman who sought new paths and found fulfillment in both search and discovery.

Discovery of Zionism*

IRMA L. LINDHEIM

WHEN THE UNITED STATES went to war with Germany, the general eddying restlessness exploded in a determination by many women to prove in public ways that they too were as patriotic as the men. One immediate concrete expression of this attitude was an organization which, though not a part of the Army, worked in an auxiliary capacity with the Army. The Motor Corps was a force of women volunteers who drove cars and ambulances, did odd jobs for the military, and in general was on call in emergencies. Uniforms were adapted from British Army style, complete to that smart accessory originally designed for an officer's field belt by a British Army officer, General Sir Samuel James Browne, and in recognition called the Sam Browne belt.

My fourth child was five weeks old when I enlisted for active service in the Motor Corps. I drove a low-slung Cadillac touring car given me by my husband as a gift for our third son. My first assignment was as "flag car" in a parade on Fifth Avenue. The date was April 18; with a bow in the direction of Paul Revere's ride in 1775 this was called the "Paulina" Revere parade.

The atmosphere of the Motor Corps out-armied the Army, its commanding officer out-brassed the Army brass. But also she was a woman possessed of a sense of mission, a stern disciplinarian, but with the capacity to elicit obedience from a heterogeneous collection of individualistic women, most of whom were rich and spoiled.

As there was a psychological as well as practical job to do, we were drilled relentlessly to high exhibition standards. A corporal found that she had a lot to go through before she was capable of barking commands in exactly the right manner! What went into the carrying out of orders for which there had been not even

* Reprinted from *Parallel Quest,* Thomas Yoseloff, New York, 1962, 47–76.

rudimentary training was hardly to be imagined. Our commanding officer was, first of all, zealous. Thin, wiry, excruciatingly efficient, her skin tightly drawn over high cheekbones lent some
credibility to a claim of being the daughter of a father of the
English nobility, and a mother who was a South American Indian princess. She had had some medical training, and managed
to convince the Surgeon General of the Army that her women
could serve many of his Corps' needs, thereby releasing men for
other jobs. At the outset, few of the women had been able to say,
without fear of successful contradiction, that they knew one end
of a clinical thermometer from the other; but when their short
period of intensive training was done, they knew at least that
and somewhat, if not much, more.

Even so, equipped with a superficial First Aid course and, at
best, odds and ends about bandaging and how to find a vein and
(in a tailor's dummy) to administer a hypodermic, we went to
our assigned jobs with high morale. Day or night we would speed
to remote sections—on the Bowery, in Brooklyn or on Long
Island—to find out, for example, whether a soldier was gold-
bricking or really in need of medical attention; if the latter,
families confidently expected the Motor Corps women to give it
at once. Or we were detailed to ride inside an ambulance with a
delirious pneumonia case from Fort Hamilton many miles to the
City and a hospital. I must say I did this over serious protest. Para-
lized with fear and helpless when the patient grew violent, even
more panicky when he lay inert, the only way to be sure he was
still alive was—praying frantically—to pinch him.

The marvel of it all was the way in which such an unlikely
group of women submitted to tough, ruthless discipline, working
round the clock with a spirit worthy of the West Point ideal of
"The Corps!" until, welded into a well-functioning paramilitary
whole, serving to its absolute limit of capacity, it became recognized for indispensable service.

It seemed incongruous that, whereas I had sought unsuccess-
fully for such a niche in peacetime, in wartime I had found my
place in a group with a purpose, serving *as* a group in a common
cause. Whatever the job, however inconsistent with any previous

experience, it was all one and the same to me. The satisfaction I
had longed for but never before found—of belonging to a group,
and working, moreover, in service necessary to my country—was
very great. It seems quite possible that it was precisely the inoculation I needed to prepare me for a decisive experience which,
unknown to me then, was just around the corner.

For the mood of the moment was indeed one of high idealism.
Young and old alike had a desire to serve, and a willingness to
sacrifice. Were we not fighting along with the men to make the
world safe for democracy? Were not oppressed nations to be
freed, a new world order established under a League of Nations?
Was not the greatest thing of all, that this was the war to end all
wars, the last war to be experienced by mankind?

Without the wholehearted encouragement and backing of my
husband I could not have done as I did. Nor would it have been
possible, without freedom from financial problems, to employ the
help necessary to maintain the mechanics of household life. As it
was, I was fortunate to encounter all manner of new people and
experiences and, through sharing them, introduce the children to
vicarious participation in the war effort.

Of course there were moments of misgiving. One day I was
detailed to drive a boxing champion, "Kid" McCoy—somewhat
confusingly explained to me as a welterweight who outgrew his
class—to Wall Street: I parked in front of the Treasury Building,
and he made a rousing recruitment speech from the back of my
car. I could only hope that, at the moment the boxer roared
"Give your name to the corporal here!"—the opening and closing cry of his speech, learned letter perfect—my husband
wouldn't chance to emerge from the building where he had his
offices, only to discover that "the corporal" was, in private life,
his wife!

Actually my husband was considerate to a fault about this
venture of mine; however, I had no desire, at this early stage of
working with the Motor Corps, to put his generosity to too severe
a test. Nor did I deem it wise later to make any point of the fact
that, in the line of duty, it had been necessary to lunch at Coney
Island with not only Kid McCoy, but an assortment of fistic

cronies including the heavyweight—and I was told, first Marquis of Queensbury champion—the Kid's contemporary, Jim Corbett.

I was one of the few Jewish women then in the Motor Corps, the only one later to become one of its high officers. I felt it a debt of honor to balance time, given away from home and family to Motor Corps service, with creative attention to my children. I was appalled at the way some women used war work as a welcome relief from family responsibilities; it gave me the consciousness that, whatever I could contribute of time and work to the war effort, I must make doubly sure not to neglect the rights and needs of my family.

Our eldest son had begun lessons at home when he was six, to learn something of his people's history. My husband and I had agreed that he was not to be a spiritual parvenu. Therefore he received instruction in the history, the legends, and the customs of the Jews from a well-qualified teacher, able to impart knowledge according to the boy's capacity, not his age. A child should at the very least become acquainted with the line of his inheritance, historical and individual. Well remembering that questions of my childhood and teen years had received answers which did not satisfy me at all, unlike my parents with their children, I decided that I too must study, to fit myself to answer questions as they would inevitably arise.

Available at the time was a course of lectures by a leader of the Ethical Culture Movement. The subject was "The Bible as Literature," the group composed mostly of Jewish women.

Discussing the Book of Job, the lecturer said one day, "The Book of Job is to be ranked with the world's greatest literature, including the writings of Shakespeare and Goethe." He startled us then by changing abruptly from the coolly intellectual to intellectual indignation, throwing out a question shocking in its pertinence.

"Should I, a non-Jew, have to reveal to you, who are Jews, the greatness of your own literature?"

No whipped dog could have felt worse as, humiliated and inwardly disgraced, I left the lecture hall. I thought I had been studying conscientiously for some years: philosophy, history, soci-

ology, politics. But now I realized how I had neglected—perhaps
subconsciously avoided—subjects which were intrinsically Jewish. I had read the Upanishads—yet not the Bible! Early marriage having cut short formal education, and feeling the urgency
of catching up with a brilliant, highly educated husband and
fitting myself to raise our children, for me Jewish history
might as well have stopped at the fall of the Second Temple.
Even though I could recall having won a medal at Sunday School
graduation for knowing all the "answers" at the back of the
lesson book, a non-Jew had—very properly—made me feel the
disgrace of my basic ignorance as a Jew.

I then knew that I must do something positive to close the gaps
in my knowledge and understanding. But what? How?

A short time after that shattering episode in the lecture course,
I was given a weekend leave from my Motor Corps duties and
went to Baltimore to pay a brief visit to my husband's cousin, my
friend Hortense Guggenheimer Moses.

A Jewish life had developed in Baltimore which had in it
nothing of the negative, formless, creedal limitations which had
impelled me to look for new, positive answers to life. Hortense
was a leader among the younger women of the Jewish community; of exceptional intelligence, she was active, too, in the life of
the city. To her it was incomprehensible that I was not a Zionist.
In the few days of my visit, conversation revolved frequently
around that subject. To me it was equally incomprehensible
that she was a Zionist, no doubt mainly because of my antago-
nism to it, for I knew little if anything about the movement.

The final evening of my visit started out, as I thought, unevent-
fully. I took merely polite interest in my hostess' decision to
expose me to strong Zionist influence, by means of our going to
call at the home of Dr. Harry Friedenwald, an eminent Baltimore physician, and an ardent and prominent Zionist.

Another guest was Dr. Ben-Zion Mossensohn.

Introduced to me as the principal of the Gymnasium in Tel
Aviv, first institution of its kind in Palestine, he was the first
Palestinian I had ever actually met.

I was jolted out of my passive frame of mind by the first impression made upon me by this thoroughly exotic-looking man. One felt astonished by a man who seemingly might have stepped forth from the pages of a tale from *The Thousand and One Nights*. The combination of his appearance—luxuriant, meticulously square-cut, black beard; glistening black-brown, magnetic—almost mesmeric—eyes; expressive long-fingered hands: a body suggesting boundless vitality—and the manner of his talk—a remarkable vocabulary, conveyed in a soft voice of great resonance—was saved from melodramatics only by a tremendous sincerity and conviction. All this was bound to be fascinating to any woman, a fact pointedly noted sometime later by my mother-in-law, who seemed well informed as to his romantic reputation and feared its effect on a daughter-in-law whom she considered woefully impressionable.

Oddly enough, his conversation that evening with Dr. Friedenwald about Zionism—to which it was intended I should listen and learn from—was boring to me at first, and I heard it with only surface attention.

However, I could certainly not deny to myself that I felt emotionally stirred by this apparition among men. Subtly, however, it became as though my mind were being exposed to a slowly unrolling scroll, silken, marvelously illuminated. I was presented with a series of images, the best of Zionist literature and thought, taken like rubbings of ancient tablets. With consummate skill Dr. Mossensohn gave to forces and events the status of oracle. The combined impact of personality, intellect, and dedication was enormous. Perhaps the effect on me was secondarily intellectual, due to some unreckoned vulnerability within me.

As I knew myself, one side of my nature was wonderfully and completely satisfied in my marriage. Another side, engrossed in a drive for self-fulfillment, was acutely receptive to external impression, like copper plate under the engraver's burin. My thinking still leaned to the abstract and the philosophical. Though little recognized as such by myself, deep within my being ran a revivalist's rushing fervor. Restrained, kept within bounds by the calm rationalistic atmosphere of our home, and a strong streak of

inherent common sense, I was protected against the dangers of
ever going off at "religious" tangents.

Later, looking back with objectivity on that evening at Dr.
Friedenwald's home, it was possible to realize that my host as
well as Dr. Mossensohn had deliberately plowed up a spirit and
mind they divined to be ready to be sown with the right seed;
they divined also, in a person showing few outward points of
contact with the Jewish heritage, that some spark lay deep, still,
which in time might be fanned into flame.

I left for New York the following morning. Boarding the train
I can recall my state of mind as only one of *waiting*. I had a misty
sense of something coming toward me, but no premonition as to
what it might be.

I opened a book, let my eyes follow lines of print, looked out
the window, absently took my tickets from my purse. The train
rushed along; it passed a red barn, a white wooden church, a
shallow pond, cattle standing placidly in lush meadowland.

A Morse Code of facts, ideas, questions, answers, arguments,
hummed along my mind. *National being of a people, captive for
centuries. . . . Isn't it enough to be an American? Untrue that
Jews are not a people, only a religion. . . . Jews are victims of
their homelessness. . . . If I am an American, am I at the same
time a Jew? Where does my allegiance, my responsibility lie?*

Without being able to identify what was happening to me, I
had the feeling of growing bigger than I knew how to be—

Must not I, so wanting to be free and to find fulfillment, be
part of the drive of a people to be free, to reassert their creativity
in a homeland of their own? *I am an American. . . . I am a Jew.
. . . Instead of an enigma to myself, am I not thereby doubly
blessed, doubly responsible? What better fulfillment than to take
my place with those who have suffered for centuries for their
beliefs? To share in rebuilding a national life in the land where
our forefathers held that very concept of freedom, equality,
brotherhood on which the greatness of America—my America?
—is built?*

So went the stream of my consciousness as I looked out at the countryside and saw it only vaguely, looked at lines of print in a book without taking in their meaning. Looked—and waited—

If, as the Zionists such as Dr. Friedenwald and this Dr. Mossensohn held, Jews retained the courage, the vision, and energy to rebuild a home in the land of their beginnings, how could I look for greater fulfillment than to be part of the great adventure?

Bits and pieces of old prejudices and antagonisms swam past the lens of my mind like motes in a shaft of sunlight—and passed into a sudden nothingness. *Zionism is not an abstract term, framed in space,* I thought. *Zionism is a saving way of life to a people, Zionism is alive—*

To what moment can one point, saying, *There in that moment my life was mystically changed?* That then one experienced the awakening, as from the unconsciousness of long sleep, to the spiritual revelation of a purpose which could become a lodestar for the rest of one's life? How express the experience in terms of a chemical composition of emotional and intellectual parts?

What had been coming toward me happened, while the train rushed onward. Zionism reached out to me and took my hand. A new way opened in front of me and there was no fear. Mystically, yet it seemed tangibly as sunlight, a great purpose and its glory touched me.

Reason murmured in my mind, *There will be conditions.* Of course. Great purpose is never without conditions.

For example, how to convey to my husband, at the end of this train ride within an hour or so, even a fraction of the vision I had caught, with its accompanying marvelous evaporation of inhibitions, doubts? How make real to those I loved, and who loved me, what was now so real to me? I so wanted my family to travel with me, side by side. How present this way to them, so that of their own accord they would want to travel it with me?

Unbidden, my mind moved back to my confirmation. How I had been exalted by it! And how far I had strayed from the font of my exaltation!

Now I was returning home. This was my conversion.

As love released me years earlier from the confines of my stammering, now the signs and symptoms of love were again all around me. I had a matchless feeling of weightlessness, of freshness of spirit, an essence of spring. Life was falling into a mosaic. There were depth, breadth, harmony, beauty in prismatic color. Puissance flowed through me.

The train crossed the Jersey marshes. My husband would be at the station to meet me. I could face him in the security of discovery that my life had reached a threshold of true purpose. No atheist ever had farther to come, or arrived with greater certitude.

When I told my husband that I had experienced a conversion and become a Zionist, would he understand?

A more phlegmatic—or less uplifted—person doubtless would have waited to get home, or at least into the privacy of the family automobile, before conveying to a quite unprepared husband so vital a piece of news; besides its inherent importance as deep human experience, it inevitably must affect the life of our family.

As it was, stepping from the train, I said, "Darling, I'm a Zionist."

His answer was equally direct. "You mean you want to live in a ghetto?" A few short days earlier, if he had been the one to make an announcement like mine, my reaction would probably have been no different than was his.

I was not disturbed. In our ten years of marriage I had learned to rely on osmosis as a method to overcome certain essential differences between us in approaches to things. In his question I had caught an edge of irony. But it would take more than irony to swerve me from the course on which—so inexplicably—I had been set. I was convinced that he could and would be won over. In terms of his own personality, the way his mind worked, it would not come about in a hurry. Time, reason, circumstances, and great caring must be given opportunity to work changes.

Though our mental processes and methods of learning and expression were quite dissimilar, my inquiring mind and intellectual capacity had earned his respect. He watched with approval how I chose my courses for study although, since his own way was that of reason and evidence, the instinctive way I reached conclusions was outside his experience and correspondingly difficult for him to understand. When it came to public speaking, which in time I was pressed to do, the success this met seemed the more extraordinary to him because I was completely untrained and extemporaneous, whereas he was an accomplished speaker, but he had been highly trained in that skill.

Unlike as our processes often were, his mind was the whetstone on which I ground my mind to a fine edge of mental discipline; it set a standard for me and was of significance because invariably I applied such a standard, and made it a fixed star by which to be guided—whether in association with a Henrietta Szold or later with the highly trained mentalities of the Hashomer Hatzair youth movement—the most intellectually self-disciplined group I have ever met.

I now began meeting a circle of new people—dedicated people —and reading books that not only were alive and interesting, but inspired. Magically, walls which had enclosed my outlook within bounds limited to our environment seemed to dissolve, allowing a new world with its people and problems to come close to my own life. For example, I grew able to see India's struggle for freedom, and the rebellion of Ireland against British domination, as akin to the Jewish struggle for nationhood and a home of its own. The self-determination of peoples was no longer just one among President Wilson's Fourteen Points; it shone as a principle and concrete purpose for which it was essential to work, if necessary to fight. Bringing it close to home, such issues were in line with my husband's passionate championing of freedom of the seas and of the right of free speech.

I became acquainted with the writings of Gandhi and of Nehru; George Russell's *National Being* presented Irish problems to my mind which in some ways were analogous to Jewish Palestine's struggle for rebirth. Such books occupied my mind alongside Moses Hess' *Rome and Jerusalem*, Herzl's *Jewish State*, and Pinsker's *Auto-Emancipation*.

As illuminating to me as these books were the people who guided me to them. Wisely they tended to lead me away from too

mystical an interpretation of my restoration to Jewish identity.
They gave me the beginnings of an understanding of the realities
of Jewish life, and the complex political factors of building a
Jewish homeland in Palestine.

At the outset of what might be called my period of orientation,
it was not so much the leaders of the Zionist Movement I met
who influenced me most as it was those who were parts of its
active nucleus. Boris Katzman and Charles Cowen were two
among many.

Head of the Society of Engineers for Palestine, Boris Katzman
—tall, lean, with a countenance as classic in its beauty as that of
a legendary Greek god—was a man noble in his single-minded
purpose, as self-effacing as he was exemplary in his dedication.

A scientist of first rank in his field, he had been engaged in
research for a major food concern in the United States. His
position and future were secure. All of this he gave up voluntarily to pursue his dream, working out in minutest detail with
his fellow engineers a scheme for settling in Palestine a carefully-
selected, self-contained nucleus of 100,000 Jews. Every skill and
profession to support its needs—"the butcher, the baker, the
candlestick maker"—was to be represented. When the plan was
ready to be put into execution he himself would immigrate.
Until it was complete he would not go, for he felt that heterogeneous and random immigration could only result in futility.

Not knowing the meaning of compromise, he failed to grasp
that the disciplined men and women on whom the success of his
plan depended were not to be found in sufficient numbers
amongst the Jews of this period, a period in which those turning
toward Palestine in thought and action were rather the atypical
and exceptional men and women, different from their families
and friends, and tending to group together when their common
objectives of settling and building in Palestine could be removed
from the realm of theory and be made fact.

Boris Katzman was of Russian origin, a son of a wealthy family
living outside the Pale, and therefore able to attend the universities of the country. While still quite a young boy he was turned
away from the assimilationist trend of his background through

reading Grace Aguilar's *Vale of Cedars*. This book, he told me, changed his life. Reading of the Inquisition and the fate of Jews in Spain sensitized him to what was going on around him amongst the Jews in Russia also, and to the gravity of the Jewish dilemma in general.

At once he had begun planning his own education along lines which would fit him to participate in the rescue of his people. Temperamentally he was unreservedly willing to make any sacrifice, however personal—even family ties—to achieve his purpose. It was easy for some to mark him as a fanatic. Certainly he was of the stuff of which great religions and causes—and sometimes martyrs as well—are made.

For the first time, then, I was confronted with a contradiction—single-minded dedication to a cause that could only result in action which would be right, necessary, and even noble to some, and to others represent only flagrant disloyalty and betrayal in desertion.

The facts of Boris Katzman's service in the cause posed a question of serious importance. In his case a premarital arrangement had been agreed upon which provided that he was to remain free of any personal bonds which would limit or hamper his work for Palestine. Complications arose when he had to choose between putting the cause first, and thus leave lucrative work, to develop his unit plan for Palestine. In this his wife would not follow him. A dentist by profession, she had now to become the mainstay of the support of her two children. Without his driving purpose, she saw him not as saint but as sinner.

I asked myself whether such conflicts must necessarily rise to plague dedication to a cause? In my own case, what of possible conflict between my primary and chosen obligation to my family and my ever deepening dedication to Zionism? Could I serve both with full justice to each?

Emotionally and intellectually stirred, I had plunged into deep, unknown waters, and now needed the support of the greater knowledge, experience, and strong convictions of these new friends, until I could develop power of my own to swim strongly in the many currents. In a sense, forces of the times, and

events, placed me in an advantageous position to "go somewhere." By means of the Motor Corps service and other liberat-
ing influences I had begun tasting the first fruits of the growing
emancipation of women; through Hortense Moses, Ben-Zion
Mossensohn, and others I had glimpsed the seriousness of the
chasm between the lives of families in our social and economic
status, and the lives of the great Jewish masses whose depressed
existence was still carried on in the shadow of persecution and
collective homelessness. I had begun to be aware of the psychic
distance between New York and Palestine, and to feel that it
presented me at once with opportunity and obligation. I had a
gathering sense of reaching what I had longed for all my life, *of
belonging*, of being a part of a great movement and, receiving of
the strength of the group, becoming capable gradually of accom-
plishing things which, as an individual, I would not previously
have thought myself capable.

Late in the year I was drafted to talk, before a group of
women, on the meaning of Zionism. Since I was scarcely six
months old in the movement, it may appear to have been rushing
things, but in a sense the majority was learning how to walk in
knowledge and understanding, and so those who were thought to
have gifts of speech, to be able to move the convictions and
action of others, were useful even when lacking experience.

I felt genuinely fearful. I, so recently a stutterer, how could I
stand before people and speak acceptably? Yet, inspired by an
opportunity to serve which transcended any mere self, I put fear
behind me, and purpose before me—and simply spoke.

Never will I forget that moment! It was as though my tongue
were touched at last with the coal of fire I had dreamed of and
prayed for during that mystic period of my confirmation, so
clouded by my miserable stuttering. Like Isaiah, I had been un-
shackled then by what seemed to me a miracle. Now, by a new
miracle, I found myself released from fear—except for that edge
of healthy fear which is its own kind of insurance against failure
—and able to convey to an audience the precious insight I
had received. And yet then, as always thereafter, it seemed as

though someone outside myself and not I were speaking—someone to whom I found myself listening, knowing they would not fail me.

My inner transformation quickly produced outward effects, naturally first and most particularly in the life of the family. Besides those of my husband and the children, I could not but be sharply aware of the reaction of my mother-in-law, for my action struck against deep-lying and ineradicable attitudes of hers. Our hard-won compatibility was, at times, sorely tried. The gap between her lifelong world and my newly discovered world of Palestine and the Zionist movement was far too great to expect her to be able easily to bridge it. Virginia-born and bred, in spirit she was far from all things Jewish. She had never met and did not now care to meet Jews, especially such as those who now were acquainting me with this new world with which I had chosen to ally myself. For example, it was as inconceivable to her as any aberration that, influenced by Ben-Zion Mossensohn, I had read Moses Hess' *Rome and Jerusalem* over and over until it became my second Bible. Nor could she comprehend my excited interest at gleaning from Charles Cowen, a Jew, an awareness of the awakening nationalisms in the world. How could such extraneous matters possibly concern me? How could I look for guidance to one who had no business or profession and was without visible means of support? Unaware of the traditionally high status of the perennial scholar in Jewish life, she had nothing but contempt for one who fitted into no recognizable category.

For his part, Charles Cowen had no difficulties about divided responsibilities. At the time a bachelor, he was kept to a lecturer's schedule only in the evenings. If he chose, he could read all night—which he did—and sleep all day. In consequence he made himself into a walking encyclopedia, with a catholicity of taste as wide as mankind. From him I gained a perspective of the renascence of the Jewish people and the building of their homeland in Palestine—not as an isolated incident but as in the stream of world movement, one of the tremendous historical affirmations of our time.

For reasons of background and training my husband could not agree of a sudden with all I had espoused. On the other hand, if he could prevent it no one was to be allowed to interfere with the translation of my convictions into action. He, like Voltaire, might disapprove of what I said, but would defend to the death my right to say it.

Knowing him as I did, a man dedicated to the steady extension of freedom, I had no anxiety about his eventually recognizing the true nature of the Jews' struggle to wrest freedom from a world so long opposed to granting it. The pioneer spirit of Palestine would come to appeal to him for its analogy to the early struggles of his own country. Once the various elements were related in his mind, we would be able to travel the way together as allies.

Meanwhile I understood thoroughly that my individual struggle was only beginning. More thought, dedication, and effort than I had ever before expended would be needed, to cultivate and maintain my Jewishness now that I had glimpsed it, and to convey it—I hoped for their emulation—to my loved ones.

My husband did not wait to be completely convinced before putting his faith in my judgment into practice. Immediately after the parade celebrating the Balfour Declaration, it was decided to give a mammoth concert at the Metropolitan Opera House—in two days' time! Very few people refrained from saying bluntly that it couldn't be done. Seemingly, however, along with my faith I had discovered that there is no such thing as "impossible." At least two of us believed it could be done—Abraham Baron, music critic of one of the Yiddish daily papers, and myself —with my husband to take our word for it.

There was only one mishap in our otherwise sensationally successful victory celebration, and that only momentary. Someone, unnerved by the numbers and volatile spirit of the crowds converging on the Opera House, put in a riot call, with the result that no one—myself included—could enter the building. But, in his inimitable, authoritative way, my husband carried conviction with the police officer in charge, who quickly ordered his men to clear the way and allow the wildly enthusiastic, happy, but orderly audience to enter and give rapt attention to an epochal concert.

I could not conceal from myself that there were very great odds against successfully infusing into our family life any such unfamiliar way of life as now occupied my every waking thought. We spent our first summer in our newly acquired estate in Glen Cove. I must admit that the atmosphere could hardly have been less conducive to making real to my family the ideal of Spartan sacrifice to a purpose which had taken possession of me. How could the luxurious life, the peace and security of a well-staffed country home possibly be related to horrors daily being faced by a homeless people? How could we, who had nothing but freedom in our daily lives, relate ourselves to people forced to flee from cellar to cellar, city to city, country to country, endlessly seeking even momentary refuge for themselves and their rootless children?

Here at Glen Cove the air was alive with the laughter of confident children at play amid the joyous barking of their dogs; here, guarded by the sheltering beauty and protection of sentinel trees, they could romp freely; scarcely a world in which to make even imaginable, however, a world where children, ill-fed and ill-housed, could know neither safety nor freedom; where "play" was a word without meaning. It was a grave matter, indeed, to find the right method to counteract the softening effects on the children of a daily existence which took for granted servants to supply their every need, making any effort on their part superfluous.

As yet I had only the broad idea of what must come about; no more than my husband had I discovered the method. It was more apparent to me, though, then it was to him that it would take time, combined with slowly maturing perspective, wisdom, and judgment, to see in just what practical ways a cushioned and protected life such as obtained in our home could be, in fact, a mixed blessing. It was too comforting and comfortable a life, and it limited the children's outlook, giving them no hint that a world outside was filled with dissonances which they would encounter sooner or later and would need to comprehend.

I became increasingly aware, therefore, that it would be very wrong for our children to be kept sheltered from any other way of life than one in which they received everything without knowing the need to work for any of it. As it was, they were without any need of the sharp cutting edge which a competitive world would ultimately require of them, in the form of initiative, selective judgment, independent skills. A day would come when mere physical and material comfort must be laid aside in order to venture forth in a real world, to find for themselves the boon and responsibilities of independent creative living. No longer could there be any question that the old order was passing; the world they would have to meet when grown would be altogether different from the one in which they had been born. How were they to be readied to meet it when the time came? In the face of so easy and ordered a life, how instill in them a living sense of the pioneering spirit which, though it must seem to them largely as something from a storybook, had formed the country of their birth and was the same spirit of pioneering which now was stirring in the land of their ancestors? How were they to develop the stamina which, closer to home, had enabled their grandfathers to come to America as friendless, penniless boys of seventeen, and find the initiative and courage to achieve their ambition to succeed in the competitive society they had had to face?

It was inevitable that there would be false starts, in finding—or inventing—the first creatively useful activities for the children. For instance—though both artificially and unnecessarily—the children and I decided that we would bake our own bread at home, instead of buying it from the baker. We proceeded under the cold, disdainful eyes of the cook and kitchen maid. The children were interested in taking turns at kneading the dough, but were really only playing along with their mother at the new game; indulgently, my husband waited for me to see for myself that it was nonsensical, to say nothing of the fact that bought bread tasted better, and was cheaper too.

In time, by trial and error, the "individual responsibilities" narrowed down to the irreducible minimum for each child, that of making his or her own bed when old enough, and keeping the room in order. My mother-in-law regally if pointedly ridiculed the whole device, assuring the boys that they were allowing themselves to be changed into sissies; she exchanged meaningful glances with my husband who, as long as he lived in his boyhood home, had never been required to so much as pick up after himself or close a bureau drawer.

An exception to my necessarily losing battle against the realities of our environment came with the family camping trips. Even on these, my husband considered an army of guides indispensable; yet the children found life in the woods giving them all kinds of opportunties to be on their own and use their initiative, happily doing the thousand and one manual jobs needed around the camp. In the out of doors they had their father setting an example—it was a point of honor with him to carry as heavy loads over the portages as the guides themselves carried. Here was what I had sought for—their father leading the family in our home.

Into this complicated and rather hit-or-miss effort to weave some serious unfrivolous elements into our existence, entered my new outlook on life. Without that I would have been beaten before I started. Even so, it could not have played the decisive role it did, had not my Zionism been based on more than pity for cruelty which long had been, and continued to be, visited on the Jews. Race hatred, discrimination—these by themselves were too far removed from my own and my family's daily experience to provide any of us with a durable urge to identify ourselves, as Jews, with the fate of the Jewish people.

However, what pity could not motivate, the pioneering spirit of Palestine could and did. And the first to become converted to my "conversion" was our eldest son, then approaching the age of ten.

Sometimes important stages of growth show themselves in apparently irrelevant ways.

Undoubtedly influenced by my entrancing experiences in Lynchburg, we had followed the custom of observing Christmas in our home as Americans, in the American way, with a tree. It was one of the things about which Ben-Zion Mossensohn challenged me. He demanded that I explain how—believing as I now did—I could conceive of this kind of celebration of Christmas in our home? How could I explain it, justify it before the children? Was I sincere after all, about giving them back their Jewish heritage? If so, how could I, on the one hand, raise them as Jews, at the same time holding out to them on the other the utter inconsistency of Christmas as *their* holiday?

It was of little avail to explain to a man of such intensity that Christmas was really nonsectarian, that it was far bigger than just a Christian holiday, as I soon found out when I applied myself to meet the challenge of his objections. True, it had become so commercialized that sometimes it seemed difficult even to get through to its deeper significance. I had to admit, of course, that any Christian would rightly find such a rationalization devious; and, to tell the truth, I myself was no longer able unreservedly to accept the shallow "American holiday" explanation of a day when I well knew its significance to be deeply holy for so many.

Yet when it came to the established custom of our own home, could I now just suddenly take away from the children something delightful and warm which had been built gradually for them? Since my first visit to Lynchburg, no fir tree had ever been too tall and handsome, no trimmings too gay and ornamental, no gifts too entrancing to mark Christmas for them. To my daughter and the younger boys—still only five, three, and not quite a year old, respectively—it would not mean so much if the tree were omitted. But to Norvin, Jr., it would mean a sharp, bewildering change and privation—or so I thought.

Therefore, that year of 1917 I compromised. Let the permanent solution wait on a little more wisdom. Meantime I would not take away the familiar celebration of Christmas time before I was prepared to replace it with another which was more fitting.

Indeed I needed time myself; I must discover and study the real meaning of Hanukkah, not let it be merely what it had been to me when I was young—a matter of a "gift" handed out to us at Sunday School, in the form of a half-pound box of candy. I was absolutely unwilling to work the change in a way which would place a vacuum where previously there had been so much sheer joy. I deeply wanted my children to come to love—not hate—being Jews.

Like many another parent, I found I had underestimated the sensitivity of her child. In front of the biggest brightest tree the Lindheims had ever had, Norvin, Jr., turned suddenly to me and said, "Mother, I want us to never have another Christmas tree, Never. Today it has made me feel ashamed." In that moment I knew that already something of the ideal and idea which had become so real to me had begun to take hold in him. My mind went back to the time when, on the train from Baltimore, I had asked myself how I could communicate to those I loved, and who loved me, this great thing that had laid hold on my life. I could not yet know precisely how it had been transmitted to him and begun to work its effect. I could only tell from our son's unexpected and impassioned announcement that, somehow, it had.

In 1918 we celebrated Hanukkah for the first time in our home. I had pored over Charles' two-volume edition of the Books of the Maccabees, and marked the salient and dramatic passages which I knew the children would love. Then I had gone over them with Norvin, Jr., so that he could read them understandingly to the children—others beside our own, for we had invited some non-Jewish as well as Jewish children to our first family Hanukkah celebration.

What story lends itself more dramatically, more inspiringly, to a child's imagination than the story of the Maccabees? The struggle of a small, inconsequential people, planted on a strategic highway between powerful forces fighting each other for supremacy in the region, daring to rise and take up arms against one of these, not for conquest or territorial gain, but for the right to live according to their own beliefs and in the manner that their fathers and forefathers had taught them was good?

They were farmers and shepherds, these people of Judea, who wanted nothing more than to till their lands and tend their flocks in peace. But when the forces of the Hellenistic Empire, under Antiochus Epiphanes' leadership, demanded not only oppressive tribute from them, but that they live and dress and worship contrary to their own laws and customs; that, against every tenet of their religion, they sacrifice swine, to them the filthiest of all animals, on altars dedicated to their God, they rebelled. When Matthathias, venerable father of five sons, killed the officer who tried to force the sacrifice of a pig on the altar of his village, Modin, then his sons rose and, with the men of Judea following them, went into the hills, formed guerrilla bands and harassed the enemy from mountain passes and ambush. After many years of hard living and heavy sacrifices of life and fortune, this tiny people had triumphed, under Judas Maccabeus' leadership, over the hosts of a colossal enemy.

No broad outline of a story is enough to fire the imagination and enthusiasm of a child. I therefore translated and adapted a number of passages from the story into dramatic action. Looking back into my own childhood, I recalled that the most exciting things were the mysterious bumps in my Christmas stocking, and I took over this idea. When the Maccabees and their guerrillas fled into the hills, assuredly they would have had to take a few things with them, probably in sacks slung over their backs. So I translated the "Christmas stocking" delight into the pack the Maccabees carried on their backs into the hills. One obvious advantage of the sack over the mere stocking was size—how much more the sack could hold, gifts and good things to eat!

The "cast of characters" assembled in our room upstairs, in costume, their sacks on their back. Each with a tall, lighted candle held in the free hand, they descended the staircase in single file, singing "Rock of Ages." The library was banked with greens, in the center a Hanukkah eight-branched candlestick into which the children, still singing were helped to place their lighted candles. Then, with the children sitting around him on the floor, Norvin, Jr., read the story of the Maccabees from the original.

Next came the lighting of the first candle by the youngest child, the blessing of the lights by the oldest, another song, then presents for all. What seemed to the children the most miraculous of anything was that, according with the number of lights, there were gifts for eight nights, instead of just a single night of Christmas gifts.

In subsequent years, when we lived at Glen Cove the year round and our children went to the Quaker School in Locust Valley, the non-Jewish children invited to share our Hanukkah celebration were not a little envious of the Jewish children whose "Christmas" lasted eight days instead of one! And Mr. and Mrs. Blackburn, headmaster and headmistress of the school, liked to come to our various Jewish celebrations, particularly on Friday nights when we lighted the Sabbath candles at the dinner table.

All of these ceremonies were completely unorthodox and not in accordance with tradition, of course, for I had no tradition to take up, never having even seen the lighting of the Sabbath candles at home, or celebrated Hanukkah. The important thing was that I had become consciously and joyously a Jew and wanted my children, as well, to take delight in giving expression to their heritage.

My persistent need was to harness my aspirations. It is all well and good to think correctly, but useless until something is done which translates thinking into action. Therefore I was looking for service. This led me after months of study to visit the offices of the Zionist organization where, for the first time, I met Henrietta Szold.

At the head of the Zionist movement then stood Louis Dembitz Brandeis, one of the great Americans of his or any other time. As it turned out, I was later to be brought into close and infinitely inspiring contact with him in matters concerning Zionism.

In the newly re-organized movement, Henrietta Szold was head of its cultural division. It would be fair to say that not only was she part of the human bridge between American Jewry and the settlers of Palestine but was, in effect, one of the pioneer builders of this bridge.

Born in Baltimore, after graduating from high school she organized the first "Americanization" classes for immigrants who came to live in her city. Not only did she teach these newcomers

English, but she conveyed to them an understanding of the
greatness of the country with which they were casting their lot.
For reasons of humanity, temperament, and patriotic devotion,
no one could better instill the values of the country she so passionately loved. Similarly no one, I was to find, could better pass
along these values to the great dream of building a Jewish homeland.

She had visited Palestine first in 1909. One of the things which
struck her forcibly was the inadequacy of medical service in the
country, and she resolved to give her life to bringing this need to
the attention of American Jewish women so as to bring healing
to their people.

The first time I saw her she was sitting at her office desk in
New York. The office was modest in size and simply furnished,
and she was as modest and unassuming as her surroundings.

It was good, she said to me contemplatively, that I had found
my way to Zionism. Increasing numbers of young American Jews
were needed to support those of European background and experience in America who had made a sacred trust and personal
responsibility of rebuilding Palestine into a Jewish homeland.

As Henrietta Szold and I talked, and I poured out to her the
glory and purpose that had come into my life with my awakening
to my Jewish heritage and the opportunity for its expression
through Zionism, I no longer saw before me an overworked, gray-
ing woman; I saw a great force in human guise. Her searching
eyes were young and full of fire, her manner dynamic, her words
a ringing call to action.

"We must find the right place for you, my dear," she said to
me, simply.

It made no difference that the first task she set me was seemingly a trifling incidental one; very likely she selected it as a test
to clarify my understanding of the issues involved.

It seemed that a leading Jewish woman in the San Francisco
community had resigned with asperity from the Women's Zionist Organization of America, Hadassah. She gave as her reason
the fact that there had recently been printed on the back of its
membership cards the aims of Zionism as defined and adopted at

the Basle Congress: "To have a publicly assured, legally secured Jewish homeland in Palestine."

This, it seemed to her, had too political a connotation to be an aim for a welfare organization such as Hadassah. Therefore she resigned her membership.

As I worked away at the answer Miss Szold directed me to frame to this letter, I learned what an instinctive pedagogue she was. Vague thoughts must be made clear, objectives defined, ideas made graphic. It occurred to me to compare the present status of the Jewish people, in relation to their deep need for a homeland, to many small deposits of coal scattered here, there, and everywhere around the world, their dispersed energies therefore dormant and wasted. Gather the deposits together within the space where their energy was needed and, like coal ignited in a well-built furnace, they would produce their propulsive power.

Whereas Miss Szold went immediately to work on this means of making use of me, I had the feeling, however, of not being taken very seriously by others in the executive positions of the movement. They were, perhaps understandably, wary of a very young woman who just might be taking up a passing fad, indulging a transient enthusiasm; perhaps a problem was posed too, when a young woman was not too plain looking, and rather unusually well dressed.

Louis Lipsky, Jacob de Haas, and others were polite, bidding me welcome. But what to do with me as a worker in the movement? Though they surely did not voice it, they probably thought briefly that possibly the best use for me in the future would be as window dressing.

I was anxious not to spoil my aspirations and hopes by impulsiveness, and I carefully bided my time. I kept up my service in the Motor Corps, taking care to keep the pockets in my car well stocked with literature concerning Palestine and the movement, and reading diligently when I must wait for passengers or orders.

My dream and my resolve were gradually stabilizing and strengthening. Zionists put me in touch with other Zionists. I knew I was often as much of a phenomenon in their lives as they were in mine. I was young—only thirty, by now. The cause needed young spirit, young minds and hearts, young energies. But those who were not quite clear as to why a wealthy and assimilated young person would be concerning herself with unsung service for this particular movement, nevertheless suffered me gladly, finding me worth bothering about, if only for my potential value.

ANZIA YEZIERSKA

*Anzia Yezierska was one of the first American Jewish immigrant
writers to make an impact on the mass magazines of her day. She
was born in Poland in 1885 and came to the United States in
1901. Before she became a writer at the age of thirty-three, she
worked in sweatshops, as a waitress, as a cook and, finally, as a
teacher. She died in New York City in 1970.*

*In 1919, a story of hers, "The Fat of the Land," was published
in the then-popular* Century Magazine, *and it was praised by
Edward J. O'Brien, a specialist in the short story, as one of the
finest of its year. Miss Yezierska's book* Hungry Hearts *was a
national success, and she sold the novel to Samuel Goldwyn, who
made a Hollywood movie of it. Her experiences in Hollywood
are described in the selection which follows, taken from her autobiography* Red Ribbon on a White Horse, *published in 1950
when Miss Yezierska was sixty-five years old. Some of her other
important books are* Children of Loneliness, Salome of the Tenements, *and* Bread Givers.

Hester Street*

ANZIA YEZIERSKA

I PAUSED in front of my rooming house on Hester Street. This was 1920, when Hester Street was the pushcart center of the East Side. The air reeked with the smell of fish and overripe fruit from the carts in front of the house. I peeked into the basement window. The landlady was not there to nag me for the rent. I crept into her kitchen, filled my pitcher with water and hurried out. In my room I set the kettle boiling. There wasn't much taste to the stale tea leaves but the hot water warmed me. I was still sipping my tea, thankful for this short reprieve from my landlady, when I heard my name shouted outside the door.

The angel of death, I thought, my landlady had come to put me out! And Hester Street had gathered to watch another eviction. I opened the door with fear.

Mrs. Katz with her baby in her arms, Mrs. Rubin drying her wet hands on her apron, and Zalmon Shlomoh, the fish peddler, crowded into my room, pushing forward a Western Union messenger who handed me a yellow envelope.

"Oi-oi weh! A telegram!" Mrs. Rubin wailed. "Somebody died?"

Their eyes gleamed with prying curiosity. "Read—read already!" they clamored.

I ripped open the envelope and read:

TELEPHONE IMMEDIATELY FOR AN APPOINTMENT TO DISCUSS MOTION PICTURE RIGHTS OF "HUNGRY HEARTS"

R. L. GIFFEN

"Who died?" they demanded.

"Nobody died. It's only a place for a job," I said, shooing them out of the room.

* Reprinted from *Red Ribbon on a White Horse,* Charles Scribner's Sons, New York, 1950, pp. 25–40.

I reread the message. "Telephone immediately!" It was from one of the big moving-picture agents. In those days Hollywood was still busy with Westerns and Pollyanna romances. The studios seldom bought stories from life. This was like winning a ticket on a lottery.

Hungry Hearts had been my first book. It had been praised by the critics, esteemed as literature. That meant it didn't sell. After spending the two hundred dollars I had received in royalties, I was even poorer than when I had started writing.

And now movie rights! Money! Wealth! I could get the world for the price of a telephone call. But if I had had a nickel for a telephone I wouldn't have fooled a starving stomach with stewed-over tea leaves. I needed a nickel for telephoning, ten cents for carfare—fifteen cents! What could I pawn to get fifteen cents?

I looked about my room. The rickety cot didn't belong to me. The rusty gas plate on the window sill? My typewriter? The trunk that was my table? Then I saw the shawl, my mother's shawl that served as a blanket and a cover for my cot.

Nobody in our village in Poland had had a shawl like it. It had been Mother's wedding present from her rich uncle in Warsaw. It had been her Sabbath, her holiday. . . . When she put it on she outshone all the other women on the way to the synagogue.

Old and worn—it held memories of my childhood, put space and color in my drab little room. It redeemed the squalor in which I had to live. But this might be the last time I'd have to pawn it. I seized the shawl and rushed with it to the pawnshop.

Zaretzky, the pawnbroker, was a bald-headed dwarf, grown gray with the years in the dark basement—tight-skinned and crooked from squeezing pennies out of despairing people.

I watched his dirty, bony fingers appraise the shawl. "An old rag!" he grunted, peering at me through his thick-rimmed glasses. He had always intimidated me before, but this time the telegram in my hand made me bold.

"See here, Zaretzky," I said, "this shawl is rarer than diamonds —an antique from Poland, pure wool. The older it gets, the finer—the softer the colors—"

He spread it out and held it up to the light. "A moth-eaten rag full of holes!"

"You talk as if I were a new customer. You make nothing of the best things. As you did with my samovar."

"A samovar is yet something. But this!" He pushed the shawl from him. "A quarter. Take it or leave it."

"This was the finest shawl in Plinsk. It's hand-woven, hand-dyed. People's lives are woven into it."

"For what is past nobody pays. Now it's junk—falling apart."

"I'm only asking a dollar. It's worth ten times that much. Only a dollar!"

"A quarter. You want it? Yes or no?"

I grabbed the quarter and fled.

Within a half-hour I was at the agent's office.

"I've great news for you," he said, drawing up a chair near his desk. "I've practically sold your book to Hollywood. Goldwyn wants it. Fox is making offers, too, but I think Goldwyn is our best bet. They offered five thousand dollars. I'm holding out for ten."

I had pawned Mother's shawl to get there, and this man talked of thousands of dollars. Five, ten thousand dollars was a fortune in 1920. I was suddenly aware of my hunger. I saw myself biting into thick, juicy steaks, dipping fresh rolls into mounds of butter, swallowing whole platters of French fried potatoes in one gulp.

"If we settle with Goldwyn," Mr. Giffen said, "He will want you to go to Hollywood to collaborate on the script."

I stood up to go, dizzy from lack of food and so much excitement.

"Maybe what you're saying is real," I said. "If it is, then can you advance me one dollar on all these thousands?"

Smiling, he handed me a bill.

I walked out of his office staring at the ten-dollar bill in my hand. Directly across the street was the white-tiled front of a Child's restaurant. How often I had stood outside this same restaurant, watching the waitresses clear away leftover food and wanting to cry out, "Don't throw it away! Give it to me. I'm hungry!" I stumbled through the door, sank into the first vacant chair and ordered the most expensive steak on the menu. A platter was set before me—porterhouse steak, onions, potatoes, rolls, butter. I couldn't eat fast enough. Before I was half through, my throat tightened. My head bent over my plate, tears rolled down my cheeks onto the uneaten food.

When I hadn't had a penny for a roll I had had the appetite of a wolf that could devour the earth. Now that I could treat myself to a dollar dinner, I couldn't take another bite. But just having something to eat, even though I could only half eat it, made me see the world with new eyes. If only Father and Mother were alive now! How I longed to be at peace with them!

I had not meant to abandon them when I left home—I had only wanted to get to the place where I belonged. To do it, I had to strike out alone.

If my mother could only have lived long enough to see that I was not the heartless creature I seemed to be! As for my father— would he forgive me even now?

Now that there was no longer reason to feel sorry for myself, my self-pity turned to regret for all that I did not do and might have done for them.

The waitress started to remove the dishes.

"I'm not through!" I held onto the plate, still starved for the steak and potatoes I could not eat. The agent's talk of Holly- wood might have been only a dream. But steak was real. When no one was looking, I took out my handkerchief, thrust the meat and cold potatoes into it, covered it with my newspaper and sneaked out like a thief with the food for which I had paid.

Back in my room I opened the newspaper bundle, still too excited with the prospect of Hollywood to be able to eat. "God! What a hoarding creature I've become!" I cried out in self-dis- gust. In my purse was the change from the ten-dollar bill the agent had given me. More than enough for a dozen meals. And yet the hoarding habit of poverty was so deep in my bones that I had to bring home the food that I could not eat.

I leaned out of the window. Lily, the alley cat, was scavenging the garbage can as usual. I had named her Lily because she had nothing but garbage to eat and yet somehow looked white and beautiful like the lilies that rise out of dunghills.

"Lily!" I called to her, holding up the steak. The next moment she bounded up on my window sill, devouring the steak and potatoes in huge gulps.

"I've been a pauper all my life," I told Lily as I watched her eat. "But I'll be a pauper no longer. I'll have money, plenty of it. I'll not only have money to buy food when I'm hungry, but I'll have men who'll love me on my terms. An end to hoarding food, or hoarding love!"

I threw open the trunk, dug down and yanked out the box of John Morrow's letters, determined to tear them up and shed the memory of them once and for all. For years those letters had been to me music and poetry. I had stayed up nights to console my loneliness reading and rereading them, drugged with the opiate of his words.

But now, with the prospect of Hollywood, I began to hate those letters. Why hang on to words when the love that had inspired them was dead? In Hollywood there would be new people. There would be other men.

I seized the first letter and began tearing it. But a panicky fear of loss stopped me. Money could buy meat and mink, rye bread and rubies, but not the beauty of his words. Those letters were my assurance that I was a woman who could love and be loved. Without them, I was again the oddity of Hester Street, an object of pity and laughter.

"Poor thing! I can't stand the starved-dog look in her eyes," I had overheard one of the men in the shop say to another.

"Well, if you're so sorry for her, marry her," came the jeering retort.

"Marry her? Oi-i-i! Oi-yoi! That *meshugeneh?* That redheaded witch? Her head is on wheels, riding on air. She's not a woman. She has a *dybbuk,* a devil, a book for a heart."

But when I met John Morrow, the *dybbuk* that drove away other men had drawn him to me. He saw my people in me, struggling for a voice. I could no more tear up those letters than I could root out the memory of him!

I slipped the torn pieces of the letter into the envelope, put it back with the others in the box and stuck it at the bottom of my trunk, under my old clothes.

A week later Mr. Giffen asked me to lunch to talk over the movie contract I was to sign.

After I had signed a twenty-page contract, Giffen handed me a check—a check made out to me—a check for nine thousand dollars.

"I've deducted one thousand for my ten per cent," he explained.

I looked at the check. Nine thousand dollars!

"Riches for a lifetime!" I cried.

Giffen smiled. "It's only the beginning. When you're in Hollywood you'll see the more you have, the more you'll get."

He took out my railroad reservation from his wallet and handed it to me. "They want you to assist in the production of the book. You're to get two hundred a week and all your expenses while there."

He gave me another check for a hundred dollars. "This is for your incidentals on the train. Meals for three and a half days—one hundred dollars. Not so bad!" He patted my hand. "Young lady! You go on salary the moment you step on the train."

I told him I could be ready as soon as I got something out of a pawnshop.

With my purse full of money, I hurried to Zaretzky's to redeem my shawl.

"Zaretzky!" I charged into the basement. "I forgot to take my receipt for the shawl!"

"Forgot nothing! I gave it to you in your hand."

"I swear to you, I left it on the counter."

"If you were crazy enough to lose it, it's not my fault."

I took out a five-dollar bill. "Here's five dollars for your quarter," I said. "What more do you want?"

He made no move. He stood like stone staring at me.

"Shylock! Here's ten dollars! I have no time to bargain with you. If that's not enough, here's twice ten dollars! Twenty dollars for your twenty-five cents!"

There was a flicker in the black pinpoints of his eyes. He took out a signed receipt from the money box. "I sold it the day you brought it here for five dollars," he groaned, his face distorted by frustrated greed.

The next day I packed my belongings without the shawl that had gone with me everywhere I went. The loss of that one beautiful thing which all my money could not reclaim shadowed my prospective trip to Hollywood.

The distrust of good fortune always in the marrow of my bones made me think of my father. While I was struggling with hunger and want, trying to write, I feared to go near him. I couldn't stand his condemnation of my lawless, godless, selfish existence. But now, with Hollywood ahead of me, I had the courage to face him. As I entered the dark hallway of the tenement where he lived, I heard his voice chanting.

"And a man shall be as a hiding place from the wind, and covert from the tempest; as rivers of water in a dry place, as the shadow of a great rock in a weary land . . ."

Since earliest childhood I had heard this chant of Isaiah. It was as familiar to me as Mother Goose rhymes to other children. Hearing it again after so many years, I was struck for the first time by the beauty of the words. Though my father was poor and had nothing, the Torah, the poetry of prophets, was his daily bread.

He was still chanting as I entered, a gray-bearded man in a black skullcap.

"And the eyes of them that see shall not be dim, and the ears of them that hear shall hearken. The heart of the rash shall understand knowledge, and the tongue of the stammerers shall be ready to speak plainly . . ."

As I stood there, waiting for him to see me, I noticed the aging stoop of his shoulders. He was getting paler, thinner. The frail body accused me for having been away so long. But in the same moment of guilt the smells of the musty room in which he wouldn't permit a window to be opened or a book to be dusted made me want to run. On the table piled high with his papers and dust-laden books were dishes with remains of his last meal—cabbage soup and pumpernickel. He was as unaware of the squalor around him as a medieval monk.

Dimly I realized that this new world didn't want his kind. He had no choice but to live for God. And I, his daughter, who abandoned him for the things of this world, had joined the world against him.

He looked up and saw me.

"So you've come at last? You've come to see your old father?"

"I was so busy . . ." I mumbled. And then, hastily, to halt his reproaches, I reached into my bag and dropped ten ten-dollar bills on the open page of his book. He pushed aside the bills as if they would contaminate the holiness of the script.

"Months, almost a year, you've been away. . . ."

"Bessie, Fannie live right near here, they promised to look after you. . . ."

"They have their own husbands to look after. You're my only unmarried daughter. Your first duty to God is to serve your father. But what's an old father to an *Amerikanerin*, a daughter of Babylon?"

"Your daughter of Babylon brought you a hundred dollars."

"Can your money make up for your duty as a daughter? In America, money takes the place of God."

"But I earned that money with my writing." For all his scorn of my godlessness, I thought he would take a father's pride in my success. "Ten thousand they paid me. . . ."

He wouldn't let me finish. He shook a warning finger in my face. "Can you touch pitch without being defiled? Neither can you hold on to all that money without losing your soul."

Even in the street, his words still rang in my ears. "Daughter of Babylon! You've polluted your inheritance. . . . You'll wander in darkness and none shall be there to save you. . . ."

His old God could not save me in a new world, I told myself. Why did we come to America, if not to achieve all that had been denied us for centuries in Europe? Fear and poverty were behind me. I was going into a new world of plenty. I would learn to live in the now . . . not in the next world.

I had but to open my purse, look at my reservation for a drawing room on the fastest flyer to Hollywood, think of the fabulous salary I was to be paid even while traveling, and no hope in which I might indulge was too high, no longing too visionary.

Grand Central Station, where I waited for my train, seemed an unreal place. Within the vast marble structure people rushed in and out, meeting, parting and hurrying on, each in pursuit of his own dream. As I stood lost in my thoughts, every man I saw seemed John Morrow coming to see me off. If so incredible a thing could happen as my going to Hollywood, surely John Morrow could appear. He must know *Hungry Hearts* was written for him. He must sense my need to share my wealth with him even more than I had needed him in poverty.

The gates opened. My train was called. I picked up my bundle, started through the gate, still looking back, still expecting the miracle. I could not give up the hope that love as great as his had been could ever cease.

The first days and nights on the train I was too dazed by the sudden turn of events to notice the view from my window. Miles of beautiful country I saw, unaware of what I was seeing. Then one morning I woke up and saw the desert stretching out on both sides. The train raced through the wide monotonous landscape at a terrific pace to reach its destination on scheduled time.

It was getting hotter and hotter. Sand sifted through the screened air vents and closed doors. The train stopped at the station to refuel. Passengers stepped out to buy trinkets from the Indians squatting on the platform. Over the entrance of an adobe building I read in gilt letters the inscription:

THE DESERT WAITED, SILENT AND HOT AND FIERCE IN ITS DESOLA-LATION, HOLDING ITS TREASURES UNDER SEAL OF DEATH AGAINST THE COMING OF THE STRONG ONE.

I looked across the vast space and thought of the time when all this silent sand was a rolling ocean. What eons had to pass for the ocean to dry into this arid waste! In the immensity of the desert the whirl of trivialities which I had so magnified all fell away. I was suspended in timelessness—sand, sky, and space.

What a relief it was to let go—not to think—not to feel, but rest, silent—past, present and future stretching to infinity.

Slowly, imperceptibly, the dry desert air receded before the humid, subtropical warmth of southern California. The sense of time and the concern with self stirred again. Green hills, dazzling gardens and orange groves, towering date palms ushered in the great adventure ahead of me.

At the Los Angeles station I was met by a man who introduced himself as Mr. Irving Lenz, chief of Goldwyn's publicity department.

"Where's your baggage?" he asked.

I pointed to my bundles. There had been no time to buy luggage or anything else.

In the midst of the crowd coming and going to the trains I found myself surrounded by curious-eyed men and women. Pencils and notebooks were pulled out, cameras opened.

"Who are all these people?" I asked.

"Reporters to interview you," Lenz said.

They stared at me as if I were some strange animal on the way to the zoo.

"To what do you attribute your success?" one of the reporters began.

I looked at him. For days and nights I had been whirled in a Niagara of unreality, wondering what it was all about. And he asked for a formula of success.

"What are you going to do with all your money?" another went on.

While I stood panic-stricken, tongue-tied, cameras clicked, flashlights exploded.

"Take me out of this," I appealed to Mr. Lenz.

"Why, this is part of the game," Lenz laughed. "A million-dollar build-up for your book."

With the cameras still clicking, he took my arm and led me to an automobile.

In one of those limousines which I had always condemned as a criminal luxury, I was driven to the Miramar Hotel. A basket of roses greeted me when I walked into my apartment. No one had ever put flowers in a room for me before. I lifted the roses high in the air, then hugged them to me.

There was a knock at the door. A maid in black and white came in. "Does Madame wish any help in unpacking? Or perhaps in dressing for dinner?"

I was wearing the only clothes I had—blue serge skirt and cotton blouse bought at a basement bargain counter. They were rumpled from travel.

"No, no, I need nothing," I stammered.

With one swift glance she appraised the cheapness and roughness of my clothes and withdrew.

As the door closed behind her, I walked into the bedroom. More flowers. I touched the bed. Clean, soft, smooth. I lifted the bedspread, feasting my eyes on the white sheets, the wool blankets. Who could lie down and disturb this delicate perfection?

Another door. Bathtub, washbowl, and toilet. My own. White-tiled walls. Sunlight streaming in through clean, glass windows. Racks with towels—towels big as blankets, bath towels, hand towels. Bath salts in crystal bottles. Soap wrapped in silver foil. Toilet paper, canary-colored to match the towels.

I looked down for the imprint of my shoes on the white-tiled floor. How could I desecrate the cleanliness of that tub with my dirty body? I thought of the hours I had to stand in line at the public bathhouse before Passover and the New Year—and the greasy tub smelling of the sweat of the crowd. The iron sink in the hall on Hester Street. One faucet for eight families. Here were two faucets. Hot water, cold water, all the water in the world. I turned on both faucets and let them run for the sheer joy of it.

I danced across the fawn-colored carpet in the sitting room and flopped down into one easy chair after another. Then up and out to the balcony, down the terrace to the private beach washed by the ocean waves. I looked at the shimmering water dotted with white yachts. The Atlantic led back to Poland. The Pacific stretched to the home of Kubla Khan.

It was too big, too beautiful. Could I ever get used to living in such comfort? Could I enjoy such affluence unless I could forget the poverty back of me? Forget? The real world, the tenement where I had lived, blotted out the sun and sky. I saw myself, a scrawny child of twelve, always hungry, always asking questions. It was soon after we had come to America. We lived on Hester Street in a railroad flat that was always dark. One morning my mother was in the kitchen, bent over the washtub, rubbing clothes.

"When was I born?" I asked, pulling her apron. "When is my birthday?"

She gave no sign that she had heard me.

"Minnie, the janitor's daughter, will have a party. A cake with candles on it for a birthday. All children have birthdays. Everybody on the block knows her age but me." I pounded the table with my fist. "I must have a birthday like other children."

"Birthdays?" Mother stopped washing and looked at me, her eyes black with gloom. "A birthday wills itself in you? What is with you the great joy? No shirt on your back—no shoes on your feet—not a penny in the house to buy bread—and you want yet birthdays? The landlord's daughter can have birthdays. For her, the music plays. For her, life is a feast. For you—a funeral. Bury yourself in ashes and weep because you were born in this world."

Like a driven horse feeling the whip behind him, she rubbed the clothes savagely.

"Have you a father like other fathers? Does his wife or his children lay in his head?" Mother wiped the sweat from her face with a heavy hand. "Woe is me! Your father worked for God and His Torah like other fathers work for their wives and children. You ought to light a black candle on your birthday. You ought to lie on your face and cry and curse the day your were born!"

The black curse of poverty followed me during my brief, few days in an American school. I had walked into the classroom without knowing a word of English. The teacher was talking to the children. They knew what she was saying and I knew nothing. I felt like the village idiot in my immigrant clothes so different from the clothes of the other children. But more than the difference of appearance was the unfamiliar language. The sound of every foreign word hammered into me: You'll never know, you'll never learn. . . . And before I could learn, poverty thrust me into the sweatshop.

But that was long ago. Now the sun was shining, laughing at my fears. For the first time in my life I had every reason to be happy. I had pushed my way up out of the darkness into light. I had earned my place in the sun. No backward glances! I would shed the very thought of poverty as I had shed my immigrant's shawl. I had learned to abase myself; now I would learn to lift up my head and look the world in the face.

To begin with, I would eat in state in the dining room. I had no clothes for the occasion. But I was too happy to care about my appearance. My shirtwaist and skirt would have to do.

The headwaiter led me to a central table. Music, soft lights, the gleam of silver and glass on snowy linen. Never had I seen such a shimmer of lovely gowns.

I picked up the gilded menu. What a feast! Ten entrées, a dozen roasts, twice as many desserts. Breaking my resolve to forget, I thought of the blocks I used to walk for stale bread to save two cents. The way I bargained at the pushcarts when the Friday rush was over to get the leftover herring a penny cheaper.

And now—choose! Gorge yourself on Terrine de Pâté de Foie Gras, Green Turtle Soup au Sherry, Jumbo Pigeon on Toast, Canapé Royale Princesse—whatever that is! Choose!

The waiter smiled at me as if he had read my thoughts, and offered me the evening papers. "Your office sent them."

I glanced at the headlines: "Immigrant Wins Fortune in Movies." "Sweatshop Cinderella at the Miramar Hotel." "From Hester Street to Hollywood."

There was a picture of me above those captions, but I couldn't recognize myself in it, any more than I could recognize my own life in the newspapers' stories of my "success."

FELIX FRANKFURTER

Former U. S. Supreme Court Justice Felix Frankfurter has enjoyed one of the most distinguished juridical careers in America. Born in Vienna in 1882, he came to the United States at the age of twelve, and was graduated from Harvard Law School in 1906. He was an Assistant United States Attorney under Henry L. Stimson, who was then United States Attorney. Frankfurter left this post to join the Bureau of Insular Affairs then attached to the War Department. When he departed from this post, at the end of the Taft Administration, he became a professor at Harvard Law School.

A close friend of several Presidents of the United States, Frankfurter was chairman, in 1918, of the War Labor Policies Board, working with President Wilson. From 1920 to 1928 he taught at Harvard Law School and helped place many of his outstanding students in Government posts. Under Franklin D. Roosevelt's New Deal, many of his former students held important positions and he himself wielded great influence. He was named to the Supreme Court by President Roosevelt in 1939. He retired because of ill health in 1962 and died in 1965.

Justice Frankfurter was a Zionist, and in 1919 he served as legal adviser to the Zionist delegation at the Versailles Peace Conference. He corresponded with Emir Feisal to bring about peaceful relations between Jews and Arabs in Palestine.

In Felix Frankfurter Reminisces, Dr. Harlan B. Phillips recorded talks with the Justice on a wide spectrum of subjects. In this excerpt Justice Frankfurter, in response to a question on Zionism, recalls his experiences in the Zionist movement and offers his impressions of Dr. Chaim Weizmann, Lord Balfour, and other important personalities of the 1920's.

Zionist Movement*

FELIX FRANKFURTER

I hope you will surround the correspondence I've shown you relative to the proposed elimination of yourself and others of the Brandeis-Mack group from Zionist councils, made apparently at the Cleveland Convention in 1921, with more in the way of illuminating insight.

I DO NOT know what interests will be served, or who would pursue the interest of the ins and outs of Zionist personalities, difficulties and policies from the time a divergence emerged between the rigorous, economically oriented outlook of Justice Brandeis and the entire consequence of the disciplined, even if inspired, mind that he was, and the kind of passionate, romantic, quasi-Messianic temperament of Weizmann so far as the realization of Herzl's dream of a Jewish Palestine. That doesn't mean that Weizmann wasn't shrewd, that he wasn't hard-headed, that he wasn't even in some respects cunning and crafty, and it doesn't mean that he wasn't a disciplined scientist, as he was, but when it came to the promotion of Zionist interests he wasn't pre-eminently a scientist. He was pre-eminently a man filled with a great dream which because of its adventuresomeness, daring to his mind and anyone's mind, required something more and beyond the careful calculation of an enterprise influenced by economic considerations, or the kind of hard-headed regard for details that was so characteristic of Mr. Justice Brandeis. That doesn't mean that Brandeis wasn't a dreamer too, but the whole bent of, not his temperament, but certainly what experience had done to his temperament, made him not oratorical, not passion stirring, not sky-scaling in his speech and even in his

* Reprinted from *Felix Frankfurter Reminisces*, recorded in talks with Dr. Harlan B. Phillips, Reynal & Co., New York, 1960, pp. 178–188.

thinking, but made him so much more—what shall I say, well, disciplined is the word, than Weizmann. Different pressures had molded the two men. Brandeis's pressures were intellectual and the pressures of imagination. They weren't the pressures of felt anti-Semitism, the pressures of the whole background of the Russian Pale, the pressures of actually being in communion with masses of Jews in Europe under the awful weight of squalid conditions, triumphing over them by a spiritual serenity. They were indeed—Jews in the mass are not now—people of the Book, and there was this sense of immediacy, or urgency, of not counting costs financially speaking but having a daring, micawberish outlook on life, that somehow or other God will provide, that the Messianic grant given by Providence to the Jews will somehow or other answer the difficulties. Brandeis wanted it answered by a balance sheet.

In addition to that there was the inevitable clash of two powerful personalities and also, I suppose ever so much more in Weizmann's case than in Brandeis's case, the sense of rivalry. The notion of leadership in the Zionist Movement was a very potent factor in the movement. Theodor Herzl was the undisputed leader—magnificent, handsome creature that he must have been. Herzl was succeeded by other people, and then by Weizmann through the force of circumstances, his own genius, his relationship to the British Government in World War I, the way in which he fired the imagination and, if not phlegmatic, certainly skeptical natures of people like Balfour whose imagination was not easily fired, or a hard-headed fellow like Smuts. These were great triumphs which vindicated to Weizmann the sense of power which he must have felt. Out of the West comes not young Lochinvar, but a judge with a composed temperament, a nonoratorical temperament, and almost inevitably challenges Weizmann's predominance, Weizmann's position of leadership.

I saw that very early. I became thick with Weizmann early and realized that through circumstances this jealousy would develop without anyone wanting it to develop. The temperaments were different. I saw early that they would clash since each naturally felt that he was a master of his respective situation. Moreover,

Jewry in eastern Europe, theretofore the mainstay of Zionism, more or less collapsed; at least it was weakened in its resources, its facilities, its strength and therefore in its total influence by virtue of World War I. All that was transferred to America. The center of the Zionist Movement had been Berlin, and the war had made it impossible for the center of the movement to remain there. America was becoming increasingly the power that called the tune. There was the same strain between European leaders, Weizmann particularly, and Brandeis and the Americans that there was between the leaders of the English Government and the leaders of the American Government, just a natural friction. Almost in the nature of the situation there was involved a certain amount of subordination on the part of those who were previously on top.

Weizmann knew I was a Brandeis man, and he couldn't indulge in open warfare against Brandeis. Brandeis had too much authority with the other European leaders. Naturally you go after the subordinates, and he thought that I was probably as close to Brandeis as anybody. Our relations, Weizmann's and mine, were never strained. In the Cleveland Convention the Brandeis-Mack group were displaced by those who supported Weizmann in the contest between the Brandeis view and the Weizmann view so far as there was a difference in the plan for the development of Palestine. Brandeis wanted all the organs of the movement, the banks, the funds, everything to be as conservatively competent as the National City Bank, then the leading bank in New York. Weizmann's relations with me never had any strain, though since he was for ousting the Brandeis-Mack group naturally I was on the other side.

I remember vividly partly his shrewdness, partly his gregariousness—he was a very gregarious person, but he could also retire into a deep groove. He was a temperamental fellow. On the whole he was much more manic than depressive, but I remember that as we were about to go into the hall where the convention was held, and according to the order of events I was to make a speech that night attacking his crowd, defending the administration as it was called, the Brandeis-Mack group, he warmly shook hands with me, and I felt, "How shrewd that was. You can't attack a man who warmly shook your hand two minutes before— at least I can't."

But I had a very good time because I was on my feet for four hours—four full hours!—and they tried to hoot me down and generally behaved the way the Irish contingent did in the House of Commons when Parnell was their leader, that is, make us as much trouble as possible. I remember saying, "I have as much time at my disposal as you have. I can stick this out just as long as you will, so you'd better listen."

There I was—four hours! But I don't think that Weizmann ever harbored any ill feelings toward me. Quite the contrary. We became after a while even closer friends than ever before. He was very eager to try to persuade me to move to Palestine. There was a breach between him and Brandeis that was never healed because Brandeis thought he was guilty of a sharp practice in a certain negotiation. A man once asked Brandeis to "forgive and forget," and Brandeis said, "I can forgive, but if you ask me to forget, you ask me to give up experience."

De Haas is a different story. He was an Englishman, an early disciple of Herzl. I don't know how or when he came to this country, but he was the editor of a Jewish paper in Boston. Justice Brandeis was a man of great loyalty and personal devotion. He had a sense of indebtedness to de Haas because it was de Haas who really, effectively, got him interested in Zionism. De Haas was a man of very considerable ability, but also of very considerable irritabilities. Irritability implies that he was irritable. What I want to convey is that he irritated other people. He had very few friends. The only people who were really for him in the movement were Justice Brandeis, Judge Mack and I. I think I can fairly say that we were less perturbed than others by his egotism. With full awareness of the limitation of a man we go for his qualities. De Haas was a little crude. He lacked tact. He didn't realize that there are various ways of skinning a cat, and he would skin the cat the hard way, the insensitive way. Instead of saying, "Well, I hadn't thought of it that way," he'd say, "You're wrong!"

Instead of leaving the impression on his hearer that he was wrong, he took a meat axe with which to demonstrate that he was wrong. Also he was absolutely devoted to Brandeis and regarded Weizmann as an unworthy rival of his hero, just as Harry Hopkins had a feeling of a mistress toward President Roosevelt which had to be taken note of. In the first encounter between Hopkins and Churchill, Churchill was made to realize that he mustn't say anything that would make Harry Hopkins feel that he, Churchill, was as good as Roosevelt. De Haas had this feeling, that he was the servant of the great man, and Weizmann was a rival.

Also there was a period in the Zionist Movement when the British Government proposed a vast tract of Uganda as a homeland for the Jewish people. The British Government was going to work that out with the Jewish leaders. That begot a great schism in the movement between the Ugandists and the anti-Ugandists, those who thought that Palestine has a spiritual, inherent historic connection with the Jewish people, while Uganda was merely a piece of land. Palestine wasn't a piece of land. As a young man de Haas was against Uganda, and I think Weizmann came, as a very young man, to the note of the Jewish leaders through his opposition to Herzl on that score. The difficulties between de Haas and Weizmann dated back to some historic rivalry at the Jewish Congress. There was friction between those two people, and Weizmann was less than wise in dealing with de Haas, and de Haas was less than tactful in dealing with Weizmann, so the request for de Haas's elimination was not a surprising thing because he got on the nerves of most American leaders.

De Haas by virtue of his close relation to Brandeis would arrogate to himself the right to speak for him. Some people resented that. They would take it from Brandeis, but they wouldn't take it second hand, sometimes suspecting, not knowing whether he professed to speak with authority, or underwrote his authority by claiming that he spoke on behalf of Brandeis—oh, the kind of frictions among personalities, the kind of rivalries and difficulties that exist in every movement, every collectivity. These men were concerned with Palestine, the achievement of securing a declaration which became the Balfour Declaration, then getting it formalized, institutionalized, internationalized through the peace conference and finally, actually making the thing move in Palestine. Well, whether it's this or that, or whether it's the Republican Party or the Democratic Party, or the Labor movement, internal difficulties are the history of every movement.

Weizmann had a very charming wife. She was herself a minor scientist. They were studying science when they met at one of the Swiss universities where they married. She was a very handsome, distinguished-looking creature—absolutely, whole-souledly absorbed by him, devoted to him, a person quite in her own right who absolutely fused her life with his. I've seldom seen so striking an illustration of a woman having an important and full life though not having a job of her own. Unlike so many American women of lesser quality, she thought she could be a person even though she fused her life with his. She didn't fuse her independence. She didn't think that she could only sustain her independence by licking stamps, envelopes, doing bell ringing for somebody else.

Weizmann was a man of great charm. He was linguistically very gifted. I don't know how many languages he mastered thoroughly so that he could make eloquent speeches in all of them. He was an excellent debater in German, French, Hebrew, Russian and I believe Italian too. He was very persuasive and very quick. He put his hooks into Balfour whom he met at Manchester when he was a reader in chemistry at the University of Manchester. I think that it was through C. P. Scott, the editor of the *Manchester Guardian,* that he met Balfour who got talking with this interesting youngish man and asked him, "Well why do you want to settle in Jerusalem? Why don't you want to settle in this large available land in Uganda?"

Weizmann turned to Balfour and said, "Why do you want London? Why don't you go somewhere else?"

"Oh, we have London," said Balfour.

"Well, the Jews once had Jerusalem."

That made Balfour sit up. He was this kind of a detached aristocrat and liked great self-confidence, daring and challenge, and they became great friends. Weizmann was a most persuasive person. He was of a very affectionate nature. He radiated authority. He was temperamental. He would move from gaiety to ferocity of speech. The gamut of his powers was very extensive. I suppose you have to count him among the great men of our time without any question; indeed, my friend, Isaiah Berlin, who became enamored of him, thinks that he was the greatest of all these people, was a greater personality than Churchill or Roosevelt. Berlin knew him intimately. That Weizmann should affect a person like Isaiah Berlin that way tells a lot. Weizmann seized the imagination and enlisted the will of people like Lloyd George, Balfour, Winston Churchill and Smuts. Winston Churchill was devoted to him. Weizmann had entree to all these people. His passion was contagious. He was a wonderful raconteur, and when he stood up to make a speech, he lifted himself in such a way that he was much taller than he was. He was a sizable man: he had that something that makes a difference, that makes the great man, that something which when Toscanini ascended the podium made him a different fellow from other distinguished conductors. There was something electric about him.

He was implacable in the pursuit of his object—implacable! And also, the other thing about him—and that I should have left it out! it's the most important thing—he himself said, "I have blinders on."

Nothing else interested him except the realization of a Jewish Palestine, but he had the kind of insight, understanding and imagination that made him realize that a lot of other things were relevant to that. He was interested in everything that was relevant, but he had blinders on. He didn't care what else happened. He wouldn't read the newspapers about anything else, except insofar as his instinct told him that this, somehow or other, was related to Palestine. The whole of life became for him a function of the realization of the reclamation, the rehabilitation, the investiture of Palestine by the Jewish people. And in that respect I've often thought—I knew Weizmann of course very, very intimately—how he reminds me of another friend of mine, Jean Monnet. He too has blinders on. For the things that he's interested in he doesn't dissipate his energies, or doesn't take time off, or doesn't listen to anything else. They are very much alike, powerful wills. In government affairs the realization of objects depends on the resolution of men—that's the difference between statesmen who matter and statesmen who don't—resolution, pertinacity, patience and persistence, and in Weizmann, as in Jean Monnet, the central quality that I call resolution, will, was manifested to an extreme intensity. Most people scatter their energies, or enfeeble them, or say, "Yes, but. . . ."—well, there were no buts in Weizmann's makeup.

People said a Jewish national home was a "dream." It was Herzl who said, "If you will it, it is no dream." Weizmann realized this dream. He was a volcano either in eruption or in training, and he couldn't go on to be as old as Gladstone, or, in a totally different way, Holmes, and so there came a time when it required some other energies, another Messianic character: i.e., Ben-Gurion, the present prime minister of Israel.

At the Peace Conference was Weizmann a good organizer of other talents?

He was no organizer. He was a soloist. Weizmann was no administrator at all. He had no sense of time. When he had an appointment with the prime minister at eleven o'clock, you may be sure that he was there at eleven o'clock, but if he had an appointment for eleven o'clock with you, you may be sure he wouldn't be there. Then too he always had a devoted crew that could attend to administration.

Take TR. Talk about a good administrator. He soon found that his then Attorney General wasn't a good sound limb to lean on, a good solid oak tree, or to change my figure, that he wasn't a wise adviser, and so he paid no attention to the Attorney General, but would consult a subordinate of the Attorney General, i.e., Henry L. Stimson at the time he was United States Attorney. Or TR would read an article—this happened while I was in law school—on rate regulation. Somebody called it to his attention, or he read it. Off went a wire asking this fellow to come down, and he turned out to be a student at the Harvard Law School. In short, these are men who represent the creative in that most difficult of arts, the art of government.

I remember during the war when I was in England in 1918, finding myself at Cliveden, residence of the Astors'. Lady Astor's sister and I were friends, and I got a message to come down. Balfour was there, the second most important member of the cabinet. Lord Milner was there. It was one of these English weekends. I always thought that if I ever wrote a book on English government, I'd call it *Weekends*. Lady Astor got going on Winston Churchill, a vituperative speech against Churchill. I don't know what the source of the enmity was between them, but she got going lambasting Churchill. Churchill in World War I was involved in the Gallipoli business in which, I think, all the best thought now is that he was right, that it was simply ineffectiveness of execution through no fault of his. She went on and on and on. Balfour was sitting next to her. I was drinking all this in and finally—all things come to an end, even Nancy Astor's powers of damning Churchill—Balfour very tenderly put his hand on hers and said, "Nancy, all you say about Winston may be true, but Winston has ideas, and to a statesman with ideas much shall be forgiven."

When you have ideas and the will to translate them into action and institutions, conduct, then you've got some powerful forces. One can't think of a character less like Weizmann or Churchill than Lincoln, but I'm prepared to defend the thesis that he had as much pertinacity and also the blinders on to everything except winning the war as those two men with reference to their objectives. Nothing swayed him, no nonsense from friends, no provocation, no fuming, no vituperative onslaughts by Horace Greeley would make a difference. No outcry about emancipating the slaves until he thought the time was right. He was swerved neither to the right nor to the left on what he clearly saw. He was a quiet man. He didn't blow up. He wasn't temperamental. He wasn't ferocious in speech as Weizmann could be, nor did he weep as Winston Churchill has been known to weep, but he had that iron will, that inflexible determination to pursue the road that leads to an end.

Those qualities seem to be very rare in combination—insight, seeing the goal and realizing the long, long trail that lies ahead before you can reach the end. I suspect that it operates in all manifestations of man. Anybody can construct wonderful policies on paper. If you don't have to persuade anybody, if you don't have to overcome opposition, if you don't have to keep a show going, you may be completely uninterested, or inimical to organization, but you've got to have secretaries and typists, and they have to be paid, so that success depended on organization even though Weizmann paid no attention to it.

Weizmann was a challenging figure of great intellectual and emotional, prophetic powers. He also had some interesting idiosyncrasies, or odd talents. He never forgot a telephone number of anybody. It was perfectly fantastic! Ten years after he'd keep it in his head, "I don't know whether it's still that number—Oliver 6735." He was perfectly uncanny about telephone numbers. I think on the whole as I visualize Weizmann in my mind's eye, as I talk here, and as he comes back cinematographically, I think he got more childish pleasure out of that quiddity of his than almost anything else, a kind of stunt—you know, like the fellow who could keep ten balls in the air. This was in London, and he'd remember the New York numbers of so-and-so. He'd never carry a book. It was all in his head.

Was there much humor to this man?

He was a very witty man—oh, yes. "Humor"—well, wit and sardonic, of the graver kind. During the Second World War I remember his coming from Portugal. He'd been in Lisbon where there was a concentration of people trying to get away from the Nazi countries, and he was describing this scene. He said, "They tell a story of an old Jew with a long beard, a very old, Orthodox Jew. There was a long line and finally he gets into the presence of the American consul in Lisbon to get on the quota list. This competent official, hardened consul, 'Your name?'

"He was very meek, humble and deferential. This fellow represents the United States, is the United States in his eye. He determines his fate, his destiny, and he gives his name.

"Where do you come from?"

"Rumania."

"Where are you a citizen of?"

"Rumania."

"Very sorry. The quota is all filled for Rumania for the next eight years. If you come back here eight years from now, you can get on the quota."

"The old Jew said, 'Eight years?' "

"Yes, eight years."

"He bows deferentially, takes off his hat, and leaves. He gets to the door and then comes back and says, 'Mr. Consul.' "

"Yes, what is it?"

"You said that I should come back eight years from today?"

"Yes, yes."

"Shall I come in the morning, or in the afternoon?"

That's what the Germans call *Galgenhumor*—humor of the gallows. The poignancy of that story!

MEYER LEVIN

Meyer Levin is one of the most prolific and dedicated of American Jewish creative writers. He was born in Chicago in 1905, and twenty years later he visited Palestine for the first time. He lived there again in 1928 and 1929, and has been living in Israel during the 1960's with his wife and children. His novel, Yehuda, *published in 1931, was the earliest novel by an American about life in modern Palestine.*

Levin is best known for his fiction, including The Old Bunch, Citizens, My Father's House, Compulsion, Eva, *and* The Fanatic. *He also has worked as a newspaperman, a war correspondent, a film maker and writer, and a dramatist.*

In Search is Levin's autobiography and is, by many of his readers, considered his most profound and rewarding book. "This is a book," he tells us, "about being a Jew." It remains one of the best autobiographies ever written by an American Jew. It is honest and it reports on one Jew's life in America, in Europe and in Palestine and Israel. Levin has been both observer and participant in the key experiences of the twentieth-century Jew. The material included here from In Search *tells not only of Levin's beginnings as a writer, but also offers hints of the issues that later dominated his thinking and his work.*

Education of a Young Writer*

MEYER LEVIN

MY DOMINANT CHILDHOOD MEMORY is of fear and shame at being a Jew. We lived on Racine Avenue in the notorious Bloody Nineteenth ward of Chicago. It was so known because it was the scene of a political vendetta between Italian ward chiefs. And it was at that time the incubating ground for the gunmen of Chicago's later gangster era.

Before I was born, the ward had been an Irish neighborhood, and in the classic pattern of deterioration in American cities, the Irish had moved on and been supplanted by Jews, the Jews were being supplanted by Italians, who were in turn to vacate the slums to Negroes before the area was at last cleared for a housing project.

My father was a tailor, with a hole-in-the-wall shop near the old Dearborn Station, downtown; he did pressing and mending, and a little buying and selling of used clothing, work-tools, and odds and ends possessed by South State Street derelicts. He worked twelve hours a day, and invested his savings in real estate. At that time, he had overextended himself in buying a three-story brick house containing twelve small flats, on Racine Avenue. Thus, we were landlords.

But as the Jews moved away and rents dropped there was an endless debate as to whether to allow the flats to stand vacant in the hope of keeping up the quality of the building, or whether to rent to Italians and deteriorate the property. Worried discussions of mortgages, first, second and even third mortgages, reverberated into the dark little children's bedroom while our parents sat discussing finances in the kitchen. Though we were landlords, though my father "had his own business," we somehow felt that

* Reprinted from *In Search*, Horizon Press, New York, 1950, pp. 13–30.

we were worse off than the poorest of the tenants, we were jani-
tors as well as landlords, and our living was always on the edge of
peril and collapse.

And in the same way that, as landlords, we felt superior and
inferior to our tenants, so we feared and yet somehow felt superior to the dagos and wops who were engulfing us, who had
swarms of babies, and whom we considered dirty.

We children believed ourselves to be smarter than the wops.
Yet they seemed more American. For though the Italians were
immigrants just like our own parents, their children already
seemed to have a native right over us, a right to call us sheenie
and kike which had overtones of degradation far beyond anything associated with wop or dago. Perhaps we knew that there
was something particularly inferior about being a Jew through
all the tales we absorbed in childhood, of how the lives of our
parents had been in the old country. From our earliest consciousness, we absorbed these tales of our people being kicked around
and browbeaten by drunken goyim, and we therefore knew that
with people, in no matter what country they lived, it had always
been as it was with us—we were a despised people. While we
could yell back at the dagos and wops, we knew from the beginning that our epithets only applied to their old people, who were
immigrants and who had green peppers and funny smelly sausage strings hanging in their grocery stores, but the children, we
knew, would have nothing to be ashamed of when they grew up,
they wouldn't be wops and dagos. We would still be Jews.

This unthought-out realization must have been in us from the
start, to make us feel somehow inferior to them. And then, we
were plain afraid of them. Going to school each day was like
running the gauntlet. By each house, the Italian kids might be
laying for us with stones or knives. —I'll cut your nuts off you
lousy little sheenie.

On Racine Avenue, our side was still Jewish, but the Italians
faced us from across the street. From our house to the corner we
felt nearly safe, but once we turned into Taylor Street on the
way to the Andrew Jackson school, we were in entirely Italian
territory. The first place of refuge was a friendly Italian's grocery

store where a hunchbacked boy would serve us with penny pickles out of a barrel. Then, after peering out to make sure the coast was clear, we would scuttle the rest of the way to school.

Actually, though we lived under constant derisive taunts and promises of beating, and though occasionally stones were thrown and knives flashed, I don't remember being assaulted, and recall instead that in my only fight I was the physical aggressor.

One morning as I was on the way to school some kid started shouting sheenie at me; I rushed at him in sudden rage, and to my own astonishment, knocked him down. I ran away, and for days afterward I was terrified that he would be laying for me with his gang.

I was a bookish child of the sort considered typically Jewish, and I shrank from physical encounter. It was certainly a monumental rage that overrode my fear. I suppose it may be said that I have been repeating this pattern all my life, raging at being called or fancying I was being called a sheenie. In all my life I never again struck anyone, until last year when I hit a man under a provocation curiously associated to the sheenie cry, for that man was a Jew. I shall come to the incident in its place.

There were only a handful of Jewish children left in our class, for by the time we reached the upper grades the Bloody Nineteenth was virtually all-Italian. After school, we few boys went to a Hebrew class in the old and deserted Jewish People's Institute that still functioned in the neighborhood.

One day, after coming home from Hebrew class and gym, I sat down at the kitchen table and wrote a story, passionately, in a little notebook resting on the oilcloth. After supper there was an unusual atmosphere of well-being in the flat. My father was home rather early from his store. My mother had polished the stove that afternoon: it shone, and a kettle steamed. Suddenly, standing with my back to the stove, I felt called upon to communicate to the family that I would be a writer. I opened the notebook and recited, rather than read, the story to them:

There was an innocent man who had been jailed, and he broke out of prison and hid in the tonneau of a passing car in order to get to the city to prove his innocence. There was a beautiful blonde American girl driving the car.

Many years later it appeared to me that there were obvious unconscious meanings in this little story. Wasn't the jail the restricted precinct of Jewish life to which we were innocently confined? I would break out, and in my childish fantasy I would be carried in the womb of a car driven by an American girl, to be delivered to the great city where I would establish my guiltlessness.

Thus, in my later interpretation, I was seeking an escape from my Jewishness in order to prove to the world that it was no crime. In the symbols of the fantasy, I wished for rebirth.

At the time, my simple adventure story evoked a family debate. My mother and father were aware that the fundamental goal of Jewish family life was for the son to become either a lawyer or a doctor. However, they said, they would not try to influence me or hold me back from any path I chose. They would try to help me. But, my mother worried, could one make a living as a writer?

I appealed to my father, as being in contact with the outside American world. Writers made fortunes, I pointed out. Especially since the invention of movies. Writers made fortunes because everybody bought their books, and then the movies paid them again for using their stories. (How I had already come to this knowledge is a mystery.)

Although I sensed that my parents still hoped I would study medicine or law as a safety career, my nine-year-old self understood that they were too timid to advise me because they felt that even an American child knew better than a pair of immigrants about the way of the world. All through childhood I sensed, and resented, this terrible shame and inferiority in my elders; they considered themselves as nothing, greenhorns, Jews.

Some months after my declaration of vocation I wrote a poem. I was then in eighth grade, a prodigy. My favorite class was the printshop; I suppose I had a notion that I could print my own works when I grew up.

The instructor called me Minsk, and with an amused tolerance for my zeal, he sometimes permitted me to stay after school, and to attempt color printing.

My great ambition was to use the shop's three-color border of leaves and berries, and to get the red berries to register perfectly on the ends of the stems. I had so little knowledge of nature that I didn't know this was a holly border, but I knew it had something to do with Christmas, and I was a little dubious as to whether I had a right to touch such an item.

One of my uncles was marrying, and I wrote a poem for the wedding and decided to print it myself; for this, the teacher permitted me to use the three-color border. I still recall the poem's concluding couplet:

> . . . and when once more the earth runs round,
> Behold, a newborn infant on its ground.

I set up the poem in Old English and got the border printed perfectly. The wedding was to take place at a hall on the corner of Racine Avenue and Taylor Street, and I knew there was a high point in such a festivity when the master of ceremonies stopped the music, and read out telegrams of congratulation. That was when my poem would be read.

But when we reached the wedding hall, I realized that in my excitement I had forgotten to bring along my present. It was locked up in the printshop at school.

There, from the first—even when I myself was the publisher—I seemed to have difficulty in reaching my audience. It is intriguing to wonder whether I didn't forget my gift because of an unconscious feeling that what I did there in the American school printshop, with the Christian holly border, somehow couldn't be brought together with my life amongst my own people. Perhaps the conjecture is farfetched: perhaps I am forcing an adult pattern of thought back upon my childhood.

In high school, I began at once to write stories for the school magazine, and if I recall them here it is not so much to trace literary development as for what they reveal of my inner conflicts as a child, for they were, I imagine, like those of any child already in the toils of the Jewish question, or the Negro question, or the wrong-side-of-the-tracks psychosis.

My first story, called *Chucklehead*, was about a hero-worshiper who pushed a football star out of the path of an automobile, losing his own leg in the rescue. Then came the big game when the star got all the glory.

Thus, there was on one level an early resentment of the distribution of social reward, and on another level an envy of people who could play the game and get the glory. Undoubtedly in identifying myself with *Chucklehead* I was saying I'd give my leg to share in the American way of life, in sports and easy comradeship, but even with such a sacrifice, I was saying, I'd still be out of it, I'm just not the kind.

To anyone familiar with analytical symbols, there is of course an evident fear of castration. And though I do not intend to elaborate such analysis in this book, I shall sometimes make use of it. The castration trauma was to reappear in other stories.

I became the editor of the school magazine; one day I submitted a batch of material to the faculty adviser, who approved everything except one story. That story, he declared, was plagiarized.

The story was my own, submitted under a pseudonym because I already had one story scheduled for the issue. Why, I demanded, did he think it was plagiarized?

Because no schoolboy could have written it, he declared. It was too mature.

I don't believe I ever again felt so proud. But the story had the trade-mark of my disturbance, for again there was castration. The tale was of a printshop foreman who kept after one of his workers to get a certain job finished on time, deviling him until the poor fellow, in nervous fatigue, chopped off his hand as he trimmed the sheets under the big papercutter. And I confess that some years later I wrote a story about a philosophic butcher, an Italian, picturing him from my childhood memories of Taylor Street. In search of his own inner reality, the butcher hacked off his own hand, with the obsessive cry that it was only flesh, meat such as he handled every day.

There is of course unconscious meaning in this persistent theme, as there is to the recurrent appearance of overgrown idiots in several of Steinbeck's stories. In my case as an adolescent writer it might be well to dispose first of all of the obvious guilt-reaction to self-abuse. But I had deeper guilts, as a child, and shame of my family was surely among them.

This fear of amputation, as a form of self-punishment, is like the fear of loss of function that often haunts men; in artists it can be a fear of loss of talent, and this fear can also act as a block to creativity. It is a fear that in expressing oneself one will tell something one is trying to hide, reveal one's secret shame, a shame that one knows to be unjustified, and over which one is therefore guilty. This was the child's guilt at being secretly ashamed of his people.

As an adult a phrase reverberates in my mind, linked to tales of the cutting-off of hands—"If I Forget Thee, O Jerusalem, may my right hand forget its cunning!" Thus the child's fear seems bedded in antiquity, in a tribal injunction against the desertion of one's people, a fear of the wrath of Jehovah, the powerful father in heaven who holds one to account for this great sin.

Has my long search in adult years been a result of this inner guilt and trembling, this plague of so many Jewish children, indeed of so many immigrant children who suffer a conflict because of their sense of owing duty and respect to their parents, even while they feel a kind of superiority to their parents through their own status as natives instead of greenhorns? Has my compulsion in adult years to retrace the steps of my people in exile been a penance for that early conflict? Does the logic of it lead back to the prayershawl and phylacteries?

The high school faculty adviser could scarcely have been aware of all these implications in my little story; to him the tale of the amputated hand seemed too morbid to have come directly out of the brain of a twelve year old. I confessed the authorship and he accepted my word that the story was original.

We moved to the Douglas Park district, where the Jews had once more caught up with the Irish. Early in the evenings, we kids used to roam up and down Twelfth Street, feeling the excitement of the restless neighborhood swarm. We would stand pressed in the crowd on the corner of St. Louis Avenue, listening to Aaron, the atheistic soap-box orator. One evening, directly on coming home, I sat down and wrote a sketch about the orator and the needle-trades workers in the crowd, the arguments about Ingersoll and philosophy, the dreamy wish of the little Jews some day to go away and seek the answer to all these questions— "Maybe tomorrow . . . but no, tomorrow they had to go to work."

At that time, Ben Hecht was the local literary idol. He was writing his sketches called *A Thousand And One Afternoons In Chicago*; they appeared on the back page of the *Daily News*. My street-corner story was in the same form, though less romantic in manner. I sent the sketch to him, and received it back with a sheet of scrawled praise saying, "You can write," and advising me to send my story to the greatest god of all, H. L. Mencken.

I was certain that I had arrived. I sent the sketch to Mencken at the new *American Mercury*, and it came back with a kindly note.

Now I began sending out stories to the magazines. I knew nothing of agents or professional methods, except for what I had read in *Martin Eden*. This book had a terrifying effect on me, as I completely identified myself with the struggling author and absorbed the conviction that the life of a writer consisted in mailing out fat envelopes and watching for thin ones to come back but receiving only fat ones.

I was soon enough aware that the big magazines didn't buy stories about Jews. Of course the stories I was sending out were probably unusable for other reasons, but the awareness of this taboo was to have a real effect on my life. On the one hand, I absorbed the basic writing axiom, "Write about what you know about," and on the other hand I was barred from communicating exactly that.

My encounter with this taboo was undoubtedly parallel to

racial encounters with barriers in various professions, schools, housing areas and in government. In the beginning, I reacted by stubbornly sending out stories of Jewish content. Later I was to give my Jewish characters names out of that special nonesuch category in American magazines, where everyone is Terrell, Fenton, Denton, Dale, Glenn, Alicia, or Kent. What I did in fiction, many sons of immigrants did in life. And a curious conversion of this subterfuge was to take place in later years, after writers like Saroyan had proved that immigrants could be quaint, when Jewish writers began to disguise sheenies as more acceptable Poles or Greeks, turning Rabinovitch into Theodopoulos. At one stroke they were propagating the idea that Jews were just like everybody else, and making their work a bit more salable.

But in my high school days I was still trying to find publications that had no taboos, no *numerus clausus* about Jewish stories. One summer, working as a name-sorter in the telephone directory shop, I discovered that the lad next to me was also a would-be writer, and in our professional market discussions he called my attention to the *Ten Story Book,* a lurid little magazine published in Chicago, with the subhead, "a magazine for iconoclasts." My friend was sure such a magazine would have no taboos. I didn't want to be seen buying the sexy periodical, but accomplished the act furtively one day on South State Street, in order to secure the editorial address.

The story I sent them was a sort of Fannie Hurst ghetto tale about a Jewish boy who was ashamed to have his gentile sweetheart encounter his Maxwell Street family. One day his girl insisted that they go slumming along the pushcart ghetto street, and when she stopped to bargain at his father's stand, he pretended not to know his own father. I received ten dollars for this unconscious bit of autobiography, and a warm note from the editor, Harry Stephen Keeler, later known as a writer of detective novels.

Now I entered the University of Chicago. In the class of James Weber Linn, in my second year, I began writing a series of interrelated stories, each of which concerned a failure in one of the arts. Linn himself occasionally referred to the novels he had published in his younger days; he was a character on the campus, noted for his vigorous language, and for the cigarette that dangled perpetually from his lips. Looking at him, I wondered and feared for my life as a writer, for what made a writer stop? This terror of an imperfect or fading talent possessed me. This sense of doom could be partly explained on the basis of youthful Weltschmertz, but the stories themselves showed my maladjustment.

The first tale was about a poet with a compulsive sense of form. He was most sensitive to beauty in modern mechanical objects, and in his rambles around Chicago the artist loved to watch the movements of railway semaphores, imagining them in dancing attitudes. One night he changed the arrangement of a semaphore arm, to conform to a pattern in his mind, regardless of the wreck that might follow.

I had no idea that my story revealed a belief that the artist was in conflict with society, that he had to rearrange the signals even if his vision proved destructive.

My story achieved the distinction of being read on top of the daily pile. A literary magazine was being started on the campus. A class ahead of me was a book-lover named John Gunther who was said to be in direct communication with H. L. Mencken. Around Gunther were lesser literary lights who joined in founding *The Circle*. Now, on emerging from Linn's classroom, one of these said, "Of course you'll give us the story for *The Circle*." He was a Jewish intellectual, but of a sort I had not known on the west side. He was a German Jew, and a fraternity man.

It was then, in college—as happens in the lives of so many Americans—that I made some social discoveries. I suppose these discoveries come in college because it is there that we first encounter people from other communities. Many years ago, Vincent Sheean wrote how his first deep awareness of prejudice came at the University of Chicago when he discovered that Jews could not be accepted into his fraternity. To a Jew, the discovery came on still another level. For after finding that there were gentile and Jewish fraternities, I realized that there were the "better"

Jewish fraternities, and that the distance between a south-side German Jew and a west-side Russian Jew was as the distance between the society page of the *Chicago Tribune* and the *Daily Jewish Forward.*

And I made a parallel discovery in college: by becoming a member of the intelligentsia one could achieve a semblance of equality on many planes; one even became acceptable to fraternity folk, Jew and gentile. The intellectual's conventional attitude of protest was to declare that he was not a fraternity man, on principle. Actually this covered a fearful dismay over the first encounter with schematized prejudice in people toward whom one felt otherwise attracted.

Thus, through the German Jewish friend who had real American friends, I felt myself raised to the level of fraternity men; I had proved to myself that there was truth in the Amercan principle that a man was measured by his ability. There was a purer kind of reward for writing, which I tasted when my story, *The Poet*, appeared in *The Circle*. I saw a girl sitting on a bench reading the magazine. Passing, behind her, I noticed that it was my story that held her spellbound. I lurked in the background; when she came to the end she breathed deeply, and looked far off, dreamily. It was as though she had said aloud, "It's beautiful." I went on my way, content.

When I had completed my series of stories I put them together in a book called *Septagon,* and carried it downtown to Ben Hecht. Hecht and Maxwell Bodenheim were then publishing a weekly paper called *The Chicago Literary Times,* which I considered I had wittily paraphrased as the *Literary Dimes.* Some days later I sidled into their little Clark Street office for the verdict. The team was in good form, and the solemn college kid was legitimate prey.

"What do you want to get published for?" Hecht demanded.

I could think of no answer, being as yet inarticulate of the intense need for contact and interplay between artist and audience. Indeed, those first stories, involved with my own inner fears, were something of a cry for reassurance. Hecht continued cleverly to describe the futility of being published, to laud the pure artist's goal of creation for oneself, rather than to submit one's works to the booboisie for desecration. I babbled something and fled.

It is curious that these two literary men suffered fates illustrative of the opposite poles of our schema. Bodenheim retained the attitude of the garret artist; he continued to live in Greenwich village, became a legendary figure in the bohemian haunts, and was reported at one time to have been found collapsed in the street. Hecht became one of the highest-paid writers in Hollywood.

Despite Hecht's sermon, I took my manuscript to his own publisher, Pascal Covici, who presided over a basement bookshop on Randolph Street. It was Covici who had brought out *A Thousand And One Afternoons in Chicago,* and his shop, a block from the *Chicago Daily News*, had become the Mecca for young literati.

My first little book of course didn't get published. I knew this was as it should be. I had to develop. I was in the city of the great American literary tradition, the city of Dreiser and Sandburg. Every week, Harry Hansen informed me on the book page of the *Chicago Daily News* that the city was the literary capital of America and that it was in the height of a literary renaissance. The litany was repeated, Dreiser, Sandburg, Edgar Lee Masters, Vachel Lindsay, Harriet Monroe, Floyd Dell, Ben Hecht, Maxwell Bodenheim. Many of these writers had worked on the *Chicago Daily News*. One's development as a writer therefore required an apprenticeship on the *News*. And so one day I went there to look for a job.

Actually there was no real need for me to earn money while in college; at this period our family was comparatively affluent. My father had traded his real estate upward until he now owned a six-flat building on Independence Boulevard, the fanciest street on the west side. And we had a Buick.

I was impelled to seek a job not only by literary consideration. I was impelled by the fear that was in every child: would I ever be able to hold my own, to earn a living in the world of men? I was impatient to try myself, a west-side Jew in the downtown world. Perhaps this fear is exaggerated in us because of the saturated climate of competition in which we grow, hearing ceaselessly the legends of self-made men, of newsboys who fought their way to riches, and of price-winning scholars who worked their way through college and yet found time to captain the football team.

One afternoon I took the El downtown, and stumbled through the ancient corridors of the *Daily News*. The paper was then housed in a patchwork of decaying buildings, all leaning upon each other. They were connected by enormous squeaky firedoors, and the connecting rooms were on different levels so that one either tumbled or stubbed one's toes in passing from one room to another.

A one-armed Lithuanian, operating a pull-rope elevator, had deposited me on the fourth floor where I was confronted by a half-paralyzed old man at a reception desk. He was deaf. I yelled that I wanted to see the editor, and in the same roar had to announce that I was seeking a job. He went away, and presently a large-headed, waist-high hunchback appeared. Questioning me, he discovered that I had been born in the Bloody Nineteenth. And then it turned out that it was his family that had kept the grocery store on Taylor Street where my sisters and I had bought penny pickles, and it was he who had served us. Now, Simon Morocco was secretary to the editor of the *News*, Henry Justin Smith. Winking conspiratorially, Simon led me through a series of firedoors to the desk of a black-garbed man who seemed to be made of pressed wood. This was the famous editor who had made the *News* a literary center.

In those days one didn't apply for a newspaper job in order to become a journalist. At least, not on the *Chicago Daily News*. One applied in order to become an author. A reporter's job was merely a way of earning a living while one "wrote."

I showed Smith my testimonial from Ben Hecht saying I could write, and secured a part-time job in the traditional starting place, as a picture chaser.

Simon Morocco conducted me through more gloomy corridors,

turning me over to an individual who was even thinner than Smith. The cadaverous picture editor, named Hume Whitaker, also, as I soon learned, dreamed of being a writer, and composed his picture captions as though they were free-verse poems.

So there I was in the incubator of Chicago authors.

I continued on the *News* as a picture chaser, campus reporter, and presently as a feature writer. The paper has since then passed through several changes of ownership; it is now housed in a modern skyscraper and devoted largely to sensationalism. Smith is dead, and the imposing names have disappeared from the editorial and book pages, and the once remarkable foreign service has disintegrated. But even in my time the atmosphere around the paper was not the boisterous front-page roar that one might expect from the legend of Chicago, but sickly and decayed and cynical; I was no doubt deeply affected by it.

In the editorial rooms there was a collection of individuals who were like a symbolic show of the thwarted, sickly, inner self of the city. At the center of the copy desk sat an epileptic who had every few weeks to be carried out to his hotel. Another copy reader had a deformed palate, and when excited gave out strange gurgling hollow roars. One of the reporters limped severely. One of the editors suffered from a severe gastric disorder, and lived only on large doses of soda, which he spooned into himself at intervals from a jar on his desk. Another of the reporters suffered from war nerves and occasionally collapsed in taxicabs.

Looking around the newsroom, one sometimes had the impression of living in a sick, crippled world. At other times one felt that all these individuals had been gathered by a tender spirit, and indeed Smith was the conventional figure of an executive with a forbidding exterior, all sentiment within. It was a Sherwood Anderson world.

Though Smith rarely talked to me, I had the feeling that his watchful eye was upon me, and that I was one of his boys, under remote control. Yet I felt that I had come too late for the warm literary group life around the *News*. I did not dare intrude in the sacred precincts of Shlogl's restaurant, where such wits as

Keith Preston, Harry Hansen, Smith and Sandburg were said to gather daily at a round table. I was intimidated not only by the prices but by the feeling that I lacked worldliness. I lunched, instead, across the street at a little delicatessen counter where one could get a real, west-side corned beef sandwich.

During summer vacations I worked as a full-time reporter. Ben Hecht had moved to New York, and I became the star feature reporter, feeling like the inheritor of an oversized mantle. My work consisted largely of two-minute railway station interviews with movie stars who were passing through Chicago; I was also called upon for detailed descriptions of gangster funerals, for that era had begun.

Then came the Leopold-Loeb case.

From the day of the finding of the mutilated body of the little boy Franks, this crime fascinated the world, and little else occupied our minds in Chicago. It seemed to us that we were in the center of the world through its purest crime—a crime, as we thought, for crime's sake. It was an intellectual crime, committed by two brilliant university boys in, it seemed to us, an almost abstract experiment in immorality, for the element of sexual perversion was not then generally understood. And we of the *News* felt ourselves to be at the epicenter of this crime of intellect, for two of our reporters, Mulroy and Goldstein, broke the case by matching the ransom note to the typewriter that connected Leopold and Loeb with the murder.

The murder stood before me as a personal lesson in morality, for both criminals were precocious students at the University of Chicago, like myself, and of my own age. Both were readers of Nietzsche, Cabell, Schopenhauer. I was not personally acquainted with them, as they, like their victim, were members of extremely wealthy south-side Jewish families. But it was inevitable that their "crime of decadence" should appear to me as a symbol. I, the west-side boy, had turned my precocious energy into accomplishment; they, the rich south siders, turned the same qualities toward destruction.

In the Jewish community there was one gruesome note of relief in this affair. One heard it, uttered only amongst ourselves—a relief that the victim too had been Jewish. Though racial aspects were never overtly raised in the case, being perhaps eclipsed by the sensational suggestions of perversion, we were never free of the thought that the murderers were Jews. And I believe that beneath the very real horror that the case inspired, the horror in realizing that human beings carried in them murderous motives beyond the simple motives of lust and greed and hatred, beneath all this was a suppressed sense of pride in the brilliance of these boys, a sympathy for them in being slaves of their intellectual curiosities, a pride that this particular new level of crime, even this should have been reached by Jews.

In a confused and awed way, and in the momentary fashionableness of "lust for experience," I felt that I understood them, that I, particularly, being a young intellectual Jew, had a kinship with them.

When the trial hearings began, I was sent to write features. The father of one of the boys sat shaking his head, muttering over and over, "Why me? I didn't do anything. Why does it come on me? What did I do?"

Remotely, I felt then and have always felt that this was a clue, and that it was related in some way to myself, to my people. I know nothing of the upbringing of Leopold and Loeb, only of their crime, but in itself it seemed to me to show a need for contact that expressed itself in violence. Their act was an extreme expression of an unwholesomeness perhaps due to our being strangers to our parents and our past, unsure of our place in society.

It is possible that I have forced this event, too, into the mold of my own preoccupation. But I believe there was a subterranean connection between this crime and the theme of my first long piece of writing, done at this time.

While I was under the paternal eye of Smith, downtown, I had at last reached the class of Robert Morse Lovett, at the university. This was the final course in English composition, devoted to major writing projects; I was writing a play.

Following the axiom to write about what I knew, I was using my west-side background. The theme of the play must have emerged from my subconscious troubling, for it was of a father and son search, surely related to the sense that we, of the generation born in America, had lost contact with our immigrant parents.

The central figure of the play was an old man who had fled Russia's long-term military conscription in his youth, and had somehow become separated from his wife and child. Now in America he was obsessed with the idea that his lost son was grown into a great man. He sat by a window, dreaming that some day his son would walk by and that he would by instinct recognize his offspring.

The son, in my conception, was a simple baker, a good man, and therefore great. I was reading Gorki and Dostoievsky; the Moscow Art Theater had passed through Chicago. But aside from these influences, there was certainly a source in the Jewish legends I had heard in my childhood about the *tsadikim*, the innocent souls for the sake of whose virtue the world was left undestroyed. All unknowingly, these legends formed the basis of my standard of value.

I felt even then that the subject of my play represented a great troubling within me, an effort to link myself to the generations that came before America, to the whole past of Jewish life. It seems to me now that this play was a way of saying I was a lost son, and that somewhere my father, the father of my people, was waiting for me. This same theme was to recur, in another form, much later in my writing.

It was the fashion in those days to pretend that one could get nothing out of college and that the best idea was to double up on courses and graduate as quickly as possible. And indeed, I recall that one had to stumble on a great deal that was of primary interest and that should have been taught. I became curious about Marx and drew *Das Kapital* out of the library; I ploughed through most of it but felt that the book was repetitious and that I had grasped the main idea. Then I began to fear that I was a surface reader and a surface writer.

Aside from Lovett, I felt no contact whatever with my instructors. Lovett is regarded as one of America's greatest teachers of writing. With him, as with Smith, I felt chiefly the warmth of encouragement, and I suppose in the end that is all a teacher can give a young writer. The teacher can confirm the beginner's feeling that he has some talent, and can make him feel that he should go on writing, that an older man is standing and watching over his shoulder, and will let him know if he heads into a wrong direction. In the case of the youngster working in fields unknown to his parents—not only the immigrant's child, but, in the dynamism of modern society, any child who goes beyond the social and intellectual limits to which his family has been confined—this leads to a seeking of a father-substitute in the teacher. Nearly everyone has known this to some extent, for with it comes an obscure sense of disloyalty to the parent, who is somehow made inferior. And the guilt grows. In my case, both the teacher and my mentor downtown were obviously substitute fathers and there must have been an additional guilt in me, for they were gentiles.

As a result of my stories in *The Circle,* I one day received a letter from a magazine called *The Menorah Journal.* I was asked to submit material to this cultural magazine of Jewish life. Several of my west-side sketches were accepted. I discovered that the magazine stood very high in O'Brien's annual short story rating, that it was a kind of *Dial* magazine for the Jews. I felt a slight uneasiness that my first serious acceptance should be in what I considered a limited world, for all that I wrote seemed to flow into this side channel. Yet according to what I had been brought up to believe, America was a melting pot. Later, I supposed, I would develop into an American writer.

INDEX